I0761169

LITERARY DALLAS

LITERARY DALLAS

Edited by Frances Brannen Vick

TCU Press • Fort Worth, Texas

Library of Congress Cataloging-in-Publication Data

Literary Dallas / Frances Brannen Vick, editor.
p. cm.
Includes bibliographical references (p. 473) and index.
ISBN 978-0-87565-383-9 (alk. paper)
1. Dallas (Tex.)--Literary collections. 2. Dallas (Tex.)--In literature. 3. City and town life in literature. 4. American literature--Texas--Dallas. 5. Dallas (Tex.)--History. 6. Dallas (Tex.)--Description and travel. 7. City and town life--Texas--Dallas--History. I. Vick, Frances Brannen, 1935-
PS549.D35L58 2008
810'.8097642812--dc22
2008010394

TCU Press
P. O. Box 298300
Fort Worth, Texas 76129
817.257.7822
http://www.prs.tcu.edu

To order books: 800.826.8911

Jacket & Book design/Margie Adkins Graphic Design

Photograph of the Dallas skyline is courtesy of the Dallas Convention and Visitors Bureau.

Dedicated to
Courtney Leigh, Katharine Bess, Taylor Mathews,
Ross Vick IV, Brannen Elizabeth, Virginia Bess,
who have brought me great joy and
who all have ties to Dallas, if nothing else,
through their grandmother
who adores them.

Contents

Introduction: The Emerald City

All the cities of Texas and indeed all parts of Texas are blessed with writers and perusers of the landscape, the culture, the history, and the minds and souls of the people therein. It is a rich heritage, this writing of our Texas world. Dallas has its own rich heritage peculiar to its founding on the prairies and the Trinity River, whose headwaters begin just to the north of Dallas and flow downstream through my part of East Texas to Trinity Bay. For years there was talk of the Trinity being made navigable all the way to the Gulf and thus making Dallas an inland port for moving goods. That didn't happen, but then it didn't need to as other forms of transportation blessed and brought prosperity to Dallas.

It has been said that if Fort Worth is where the West begins, Dallas is where the South ends. However, just to set things straight, plenty of cattle were trailed through Dallas on the Shawnee Trail, or Texas Road as it was often called. It is now called Preston Road and was indeed the road to Preston in the old days. It is now the street off Northwest Highway that I use to identify the spot where I live to visitors. The Shawnee was the first cattle trail of its kind in Texas, taking cattle from the 1840s until after the Civil War up to northern markets in St. Joseph and St. Louis, Missouri. Pioneer Plaza in Dallas celebrates this with a flowing stream, a waterfall, native plants and trees, and a re-creation of a longhorn cattle drive with some forty-nine bronze longhorns. I am told this is the largest bronze monument in the world, and Pioneer Plaza itself is some four acres in the heart of Dallas.

What other city can boast of some of the most outstanding contemporary sculpture in the world—in a shopping mall? Dallas can in NorthPark Mall, built by Ray Nasher, who with his wife Patsy accumulated a world-class collection and shared it with the public in his mall and then built the world-class and internationally known Nasher Sculpture Center to house the rest of it. Of course Dallas had La Réunion colony before that time to bring people who were artists, artisans, and intellectuals to the area so it would become a ready place for the Nashers and others like them in later years who would bring culture to Dallas.

Natalie Ornish writes of the great merchant princes who made Dallas a merchant center, a city of high fashion to go with the search for the "finer things in life," and they made it a world trade center for moving goods—a trading post, as it were—bringing those goods in and out of the city. The financial giants came with them to provide more grist for the mill. Of course the writers were observing and writing about all of this activity.

The poets were here early on, as were the writers and artists and purveyors of culture and those who backed them, bringing support for a new school to be called Southern Methodist University, and the Dallas Public Library, and the museums, the opera, the theater. Spencer Williams was making movies for African American audiences in South Dallas, and Deep Ellum was there, too, with its blues and the beginnings of jazz and Big Bands. Matter of fact, Dallas has had an abundance of songs written about it, maybe more than any city in Texas. John T. Davis listed some of them in a *Texas Highways* article: "Big D, My oh Yes!"; "D/FW" by Jimmie Vaughan; "Dallas" by Jimmie Dale Gilmore; "Dallas" by Jackson/Stegall; *Dallas*—TV Theme by Jerrold Immel; "Dallas," Roger Bartlett; "Dallas Blues" by Garrett/Wand; "Dallas Rag," unknown; "Dallas 1 p.m.," by Biff Byford; "Dallas Jam," by Phish; "Goin' to Dallas," by Lightnin' Hopkins; "Don't go to Dallas," unknown; "Dallas Alice," by Doug Sahm; "Alice from Dallas," by Buster Jones; "Dallas, Texas," by Hank Card; "Dallas After Midnight," by Ray Wiley Hubbard. An impressive list you have to admit.

We have also had our share of gunslingers, two of them being legendary women of Texas—Belle Starr and Bonnie Parker. Bonnie was, of course, running with Clyde Barrow, and Belle was running with Cole Younger, Blue Duck, and several other unsavory characters of the time. Dallas also had its characters such as Toy Woolley, who shot his wife accidentally, the jury ruled, with the gun that would later be used in the ambush of Bonnie and Clyde. Ted Dealey introduces us to Colonel Bill Sterett, both of them characters in their own right. All of them had to be written about, among other characters. I chose many of these pieces because they were by or about the people who made Dallas the city it is.

In my quest for *Literary Dallas,* I must confess that I was governed by what I *did not* know as much as what I did know. Thus there are pieces in here that may have been lost but I found them and thought they should be included. They show the attitudes of the people living at that time and in this place—Dallas—and that made them important to me, if not to the rest of the literary world. The historians of Dallas have written some inspiring pieces so I thought they should be here. The journalists in Dallas have been outstanding writers, from the very beginning, it seems. If they lived here, or wrote about Dallas and I found them, I included them. Thus you will find A. C. Greene, Bob Compton, Stanley Walker, Bryan Woolley, Kent Biffle, and Jay Milner among others. I had heard about Paul Crume even before I moved to Dallas, so when I discovered columns collected by his wife, I was delighted. I sat down to read them and alternated between laughing and crying. What a jewel he was for the city. I have been told that when *The Dallas Morning News* arrived at peoples' homes, the first thing they turned to was Paul Crume's column. I can see why.

I have included some writers who have not written about Dallas but are *of* Dallas and I felt should be included in any book about the writing done in Dallas. James DeShields and his interest in Cynthia Ann Parker, among other Texas history subjects, is one of them. Jon Bauman is another of them. He was schooled in Dallas and after college and stints as a journalist became a lawyer and then a writer. His work has been included as a Dallas writer. Some of the Dallas writers were written about by other writers, thus you will find a mixture of writers being written about as well as their writing itself.

As I began to explore possibilities, I became excited about the deep richness of Dallas's literary background. It began early, as is attested to by the *WPA Dallas Guide and History,* published by the University of North Texas Press, thanks to A. C. Greene's suggestion, who had discovered its presence at the Dallas Public Library and had used it for years, as had many others. I was impressed once again with the work done by those long ago writers, historians, and artists who left that manuscript, complete with the design and illustrations, just waiting to be found and published.

The biographies of the people who made Dallas the place it is, with its own unique personality, were included. How could I not? There was C.C. Slaughter who helped make Dallas a banking center; John Rosenfield, whose critiques and support made his city what he wanted it to be—a place with opera, theater, and symphony—and he did it through his writing. His good friend Evelyn Oppenheimer made her career reviewing books but also turned her hand to writing and editing, so she is included here. Frank X. Tolbert, a journalist, writer of fiction, and the Chili King—how could one leave him out?

Dallas has had its ups and downs during its history, with the biggest down being the assassination of President Kennedy in 1963. It was such a crucible that the way the city reacted was worth revisiting—from the police, reporters, bystanders, and the participants in the events. The writers who tackled this subject—from the journalists to the fiction writers, poets, and observers—included Hugh Aynesworth, Stephen Michaud, Pulitzer Prize winner Lawrence Wright, bestselling author Ed Shrake, Bryan Woolley, Wes Wise, Jim Lehrer, Darwin Payne, to name a few who were caught up in those traumatic days in Dallas.

The city has also been incredibly blessed with far-sighted men and women who always managed to get the city back on track when it went off course. They are written about or have written themselves and been included. Stanley Marcus would have to be in this group as being one of the moral compasses of the city. There are others, including the Cullum brothers, and more.

Fiction set in Dallas has been wide and deep. From short stories to novels, writers have covered all parts of the city. From a nursing home with Tracy Daugherty to a Catholic church with Jane Roberts Wood; from a mini-warehouse with Ed Garcia to the secretarial pools of Pat Ellis Taylor; from a classroom with C. W. Smith to an English manor with Caroline Rose Hunt;

from a doctor's office with Marsh Terry to bars with Clay Reynolds—and all the places in between—Dallas is covered.

The book is arranged chronologically by the subject's time period, rather than the years during which the author wrote. This arrangement will put some writers in more than one place. This chronological approach by the time written about seemed logical to me so that is the path I followed. Thus the written word itself is what established the format of this book. I know that I have left out many writers who should be in here. Some of them I did not find, some of them I ran out of time to include, and the manuscript was becoming fearfully large so I had to stop somewhere. Forgive me, all of you Dallas writers, who are not within these pages. Surely another volume of *Literary Dallas* will come along in the future.

I have found many misconceptions about Dallas. For example, when James Ward Lee comes to Dallas, this man, who since his retirement from professoring and departmental chairmaning, has adopted sports shirts and slacks for his daily attire, puts on a coat and tie. When I asked why, he replied, "I was coming to Dallas," as if that were explanation enough. Is it because of Stanley Marcus and his impeccable suits and ties and the premiere store in Texas—Neiman-Marcus? It is indeed true that Dallas has some of the best-dressed men and women in the world. Haute couture is not a stranger in this city, but as Prudence Macintosh points out, it is possible to live a perfectly happy life in Dallas and never wear a ball gown, or even own one, for that matter.

I have been incredibly blessed with friends in my life. Two of them are my colleagues in publishing. Judy Alter, Director of TCU Press, and James Ward Lee, who invited me to come help him start the University of North Texas Press. Both of them have remained friends through thick and thin, to the point of asking me to edit *Literary Dallas* as a part of the series they were publishing from TCU Press. They had edited *Literary Fort Worth,* so the challenge was daunting. Jim Lee knows a lot about Texas writers and Texas literature, even if he did start life in Alabama. I naturally turned to him for all sorts of help and advice, which he, as always, gave willingly and freely. Jim and Judy are formidably experienced writers and I did want to do justice to my adopted city. My good friend Bob Compton steered me in the right direction in many cases, as did many other friends, but Compton, with his incredible knowledge of Texas writing and writers from his years as the book editor at *The Dallas Morning News,* was a tremendous help. As always I have had a lot of friends and family rooting for me on the sidelines. I would be lost without all of you. You all know who you are and also know that if I start naming you there will be no end to it, so I have not started, at least not here.

I have found Dallas full of all the things that I expected and more when I came here almost thirty years ago—theater, opera, symphony, art, and those who ardently support those things. Most of all, there were the writers and those who enjoy writers—writers of fiction, poetry, history, folklore, and current events. What a cornucopia!

They have been my friends, either literally or through their written words, and they have enriched my life unbelievably. My hope is that this book gives credit to their substantial talents and once again draws attention to their works and their contribution to the building of Dallas.

I have heard Dallas called the "Emerald City," as in the Wizard of Oz, I suppose, and maybe because of the marvelous green skyscraper I see from my living room window, and for me, partly because of the magic I have found here. So, here's to you, Dallas, and the ones who wrote about you and lived within you. You are one in a million as far as I am concerned. I'm proud to be a part of you.

—Frances B. Vick
Dallas, Texas

Part One

From the Beginnings to 1963

A. C. Greene

A. C. Greene (1923–2002) was so well known to Dallasites that it seems almost ridiculous to explain who he was and how much he has done. But for those who missed this Texas raconteur, here are just a few of his accomplishments. He wrote many books, several on his adopted city of Dallas. His classic *A Personal Country* is still in print; his *Fifty Best Books on Texas* and *Fifty + Best Books on Texas* are musts for Texana collectors. His *Santa Claus Bank Robbery* is still in print and stacks up well against the Bonnie and Clyde books for rogues on the run. He served as book editor and editorial page editor of the *Dallas Times Herald,* published numerous articles in *Texas Monthly; Atlantic; Southwest Review*; and *Southwestern Historical Quarterly.* He was a fellow in the Texas Institute of Letters and in the Texas State Historical Association. Upon A. C.'s death, Gerald Saxon wrote: "A. C. Greene [was] often called the 'dean of Texas letters'. . . . He was . . . the individual to whom news and other media organizations turned for quotes about, and analysis of, the Texas experience." Jim Lehrer eulogized his good friend on his *NewsHour,* where A. C. had written many essays. The University of North Texas Press established an A. C. Greene series to honor his help in establishing that press. The Dallas Public Library, which gives an A. C. Greene award each year, has forty-five listings under "A. C. Greene," including three books on Dallas: *Dallas the Deciding Years: A Historical Portrait; Dallas U S A; A Place Called Dallas: The Pioneering Years of a Continuing Metropolis.* He was a great friend and his delightful tales and conversations are greatly missed. At his graveside at the Greene Ranch in Albany, I ended my eulogy with these words: "He was one of the state's most prolific writers. And I cannot find a bad book in the lot. He moved from history to short story to novel to sketches to poetry and back again, just as easily as most folks breathe. He was a marvelous wordsmith and a good friend. I will miss him terribly. So will Abilene and Albany and Salado and Dallas and all of Texas." His pieces here give the story of the founding of Dallas.

From *Texas Sketches*: John Neely Bryan: Father of Dallas

THE "FATHER" OF DALLAS WAS JOHN NEELY Bryan, a thirty-one-year-old bachelor from Tennessee. Although he first visited Texas in 1835, Bryan didn't get to "The Three Forks," as the upper Trinity River region was called, until about 1840, when he rode what is now Preston Road to look over the country. He found what he was looking for: an eighteen-foot bluff, where he felt he could develop a town. It was the head of navigation of the Trinity and a well-known crossing of the river. He is said to have burned his name on pieces of hide and staked out a claim before going back to the Red River settlements, but this seems to be legend, and was not the method used in "staking claims" in Texas.

Bryan returned . . . around November 9, 1841, with four other bachelors, [and] attempted to start his town. One of his companions remembered the first structure they lived in as "an open face hunters lean-to."

Neely Bryan rode a horse with the Choctaw Indian name of Neshoba, which meant gray wolf, and he was accompanied by a bear-dog he called Tubby. The dog wasn't fat. It was named for a Choctaw chief, either Moshulatubbee or Higholetubbee ("tubbee" was a Choctaw war name, signifying "killer"). Bryan confused historians by naming several mounts "Neshoba," thus appearing to ride the same horse for decades.

Bryan's bluff is now Dealey Plaza in downtown Dallas. In 1841 the river ran about where the Triple Underpass is today. He lived in a dugout, but when he married Margaret Beeman in February of 1843, he had a log cabin built for her there on the bluff. However, this is not the same "Bryan Cabin" on display at Memorial Plaza today.

Bryan had clerked at Holland Coffee's station on the Red River, and had lived and traded with the Cherokee and Choctaw Indians, reputedly speaking seven dialects. He was said to be a lawyer but no record of his license has been found. . . . Bryan was apparently well educated and brought several books with him to his frontier home. ★

From *Texas Sketches*: The Name of Dallas

DALLAS COUNTY WAS NAMED IN 1846 FOR VICE President George Mifflin Dallas. But who was the City of Dallas named for? For nearly a century, the question plagued historians, several names being suggested. We now have a historically sound idea.

George Mifflin Dallas was a Philadelphia lawyer, hardly known outside his home until he was put on the presidential ticket with James K. Polk in mid-1844. He and Polk successfully campaigned for the annexation of Texas to the United States, and that's why Dallas County honors him. But the town was called "Dallas" well before George Mifflin Dallas gained prominence. A deed filed in August of 1842 is for a lot in "Bryan's town of Dallas," and the name had obviously been chosen earlier. It is highly unlikely that John Neely Bryan, the founder of Dallas, would have known the Philadelphia lawyer, but his older brother, U.S. Navy commodore Alexander James Dallas, is another matter.

New historical evidence suggests Bryan staged a contest, offering a town lot to whoever supplied a name for his proposed town. The contest was won by Charity Gilbert, the first white female to live in Dallas and wife of Captain Mabel Gilbert. Since Bryan proposed his new town should be a river port, she suggested "Dallas" to honor Commodore Dallas, commander of the U.S. Navy's Gulf of Mexico squadron. (The deed to the lot Bryan gave her has been found.)

Mrs. Gilbert was a member of the Morris family of Pennsylvania, friends of the Dallas family. Commodore Dallas, a national hero who fired the first return shot in the War of 1812, had been stationed at New Orleans and was a friend of her husband and his brother, both riverboat captains. Bryan chose the site primarily because it was the head of navigation for the Trinity River; his interest in having Gilbert, the riverboat captain, move to his "town" was not random. Coincidentally, Charity and Mabel had with them a parrot, Jocko, when they arrived at Bryan's bluff on March 1, 1842. And where do you think the parrot came from? It was a gift from Commodore Dallas. ★

From *Texas Sketches:* Cedar Springs in Dallas

Cedar Springs, as a place and a name, is older than Dallas. An Indian village had been on the site prior to 1840. In February 1841, when soldiers of the Republic of Texas erected a temporary post at Cedar Springs, the location was already well known. Dallas began (if four or five bachelor hunters make a beginning) nine months later. The post at the springs was the first structure erected by white men in Dallas County. Apparently it never was garrisoned, but was used by troops laying out the Military Road, which stretched from Holland Coffee's Station on the Red River, via Cedar Springs and the Kickapoo Crossing of the Trinity (in downtown Dallas), to Austin.

When Dr. John Cole and his five sons arrived at Cedar Springs in the fall of 1843, Dr. Cole planned to claim the springs as part of his Peters Colony grant. But he discovered the area had already been granted to Crawford Grigsby, a Texas Revolutionary veteran. Cole had to pay $160 (about one dollar an acre) to the Grigsby heirs to obtain ownership of the springs.

The doctor put up a log mercantile establishment and drug store, and a town with church, school, and racetrack began to grow along the creek formed by the springs. After Cole's death in 1850, Cedar Springs Institute opened. Gold and Donaldson built a distillery in conjunction with their gristmill at the springs, producing a reputable grade of whiskey selling for 50 cents a gallon. William A. Gold died and Donaldson sold out to a Mr. Wheeler, referred to as "a northern man." Wheeler ran the mill and distillery successfully for about two years, then both burned. Wheeler attempted to rebuild but before he could complete the work, he was thrown from a horse and killed. Cedar Springs whiskey remained a Dallas staple until after the Civil War, however.

In 1850 Dallas beat out Hord's Ridge and Cedar Springs in the county seat election, although citizens cried foul: Dallas, they claimed, had gotten the Cedar Springs voters drunk. Today, Cedar Springs Road remains a major Dallas street, and some of the springs still flow, although now submerged in the creek. The town site was mainly situated around the modern crossing of Cedar Springs and Kings Road. ★

WAYNE GARD

Wayne Gard (1899-1986) received his BA degree from Illinois College, an MA in journalism from Northwestern University, and did further graduate work at Columbia University. He received an honorary doctorate in literature from Illinois College. He became a copy editor for *The Dallas Morning News* in 1933 and then moved to editorial writing until his retirement in 1963. While there he grew fascinated with the history of Texas and the Southwest. His first book was *Sam Bass,* followed by *Frontier Justice; Chisholm Trail; The Great Buffalo Hunt; Rawhide Texas;* and *Reminiscences of Range Life. Rawhide Texas* won the Summerfield G. Roberts Award from the Sons of the Republic of Texas. He also wrote articles and reviews for such publications as *American Heritage; Reader's Digest; American Mercury; Cattleman;* and *Vanity Fair.* Gard was president of the Texas State Historical Association, and a member of the Texas Institute of Letters; Texas Folklore Society; Western History Association; and Press Club of Dallas. His piece shows that one of the first—if not *the* first—cattle trails was through Dallas, Texas.

From *The Chisholm Trail*

"SEVERAL DROVES OF CATTLE HAVE PASSED through this place en route to Missouri," reported the Dallas *Herald* in June 1850. "They are brought mostly from the upper Brazos and are carried to Missouri to be sold for beef or to furnish teams for California emigrants."

This trailing to northern markets, which mounted steadily during the 1850s, generally followed a route that Indians, traders, and emigrants already had well established. Red Men had used it for decades. They had ridden over it in hunting buffaloes and in raiding the early white settlements in central Texas to steal horses and to capture prisoners for ransom. Many pioneer settlers, coming down through the Indian Territory in Conestoga wagons, had entered Texas by this trail. They called it the Texas Road. In the early spring of

1845, more than a thousand wagons were said to have crossed the Red River into Texas in six weeks.

This route, which some drovers came to call the Shawnee Trail, led from the ranges of southern and southwestern Texas past Austin, Waco, and Dallas. On to the north, it kept to the high prairies, skirting the post-oak cross-timbers. The herds swam the Red River at Rock Bluff Crossing, near Preston, in Grayson County. This crossing was popular because a natural rock formation served as a chute into the water and because a gentle slope on the opposite side made it easy for the cattle to come out.

Texas drovers who used this route in the 1850s called it the cattle trail, the Kansas Trail, or merely the trail. Just when or how some began to call it the Shawnee Trail is uncertain. That name appeared in print at least as early as 1874 and presumably was used much earlier. The name could have been suggested by an Indian village, called Shawneetown, on the Texas bank of the Red River just below the trail crossing. Or by the Shawnee Hills, which the route skirted on their eastern side before crossing the Canadian River.

In Dallas, where herds of bawling longhorns raised clouds of dust in the streets, people knew the section of the trail from their town to the Red River as the Preston Road. This road and that into Dallas from the south had been surveyed in 1840, in the days of the republic. In the fall of 1839, under an act the Congress of Texas had passed a year earlier, Albert Sidney Johnston, secretary of war, had sent north a company of soldiers under the command of Colonel William G. Cooke. The purpose was to lay out a military road from the Brazos to the Red River and to establish small forts for protecting the settlers against Indian raids. . . .

On the Red River, Colonel Cooke had his men build a stockade called Fort Johnson, midway between Holland Coffee's trading station and Basin Springs. He also opened a supply post that became known as Fort Preston. It took its name from that of Captain William G. Preston, who was in charge of a company of men there in 1840. Later the village that grew up about the fort was called Preston Bend or Preston. . . .

The Shawnee Trail was an unusually wide road. It needed to be to accommodate its heavy and varied traffic. Besides the long lines of settlers' wagons, there were military supply caravans and companies of freighters. On their return north, many of the freighters carried buffalo robes or other pelts. And along with the northbound cattle were occasional herds of mustang ponies and Mexican mules. As deep ruts made parts of the road impassable, teamsters and drovers went to one side or the other, thus widening the trail.

By 1854 the Shawnee Trail was a recognized and important cattle route. In early June of that year, the exploring and surveying expedition of Captain Randolph B. Marcy headed southward, passed an estimated ten thousand longhorns, plodding in the opposite direction, between Fort Washita and Boggy Depot. The cattle were on the way to Missouri and Illinois.

The rapid increase in the trailing of longhorns from Texas to Missouri drew comment from the *Texas State Gazette* two months later. Fifty thousand head, it reported in its issue of August 5, had crossed the Red River at Preston that season. ★

A. C. Greene

From *A Place Called Dallas*

Something happened in 1854 which was uncommon on the frontier and left Dallas a different sort of town—a difference appreciated more well over a century later than when it took place. On April 26 of that year the first arrivals, a dozen men, came to arrange for a Fourierest colony just west of Dallas to be called La Réunion. Victor Considerant, the head of the group, had already visited the Three Forks region and had gone back to France and written a book about it titled *Au Texas.* It was an altogether too ebullient little volume . . . which created a zealous "phlange" of French, Swiss, and Belgian Fourierests, eager to come to the paradise at Dallas.

The main body of European settlers arrived the next June and moved onto 1,200 acres of land. The founders had picked the worst land for agriculture. The French leaders were said to have liked this chalky soil because it resembled the great French wine soils. At any rate, the work of the settlement fell victim to philosophy. The people were a curious mixture of artists, aristocrats, physicians, editors, and political figures who had been forced to leave their various countries when governments changed. (The Fourier movement was communistic in principle, believing in sharing everything including work, but most of the colonists seemed to care little for this feature of their utopianism.) Texas turned on one of its fiercest weather cycles: a terrible drought, then an equally terrible winter in which even the Trinity froze. Not knowing local agricultural traditions, the La Réunionists couldn't even raise vegetables in their kitchen gardens.

Kalikst Wolski, a Pole who had lived in France many years, joined La Réunion in May 1855 and wrote a candid memoir. Wolski's book contains two chapters on La Réunion which was especially valuable for their description of the social scene taking place on the Dallas frontier at the time. A short while after he arrived in Dallas, Wolski writes with great relief that some aristocratic ladies had arrived:

> Considerant . . . with his wife, his wife's mother, Madame Vigoreux, and the wife of (Francois) Cantagrel . . . accompanied by two ex-members of the French legislature, who under the Second Empire had been exiled—also several editors of various Brussels and Paris newspapers . . . with the arrival of this party, our life at the colony became pleasanter. The high culture of those who have now joined us will make the hardships, discomforts, and lack of many material things to which each of us . . . had become accustomed, more endurable. The ladies are of the highest Parisian society, and so, with their coming, life will flow more freely.

Madame Considerant sensed the importance to the colony of intellectual stimulation, and she discovered a grove of cedars near the Trinity and transformed it into a salon comparable in tone to anything the group had left in Europe. Wolski describes it colorfully:

> In her cedar salon the floor was covered with a rug of natural green. . . . Above the branches spread their thick, broad leaves . . . the moon—or millions of glittering stars—took the place of a lamp [and] in place of the tones of a piano, we had the . . . harmonious singing of masses of birds. Hammocks were hung from trees, or nets of thick twine served as couches.
>
> After nine o'clock in the evening, there would gather here not a large, but at least a select company of the colonists. The rest period of five hours in the middle of the day almost sufficed us for sleeping, and permitted us the luxury of reveling in the marvelously beautiful nights beneath the Texas sky in an enlightened and congenial company. Often these gatherings lasted until one or two in the morning . . . where extraordinarily captivating and often highly erudite conversations went on, though more often the talk was of a light and witty nature, with anecdotes exchanged back and forth.

The lack of industry, knowledge of Texas agriculture, and of coordination within the group doomed the utopian plan, even more than the vagaries of Texas weather. Within three years many of the leaders had returned to Europe, and others, including thirty Swiss farmers, had separated themselves from the colony and moved to their own farms and settlements. Less than a decade after it was begun, La Réunion, as a colony, had completely disbanded. But what it added to Dallas was an intangible attitude which without doubt became a part of that indescribable quality which pulled Dallas, the city without nature's blessings, through to international importance. Because of La Réunion, Dallas even as a raw Texas village had fine tailors, lithographers, dressmakers, weavers, watchmakers, jewelers, dancing masters, printers, chefs, vintners, scientists, and innumerable trades which the ordinary American village would seldom attract. A great many of the La Réunion settlers could not afford to return to Europe or did not desire to, and moved into the town of Dallas to form part of the life of the place. Two of the colonists, Julien Reverchon and Jacob Boll, were naturalists who became the first internationally recognized citizens of Dallas. The family names of those who remained are woven like bright, foreign threads throughout Dallas history: Barbier, Capy, Raymond, Michell, Loupot, Santerre, Gouffre, Henry, Frichot, Nussbaumer. Who knows what part of Dallas self-esteem as a cultural center stems from that ill-fated, but ultimately happy, undertaking? ★

Benjamin Capps

Benjamin Capps (1922–2001), a distinguished writer from Grand Prairie, Texas, has captured the La Réunion spirit in his novel *The Brothers of Uterica,* published in 1967. James Ward Lee in his *Classics of Texas Fiction* describes the novel: "The 'brothers' of the title are French colonists who come to Texas to set up a Utopia on the banks of the Trinity. The colonists were more interested in making lists of noble ideals than in confronting the wilderness and making provisions for survival." Capps received bachelors and masters degrees and Phi Beta Kappa from the University of Texas and taught for a year before leaving teaching to write. He wrote several novels—*Comanche Wells; The Trail to Ogallala; Sam Chance; A Woman of the People; The White Man's Road; The True Memoirs of Charley Blankenship;* and *Woman Chief.* His nonfiction includes: *The Indians* and *The Great Chiefs* in the Time/Life series, and *The Warren Wagon-train Raid.* He won several awards from the Western Writers of America and was named an Honorary Life Member of the Western Literature Association. Capps gives the novelist's account of the founding of La Réunion.

From *The Brothers of Uterica*

The wagons creaked to the patient pull of the ox teams, and the wheels clonked from side to side as they turned against the bumpy, roadless land, marking it with the first wheel tracks it had felt since the beginning of time. From somewhere toward the rear of the caravan came the occasional short, shrill whistle of a German boy, who used that sound along with a switch to urge his oxen on, and walking just ahead of me one of the American employees sometimes shouted, "Hup! ah! Hup! ah!" at his team. At the head of the column went the massive wagons belonging to the freighters from Shreveport. In days past they had become aggravated with the clumsy wagon-handling of some of the colonists, and now they would lead off each morning, never looking behind them unless they were halted by someone in authority, expecting us to bring our lighter wagons wherever they could take their heavier ones.

Out to the left I could see our herds of horses and milk cows, separate, each driven by three horsemen, and farther back the sheep, coming like a lumpy, gray carpet dragged along the land. They were herded by more than a dozen women and children on foot and one dog. The women wore simple long dresses and bonnets they had fashioned as protection against the sun. Except for a half dozen colonists who were sick, none of them rode; they herded loose stock or goaded oxen and trailed wagons, ready to push. Ironically, now that we neared our destination, we were becoming an efficient caravan.

I can hardly put into words how I felt, looking at the land ahead. It was promising country with gentle hills rising all around, but with long, fine slopes for farming, some of these covered with tall, dry buffalo grass. On this spring afternoon, it lay under a brilliant sun, vivid, almost sparkling. The post oak trees which covered a quarter of the hilly expanse still carried some old leaves of the year before in dusty tan clumps, mostly low down where the wind had been unable to dislodge them. Other trees were completely bare. But in certain protected sunny spots tender new grass was pushing up, also the bright, fragile flowers of early spring. It was as if the life in the earth was eager to burst through the gray remnants of winter. But those kinds of things happen also in a civilized land. There was more here. This was vast, strange, uncertain. We had left the settlements far behind. What lay ahead was extensive and grand, as august as the oceans, as colossal, also as mysterious; it set us a challenge, but also suggested faintly some tragic possibility. It seemed a young land, yet the solitude that lay over it seemed as old as anything on earth. . . .

The lead wagon stuck in a small gulley, and the freighters broke out picks and shovels to free the wagon and improve the small crossing. One of the American employees walked up to see whether any help was needed, and he and I and one of the freighters stood talking during the short delay. The freighter was a rough fellow with untrimmed beard and floppy hat, with the insolent self-assurance of a man who knows his job and accepts no other responsibilities.

"I saw you holding a lot of parley-voo with that little Frenchy last night," the employee said. "What's he doing? Converting you to socialism?"

"Naw," the freighter said. "We talked about painters."

"Painters?"

"Yeah."

"What does he know about painters?"

"He don't know nothing. Calls 'em panthers. Asked me did I ever hear one scream."

"Did you?"

"I told him they sound like a woman wailing, only worse." He grinned.

"Did you ever hear one?" I asked him.

"Can't say as I did, but I lived in painter country all my life, and anybody knows that's the way they sound, like a woman wailing, only worse. They say you can hear one three, four miles."

The employee asked, "What did the little Frenchy say to that?"

"Et it up. Hell, I told him about horn snakes, too, how they got that poison horn in their tail and all. You think he never et that up. Hell, might as well tell 'em the worst, I say, let 'em know what they're up against out here." He was half serious, half joking.

"You been out here before?" the employee asked.

"Naw, and I ain't staying out here this time a minute more than I can help. I get that load off that wagon, I'm long gone, I tell you."

The employee winked at me. "Damned if I don't think he's scared of this country."

"Scared of greenhorns, you mean," the freighter said. He looked around to see who was in hearing distance, then confided, "This here is the queerest crew of people, taken all in all, I ever run up against. You ever see the like?" He shook his head in wonderment, then, not waiting for an answer to his question, walked toward the front of the caravan.

We were more queer than such a man as the freighter could believe. A half dozen of the queer greenhorns among the colonists had been professors in the great universities of Europe, others doctors, lawyers, writers, government officials. How could he understand?

There in the wagons, in the trunks and boxes and purses, in the places where keepsakes and letters and private treasures were kept, each of us colonists preserved a single sheet of paper. It was printed in small type with this heading: "Goals of Our Common Faith." But we called it the Covenant. It listed these points:

1. All those forms of private ownership which lead to inequality and special privilege are to be abolished.
2. Every form of honest toil is ennobling, and each colonist shall take his turn at physical labor.
3. Universal suffrage shall be observed. Every male and female colonist old enough to do the work of an adult shall have the privilege and responsibility of voting.
4. Every person shall have a portion of leisure. Intellectual pursuits as well as all the arts will be encouraged.
5. Education is the birthright of every person. We shall establish free public education for adults and children. Poetry or legend teaching old irrational beliefs will not be taught. Teachers shall devise stories which teach virtue.
6. There shall be no title based on pride and privilege. Titles may be used only to designate the occupation of the holder.
7. Money as a private holding and in any dealing between colonists shall be considered valueless.
8. Everyone shall have complete religious liberty and the liberty of his own conscience.
9. Every colonist shall take from the common storehouse according to his desires without restraint, and there shall be no locks on any doors.
10. Governmental and legal procedures shall not have such contrived intricacy as to delay and thwart justice, but shall be so simple that every person may be his own lawyer.
11. We seek a life ordered by reason and good will; we expect to find such life amid the beauties and common virtues of nature.
12. Care in old age or ill health or misfortune is the right of every human

being.

13. English shall be the official language of the colony; but it is our faith that every nationality and race of man is equal.
14. The rewards of toil should go not to those who inherit wealth, but to those who toil.
15. We denounce the kind of pleasure which comes from observing the discomforts and miseries of less fortunate people, but we believe in human happiness and recreation. We shall have music, enjoyment of nature, wholesome conversation, lectures, and games, some of which shall be devised so as to teach to children the rewards of virtue.
16. At the end of five years or at such time as the New Socialist Colonization Company shall be reimbursed for its investment, all the property derived from the Company shall be the property of each and all of the citizens of the colony. . . .

The journey had been a rough initiation for them. They were intellectuals and the kinds of artisans that work in civilized countries. There was not a jack-of-all-trades among them. These gentlemen had found themselves faced with an adversary so simple, so elemental, so difficult, that it was agonizing: mud. The land of east Texas looked beautiful if you didn't touch it; when it felt the weight of a loaded wagon, it became an enemy. So we had pushed and tugged and pried and cursed in several languages, sometimes using three ox teams for one wagon. The prairies of blackland had been the worst; the soil gripped the wheels like a vise and it was bottomless. Those who wore their wooden shoes had a pitiful time of it, for the shoes kept coming off ten inches underground. Some of them had brought sickness from the lowlands, too—ague, diarrhea, boils on the feet.

Their introduction to Texas had been a cruel contrast: on the one hand, a virgin prairie that grew flowers as early as February; on the other, mud and boils on the feet. ★

Faye Carr Adams

Faye Carr Adams has served as an officer of the Poetry Society of Texas for many years. Born in Lavon, the poet and prose writer has been involved with Southwestern literature since she was a child. She has been included in such publications as *The Christian Science Monitor; The Land; The Texas Anthology; Behold Texas: As Seen by Texas Poets;* and *From Hide and Horn: A Sesquicentennial Anthology of Texas Poets.* Her books of poetry are *Sweet Is the Homing Hour* and *More Than a Loaf.* She has been the state poet laureate alternate twice, in 1970–71 and 1971–72.

La Réunion

Victor Considerant seeking a place to establish a commune,
Chose the hills west of the village of Dallas;
he returned to his native France to recruit immigrants;
embellished by his oratory, his land of promise became a reality
when French, Swiss, and Belgian families joined the project.
The first group arrived in April 1854, they were not farmers
or tradesmen but aristocrats, musicians, artists and jewelers
and physicians; this socialistic commune was to share and share alike,
raise their food from the land and build their houses working together.
Difficulties developed, the soil was shallow over rocks, not suited
to producing, droughts came, winters were harsh, the people suffered
hardships; they became discontented with the colony life.
In 1857 the commune was a failure and it was dissolved.
Some of the families returned to their native land, others
relocated in other parts of Texas, and New Orleans claimed some.
Some joined the inhabitants of the Dallas village of farmers,

tradesmen, cowboys and other pioneers, reverting to their individual talents, these artisans of the dissolved commune, became physicians, musicians, artists and forgot the Utopia promised by Victor Considerant, the community of Dallas grew; Reverchon, a botanist, had a park named for him, the names of Santerre, Allrye Bureau, Ben Lang, Brisbane and others were woven into the history of Dallas, leaving footprints of their culture in their contribution to the Dallas village.
The descendants of La Réunion colonists can be found today but the only remaining landmark of the French colony is the Fishtrap Cemetery, a grim reminder of the past. ★

James T. DeShields

James T. DeShields (1861–1948) wrote several books of the tales of pioneer days that had captured his imagination as a boy and contributed articles on the subject to newspapers, including *The Dallas Morning News.* DeShields set down the stories of frontiersmen he knew and dug historical material from newspaper files and other sources. His *Border Wars of Texas* recounted many Indian engagements. In 1914 he moved to Dallas, set up a dry-goods business, and continued to write in his spare time. He wrote many articles on such subjects as Stephen F. Austin, Sam Houston, John Coffee (Jack) Hays, the battle of the Alamo, the story of the Texas Revolution, Texas border tales, riding and fighting with the Texas Rangers, and the lure of the frontier. He died in Dallas on February 8, 1948. His account of Cynthia Ann's capture first appeared in 1886. Her abduction by the Comanche Indians in 1836 during the bloody raid on Fort Parker was of great interest and was widely known. Cynthia Ann's great tragedy was being ripped from the arms of her family at Fort Parker, being carried into captivity, and finally becoming assimilated into that new "family," marrying Chief Peta Nocona and having children with him. Then, she was once again ripped from the arms of her Indian family and taken back to her white family where she could not assimilate this time. She died of a broken heart shortly after her daughter Prairie Flower died. Her son Quanah was the last of the great Comanche war chiefs. This Dallas writer captures the tragedy of the almost mythical Texas woman.

From *Cynthia Ann Parker*

Contemporary with, and among the earliest of the daring and hardy pioneers that penetrated the eastern portion of the Mexican province of Texas, were the "Parker family," who immigrated from Cole County, Illinois, in the fall of the year 1833, settling on the west side of the Navasota creek, near the site of the present town of Groesbeck, in Limestone county. . . .

These families were truly the advance guard of civilization of that part of our frontier; Fort Houston, in Anderson county, being the nearest protection, except their own trusty rifles. . . .

On the night of May 18, 1836, all slept at the Fort, James W. Parker, Nixon, and Plummer repairing to their field a mile distant on the Navasota, early next morning, little thinking of the great calamity that was soon to befall them.

About nine o'clock A.M. the fort was visited by several hundred Comanche and Kiowa Indians. On approaching to within about three hundred yards of the fort the Indians halted in the prairie, presenting a white flag, at the same time making signs of friendship. . . .

Not daring to resent so formidable a body of savages, or refuse to comply with their requests, Mr. Benjamin F. Parker went out to them, had a talk and returned, expressing the opinion that the Indians were hostile and intended to fight, but added that he would go back and try to avert it. His brother Silas remonstrated, but he persisted in going, and was immediately surrounded and killed, whereupon the whole force—their savage instincts aroused by the sight of blood—charged upon the works, uttering the most terrific and unearthly yells that ever greeted the ears of mortals. Cries and confusion reigned. The sickening and bloody tragedy was soon enacted. Brave Silas M. Parker fell on the outside of the fort, while he was gallantly fighting to save Mrs. Plummer. Mrs. Plummer made a most manful resistance, but was soon overpowered, knocked down with a hoe, and made captive. Samuel F. Frost and his son Robert met their fate while heroically defending the women and children inside the stockade. Old Granny Parker was outraged, stabbed, and left for dead. Elder John Parker, wife, and Mrs. Kellogg attempted to make their escape, and in the effort had gone about three-fourths of a mile when they were overtaken and driven back near to the fort where the old gentleman was stripped, murdered, scalped, and horribly mutilated. Mrs. Parker was stripped, speared, and left for dead, but by feigning death escaped, as will be seen further on. Mrs. Kellogg was spared as a captive. . . .

At twilight Abram Anglin and Evan Faulkenberry started back to the fort to succor the wounded and those who might have escaped. On their way, and just as they were passing Faulkenberry's cabin, Anglin saw his first and only ghost. He says, "It was dressed in white with long, white streaming down its back. I admit that I was worse scared at this moment than when the Indians were yelling and charging us. Seeing me hesitate, my ghost now beckoned me to come on. Approaching the object it proved to be old Granny Parker, whom the Indians had wounded and stripped, with the exception of her underwear. She had made her way to the house from the fort by crawling the entire distance. I took some bed clothing, and carrying her some distance from the house, made her a bed, covered her up, and left her until we should return from the fort. On arriving at the fort we could not see a single individual alive or hear a human sound. But the dogs were barking, the cattle lowing, the horses neighing, and the hogs squealing, making a hideous and strange medley of sounds. Mrs. Parker had told me where she had left some silver, $106.50. This I found under a hickory bush by moonlight. Finding no one at the fort we returned to where I had hid Granny Parker. On taking her up behind me, we made our way back to our hiding place in the bottom. . . ."

A burial party of twelve men from Fort Houston went up and buried the dead. Their remains now repose near the site of old Fort Parker. Peace to their memories. . . .

From May 19th, 1836, to December 18th, 1860, was twenty-four years and seven months. Add to this nine years, her age when captured, and at the later date Cynthia Ann Parker was in her thirty-fourth year. During the last ten years of this quarter of a century, which she spent as a captive among the Comanches, no tidings had been received of her. She had long been given up as dead or irretrievably lost to civilisation.

Notwithstanding the long lapse of time which had intervened since the capture of Cynthia Ann Parker, [Lawrence Sullivan] Ross, as he interrogated his "blue-eyed" but bronzed captive, more than suspected that she was the veritable "Cynthia Ann Parker," of which he had heard so much from his boyhood. . . . So sure was Ross of her identity that . . . he at once dispatched a messenger to her uncle, the venerable Isaac Parker. . . .

Upon the arrival of Colonel Parker at Fort Cooper, interrogations were made her through the Mexican interpreter, for she remembered not one word of English, respecting her identity; but she had forgotten absolutely everything, apparently, at all connected with her family or past history.

In dispair [*sic*] of being able to reach a conclusion, Colonel Parker was about to leave, when he said, "The name of my niece was Cynthia Ann." The sound of the once familiar name, doubtless the last lingering memento of the old home at the fort, seemed to touch a responsive chord in her nature, when a sign of intelligence lighted up her countenance, as memory by some mystic inspiration resumed its cunning as she looked up, and patting her breast, said, "Cynthia Ann! Cynthia Ann!" At the awakening of this single spark of reminiscence, the sole gleam in the mental gloom of many years, her countenance brightened with a pleasant smile in place of the sullen expression which habitually characterizes the look of an Indian restrained of freedom. There was now no longer any doubt as to her identity with the little girl lost and mourned so long. It was in reality Cynthia Ann Parker—but, O so changed!

But as savagelike and dark of complexion as she was, Cynthia Ann was still dear to her overjoyed uncle, and was welcomed home by relatives with all the joyous transports with which the prodigal son was hailed upon his miserable return to the parental roof. As thorough an Indian in manner and looks as if she had been so born, she sought every opportunity to escape, and had to be closely watched for some time. Her uncle carried herself and child to his home. . . .

The ruling passion of her bosom seemed to be the maternal instinct, and she cherished the hope that when the war was concluded she would at least succeed in reclaiming her two children who were still with the Indians. But it was written otherwise, and Cynthia Ann and her little "barbarian" were called hence ere "the cruel war was over." She died at her brother's in Anderson County, Texas, in 1864, preceded a short time by her sprightly little daughter, "Prairie Flower."

Thus ended the sad story of a woman far famed along the border. ★

Frank X. Tolbert

Frank X. Tolbert (1912–1984) was a Dallas institution and larger than life. He was first and foremost a historian and a storyteller. He wrote a regular column, "Tolbert's Texas," that ran for thirty years in *The Dallas Morning News* and was read by thousands. He was also a popular restaurateur in the city, a tradition his children kept up. It was and is mighty fine eating. He founded an annual chili cook-off in Terlingua, Texas. His books include *Informal History of Texas; The Day of San Jacinto; Dick Dowling at Sabine Pass; Bigamy Jones*; and *The Staked Plain.* Tolbert says of *The Staked Plain* in the preface: "This book is written in a style of fiction. Yet it is the truth as some poets remembered it. The poets were frontiersmen I talked with over a period of thirty years." His book, *A Bowl of Red,* about one of his favorite foods—chili—appealed worldwide. Frank wrote short stories for *Collier's; Blue Book; Liberty; Saturday Evening Post; Reader's Digest; Esquire;* and *Argosy.* He wrote for *Leatherneck* during World War II, and became managing editor in 1945. He served stints at newspapers in Lubbock, Wichita Falls, Fort Worth, and finally Dallas at *The Dallas Morning News* where his columns evolved into *Tolbert of Texas: The Man and His Work,* edited by his great supporter and friend, Evelyn Oppenheimer. Tolbert's fiction is not often seen, thus the inclusion of this piece.

From *Tolbert of Texas*: *The Man and His Work:* The Staked Plain

It was very early in the morning and only a slim streak of red showed on the dark skyline when the girl called Woman left the camp of the Tonkawas. . . . Woman was nineteen, a little less than tall, and because of some Spanish blood she had softer, less sculptured features than the other Tonkawa women. Except for a one-year interruption as a house servant in the home of the Quaker Indian agent at Fort Sill, she had been a scout for cavalry regiments on the Texas frontier since she was fifteen.

It was not unusual for Indian women to go on long combat expeditions with the soldiers. The Indian scouts were permitted by some commanding officers to take along their wives as cooks. Woman, though, as an aristocrat of the Tonkawa nation was an individualist, and she insisted on a man's combat duties. She demanded and got the same status and pay as the male scouts. And, up until that early morning in 1871, she had never been cook or bedfellow for any man, red or white.

The fellow who came too close to her found her ready with revolver and scalping knife. Even Lieutenant Kramer, commanding the 4th's Indian scouts, and a man who considered himself a very devil with the women, seemed to have no attraction for the girl.

The Tonkawa language is an agglutinative one. One Tonk verbal phrase meaning love-making is translated into English as, simply, "he-and-she" or "heing-and-sheing." When Lieutenant Kramer made one of his frequent plays for her, Woman would reply in the biblical English she had learned while living with the Quakers. She would say, "I will not he-and-she with thee, Father Kramer. . . ."

On this early morning, though, Woman was as sad as she'd ever been in her young life. For she had been fired. She had been ordered to leave Fort Griffin and never return to the command. The orders were from the new colonel of the 4th, Ranald Slidell Mackenzie. Stories had been poured into the new colonel's ears and he suspected Woman of being a cannibal priestess at Tonkawa wolfskin dances, of being a prostitute, and a general distracting influence. . . .

Woman's friends the Quakers had great influence on her, especially on the Old Testament way she spoke English. Except for a slight weakness for stealing colored cloth when she got the chance, Woman was a kind of prim, capable little Quaker girl.

This morning, for want of a better objective on that wild frontier, she was going to head for Fort Sill. The Quakers would be glad to take her back, for she was a good domestic worker. . . .

Woman had found Mackenzie, the new colonel of the 4th Cavalry, to be much more severe than her former bosses, Generals Custer and Grierson, though she hadn't actually had any conversations with Mackenzie. Custer had taken his 7th Cavalry to the north. Maybe she might catch on again with Grierson's regiment at Fort Sill. If not there were always the Quakers, and maybe she could learn to read.

She would have liked to read the carefully folded note which she carried in a pocket of her buckskin jacket. When she was ordered the day before from the 4th Cavalry, she'd asked Lieutenant Kramer to write her a sort of letter of introduction. This might help her if she were stopped by U.S. troops or Texas Rangers on the dangerous miles between forts Griffin and Sill. White men were very ignorant about Indians, and many might take her for a Comanche or Kiowa.

The chief of scouts, a mischievous, blond young fellow, and still miffed because she hadn't seemed to find him attractive, had obliged with this letter in tall, boldly written script:

> TO WHOM IT MAY CONCERN: This will introduce Woman of the Tonkawa Indian tribe, which has always been more or less friendly with the whites, mainly because they are a lazy, drunken bunch and want someone to look out for them. She has worked for the agent at Sill and can speak a fair English but can't read, of course. She will tell you she has been a combat scout for three U.S. cavalry regiments. This is true. And she is a she-devil in a fight. Some say she is a cannibal. This is probably true, for she's a Tonk. She will lie, steal, and cut out your heart if she takes a notion. Watch her like a hawk!

Kramer didn't sign the note.

Though she couldn't read, Woman treasured the piece of writing from the handsome lieutenant. . . .

Dulce Deno [and] Woman . . . were very good friends, and Woman had heard that Dulce had returned to Griffin Town the afternoon before. Before leaving, Woman stopped to say good-bye to Dulce and to get the white woman to read the lieutenant's letter. . . .

When Woman came in, Dulce and Lonnie Nabors were dancing. . . .

Soon after Woman arrived, Pruitt and his bunch left Griffin Town.

It was pretty well known, though never proved, that Dripping Pruitt was the leader of a gang of white badmen who usually disguised themselves in paint and feathers and buckskin when they raided ranches or attacked trail herds of cattle. This way they put the blame on Indians. Then they would drive their stolen livestock to southern New Mexico. . . .

Miss Deno, after she talked in low tones with Woman, went over to a lamp by the bar to read the letter. Lonnie got up and walked over to the girl. He took off her silk hat and he took her in his arms. The Mexican trio was playing a waltz. Usually, Woman would have knifed any man who did this to her. Yet she did nothing this time except try to waltz. When he saw that the steps were strange to her, he moved more slowly. And she found she could follow the guidance of his hands and the movements of his big body and do what the soft music was bidding them. . . . After a few minutes of this, though, she slipped out of his arms and . . . went over to Dulce at the bar.

"This letter isn't good, honey. I'm going to tell you the truth. The lieutenant was just playing a little joke. Don't show it to anyone else." . . . She read the letter out loud. . . .

The sun was rising out of the bluffs over the Clear Fork. Tonk women had their cook fires going. Through the open door of the saloon, Dulce and Woman and Lonnie could see a spring wagon come down the caliche road that ran from the fort down the hill and into Griffin Avenue. At first, Lonnie and Dulce thought it was General Sherman's rig, some hours ahead of schedule. Then, when it passed down Griffin Avenue, Miss Deno and Woman saw that it was Ranald Mackenzie, colonel of the 4th Regiment, and Lieutenant Kramer riding in the wagon with their saddle horses trailing and with only two cavalrymen for an escort. They were hurrying to Fort Richardson, where most of Mackenzie's squadrons were based, and where he would receive General Sherman late that evening. . . .

"Mr. Nabors here is taking a string of trading horses to Jacksboro Town and Fort Richardson this morning. Miss Placido, I'd feel better if you rode with him for protection. I like you both. There are too many graves in Lost Valley already. . . ."

"I will be glad to ride with thee," said Woman to Nabors. . . .

A young Comanche, leading a painted war horse, came through the trees. It was Crow Appearing. . . .

"We followed you since you left Griffin—Forty Young Antelopes and I—Something has happened over the ridge. . . . Come I will show you. . . ."

In the clearing below was a scene which told a complete story:

The colonel and Lieutenant Kramer were stripped down to their long-handled cotton underwear and each was tied to a wheel of the spring wagon. They were alive and not even hurt, apparently, though their eyes were bandaged. The two escort cavalrymen were dead on the ground with their horses cropping grass near their bodies.

Dripping Pruitt was partially dressed in long-fringed Comanche buckskins. His ruddy face was streaked with war paint. He was rather awkwardly trying to scalp a dead cavalryman. One of his six men was unhitching the mules from the Daugherty ambulance. The others were on the ridge, not twenty yards from where Woman lay in the bush, looking back down the wagon trail toward Griffin. . . .

Woman, Nabors, and Crow Appearing all knew what was next on Pruitt's program.

He would torture the two officers to make things look realistic. Perhaps he might even scalp them before killing them. Then he'd run off the stock, and it would look like another job of the Plains Indians when the 4th Regiment patrol came along. . . .

Lonnie whispered to Woman, "Shoot at Pruitt and the man unhitching the team. My friend here and I will take care of those on the ridge."

They shot at the same time and it sounded like only about five volleys, though many were fired. There were only seconds between the deaths of Pruitt and his men.

The officers tied to the wheels fought at their bonds and shouted things like "Who in the devil are you? Speak up! . . ."

When she was sure Lonnie and the Comanche youth had time to leave, she went down the ridge, too, and got her stock and rode over the ridge with the silk hat set at a smart angle on her pretty head.

The men tied to the wagon wheels were taut with anxiety. She took the bandages off their eyes.

Lieutenant Kramer was the first to speak.

"Thank God, sir! It's our little gal."

"Our little girl, indeed," thought Woman. She said to Kramer, "I am not thine."

"Where are the others?" asked the colonel. "That was quite a volley."

"No others, sir. Thee sent me away alone," said Woman. "I had more than one weapon."

"Most happy to see you," said the colonel, mumbling, for when Pruitt had tied him he had run a tight rope back of the officer's neck, bringing his head far down on his chest.

As the girl made no move to untie him, the colonel surveyed the bodies of the dead men around him and said in his bargaining tones, "You are most welcome to keep the horses of Pruitt and his people for your trouble. Maybe heap reward, too, for killing these fellows."

"Thee do not have to speak baby talk to me, sir," said Woman.

"She's the one you ordered out of camp yesterday, sir," said Kramer in a low voice. "I think you'd better take her back."

The colonel dropped the bargaining tones and said, "I know who she is. The order has been issued, though. No woman will ride as a scout in my command."

It was then that the girl took Kramer's letter from the buckskin case. In her quaint English, struggling to remember, she recited pretty much what Dulce had read to her. Her memory was best on the part where Kramer had written:

"Some say she is a cannibal. This is probably true. . . . She will lie, steal, and cut out thy heart if she takes a notion. . . ."

"One of the most stupid letters ever written, Kramer," was the colonel's mumbled verdict when she had finished her recitation.

The colonel then spoke very crossly. "Young woman, when are you going to get around to untying us?" For he had begun to make mind pictures of the sorry sight he made to the girl, trussed up, and wearing only his underwear.

Woman answered nothing. She tied her riding horse and the mules to the wagon, on the off side from the bound men. She walked up on the ridge and came down with an armload of dried post-oak sticks. She arranged these like a campfire, though she didn't light it right then. She took the big copper pot from one of the pack saddles and poured water in it from a canteen on the ambulance. She put the copper pot on the mound of sticks.

She tried to make her young face look very fierce as she stood near the helpless army officers and spoke some ominous-sounding nonsense in Tonkanese.

She took out her scalping knife and touched the sharp point lightly to the colonel's breast. She traced a heartlike pattern on the underwear near his heart.

"She's just joking, sir," said Kramer. "She's acting out my letter. About me calling her a cannibal and saying she'd cut out a man's heart. She's just trying to scare you, sir."

"She is scaring me. Shut up, Kramer," said the colonel. "You must have had some thought that she was a cannibal or you wouldn't have written that stuff."

The colonel was again in his bargaining tone as he said, "What do you want, girl? Name it."

"My job back," said Woman. "I would ride with thee."

"You've got your job back. You have my word. Now untie me. Take your time untying Kramer here."

"How can I trust thee?" asked Woman. . . .

Woman was a very careful girl. She took out the Bible the Quakers had given her. And she made the colonel place a bound hand, purple from loss of circulation, on The Book and swear she'd never lose her job as long as he was in command.

Only then did she release them.

She lashed the cook pot back on the pack mule and hitched the four Missouri mules to the Daugherty ambulance. She rounded up the stray stock. All this while the numbed officers were struggling into their uniforms.

They put the bodies of the dead cavalrymen in the back of the ambulance. Dripping Pruitt and his boys were left for the buzzards and wolves.

Then Woman, permanent scout for the 4th U.S. Cavalry, rode escort on to Fort Richardson. ★

Elizabeth York Enstam

Elizabeth York Enstam is an independent scholar of urban, community, and women's history. Her books include *When Dallas Became a City: Letters of John Milton McCoy 1870–1881; Using Memoirs to Write Local History*; and numerous essays. She serves as a contributing editor of *Legacies: A History Journal for Dallas and North Central Texas.* She received her PhD in history from Duke University and now lives in Dallas.

From *Women and the Creation of Urban Life: Dallas, Texas, 1843-1920*

Within roughly eighty years from the time of its founding, Dallas developed through four identifiable stages to become a modern city. Always distinguished from the surrounding rural areas by its economy, Dallas by 1880 offered the financial and mercantile services and, before the turn of the century, the cultural experiences and social diversity characteristic of cities. To be sure, the pioneers of the 1850s established a genuinely urban culture, and, during the 1880s, railroads and freight wagon companies turned Dallas into a regional inland distribution center with the economic functioning of a modern commercial city. But only after 1900 could city leaders marshal the resources, whether public or private, to increase services to citizens, multiply opportunities for cultural expression, and protect the most vulnerable residents.

At every stage, women were active participants, whether incidentally in the unusual circumstances of the frontier or later in establishing the distinctive forms of urban living. Beginning in the late 1880s, middle- and upper-class women—virtually all of them married and mothers—worked to improve education and nurture the fine arts, and to alleviate, if not resolve, numerous social problems. Primarily through their initiative, Dallas acquired the agencies, institutions, and organizations to maintain standards for public health and safety, provide dependable assistance to those in need, and both preserve the cultural heritage and extend its expression in following generations. Many of the factors that classified Dallas as a modern city originated in efforts by women to improve life for families.

In that most fundamental of urban characteristics, the economy based upon trade and commerce, women labored at both the unseen, "private" domestic work that sustained the labor force and the more visible and "public" occupations of business ownership and wage employment. By 1920, work for upper- and middle-class wives consisted primarily of services and managerial tasks, changes dependent less on new products and appliances than on a family's ability to hire household help. Among blue-collar families, ever fewer women manufactured goods from raw materials they produced themselves, but higher standards of cleanliness absorbed their "free" time. The female proportion of the Dallas paid labor force grew from around one-fifth in 1880 to more than one-fourth by 1910. At the same time, women spread throughout the city's economy in virtually every occupational category, including clerical and sales jobs, the professions, ownership of businesses, positions as officers in small family-owned firms, and all levels of management in large companies. Although as late as 1920 women in the newer kinds of work barely outnumbered those in jobs related to domestic skills, the growing female presence in the marketplace was as characteristic of the modern city as the variety of employment available there. . . .

One uniquely Anglo-American organization, the voluntary association, proved to be a flexible and highly effective device, both for generating routine social functions and for achieving social change. Forming new friendships through the ladies' aid, industrial, and benevolent societies in churches and synagogues, as well as the secular literary societies and study clubs, women also organized social occasions that fostered acquaintances among their families. Such events gave men, too, contacts beyond those developed through business and trade. With oyster suppers and "evening entertainments," benefit musicales and charity balls, women initiated the community patterns that came to be typical of urban places. Characterized by association at planned events rather than by spontaneous socializing at rural barn raisings and quilting bees, community in Dallas fragmented by 1880 into interest groups based on ethnicity, class, and religion. Individuals consciously chose membership in one or several groups, or none.

For a generation, women's organizations engaged in volunteer service that did as much as the developing urban economy to create the modern city. Unlike the church groups, with their consistently denominational focus, the study clubs very quickly turned their attention beyond merely personal interests and self-improvement to the opening of a privately funded "public" library and reading room, as well as such "village improvements" as planting shrubs around the courthouse. In their subsequent founding of permanent cultural institutions such as the Dallas Public Library and the Art Museum, the clubwomen provided evidence of a new division of civic labor by gender. First emerging in the 1880s and tacitly accepted during the 1890s, the first traces of this profound alteration in community duties appeared with the economic changes accompanying the railroads. The reversal in public gender roles occurred as men abandoned, and women assumed, responsibilities within the city's aesthetic life.

During these years, women also began to extend their customary obligations beyond traditional concepts of charity and benevolence. More than "taking care of our own" with seasonal or occasional "handouts," Dallas clubwomen initiated programs in health care for infants and children, and then for entire families. They sought, too, to "help others help themselves" with preschool education and, for mothers, training in child-care, sanitation, hygiene, and nutrition. Reaching across class and ethnic (and later, racial) barriers, women founded and administered more than half the institutions, organizations, and agencies for public and private assistance in Dallas, whether secular or religious in character.

These pioneering efforts to establish a modern system of regular, dependable relief drew privileged middle- and upper-class women into political activism years before they won the right to vote. Clubwomen achieved the passage of city ordinances that improved health and safety, convinced the Dallas government to create administrative offices for problems affecting women and children, increased the number of city services for children, and succeeded in getting two club leaders elected to public office. With regard to issues clearly related to domestic affairs and the private realm, women found elected officials usually receptive to their views and cooperative in implementing stated goals. Men, also, tended to accept as domestic and female the values which women espoused, although they agreed more reluctantly that women's standards should be transposed from private into public life. The voluntary associations, themselves often classified as a primary characteristic of urban places, became the means by which female energy and expertise applied female values to change public policies and alter public values.

Even the suffrage campaign in Dallas grew out of the city's club movement. Surprisingly, the most useful measure of women's relationship to the city appeared during the campaign for woman suffrage. Like the clubwomen before them, the suffragists tapped a fund of deep public interest in domestic and familial concerns. Communicating their goals through symbols and events intimately linked to local and popular culture, the city's suffragists based their campaign on the rhetoric of motherhood, children, and the home. Benefiting from the clubwomen's consistent tact and diplomacy during the past twenty years, the suffragists won approval by both city and county voters of the woman suffrage amendment to the state constitution in a May 1919 referendum. This local victory suggests readiness by a majority of Dallas voters to extend formal, legal recognition to the significance of women's traditional work, as well as to newly developed public roles for women.

Always, the relationship of women with the city was reciprocal. The urban environment changed women's lives and work, presenting them with unprecedented opportunities, but also with living conditions that were often difficult and sometimes unacceptable. In turn, privileged women worked for improvements and reform, and in the process altered and shaped the physical and social conditions of living in an urban place. Wealth generated by the urban economy's trade and commerce provided the leisure to address public concerns, to ponder and discuss issues and information received from women's organizations in other areas of Texas and the United States. The ease of intracity travel and communication fostered associations and friendships among female members of the ever-growing Dallas population, and such frequent contact encouraged women to share interests and concerns. Urban conveniences expedited the development of enduring relationships as privileged women identified first neighborhood, and then communitywide needs and problems and worked together to find remedies. . . .

The record of women's work in Dallas challenges a fond American tradition, that the frontier held great benefits for women. Statistics alone allow little argument with David Potter's observation that cities offered women employment opportunities never available in rural areas. For individuals, Potter was right, but as members of families, farmwomen benefited from their hard work and sacrifices during the period of early settlement. Aside from economic concerns, the frontier's "liberating" effects in Dallas County were temporary and shallow. Whatever their gains in familial wealth and status, female pioneers, like their men, aspired to re-create accustomed ways—to "return to normal." As soon as physical conditions allowed, women resumed their traditional "places" and reared their daughters to be southern ladies, not participants and leaders in community life. . . .

Armored against social criticism by an imagined moral superiority, yet shut out of the established dignity of the professions and the recognized authority of public offices, single and married women alike learned to wield power through the doctrines of domesticity and maternalism. The result in Dallas was a contradiction of custom and tradition. Accompanying the institutions, organizations, agencies, and services never before available was a new status for women in the form of meaningful influence over what the community became; a voice in policy decisions and allocation of community resources; and acceptance as arbiters of values for community life and of standards for public behavior.

Cities, and not the frontier, emancipated American women. Often related to women's traditional roles, pressing urban problems drew matrons out of their homes into reform efforts, much as the growing, changing marketplace pulled single women into employment. As Dallas women and men divided and shared, contended and cooperated in the interests and concerns of urban life, the public and the private "spheres" overlapped in new ways, creating the forms of modern urban life. ★

Jon R. Bauman

Jon R. Bauman was raised in Dallas and educated at the University of Texas at Austin with a BA in Latin American History and a Bachelor of Journalism. He also studied at the National University of Mexico, University of Buenos Aires. He received a juris doctor at Southern Methodist University Law School. He was a senior partner at Baker & McKenzie and at Jenkens & Gilchrist in Dallas. As a journalist, he was with United Press International in Dallas and with the Associated Press in Buenos Aires, Argentina. He is author of *The Sovereigns and the Admiral: A Biography of Isabel, Ferdinand and Columbus* and *Pioneering a Global Vision: The History of Baker & McKenzie.* His *Santa Fe Passage* was a finalist in the Spur Award for the Best First Novel for 2005. He lives in Dallas with his wife Lou, good friends both. His piece gives a look at Manifest Destiny and the move west.

From *Santa Fe Passage*

THE MAN AND THE HORSE WORKED UP A SWEAT on the trip from Georgetown to the White House. When the president's messenger had arrived at his home earlier on that hot, humid morning, Senator Thomas Hart Benton hurriedly put on a red silk vest and shoved his heavy arms into a swallowtail coat. He donned a battered beaver hat he plucked from the hat rack and heaved his bulk onto his sorrel mare. The horse sucked in a gulp of air and resigned herself to the solid block on her back, but stumbled and almost fell when she crossed the rain-slick boards of Rock Creek Bridge.

The sun came out as he cantered through the federal district, and Senator Benton guessed that something about Mexico had caused James K. Polk to summon him on a Sunday. In the White House drive, the mare stopped to nibble at a tuft of spring grass that was poking up through the gravel. Annoyed, Benton yanked her head up. At the mansion's back door, he dismounted, gave the reins to a stable boy, and followed a stately black butler to the president's office.

The president rose and motioned the senator to a chair in front of his desk. Through the window behind Polk's back, Benton had a fine view of the orange flowers on the trumpet vines and of the just-greened lawn, but the sunlight at Polk's back made it difficult for him to make out the president's features.

"Tom, I need this man—this Collins. What's his Christian name?"

"Matthew, Mr. President."

"The Mexicans have taken the bait. They attacked General Taylor's position on the Rio Grande. It's a by God act of war, and I'm going to Congress for a declaration." Polk hammered his fist on the desk so hard that his inkwell jumped and splashed black liquid onto his blotter.

Thomas Benton and James Polk had been friends and sometimes political allies for years. Benton had staunchly supported the Democratic Party's 1844 dark-horse candidate because the Tennessean had promised to push democracy from Missouri to the Pacific Ocean, and, for years, Benton's had been the loudest Senate voice calling for the westward expansion that was enriching Missouri. His home state was the jumping-off point for traders and fur trappers, and it was booming by selling wagons and oxen, beans and onions to the adventurers, and Benton was always the driving force behind any measure that would bring more money to Missouri.

"Where the hell is this Collins?" Polk asked.

"He's somewhere on the Santa Fe Trail, Jim—Mr. President—but the First Dragoons they sent from Ft. Leavenworth couldn't find him. If Collins is traveling south of the Arkansas River, he's in Mexico and our troops can't cross the border. Even if he's on the American side, the trail meanders all over hell and back and they could have passed one another without knowing it."

"Wherever he is, we've got to get this Collins to Washington in a big damned hurry. I've talked with General Scott. He's planning to invade Mexico on two fronts—from Matamoros and Veracruz. If your man Collins can't fix things for us in Santa Fe, then we've got a monumental problem."

"Mr. President," Benton said, "you'll recall that I told you that there are people in this town who will question your judgment in choosing Collins for this mission." Benton leaned forward to see whether, from the president's expression, he had picked up the senator's attempt to shift any future blame away from himself. The lanky president's thin features revealed his pique.

"Damnit, Tom, you're the one who recommended him. He's your man. You vouched for him."

Benton knew that James Polk, a veteran of backwoods, bareknuckled political wars in Tennessee, had boxed him in. The senator's only choice was to give Matthew Collins his full support. "I think he can do the job, Mr. President, but, with this war coming on, I just wanted to remind you that there are risks. Damn! Sure is humid." Sweat beads rolled down the creases in his jowls.

"Take your coat off, Tom."

Polk, Benton thought while he rose and draped his coat on the back of his chair, was, like him, a Westerner who resented the Easterners' financial stranglehold over the West. But the president knew little of the Missouri frontier and nothing of the Santa Fe Trail. "Mr. President, some of the Americans who've been out in New Mexico a long time have lost their enthusiasm for our democratic experiment. But Collins is pragmatic. He wouldn't want a shooting war that clutters up the Santa Fe trade. He's been a successful merchant on the Trail for twenty years, and he knows he'll make even more money when New Mexico joins the Union."

The senator gave Polk what was meant to be a reassuring smile, one that bared his large square teeth and gave his heavy jaw the set of a mastiff.

"If it's not him, we've got to find somebody who can get to New Mexico's governor," Polk insisted. He stood, put both hands on his desk, and leaned toward Benton. "We don't have enough money or troops to fight on three fronts, and General Scott's plans don't include a full-scale campaign in New Mexico. If we can't control Santa Fe, we can't take California."

"I think Collins will be loyal, Mr. President. I still vouch for him. I know a man here in Washington who's been up and down the Santa Fe Trail two or three times. If you'll authorize funds for his expenses, he'll find Collins."

"How much will he need?"

"Enough for the stagecoach, railroad, and steamboat fares to Independence. He can buy a good horse and tack out there. If we give him something extra for his trouble, five hundred should do."

"Done. Get him moving." Polk walked around his desk and helped Senator Benton struggle into his coat, clapped him on the shoulder, and ushered him to the door. ★

Ruthe Winegarten

Ruthe Winegarten (1929-2004), an activist author who wrote books focused mainly on Texas women's history, was born in Dallas. She began her public life working on the 1946 gubernatorial campaign of Homer Price Rainey, a former University of Texas president who was fired when he refused to censor liberal professors and texts. She received a bachelor's degree in anthropology from the University of Texas at Austin, and helped lead Dallas's Jewish Welfare Federation, served as director of the Dallas Regional Anti-Defamation League of B'nai B'rith office, and earned a master's degree in social work from University of Texas, Arlington. She became a writer in the early 1970s, being fifty before her first book was published. In twenty-five years, she wrote and cowrote eighteen books, rediscovering almost everything ever forgotten about the history of women, African Americans, Latinos, and Jews in Texas. In the early 1970s, Winegarten and fellow Dallas housewife Ann Richards started a sketch comedy group they called "Political Paranoia," which was the foundation for Winegarten's first book, the *Texas Women's History Bibliography.* That book spun off into a second, *Texas Women: A Celebration of History,* cowritten with Sherry A. Smith and Mary Beth Rogers. With black entrepreneur and activist Annie Mae Hunt, Winegarten coauthored *I Am Annie Mae.* In the following piece, Winegarten writes of one of Dallas's most legendary women.

From *Legendary Ladies of Texas*: Belle Starr: The Bandit Queen of Dallas

Belle Starr was a sexually liberated, unconventional nineteenth century woman. Unfettered by social mores and with a mind of her own, Belle refused to be locked into the traditional female roles of her society. . . .

At fifteen, Belle eloped against her father's will to "marry" an outlaw in a mock horseback ceremony. By the age of twenty-three she had two illegitimate children, and had joined a band of horse thieves. After ostracism from family and "polite" Dallas society (which was not much more high-toned than she), and with a second outlaw-lover in hiding, Belle was now on her own. She supported herself by singing in Dallas dance halls, dealing poker as a professional gambler, and running a livery stable which trafficked in stolen horses. Belle dressed flamboyantly in black velvet, long flowing skirts, white chiffon waists, and a man's Stetson hat decorated with an ostrich plume. The *Dallas News* of June 7, 1886, said, "She was a dashing horsewoman, and exceedingly graceful in the saddle," with two revolvers suspended in holsters from a cartridge belt around her waist. Apparently unprejudiced, she had a succession of Indian lovers—Jack Spaniard, Jim French, Choctaw Charlie, Blue Duck, and Jim July—finally wedding Oklahoma Cherokee Sam Starr in the only official marriage which has been verified. She forced her last lover, Jim July, to switch his name to hers, and he became Jim Starr. "Changed my name the first time. After that the men change," she boasted.

The Cleopatra of the Plains was born Myra Belle Shirley on February 5, 1848, near Carthage, Missouri. The youngest child of John and Elizabeth Shirley, stock-raising Ozark farmers, she had two brothers—Ed, eight, and Preston, ten. . . . In 1856, when Belle was eight, the Shirleys moved to Carthage (population 100) where Shirley opened a hotel and stable with horses and hacks for hire. Belle must have learned to ride and handle horses quite young, as she was a superb horsewoman. First attending a private school in the local Masonic Hall, she was remembered by a classmate as a small and dark ten year old, "a bright, intelligent girl but was of a fierce nature and would fight anyone, boy or girl, that she quarreled with." Later Belle probably attended the Carthage Female Academy, a typical frontier finishing school, where the young ladies learned a smattering of Greek, Latin, Hebrew, and French, needlework, and good manners. Belle must have also taken advantage of the optional $50-a-year piano lessons as later legends tout her musical talents. . . .

In October 1863, Carthage was burned by Confederate guerrillas. Now homeless, Belle and her parents, along with hordes of other border state emigrants, headed for Texas.

Upon arrival in the Dallas area, the Shirleys moved into a dugout with

Belle's brother Preston, who had settled several years earlier in Scyene, ten miles east of downtown. At that time, Dallas had a population of 2,000 and one main street, alternately a mud-hole and a dust bowl. The county had its water problems even then, and the clannish Shirleys made themselves unpopular with their neighbors by draining the communal well dry. John Shirley again turned to raising crops and horses. . . .

Historians disagree as to whether Belle's first lover and father of her daughter Pearl was Cole Younger or Jim Reed. Belle herself could have cleared up the mystery, but chose not to do so. In 1886, she granted interviews to correspondents with *The Dallas Morning News* (June 7) and the *Ft. Smith Elevator* (May 30). The *News* story read:

> After the surrender (end of the Civil War), Quantrill's men came to the locality and were at all times welcome guests at her father's home [John Shirley in Scyene]. When less than fifteen years of age she fell in love with one of the dashing guerrillas, whose name she said it was not necessary for her to give. Her father objected to her marriage and she ran away with her lover, being married on horseback in the presence of about twenty of her husband's companions. John Fisher, one of the most noted outlaws in the State of Texas, held her horse while the ceremony was being performed, her wedding attire being a black velvet riding habit.

Both Rascoe and Glenn Shirley believe that Cole Younger was Belle's first lover. According to Shirley: . . . dark, handsome, twenty-four-year-old Cole Younger rode into the Shirley ranch with his three brothers and Frank and Jesse James, fresh from their first bank job at Liberty, Missouri, and Myra Belle fell in love with Cole. When the outlaw rode back with his gang to Missouri in 1867, he left her pregnant with a child.

Myra Belle never saw Cole Younger again. . . . At Northfield, Minnesota, the gang was nearly annihilated; only Frank and Jesse escaped; Cole and Bob were wounded and captured and sentenced to life terms in the state prison at Stillwater. Meanwhile, Myra Belle's scandal swept the Texas countryside. Scyene society ostracized her.

She named her first child, born around 1868, Pearl Younger. Belle was too honest a woman to have given this cherished child a false name. . . . Belle, already suffering from family and local rejection for having borne Younger's child, broke finally with Dallas society and its conventions. Leaving Pearl with her parents, she entered the saloon life of Dallas as a woman on a man's terms, but asking no quarter from men. She supported herself as a singer or an entertainer in a Dallas dance hall, dealt poker and faro as a professional gambler, and did very well financially.

After awhile, Belle became known as the wife of Jim Reed, a two-bit Scyene desperado, also originally from Missouri, and served as the fence for a large band of horse thieves who preyed on Texas herds and ran them north. Belle and Jim soon had a son whom they named Ed Reed.

On November 20, 1873, the first robbery in which Belle herself (along with Reed) is supposed to have participated was that perpetrated upon a wealthy Oklahoma Creek Indian named Watt Grayson, tortured and robbed of $30,000 in gold by a gang, one of whom was a woman dressed as a man. Labeled a criminal by every chronicle, Reed went into hiding, but Belle brazenly established herself at the Planter's Hotel in Dallas.

Belle dressed and behaved in a spectacular manner. She purchased a horse and buggy, a riding horse and a stud which she kept in the stables back of the hotel, hiring a Negro as her special hostler and groom. She dressed in black velvet, with long flowing skirts when she rode side-saddle, and wore white chiffon waists, a tight black jacket, high-topped boots and a man's Stetson hat turned up in front and decorated with an ostrich plume. . . . around her waist she wore a cartridge belt from which two revolvers were suspended in holsters. She attended the races, the circus and the county fair. She would enter bars and drink like a man or take her place at gaming tables for a try of her luck at dice, cards or roulette.

When the mood struck her, she shocked the women and more respectable citizens of Dallas by changing into beaded and fringed buckskin costumes like those worn by Buffalo Bill, and riding at breakneck speed through the streets of the town, scattering everyone to the sidewalk. The constabulary and the whole town was afraid of her; and she gloried in being pointed out as the

Bandit Queen. She had nothing to fear as long as there was no warrant out for her arrest. . . .

Belle opened a livery stable on Camp Street, dealing in stolen horses, near the present location of the *Dallas Times Herald.* Flush from the Grayson robbery, she invested in a string of handsome race horses, including a black stud named Venus who was to become her favorite.

The crossing of two railroads in 1873 had catapulted Dallas, already the world's largest buffalo hide center, into a spectacular boomtown, and Belle was in her element. The teeming town was noisy and disorderly, jammed with a scruffy pack of frontier riffraff squared off in an uneasy truce with a tiny group of civic-minded, law-abiding members of the establishment. The population, now 7,000, had doubled in the last three years, and Dallas boasted the state's best bawdy houses, casinos, and taverns. Every general store had a whiskey barrel serving free drinks to the customers until the saloon keepers, who outnumbered the merchants, stopped the practice with a city ordinance. Herds of longhorns forded the Trinity River across from Dealey Plaza, and Elm Street was a sea of tall white cotton bales.

Belle and Jim were soon implicated in another sensational crime: a holdup at gunpoint of the San Antonio–Austin stagecoach on April 7, 1874. Local newspapers followed the incident with great interest and were soon pleased to announce the arrest of Jim Reed. Reed was released for insufficient evidence, nor was Belle indicted. Later that year Reed was killed trying to escape the custody of a deputy sheriff. . . .

About 1876, Belle began branching out from Dallas. . . . Sometime around 1880, Belle acquired dower rights to a share in Indian communal land by marrying Sam Starr, an Oklahoma Cherokee. The couple and Belle's children, Pearl and Ed, settled in a log cabin overlooking a curve of the Canadian River. Belle romantically named their new home "Younger's Bend. . . ."

At the age of forty-one, on February 3, 1889, Belle was murdered by an unknown assailant, blasted from behind with four buckshot in her back, as she rode near nightfall on a lonely path by her cabin. Some said she was killed by a neighbor whose advances she had rejected. But local gossip insisted that her own son Ed Reed had killed her. . . . The real murderer was never caught.

Belle was buried in her front yard, dressed in black silk skirt and white waist, clasping her favorite six-shooter. In an ancient tribal ritual, each Cherokee passing by for a last look dropped pinches of cornmeal into the coffin. Pearl commissioned the following tombstone inscription:

Shed not for her the bitter tear,
Nor give the heart to vain regret;
'Tis but the casket that lies here,
The gem that filled it sparkles yet. ★

David J. Murrah

David J. Murrah is a vice president and senior historian with Southwest Museum Services in Houston. Prior to his semiretirement in 2002, he served the company as its historian and later as General Project Manager. His major projects have included the National Museum for the Pacific War at Fredericksburg, Texas; Roanoke Island Festival Park, at Manteo, North Carolina; The Stanzel Model Aircraft Museum at Schulenburg, Texas; and the Lea County Cowboy Hall of Fame and Western Heritage Center at Hobbs, New Mexico. Murrah has written or edited six books related to Texas history and more than forty other publications. His most noted works are *C.C. Slaughter: Rancher, Banker, Baptist; Oil, Taxes;* and *Cats: A Saga of the DeVitt Family and the Mallet Ranch.* He is currently writing a centennial history for the Northwest Texas Conference of the United Methodist Church. Murrah retired in 1996 from Texas Tech University after a twenty-five-year career as archivist and director of the Southwest Collection. He holds a BA degree from Hardin-Simmons University and MA and PhD degrees in history from Texas Tech. He is a past president of the Society of Southwest Archivists (SSA) and the West Texas Historical Association. He is the recipient of SSA's Distinguished Service Award and is a lifetime member of WTHA and a Fellow of the Texas State Historical Association. The Texas Tech Ex-Students Association honored him with its Distinguished Service Award. He and his wife Ann make their home in Rockport, Texas. His story of Slaughter gives the foundation of Dallas banking and the Baylor Hospital conglomerate.

From *C. C. Slaughter: Rancher, Banker, Baptist*

C[hristopher] C[olumbus] Slaughter, [J. R.] Couts, and [William E.] Hughes were examples of the new wealth of Texas—enterprising young men who took advantage of opportunities afforded by the South's struggling but resurging economy. Having long realized Texas' desperate need for capital, the three decided to pool their resources to establish a new banking venture. Rapidly growing Dallas seemed to offer the greatest promise.

In 1873 a Dallas newspaper heralded the city as "the commercial center of North Texas." The year before the former village had doubled its population to reach seven thousand residents. More than any other factor, the arrival that year of the Houston and Texas Central railroad, the city's first, caused the tremendous boom. . . .

With the arrival of a second railroad in Dallas, the Texas and Pacific, Slaughter and his banking partners concluded that Dallas was the place to invest. On May 31, 1873, in league with an established insurance man, T. C. Jordan, Hughes, Slaughter, and Couts obtained a charter for the creation of a Dallas state bank to be capitalized at $250,000. From Weatherford, Hughes, Couts, and Slaughter secretly moved $42,000 in gold and silver in a buckboard across sixty miles of frontier roads to their new banking facilities in Dallas. Seventeen thousand dollars of the fund belonged to Hughes; C. C. Slaughter and J. R. Couts contributed $12,500 each. Named the City Bank of Dallas, the new business attracted investors. For a few months Slaughter, Couts, and Hughes remained in the background as directors. Jordan, who had practiced banking in connection with his insurance business, became the first president, and R. P. Aunspaugh was cashier.

Despite the panic of 1873, City Bank soon moved into a remodeled building, described by a newspaper as "an honor and ornament to Dallas." Financial troubles, however, forced President Jordan to sell his interest in the enterprise, and Hughes succeeded Jordan as president. C. C. Slaughter persuaded his father in 1874 to buy into the venture, and the elder Slaughter immediately moved from Kansas to booming Dallas to watch over his money.

C. C. Slaughter had already moved to Dallas. . . . Slaughter's young family adapted rapidly to its new environment. Within two years Cynthia Jowell Slaughter had achieved a measure of prominence in Dallas society. Seemingly recovered from an 1873 illness, she became involved in community activities. The five children, ranging in age from two to fourteen, kept busy with school and chores.

Tragedy, however, struck during the spring of 1876. In May, Cynthia became ill with what was termed a "complication of diseases." Though she gradually weakened, her illness for a time was not considered serious, but on May 16, while on business in Fort Worth, C. C. was suddenly called home to be with his wife. The following evening Cynthia died quietly in her sleep at the age of thirty-two. "Her sudden death was a terrible blow to the afflicted husband and five motherless children," reported the local newspaper, "and a large circle of friends [were] left to mourn her loss. . . ."

Although grief-stricken, Slaughter soon sought a new mother for his children. While on a trail drive to Kansas during the summer of 1876—his last time to herd cattle north—Slaughter . . . asked some local Emporia residents to introduce him to a lovely young lady. . . . In mid-January Slaughter returned to Kansas to claim his bride. At the Averill home in Emporia, after an all-night wedding party, he and Carrie Averill were married early in the morning of the seventeenth and immediately boarded a train for Dallas, Carrie's home until her death in 1928.

Throughout his career, Colonel Slaughter dedicated most of his time to the cattle business. Three other interests, however, attracted his attention, and to these he wholeheartedly devoted himself when presented the opportunity. They were his beloved city of Dallas, his church, and his family.

When Slaughter moved his family to Dallas in 1873, the community boasted a population of 7,054; at his death in 1919, it had 150,000 residents. Over the years his love for the city grew as rapidly as its population. He admired its busy atmosphere, its steady growth, and its abundant opportunity. In addition to his heavy investment in city property, he helped promote numerous businesses, major civic events, churches, and medical institutions.

Slaughter monitored Dallas' financial, social, and philanthropic activities through his long association with the city's banks. Following his organization of the American National Bank on March 4, 1884, Slaughter served as its vice president but rarely participated in the bank's daily business activity. . . . However, Slaughter consented to [a] merger, and for his $30,000 investment in the old bank, he received $150,000 with an option to buy into the new bank. In October 1905 he invested $50,000 in the American Exchange National and became a director and vice president, positions he held until his death.

The merger created a powerful financial institution in Dallas, and by 1910 the bank was the state's largest, with capital and surplus totaling $2,500,000. Subsequently, the American Exchange merged in 1929 with its major rival, the City National Bank, thereby creating the powerful First National Bank. . . .

C. C. Slaughter made a more important contribution to religious activities. A longtime member of the First Baptist Church of Dallas, he served on the 1890 building committee that supervised the construction of the church's present sanctuary. Of the $90,940 cost, he reportedly contributed $60,000, or about two-thirds of the total. . . .

No one did more to stir Slaughter's heart—and open his checkbook—than George Washington Truett, a dynamic young Baptist preacher who became Slaughter's pastor at Dallas in September 1897. . . . In May 1903 he influenced Slaughter to pledge $50,000 toward a new Baptist hospital. Constructed on a site where the Colonel had once bedded down cattle, the hospital opened in March 1904. Reportedly, the directors considered naming the facility in honor of its generous benefactor, "but the disadvantages of having a hospital known as the Slaughter Hospital brought the decision to find a less pointed name," the Texas Baptist Memorial Sanitarium. . . .

In November 1913, encouraged by Truett, Slaughter once again stunned Texans by pledging a challenge gift of $200,000 to the hospital. In a letter Truett read to the Baptist General Convention, philanthropist Slaughter promised to give two dollars for every three given by others in a drive to meet the "remarkable growth and urgent needs" of the sanitarium. . . . Shortly before leaving to spend six months with the United States Army in Europe, he persuaded Slaughter to cancel $162,000 he held in the hospital's bonds. According to J. B. Cranfill, the resulting cancellation of the bonded indebtedness was "the crowning achievement of C. C. Slaughter's life." The Colonel's total contributions to the sanitarium, which was renamed Baylor Hospital in 1920, may have exceeded $320,000. . . .

Colonel Slaughter was spared the agony of witnessing the final demise of his empire. On January 25, 1919, two weeks before his eighty-second birthday, the old cattleman died. . . . Within two years . . . sixty-five years of building a vast West Texas empire was undone by Slaughter's children. . . . Unfortunately, the dissolution of the vast ranching domain deprived Slaughter of the significant place in history he deserved. No longer did his far-flung cattle empire stand as a visible embodiment of his wealth and power, and the greatness of his accomplishments was forgotten as rapidly as his legacy was carved into hundreds of cotton and small grain farms. Furthermore, family disharmony, which continued beyond his own children's generation, prevented any united effort to memorialize his life. . . . Slaughter had "built his own monuments"—Baylor University and seven other Texas Baptist colleges, as a tribute to his appreciation of Christian education; Baylor Medical Center in Dallas, in 1979 a $100,000,000 complex, as evidence of his humanitarianism; and a thriving cattle industry in West Texas, as testimony of his faith in the importance of land and cattle. ★

Michael V. Hazel

Michael V. Hazel is a native Dallasite and fifth-generation Texan. He has been an adjunct professor in history at both Southern Methodist University and the University of North Texas. He has served as interim director of both the Dallas Historical Society and the Dallas County Heritage Society. Since 1989 he has edited a semiannual regional history journal, *Legacies,* focusing on Dallas and North Central Texas. He is author of *Dallas: A History of Big D* and *Dallas: A Dynamic Century,* as well as editor of *Dallas Reconsidered* and *Stanley Marcus from A to Z.* Hazel writes of the women who were instrumental in establishing the Dallas Literary system.

From *The Dallas Public Library: Celebrating a Century of Service, 1901-2001*

There had been public libraries in Dallas since the 1870s, but like most libraries in the United States, they were really private libraries, open only to those who paid a subscription. One of these, founded by Colonel John C. McCoy in 1884, began above a music store on Main Street and later moved to the city hall with more than 1,600 books. Another, under the auspices of the Pierian Club, a women's literary society, was housed in the home of Mrs. Richard W. Allen on Fairmount Street; the club later donated its volumes as the nucleus for a traveling library in rural areas. The development of the public school district after 1884 increased the demand for library facilities, especially since the only reference books in the high school library when it opened were an encyclopedia and dictionary furnished by the principal and superintendent.

"Pauline Periwinkle" (Mrs. S. Isadore Miner), a columnist for *The Dallas Morning News* . . . reminded her readers in 1897 that "the stranger in a small town is often surprised by the size and completeness of a library that gives him an opinion of the progress of its people no other enterprise could have provoked. . . ."

Andrew Carnegie's decision to donate a large part of his fortune to building public libraries provided an opportunity [for] . . . Dallas club women [to] initiate the movement, led by May Dickson Exall. . . . May enrolled in Vassar . . . [and was] probably among the minority of college-educated women in Dallas at the time, and when the Dallas Shakespeare Club was formed in 1886, its members elected her their president.

In November 1898, Mrs. Exall invited representatives of several other clubs to meet and organize a Dallas Federation of Women's Clubs. . . . The first project adopted by the Dallas Federation was the securing of a public library for Dallas.

The Friends of the Dallas Public Library continues to live up to its reputation as the best public library friends' group in the country. . . . Given the combination of a valuable product and strong support . . . Director Ramiro Salazar says, "I see a bright future for the Dallas Public Library. . . ." Lillian Bradshaw, whose association with the Dallas Public Library covers more than half its history, observes, "I want to see the Dallas Public Library be a library for all the citizens of Dallas, regardless of ethnicity. . . . It has the potential to do this, but it must continue to gather support from the entire community." If this happens, the efforts of May Exall and the other founders will be justified, and the Dallas Public Library will continue to be a crown jewel of the city for centuries to come. ★

Ted Dealey

Ted Dealey (1892–1969), journalist and publisher, in Dallas, Texas. He attended Dallas public schools, the Terrill School for Boys, and received a BA degree from the University of Texas and an MA degree in philosophy from Harvard. He began his career with *The Dallas Morning News* as a reporter and a member of the fifth generation of his mother's family in the newspaper business. Dealey became an editorial writer and editor of a Sunday magazine supplement, began his rise as a board member of the Belo Corporation and assistant to the publisher, vice president, and finally president in 1940, succeeding his father, who had established *The Dallas Morning News* in 1885. The excerpt reprinted here from "'Colonel Bill': One of the last of the old-time personal journalists" is from the October 1, 1935, Golden Jubilee Edition of *The Dallas Morning News* for private distribution to friends and associates of the writer. In it he captures the importance of the journalists to early Dallas.

From 'Colonel Bill': One of the last of the old-time personal journalists

In this day of worldwide news coverage and specialized editorial analysis, the voice of the old-time "personal" journalist has been largely stilled. And with his passing has gone some of the color of the press. But these old-timers have left a heritage of fine traditions to the present generation of newspaper writers.

Among the last of that tribe to go was Colonel William Greene Sterett of *The Dallas Morning News,* whose memory is still green in the hearts of many not only in the Southwest, but in the national capital and the country at large. It is of him that this story deals.

The colonel came to Dallas from Port Lavaca in 1872 and shortly afterward bought out the old Dallas *Times,* which he ran for several years with varying success. Even with his many qualifications, Sterett's career as an independent publisher was fraught with obstacles. In the first place, the colonel was no businessman. He simply couldn't be bothered with the details of bookkeeping, selling advertising, or collecting bills. He was essentially a writer. In the second place, his newspaper, *The Times*—an afternoon sheet—was, to say the least, undiplomatic in its treatment of the news of the day. If a killing occurred on the streets of Dallas, regardless of the prominence of the killer or the possible extenuating circumstances, such as self-defense, *The Times* on the next day would carry over the story some such headline as: "Another Cold-Blooded Murder," and would then go on with all the lurid details, sparing nothing. But the colonel was redheaded and from Kentucky and was plenty able to take care of himself. If necessity arose, he was always amply prepared to defend his own person and the independence of his newspaper with his fists, or anything else that came handy.

There were two sides to Colonel Bill Sterett. To those with whom he was not intimately acquainted, he was a trifle uncouth as to manner, way of expression, style of dress. In all he was utterly careless. He didn't care how he looked so long as he was comfortable. His Southern associations and his complete democracy—which made all men in all walks of life equal in his eyes—contributed toward a colloquial manner of speaking which was nothing short of ungrammatical at times, although Colonel Sterett wrote, and thought, like an angel. Indeed, this was one of the most noteworthy characteristics of the man. In ordinary conversation he slurred his words, mouthed them when in excess of enthusiasm or amusement, used double negatives, slang, vernacular—anything to serve his purpose. But put a pencil in his hand and a Macaulay spoke. Beneath the eccentricities of speech, raiment, and manner, the real merit of the man shone like a star. . . .

Many amusing stories have been told about Colonel Sterett and his Dallas *Times* . . . the colonel told me [stories] himself and, lest they die with me, I will here and now preserve them for posterity.

"One time," related Colonel Bill, "some famous Shakespearean actor come to town to put on a bunch o' plays. I forget now who it was. Maybe Booth or Forrest—it don't make no difference. Anyhow one o' th' plays was *Julius Caesar*, and, when it was at th' op'ry house I went to take it in an' write a review for th' paper. Well, it was a pretty good show an' I was takin' notes an' gettin' along fine with th' review I meant to print till th' Roman mob scene come on. After that, I couldn't think o' nothin' else. I couldn't git that Roman mob out o' my mind. I left th' op'ry house before th' show was over an' went to th' office an' wrote my review. It ran to about a column an' a half. In it I never mentioned th' name o' the show or what company was playin' it or th' name of th' famous Shakespearean actor that was th' leadin' man. No, I never mentioned one single, solitary thing but that Roman mob. . . . All of that mob was Irishmen from Leftwich & Jamison's brickyard acrost the river. I knew ever one of 'em personally. It fascinated me to see those big double-jointed Irishmen out there in little short skirts, with their knobby bare legs showin,' all covered with red hair. It was th' most ridiculous an,' as I say, th' most fascinatin' sight I ever saw. . . . So I sat down and wrote that column an' a half review on that Roman mob an' I didn't call 'em Romans, either. I called 'em all by their first names—Joe or Pat or Bill or Dan, or whatever th' case might be. An' I described each one of 'em's costume and how he walked and acted, an' all like that. Then, th' next day, I printed it.

"That evening late, th' manager of th' show come to th' office and called on me. He wanted to know how many extra copies o' th' paper I had. There wasn't many left, but he bought 'em all an' then had me start up th' press and run him off some more. He left town with a good-sized trunk full. He told me that that company had played all over th' world, but that they never had got no review like this one before, not never in their whole career! . . ."

[T]his is another story. I'll preface it by saying that Colonel Bill wrote probably the worst hand in the world. His handwriting was, in fact, so terrible that only the old-time printers, who were accustomed to it, could read it with any facility. In his later years, Colonel Sterett was persuaded to take up the typewriter. Always young in his ideas, he did so. For the last eight years of his life most all of his articles were produced on a machine. But, marvelous to say, his stories were just as illegible when typed as when written by hand. This may be taken by some as an extravagant statement, but it is the absolute truth. What with hitting the wrong keys, "x-ing" out mistakes, hitting the shift key or the spacing bar at the wrong time, penciled interlineations and what not,

Colonel Bill would never have been able to make a living as a stenographer. Had he written: "Now is the time for all good men to come to the aid of the party," it probably would have got to the printer in some such form as this: "now is th$time frail goOl me*n tO cOME *tVz* a ido f th-p aartyoe," with some penciled corrections that made it even worse.

So, whether the basis of this story was the fault of Colonel Sterett's own peculiar style of chirography or whether it was due to the agony of obstetrics on a typewriter makes no particular difference. The facts in the case are these:

One morning along about 1919 or 1920, Colonel Sterett came shuffling down the second floor of *The News* office—this is the editorial floor—seersucker suit, battered sandals, vari-colored Panama hat and all. His face was red and he was more than serious. He was mad.

He stopped at my desk and slapped down on it belligerently a half rolled-up newspaper and exclaimed:

"Them ——damned printers have done made me th' laughin' stock of Texas!"

"What's the matter?" I inquired respectfully.

"Looky here," exclaimed Sterett, spreading out the paper and pointing to a certain line of type in a story of his that appeared in that morning's issue. "Just look at that damn thing!"

I read a few paragraphs. The story was one on the dipping of cattle for fever ticks. And the portion of the yarn that had roused Colonel Bill's ire was one in which something was stated about dipping the steers in marble vats. It really did sound rather peculiar. The colonel waited impatiently until I had scanned a few sticks of type.

"You see!" he choked. "You see what they done . . . Who ever heard o' dipping a cow in a ——damned marble vat! People will think I've gone crazy."

"Yeah," I agreed sympathetically. "It's pretty bad. . . . But what did you write, colonel?"

"Movable vats, by God," exploded the old man, "movable vats!" ★

Willie Newbury Lewis

Willie Newbury Lewis (1891–1985) was a lifelong resident of Dallas. In addition to *Willie, A Girl from a Town Called Dallas,* she has also written *Between Sun and Sod: An Informal History of the Texas Panhandle* and *Tapadero: The Making of a Cowboy,* the biography of her husband. As you will read from the following excerpt from her candid autobiography, she wrote of a period of Dallas life that showed a city growing up. She was part of the social milieu of the city and contributed much to the culture of the city through her memberships in the Dallas Historical Society where she was a board member, president of the Dallas Shakespeare Club and the Founders' Garden Club. She was a charter member of the Dallas Women's Club and helped found the first Meals on Wheels program in the state. She was also cofounder of the Women's Council of Dallas County.

From *Willie, A Girl from a Town Called Dallas*

I was born in a cottage on Saint Louis Street in a part of town commonly known as the Cedars. In the early 1890s Dallas, although the fastest-growing community in Texas, was little more than an unsophisticated, overgrown small town. Like Mastern Street and certain parts of Ross, McKinney, and Maple avenues, the Cedars was considered one of its better residential districts. Ervay Street was a block and a half to the west of my home, Harwood Street a block to the east, and the business district within easy walking distance.

Even in the better homes, gas and electricity were not accepted parts of daily living. Houses were heated by fireplaces or by large wood-burning stoves, and air-conditioning was as yet unknown. The summers thus seemed much hotter than they do today. Some respite from the heat was achieved at night by keeping the windows open, but during the day when the sun glared down, windows were closed within an inch of the sill, and the shades were drawn. Everyone who was not working attempted to sleep during the hot afternoons. The sound of the neighborhood yardman's lawnmower, accompanied by the song of the cicadas, or katydids, as everyone called them, was prevalent everywhere.

Lamps were the commonest form of lighting. In my home there hung from the center of the living room ceiling a chandelier-like contraption composed of a central container for coal oil and five or six adjoining burners resembling candelabra. My father had a special stick that enabled him to apply a lighted match to the tips of the burners, and the lighting ceremony took place each evening at the approach of dusk.

Another ritual—though more of a weekly chore than the daily routine it is today—was bathing. According to some reminiscences, there were practically no bathtubs at that time, even in the finer homes, but I have no recollection of bathing in any way other than in a stationary, tin-lined tub in a bathroom.

Transportation at the turn of the century was also quite different from the streamlined systems of today. The three main streets of the business section—Elm, Main, and Commerce—were paved with *bois d'arc* blocks, and the other streets, having remained in their natural state, became a muddy slush when it rained. Crossing for pedestrians was possible only at intersections where a walk of planks was constructed by laying two wide planks together and placing a third on top in the center where the lower two were joined. The well-to-do in town kept horses and carriages, while the rest walked or hired a hack—or a victoria, if the occasion demanded more dignity.

In time, Dallas installed a transit system. The streetcars were mule-drawn, entirely open vehicles with a long bench on either side of the car for seating. The streetcars would follow certain routes on what were loosely termed "belt-lines." Often on Sundays, my parents would give my playmate and me a nickel apiece to amuse ourselves with a long ride.

When the recently invented telephone arrived in Dallas, it was a clumsy affair that hung on the wall. At the side was a handle that, when cranked, attracted the attention of the operator, who then made the proper connection.

Residential telephones were few, and even many business houses considered them unnecessary.

There were, of course, no supermarkets, and the grocery stores offered mainly staples such as flour, sugar, meal, coffee, and meat. Vegetables usually were procured from the vegetable man, who made daily rounds in his wagon. It was not considered good form for the mistress of the house to go out to the wagon to select her own vegetables, but my mother paid little heed to this edict, since our one maid was usually busy at more strenuous tasks.

Many prominent families lived in the Cedars, but only a few were friends of my parents. The heads of these families were older, well-established businessmen, and my parents were very young. Later, my father came to know the heads of these families very well.

My father, Henry Lee Newbury, while in his early twenties had moved with my mother, Anna Hearn Newbury, and their small son, Orren, from Pilot Point to Dallas. Father had accepted a permanent position with the Trezevant and Cochran Insurance Company, for which he had been working as an outside agent. Through the advice of Sam P. Cochran, one of the partners in the company, he later moved to a better position as cashier in the City National Bank. Eventually my father left the bank to go into business for himself. During all my younger years he was a shoe merchant, and his original store was on Elm, near Griffin. Later, he expanded to include a store in Fort Worth, the shoe department in the original Titche-Goettinger store, and a small store for used merchandise farther out on Elm. . . .

My mother was among twelve women invited to a luncheon to discuss the formation of a local garden club, and this luncheon was the initial step in the formation of the Dallas Garden Club (part of the Dallas Woman's Club). When the club published its first garden book, she contributed the chapter on classification of wildflowers. Later she was consulted by the Texas Highway Department on the subject of developing the growth of wildflowers along the state's highways.

The family home was run in about the same manner as the greenhouse. Mama was an excellent housekeeper and set a good table. I remember well the hours my mother spent each fall making quart after quart of mincemeat for winter pies. I still serve at my table today the kind of charlotte russe and snow pudding that my mother used to serve.

As comfortable and homelike as our house was, Mama was completely disinterested in beautifying it. . . . The family did, however, possess and enjoy some beautiful things: a silver tea service that had belonged to the Newbury family, beautiful knives, forks, teaspoons, and tablespoons. The tablespoons, molded from melted silver dollars, were especially prized because they had been a wedding gift at Grandpa Newbury's postwar wedding. Their unusual method of manufacture came about because no silver was available for purchase following the Civil War. We also owned an entire set of Haviland china decorated with violets, which, however, was used only on special occasions.

My mother was a member of the Saint Cecilia Choral Club, an organization promoted and managed by a busy little woman, Mrs. Jules D. Roberts. On occasion the choral society gave concerts, but its most important function was to sponsor annually in Dallas the appearances of such renowned artists as Ignace Paderewski. I accompanied my parents to the concerts and was often taken backstage to be introduced to the artist of the evening.

My mother also belonged to two neighborhood book clubs. The book club of that era enabled its members to keep abreast of numerous current novels through the purchase of only one. There were always twelve members, and after reading her own novel, each member passed it on at the first of the month to another specified member, probably her nearest neighbor. The variety of novels that arrived monthly at our house greatly encouraged my love of reading.

Both my parents loved the theater. When the old opera house burned in 1901, a new and much larger one was constructed on Commerce Street, for Dallas has always been theater oriented. Even in those early days, the best talent from New York was available on occasion, giving Dallas patrons the privilege of seeing such performances as Richard Mansfield in *Monsieur Beaucaire,* Joseph Jefferson in *Rip Van Winkle,* and James O'Neill in *The Count of Monte Cristo.* I shed copious tears over Bonaparte's farewell to Josephine and thrilled with teenage delight over fat old Chauncey Alcott's rendition of Irish love songs. As a result, the theater has never lost its fascination for me.

At that time, Dallas society was loosely divided into two sets, the "church set" and the "society set." My mother and father belonged to the former. Whether my mother's timidity was the result of temperament or of her forced adjustment, while immature, from the intimate circle of a small town into the more sophisticated life of Dallas is an undecided question. Although pretty, well mannered, well educated, and stylishly dressed, she had little self-confidence. As a result, Society with a capital S never appealed to her. Her one concession to formal society was to hire each fall a specially designed pleasure carriage for two known as a victoria, and gowned in her best, with calling cards in hand, to make the rounds of certain matrons' homes. When I became old enough, I often accompanied her. . . .

From the beginning, my parents intended that their children have the best possible education. I started school at the Columbian Public School on Akard Street, but at the end of the second year I was placed in Miss Cowart's School for Girls. I can well remember that momentous morning when my mother dressed me in the sort of uniform I was to wear through all my younger school years: a plaid woolen dress over which was worn a beruffled, clean, and starched white apron. I also wore long black stockings and, during the winter months, heavy underwear. The wearing of this apparel began on a certain date in the fall and ended on a certain date in the spring, regardless of the temperature. . . .

Most of the pupils at Cowart Hall were the daughters of parents with only one career in mind for their girls—that of marriage. Miss Lora, as we called Miss Cowart, offered the kind of education that suited that goal. In addition to the basics, she also emphasized good manners and good taste. Lessons in Latin and French began in the first grade. She taught both languages well, but unknowingly pronounced both improperly. Students conjugated Latin verbs and eventually progressed to the translation of excerpts from such works as Cicero's *Orations,* Virgil's *Aeneid,* and Ovid's *Metamorphoses.* I remember translating only one French work, Dumas's *La Tulip noire.*

We were taught to write not only legibly but in a beautiful Spencerian style. This sort of handwriting was slightly larger in form than most, slanting and extremely legible as well as attractive. . . .

In addition to all the events school brought to my life, I was busy in other ways. Even though only nine or ten, I was expected during this time to come directly home from school and, for the remainder of the afternoon, whip lace on petticoats, "drawers," and nightgowns. In this way, I became fairly proficient with the needle. A few Dallasites wore silk lingerie specially made for them by the nuns in the convent, but my mother and I wore only homemade cotton underwear, the products of a dressmaker who earned a dollar and a half a day working for the family several weeks each spring and fall. . . .

About the time I was eleven, various changes began to occur in my life. The two eldest daughters of our much-liked Jewish neighbors had married. Shortly after, their mother, Gaga, died. The youngest daughter, Bertha, was the only one left in their home, and she agreed to rent her house to us under the condition that she be allowed to remain there as our boarder until her contract with the public school where she taught had been fulfilled. Our cottage was quickly put on the market and sold, and we were soon settled in our new place of residence. It was a house of no great distinction but more comfortable and better suited to the needs of our family. It had a sitting room, parlor, dining room, and kitchen downstairs, and four large bedrooms upstairs. . . .

When I was about fourteen, my grandmother Hearn's eyesight failed, making it necessary for my grandparents to move to Dallas, where our family could help care for her. Grandpa, being well-to-do, sold his store and the home place in Pilot Point and bought a house large enough for our two families on the corner of Worth Street and Haskell Avenue. I was delighted with the move because I knew several girls in the neighborhood, the house was by far the largest I had ever lived in, and we had not only a cook and a manservant but also a carriage and a nice team of horses. . . .

Returning to school, I discovered that a new teacher, Kate Wilson, who had recently received degrees from Wellesley and the Sorbonne and who was from the Oak Cliff section of Dallas, had been added to the staff. She was a superb English teacher, and it was from her that I acquired all of my basic knowledge of serious writing. Among my prized possessions are copies of *The Scarlet Letter, Pride and Prejudice,* and *The Marble Faun,* which I read under her guidance, all three marked over with such directions as "shows character," "indication of events to come," and "development of plot. . . ."

In the fall, I entered Miss Holley's School for Girls. This experience was neither educational nor particularly pleasant. Few of my friends were there, because most of them had gone either to schools in the East or to the University at Austin. Although it would have been a financial strain for my parents, I am certain that I, too, could have gone away to school had I wished to go. I was not eager to leave, however, and my parents, like most other people, felt that higher education was not necessary for a girl. . . .

[F]all was approaching, and I began planning the social activities that were to be so much a part of the season. . . . Both my time and my thoughts were occupied with ideas for . . . entertainment, with decisions over the purchase of the necessary additions to my limited wardrobe, and with the party I was planning to have.

My father was a member of the Dallas Country Club, and the dance was scheduled to be held there. It was my wish that the dance take place a short time before the Idlewild Ball. The large new country club had not yet been built, but the comparatively small wooden structure would suffice for the one hundred fifty guests I planned to invite. I was busy making my dance list some days after making the reservation at the club when I was interrupted by a telephone call from Miss Kate, the teacher I had known at Cowart Hall. Miss Kate had not yet married the man whose wealth was to make her social position possible, and she was working as society editor for *The Dallas Morning News* . To my surprise, she was calling on what she seemed to consider serious business, and one question quickly followed another.

"Are you going to the Idlewild?"

"Yes, I have had a date for several months."

"With Ballard Burgher?"

"Are you going to have any special guests?"

"Yes, Lila McClelland, from Clarendon."

"Are you going to entertain?"

"Yes, with a comparatively small dance a week or so before the ball."

"So you are planning to make a debut?"

"No, I have never given such a thing as a formal debut a thought, but it might be fun."

"Indeed it will, and I shall immediately add your name to the list."

Thus it was that by the grace of Ballard's wanting me for a date and my knowing *The Dallas Morning News'* society editor, who happened to place much importance on the entire affair, I became one of the Idlewild debutantes of the 1911 season.

My father's response to my having a debutante ball was that it would be a pleasant experience, but he sincerely hoped I would make every effort not to be extravagant, because he simply could not afford it. Being a debutante meant formal, engraved invitations, new dresses, and numerous other expenses. . . .

My dance was held in early October, a short while before the Idlewild. My party opened the debut season. In every way I attempted to follow my father's instructions that I not be extravagant. Only a few growing green palms and rosebuds decorated the living room of the Dallas Country Club. It was the club's first official home, nothing more than a large two-story frame house on Oak Lawn Avenue. The music was furnished by a small, successful local group. Monogrammed programs announced the dances, which included cotillion figure numbers, a form of dance that was not popular for too long. A buffet supper was served at midnight.

The following morning, however, my father had a serious talk with me. He was pleased that it was a happy occasion, but warned me that if I continued in my extravagant ways, the chances were good that I would ruin the life of some worthy young man. My party, it seems, had cost the large sum of one hundred and fifty dollars. . . .

Because the Dallas Country Club was not of sufficient size, the 1911 Idlewild Ball was held in the beautiful new Jewish Columbian Club. The ball differed from my debutante party in every way; no expense had been spared. The ballroom was elaborately decorated to resemble the façade of an Italian villa. Special lights and an abundance of flowers gave the impression of dancing in an Italian moonlit garden. An orchestra from the East furnished the music. The program consisted of dances, waltzes, two-steps, and the Boston (a new and very popular dance).

Ten young ladies, daughters of prominent families of the city, and five visiting girls were considered the guests of honor. There were two refreshment tables, one serving cocktails for the men and one punch for the ladies. Two years later, the punch table was done away with, and the women then enjoyed cocktails, if they so desired. It was also a few years later that the debutantes were presented in a very formal manner. . . .

At the time of my debut, a harmless but gossipy and widely read little magazine called *Beau Monde* was circulating in Dallas. Owned and published by a Mrs. Fitzgerald, it was a weekly newspaper that, for want of a better name, shall be described as a social or gossip paper. . . . Already such articles as the following were beginning to appear:

> When Will Lewis leaves Spur for Dallas, the florists sit up and take notice, for then there is something doing in the flower market. Orchids and carnations, not by the dozen, but by the dozens, and where there are many dozens of them, there must be an American Beauty somewhere. And Will comes often, not too often, either for the trade or the other and greatest motive, but who is she?
>
> Did you know that there is a bachelor's paradise in Highland Park? That Langdon A. Smith, Paul Vandervelt, Ted Newsome, Will Lewis of Spur, and George Pattullo have a luxurious bungalow there? You will find it in the telephone book. These men call themselves the M. B. Now M. B. stands for many things, Millionaire Bunch, Modern Brigands, Merry Beggars, Mad Bachelors, and lots of things. It was whispered that they were keeping bachelor's hall, but it was quickly discovered that they have three genuine Delmonico chefs and an Oscar menu every day, and now every evening there is a beautifully appointed dinner served to a limited number. On Sunday evening, however, there are from twenty to thirty guests at the dinner table. . . .
>
> It is said that another one of the M. B.'s is anxious to follow Mr. Newsome's example. It was told to the Idler in strict confidence, and being a woman she repeats it under the same condition, absolute secrecy. One initial of the man's name is W. (and another is well-1-1-1, never mind, there is an L in it near the front end). They say—a dangerous informant but serviceable sometimes—that this man is

fond of berries, spelled New ways and old, and our advice to him is go in and win one of the sweetest girls in Dallas. This is a Spur.

Editor's note: Willie did shortly marry Will Lewis and move to the Spur Ranch in West Texas. ★

Natalie Ornish

Natalie Ornish, at the age of fourteen, enrolled in Sam Houston State University, received her BA degree in English at seventeen, and at eighteen received a master's degree from Northwestern University. She worked for the Associated Press in Chicago and Omaha, Nebraska, reporting, editing, and rewriting. A native of Galveston, this astounding woman led a bond campaign to make their library public and then she founded Galveston's first historic museum. She has served as contributing editor for magazines. In Dallas she worked for Rogers and Smith advertising agency. She became one of the nation's first female film producers and holds membership in Information Film Producers of America. She is listed in *Who's Who of American Women; Who's Who in World Jewry;* and *Foremost Women in Communications.* For years the Texas Institute of Letters gave a Natalie Ornish Prize in Poetry. In addition to *Pioneer Jewish Texans,* Ornish annotated Herman Ehrenberg's book, which had been translated from German by Peter Mollenhauer and she also has written Ehrenberg's biography *Ehrenberg: Goliad Survivor-Old West Explorer.* She has done incredible research on Jewish Texans. Without her work I fear that much of the information she imparts would have been lost. I am particularly grateful to her for her work on the Dallas merchants, without whom Dallas would be much less of the city that it is. It would be much less without Natalie Ornish, as well.

From *Pioneer Jewish Texans*: The Great Merchants

When the Texas & Pacific Railroad extended its terminus to Dallas, the small town attracted many, among them young Emanuel Meyer Kahn (pronounced Can) who in 1872 founded E. M. Kahn & Co., which continued for ninety-two years as a family-owned business.

For fifty years, E. M. Kahn served as the president; his son Laurence followed as president for nearly twenty-five years; and his grandson Eugene

Sanger served as president for seventeen years until the sale of the firm to a national organization, Eagle Clothes, in 1969. The new owners kept the name E. M. Kahn & Co. and made another grandson, Alex F. Weisberg Jr. president. In the 1970s, after ninety-two years, the stores closed.

"E. M. Kahn, besides being the oldest retail store in Dallas, had the distinction of being the first air-conditioned store in town. It was the first store west of the Mississippi to have fixed prices. One didn't bargain," said Eugene Kahn Sanger. Until the late 1930s E. M. Kahn operated as a men's clothing store; then in 1936 Laurence Kahn added women's and children's departments. In the 1950s, Kahn's branched into the suburbs. . . .

E. M. Kahn and his wife, Lily Belle (Hurst), had six children. . . . The third child, Felice Kahn, at age fifteen, became a violinist with the first Dallas Symphony Orchestra . . . She gave up her music when she married Alex Sanger of Waco and moved away from Dallas. Alex's father Sam was one of the original Sanger brothers. Alex and Felice lived in Waco forty years or more, until 1938. . . .

"Mother was never happy in Waco," her son Eugene pointed out. "There was little opportunity for music there and few cultural influences, just agriculture and the Katy train running through Waco. She felt stultified. She told me, 'If you can talk your daddy into moving to Dallas, I'll buy you a car.' So I worked at it, and my mother was in her sixties when she returned to Dallas, and my father came to live here for the first time. I got a Packard convertible."

"Every institution, like every individual, to be successful must be useful," said Edward Titche, early Dallas merchant and department store founder. And Titche lived by those words. Only a few months before his death in 1944 he purchased a Dallas mansion and presented it to the Dallas chapter of the Red Cross. Titche became a charter member of the Dallas chapter when it was organized in 1905. At that time he was a partner in Titche-Goettinger Company, then a widely known dry goods and fashion establishment, which merged with Joske's and later Dillard's. . . .

In 1894 his uncle Aaron Titche of Dallas died, leaving no heir. Edward was chosen to run the store his uncle had owned. He renamed the store The Edward Titche Company, but six years later he met Max Goettinger and the two formed a partnership and called the store Titche-Goettinger. Under this name the store achieved its greatest success. . . .

In 1922 Titche served as a charter trustee of the Dallas Historical Society. After his retirement in 1929, he served as a director of the State Fair of Texas, became a thirty-third degree Scottish Rite Mason, a vice president of the Dallas Scottish Rite Hospital for Crippled Children, and adviser to Baylor Medical Center of Dallas.

Many great merchants became philanthropists, but the Sanger brothers became the only ones whose philanthropy grew so extensive that they put themselves out of business. During the years when their firm reigned as the greatest dry goods company west of the Mississippi, the family seemed invincible. In Dallas they were the "epitome of royalty."

They left a trail of stores in many Texas villages in their progress, in an era when chains were virtually unheard of. . . . Following the railroad, in 1872 the Sanger brothers reached Dallas and made it their central location. . . . Sanger Bros. stores had covered the state from Oklahoma to the Gulf of Mexico at one time or another.

The Sangers lived like Texas royalty and laid the foundation of Dallas being a city of fashion and good taste. They set the stage for the merchant princes. The founder of Neiman-Marcus got his start as a Sanger's salesperson.

The coming of the railroad made the Sangers boom. Most Texas towns depended entirely on rail service for their prosperity. Dallas, which until 1872 was a four-week ox-wagon ride from the port of Houston, managed to secure a connection to the Houston & Texas Central line. Without this railroad connection Dallas would have remained an obscure landlocked hamlet and the vast empire of the Sanger brothers would have had another location. . . .

By the time the railroad reached Dallas in 1872, the Sanger brothers were respected throughout the state. By the turn of the century, Sanger Bros. had become the greatest dry goods company west of the Mississippi. Not only did it have retail stores, but also a wholesale business second in importance only to that of Marshall Field's in Chicago. Sanger Bros. sold saddlery and crockery, harnesses and plows, as well as clothing, "ribbons, perfumery, occasionally a fiddle or accordian."

As Dallas grew, so did the Sanger brothers' fortune. It was their job to outfit both the home and the person of the city's civic elite. And the families of the brothers, including Alexander, who had joined the operation, lived as well or better than any of their customers. The first posh section of Dallas was called "The Cedars" and both Philip and Alex owned residences there. Philip's home, nicknamed "The Mansion," became a showcase, copied after a summer mansion he had seen on the New Jersey coast. Built in 1885, the home caused writer Edna Ferber to exclaim, half a century later, "It's worth a trip to Texas just to see it."

Alex, not to be outdone, built a three-story house complete with chandeliers handmade by Louis Comfort Tiffany. The house had a butler's pantry with a sink just to wash fine crystal and a special dining room for poor relations. Joseph Sanger Linz, a grandson of Philip Sanger, one of the original brothers, remembered his weekly Saturday visits to his grandparent's "mansion," which he described as "wood with gingerbread trim." When asked what he remembered best about his uncle Alexander's home, Joseph replied, "Alex's grandchildren: Frances Sanger Mossiker and her brother Everett had a marvelous electric train set in the attic. This was around 1922," Joseph recalled more than sixty years later.

Alex Sanger served as president of the Texas State Fair in 1894. He was the first Jew to be appointed a regent of the University of Texas. In the halcyon days of their success, Alex, a civic leader, promoted the store's image through his many philanthropies. When disaster hit the Sangers with the unexpected death of Philip in 1902, the store moved forward under its own momentum for about five years. But Alex—who had established the city's first library, organized what became the United Fund, brought the first professional city planner to Dallas, and helped secure the Texas State Fair for the city—proved unable to take the stringent business tactics necessary to maintain the success of the store. He allowed the store to become more and more extended to its creditors, permitted its customers more credit than they could afford, and Sanger Bros. goes down in history because it initiated a series of firsts: the first Texas store to open a buying office in New York; the first Texas business to institute sales training; the first to offer free home delivery (which they publicized highly with photos of their many horse-drawn wagons, and later motor vehicles), and to set up gaslights in Dallas. In 1881 they bought the first Dallas telephone, which linked the store with the palatial home of Philip Sanger at Ervay and St. Louis streets. It was the first telephone in the entire state of Texas. In 1883 they installed electric lights. They installed elevators in 1889, and an escalator in 1911—other Texas firsts.

The Sanger brothers created the first dry goods empire in Texas. Their innovations, their charitable contributions, and their civic authority provided a model for later department store magnates to emulate.

In 1859 Adolph Harris arrived in Galveston from Prussia at the age of seventeen. . . . A. Harris's grandson Arthur Kramer, Jr. told his account of why Harris left Galveston, then a most important city, for Dallas, then a relatively unknown town: "Adolph Harris was a partner with his father-in-law, Grumbach, in Fellman, Grumbach & Harris in Galveston. George B. Dealey also lived there, a trusted young employee of the *Galveston News,* and Harris and Dealey were very good friends. Dealey urged Harris to leave Galveston and come to Dallas with him, and two years after *The Dallas Morning News* emerged in 1885, Harris moved to Dallas also."

In 1887 he headed Fellman, Grumbach & Harris's Dallas store. He then established A. Harris & Company in the center of downtown Dallas.

In 1910 A. Harris's daughter Camille married attorney Arthur L. Kramer, and in 1912 Kramer joined his father-in-law's company. Only one year later, when Adolph died, Kramer became president of A. Harris & Company.

Arthur L. Kramer Sr. determined, to a large degree, the way Dallas citizens looked during his thirty-seven years as president of A. Harris & Company department store.

Arthur L. Kramer was born December 17, 1880. . . . The family moved to Dallas when he was age nine. He received a law degree from the University of Texas and practiced law in the firm Hexter and Kramer from 1902 to 1912. He served as president of A. Harris & Co. from 1913 until his death in 1950.

Arthur took on not only running the business, but also promoting it. As part of his promotional efforts, he immersed himself in the arts. Kramer served as president of three arts organizations: the Dallas Symphony Society

(1925-1939); Dallas Art Association (1929-1941), and Dallas Grand Opera Association (1939-1950). He also served on the Dallas School Board, which named the Arthur Kramer Elementary School for him in 1955.

Over a period of eight years, Kramer pursued without success the idea of bringing to Dallas the Metropolitan Opera of New York. On one of these visits in January of 1939, he learned that the company planned to play in New Orleans the coming April and needed a city with which to split the week. Met officials asked Kramer if Dallas would put up a guarantee of $65,000 for four performances.

Kramer telephoned the Dallas Chamber of Commerce immediately, but they hesitated to put up so large a guarantee. Kramer asked his Met friends for a few days "to work out details" and caught the first train back to Texas. As soon as he arrived in his office, he began to call individuals and firms he thought would be interested and raised the money in a matter of hours. So successful became the annual Met tours that, during his years as president of the Grand Opera Association, he did not call on guarantors to contribute funds.

Whether these men and women of the merchant families acted from a love for the arts, from a recognition that Texas would never equal other markets until it could compete culturally, from a desire for social status, or whether those artists who wished to perform in a wider market persuaded them to raise funds for them, hardly matters in the end. There can be no doubt that these merchants were primarily the ones who put their own money into the arts and persuaded others to do so. A top salesman at A. Harris & Co., Abraham Lincoln (Al) Neiman, married the top saleswoman at A. Harris & Co., Carrie Marcus, aunt of Stanley Marcus. ★

Stanley Marcus

Stanley Marcus (1905–2002), chairman emeritus of the Neiman-Marcus stores, received a BA degree from Harvard University and also attended Harvard Business School. He was a noted lecturer who published fine press miniature books out of The Somesuch Press. His own books include *Minding the Store; Quest for the Best; Viewpoints of Stanley Marcus;* and *Stanley Marcus from A to Z,* edited by Michael V. Hazel. His value to Dallas cannot be overstated. He stepped in when the city needed him. He had learned well from those merchants who went before him. He was a great role model for anyone with whom he came in contact, particularly for me. He took a chance on a new press, the University of North Texas Press, reprinting his classic works. It turned out to be a wonderful experience for that publisher because he turned out to be one of the very best of the writers with whom to work. The impact of Neiman-Marcus on Dallas' image in the world was enormous.

From *Minding the Store*

> *"There is never a good sale for Neiman-Marcus unless it's a good buy for the customer."*

That was one of the first declarations of business philosophy I heard my father, Herbert Marcus, make soon after I came to work at Neiman-Marcus in 1926. It was reiterated so many times that it became established as an article of faith in my mind, and on numerous occasions he demonstrated his enforcement of this principle even when it meant lost sales and profits. He explained that there was a right customer for every piece of merchandise, and that part of a merchant's job was not only to bring the two together, but also to prevent the customer from making the wrong choice.

Some may regard this as sheer idealism, but having worked with my father for twenty-four years, I consider it a doctrine of idealistic pragmatism. First of all, he enjoyed doing business that way, and second, he recognized that there was no advertisement as potent as a satisfied customer. This was his way of practicing the Golden Rule, and now, almost seventy years since the founding of Neiman-Marcus, the same policy prevails.

Although every new employee goes through an orientation class, I have made it a custom, now carried on by my son, to meet with groups of them at a morning coffee to explain some of the background and ideals of the founders. I start by telling them that Neiman-Marcus was established as a result of the bad judgment of its founders, my father, Herbert Marcus, his younger sister, Carrie Marcus Neiman, and her husband, Al Neiman. This statement usually distracts my listeners from their coffee cups. I go on to explain that my father, who at twenty-five was a buyer of boys' clothing at Sanger Brothers, the leading store of the Southwest, and his sister Carrie, who at the tender age of twenty-one was the blouse buyer and top saleswoman at A. Harris & Company, another local store, were persuaded by her husband Al to leave their jobs and go with him to Atlanta, Georgia, to establish a sales promotion business. I was then six months old and, since my recall doesn't extend back that far, I am forced to rely on hearsay for what happened during the first half dozen years of my life, and some of that may be apocryphal.

The partnership they set up was directed towards helping country merchants in Georgia raise cash by staging special sales, with flamboyant signs, banners strung up across the streets, and band music to lure the crowds. They were so successful that at the end of two years they had had two offers to sell out, and here is where the bad judgment came in. One offer was for $25,000 in cash, and the other was the franchise for the state of Missouri or Kansas for a relatively new product called "Coca-Cola." They apparently were too smart to be taken in by this unknown soft drink, so they took the $25,000 in cash instead, returning to Dallas to start a business of their own, to be run in a manner they had dreamed about when they were employees of Sanger Brothers and A. Harris & Company. In retrospect, if their judgment had been better, they would have taken the Coca-Cola franchise and Neiman-Marcus would have become a famous name in Missouri or Kansas as bottlers of Coca-Cola, with a fraction of the effort required to build a fashion institution of world renown.

They came back to Dallas with their $25,000, which, combined with their savings and with funds from the sale of some minority shares to other members of their family, provided them with barely sufficient capital to pay for the fixtures, carpets, and merchandise for their new fifty-foot storefront in a building in the heart of the retail district. At that time, Sanger Brothers dominated Texas retail distribution, much as Marshall Field & Company did in the Midwest. Alex Sanger, the president of the Sanger business, had offered my father a raise of $1.87-1/2 a month to keep him from going to Atlanta, and when he heard of the proposed new venture, he urged my father to give up his foolish dream and return to the Sanger fold, where a bright and secure future could be assured.

Nonetheless, the three young hopefuls were determined to go into business for themselves and to run it in the way they felt a fashion store should be operated. It was not unusual for three young people to leave secure positions to go into business for themselves. Young people have been, and still are, venturesome enough to want to try it on their own. Of course, it took courage to come into the same town dominated by Sanger Brothers. But courage they didn't lack, nor were they bashful or overly modest in their evaluation of their own standards of good taste and fashion. On Sunday, September 8, 1907, a full-page advertisement appeared in *The Dallas Morning News* announcing "the opening of the New and Exclusive Shopping Place for Fashionable Women, devoted to the selling of Ready-to-Wear Apparel" and labeling Neiman-Marcus as "The Outer-Garment Shop." It went on to state that "Tuesday, September tenth, marks the advent of a new shopping place in Dallas—a store of Quality, a Specialty store—the only store in the City whose stocks are strictly confined to Ladies' Outer-Garments and Millinery, and presenting wider varieties and more exclusive lines than any other store in the South."

[Earlier] Herbert Marcus fortunately caught the eye of Philip Sanger, one of the Sanger brothers, who was impressed by his selling ability, ambitions, and appearance, and promoted him to the post of buyer for the boys' department. Mr. Sanger, a keen judge of talent, believed he had discovered a "comer." One observer commented that if Philip Sanger had only lived longer, there never would have been a Neiman-Marcus. He wouldn't have let Herbert Marcus get away.

Armed with a new job and an increased income, he pressed his courtship and overwhelmed Minnie [my mother] with his self-confidence. She consented to marry him on the condition that he promise to save $500 the first year they were married. He did, and that was the first money he ever saved, but only after borrowing $200 to go on their honeymoon. When mother was pregnant with me, he applied for an increase in salary. He was dissatisfied with the $1.87 1/2 per month offered him and it was then that he yielded to the persuasions of his brother-in-law to join him in the sales-promotion effort in Atlanta. It was Al's idea that he and Aunt Carrie would set up a branch office in New York, while my father would manage the head office in Atlanta. Dad did extremely well in his operation, but apparently New York wasn't ready for Al Neiman at that point, so he closed the New York office and moved to Atlanta and joined forces. The Neimans had no children, and they lavished love and affection on me as virtually their own son.

Aunt Carrie was an extraordinary woman. She was not only kind and gracious, but she possessed a queenly quality, which she carried as if to the manor born. She was devoted to her family, each and every member. She had elegance, but she never asked a maid to do something she wouldn't do herself. She was modest, but not self-deprecating. She and my father were born with an appreciation for beauty and fine quality that their home environment and education didn't provide. They were both perfectionists early in their lives, and concurred with Oscar Wilde's declaration, "I have the simplest tastes. I am easily satisfied with the best."

So this is a capsuled background of the trio, whose ages averaged twenty-six and a half years, whose credo was described so well in the opening newspaper announcement, whose self-assurance encouraged them to use advertising hyperbole to proclaim the virtues of their wares and buying skills. . . .

Why did they select Dallas as the place to go into business? Why not St. Louis, or Chicago, or New York? That's a question often asked, and I'm not sure of the answer. However, I think two of the three partners considered themselves Southerners, they felt at home in Dallas, and I surmise that after two years in Atlanta they were homesick for their families, to whom they were deeply devoted. If Sanger and A. Harris could fare so well with department stores, didn't that indicate that a specialty store might do equally well? Dallas in 1907 was a thriving metropolis of some 84,000 inhabitants, the center of the then-all important cotton distribution industry. The wealth of the Dallas Establishment was land-oriented, either in the direction of cotton or cattle. The wealthy had cotton farms, or gins, or compresses, or warehouses, or sold insurance and services to those who were so engaged. To the west were the great cattle ranches, which needed saddles and materials, supplied by the Dallas distributors. . . .

Somewhat aghast at a few of the unreasonable complaints and demands which I encountered in my first years in the business, I asked my father, "How can we afford to replace a garment which the customer has clearly abused?" I was referring to a handmade lace ball gown a customer returned after one wearing. "She should have known it was fragile." My father replied, "Yes, she should have, but since this is the first fine garment she's ever bought, she didn't. Explain to her that we will replace it, and tactfully call her attention to the fact that a delicate handmade lace will wear less well than a coarser machine-made lace. She'll know better next time." Unconvinced, I asked, "How can we afford to take such a loss? The manufacturer won't assume any of the cost." He replied very patiently, "She's not doing business with the manufacturer, she's doing business with us. It costs us over $200 to get a new customer of this woman's buying potential, and I'm not going to lose her for the $175 this dress cost us." And then he added, "When you tell her, do it with a smile." Over the years, this woman spent over $500,000 with us. I had learned one of the most important lessons in my retail career. . . .

The store continued to make modest profits during the sluggish economy induced by the European war, but it wasn't until 1918, about a year after the United States entered the war, that business began to pick up. Simultaneously, the discovery of the West Texas oil fields around Ranger, Burkburnett, and Wichita Falls brought a new stream of wealth into the Texas economy, and for the first time diversification of income sources freed the state from its complete dependence on the products of the land. The products from under the land created not only new wealth, but a new breed of customer. They were people who had made their money in a hurry, and they were in an equal hurry to spend it on some of the luxuries they had heard about all their lives. They put their confidence in Neiman-Marcus, for the reputation of the store carried a guarantee of good taste.

Actually, Dallas had little justification for being anything more than another small-town American city. It was located on a relatively flat piece of topography that was scorchingly hot in the long summer months, cold and raw in the winter. It had no surrounding lakes, no mountain views in the background, no pictorial waterfalls, or any historic tradition, as did some of the other Texas cities. In short, there was little or no reason for anyone to want to come to Dallas to visit or to take up residence, except for its geographical location as the hub of the entire southwestern region. Dallas was roughly equidistant from Houston and San Antonio to the south. El Paso to the west, Oklahoma City and Tulsa to the north, and New Orleans to the east. Thus it was an ideal central point from which to distribute farm machinery, dry goods, and other commodities to the area. Railroad transportation provided adequate service for both passengers and goods. Much of this would characterize Fort Worth, a mere forty miles to the west, except for the fact that the land on which it was built offered the relief of rolling hills. Both towns had about the same opportunity to emerge as the larger community. Fort Worth didn't; Dallas did.

Without going into a deep sociological analysis of the differences between the families that settled in the two places, I have the impression that the business leaders of Dallas in the first quarter of [that] century recognized their problems and exercised some farsighted judgment in finding the solutions. They envisioned a metropolis, and they spent time, effort, and money to compensate for the lack of natural attractions. At that point in Dallas's history, there was no single wealthy individual who dominated the city, as Amon Carter did in Fort Worth and Jesse Jones in Houston; instead there was a large group of bankers, insurance company presidents, cotton-oriented industrialists, and retail merchants who banded together to supply the vitality for attracting conventions, establishing new industries, and making Dallas a better place in which to live. ★

Frank X. Tolbert

From *Tolbert of Texas: The Man and His Work*: Mr. Stanley

Some years ago, Harold Stanley Marcus took his good-looking teenage daughter, Wendy, to one of his Harvard class reunions in Boston. At the reunion, Wendy Marcus met a youthful daughter of Governor John Davis Lodge of Connecticut.

The two little girls were discussing the progress their fathers had made since they were graduated from Harvard in 1925. The little Lodge girl mentioned, "My father is governor of Connecticut. And some day he's going to be elected vice president of the United States. And then he's going to be elected president of the United States."

To this Wendy Marcus replied, "That's nothing. My father is president of Neiman-Marcus now!"

Wendy wasn't being boastful. Like most Texas girls she can think of nothing more marvelous than presiding over the Store at Main and Ervay and Commerce.

Stanley Marcus likes his job, too.

He doesn't work at being a fabulous character. It just sort of happens. There is a new story about him almost every day. His personality pervades the store. And on a quick visit to the establishment, you get the impression that H. Stanley is a creature of almost incredible talents, industry, and interests.

You get a picture which makes it appear that Mr. Stanley can, all in one day, do all of these things:

Sell a $32,000 mink greatcoat to a celebrity, sell a $39.95 dress to a Dallas housewife, make a wise and tolerant speech to a civic group, raise money for a college or an art museum or an Eisenhower campaign, write an article for the *Atlantic Monthly,* and make—without wrinkling his high, sloping brow—a style decision on which he stands to win or lose thousands of dollars.

Certainly, Stanley Marcus is Dallas's most internationally famous citizen, unless you want to count celebrities whose folks live in Dallas, like Jennifer Jones or Linda Darnell. And Marcus's only competitor for the title of the Southwest's No. 1 businessman-intellectual is E. DeGolyer, the great Dallas geophysicist, oilman, and chairman of the board of the *Saturday Review.*

Certainly, Stanley's talent range is very wide.

Without effort, he can switch roles from store president to salesman. In fact, he makes this switch with pleasure, for he loves to sell as much as a bird dog loves to hunt.

In his modernistic office, surrounded by his collection of weird South Seas masks, Mexican and Chinese statues, he is often functioning as salesman over the telephone. Neiman's has a monopoly on many fine things, including a lot of kinds and colors of mink pelts. Almost every day Stanley talks over the telephone to fashionable women all over the world. He seems to know the sizes and tastes of every lady who calls up. When he's selling over the telephone, though, he is just a soothing baritone who chews nervously on a pencil while he's listening to the faraway lady customer.

If the lady comes onto Neiman's second floor, she's apt to get much more theatrical treatment from salesman Stanley. He's apt to fling mink coats of sixteen colors at her feet. And Neiman's is the only store which can fling so many colors of mink at the feet of a customer.

Since he got out of Harvard School of Business Administration in 1926, Stanley has sold more than $5,000,000 worth of fur coats as a sideline to his executive chores. . . .

When Stanley got out of school, Neiman thought his nephew should get some training with a well-known New York store before starting in with Neiman-Marcus. Herbert Marcus disagreed with this.

"This would just be time wasted. That boy is going to show us new ideas in merchandising that will make us all sit up and take notice."

Neiman said he wasn't convinced, "But Stanley came into the store, and justified the trust placed in him."

That first year Stanley developed the fashion shows which were the first regularly scheduled weekly style shows ever presented by an American store.

Then, years later, he dreamed up the Neiman-Marcus international fashion expositions, which are now copied by fine stores all over the world. He got heavily hooked up, too, in local cultural matters. He became a trustee of the art museum, a director of the city's symphony orchestra. He'd acquired an interest in printing at Harvard. And he started the Book Club of Texas, an organization dedicated to publishing books on Texas in distinctive typographical format. Lob Exline, head of a Dallas printing house, says, "Stanley knows more about typography than I do. He knows more about printing than almost all printers."

Maybe this is why Neiman's ads in the *Dallas News* are so elegant you feel like putting on a coat and tie before you read them. . . .

A recent skit at a Dallas Press Club Gridiron show was just pointing up a truth when it had an actor, labeled "Stanley Mark Up, Prince of Dallas Merchants," come on stage wearing crown and ermine. And all the other Dallas merchants on the stage salaamed. Meanwhile, four newspaper girls were singing some lyrics composed by the *Dallas Times-Herald*'s beauteous young book-page editor, Luise Putcamp, on the complaints of Yankee wives who've just moved to Texas. The thing, to the tune of the "Whiffenpoof Song," went like this:

"To the counters down at Neiman's
To the place where Stanley dwells,
To the dear old minks and diamonds that they sell.
See the oilmen assembled
With their checkbooks raised on high—
It's enough to make us poor folks feel like hell." ★

From *Tolbert of Texas: The Man and His Work*, Neiman-Marcus Defined

ONE NIGHT ABOUT TEN YEARS AGO A BEAUTIFUL blonde girl ghost appeared on a road near Dallas' White Rock Lake. Mr. and Mrs. Guy Malloy, directors of display for the world-famous specialty store, Neiman-Marcus, saw the girl. Only they didn't recognize her, right off, for a ghost. She had walked up from the beach. And she stood there in the headlights of the slow-moving Malloy car.

Mrs. Malloy said, "Stop, Guy. That girl seems in trouble. She must have fallen in the lake. Her dress is wet. Yet you can tell that it is a very fine dress. She certainly got it at the Store."

By "the Store," Mrs. Malloy meant the Neiman-Marcus Company of Dallas.

The girl spoke in a friendly, cultured contralto to the couple after the car had stopped. She said she'd like to be taken to an address on Gaston Avenue in the nearby Lakewood section. It was an emergency, she said. She didn't explain what had happened to her, and the Malloys were too polite to ask. She had long hair, which was beginning to dry in the night breeze. And Mrs. Malloy was now sure that the girl was wearing a Neimam-Marcus dress. She was very gracious as she slipped by Mrs. Malloy and got in the backseat of the two-door sedan.

When the car started, Mrs. Malloy turned to converse with the passenger in the Neiman-Marcus gown. The girl had vanished. There was a damp spot on the back seat.

The Malloys went to the address on Gaston Avenue. A middle-aged man answered the door. Yes, he had a daughter with long blonde hair who wore nothing but Neiman-Marcus clothes. She had been drowned about two years before when she fell off a pier at White Rock Lake.

The point of this story—for our purposes—is not that Mr. and Mrs. Guy Malloy, a hard-working, sober, no-nonsense couple, say very firmly that they saw a ghost. Other folks say they have seen the beautiful girl ghost of White Rock. The point of this story is that she was a very well-dressed ghost. And Mrs. Malloy at once identified her as wearing Neiman-Marcus clothes.

For to Dallas women—and to all style-conscious women from Paris to California and from Peru to Alaska—Neiman-Marcus is not just the name of a store which traffics in the choicest of clothes, jewels, and house furnishings. Rather, Neiman-Marcus is an adjective—and a superlative one. An unusually well-groomed woman, who rhymes tastefully with her clothes, is likely to be described as "very Neiman-Marcus-ish!"

Mrs. Mamie Eisenhower, wife of the first Texas-born president of the United Stares, is a very Neiman-Marcus-ish lady.

Before buying her clothes for the 1953 inaugural day ceremonies and celebrations, Mrs. Eisenhower went to the Smithsonian Institution in Washington to make a good study of the collection of inaugural gowns of former first ladies.

Then Mrs. Eisenhower bought both her Renoir pink gown for the two inaugural balls and her town suit for the inaugural ceremony and parade from the Neiman-Marcus Company. Neiman's commissioned Nettie Rosenstein to design the ball dress and Hattie Carnegie the suit. . . .

George Sessions Perry, a Rockdale, Texas, writer and longtime friend of the Marcus boys, strains his rhetorical milk so much when he mentions Neiman-Marcus that he has never been able to sell the magazines much about the store. Perry says, "Many folks look at Neiman-Marcus and see only a breathtakingly beautiful store. This is like a rancher looking at wildflowers and seeing only cow feed. Neiman-Marcus is a state of mind. Almost a state of grace. It isn't the biggest store on earth, but it is one of the finest and most exciting." ★

NATALIE ORNISH

From *Pioneer Jewish Texans:* Frances Sanger Mossiker

FRANCES SANGER MOSSIKER'S FAMILY HISTORY in the arts started two generations before her birth. Her grandfather, Alexander Sanger, was an active civic leader. Her parents were Elihu and Evelyn Sanger. By the time Frances was born on April 9, 1906, her family knew few hardships. This privileged little girl, whose parents' prairie mansion stood on the site where the Dallas City Hall was built decades later, seemed an unlikely candidate to be a celebrated author. . . .

Miss Fanny grew up speaking three languages—English, German, and French. In the summers she visited her mother's relatives near Strasbourg, France. At one point she tried to join the circus as a dancer, but the circus owner knew her grandfather Alex. She attended the Hockaday School, a Dallas private girls' school, and Forest Avenue High School before enrolling in Smith College in Northampton, Massachusets. . . .

Frances returned to Dallas around 1929 where, with the encouragement of Stanley Marcus, a childhood friend, she began reviewing books for WFAA radio. . . . Then she met Jacob Mossiker, who owned a retail shoe and bag company. They married in 1934. They had no children. Frances returned to travel, bridge, and reading. "I was sort of asleep. I can't tell you what I did all day. I just frittered away the time," she remembered. That life ended when in her early fifties she experienced a major trauma—a radical mastectomy. She escaped into writing books.

She went to France to research in archives there the mysterious disappearance of Marie Antoinette's million-dollar diamond necklace. The result was the nonfiction mystery, *The Queen's Necklace,* published in 1961. . . . It won the Carr P. Collins award from the Texas Institute of Letters. She followed with *Napoleon and Josephine: The Biography of a Marriage; The Affair of the Poisons,* on the loves of Louis XIV; *More than Queen: The Story of Josephine Bonaparte; Pocahontas: The Life and Legend; Madame de Sévigné: A Life and Letters.* ★

Joyce Gibson Roach

Joyce Gibson Roach (1935–) is the grande dame of Texas folklore, cowgirls, and a high-toned woman herself. She holds a BFA and an MA from Texas Christian University, where she also taught English, specializing in the Western novel and life and literature of the Southwest. She is a three-time Spur Award winner from the Western Writers of America for *The Cowgirls,* "A High Toned Woman" from *Hoein' the Short Rows,* and "Just As I Am" from *Women of the West.* She received the coveted Carr P. Collins Award for the Best Book of Nonfiction from the Texas Institute of Letters for *Eats: A Folk History of Texas Foods,* coauthored with Ernestine Sewell. She is a fellow of the Texas State Historical Association, a fellow of the Texas Folklore Society, a member of the Texas Institute of Letters and the Philosophical Society of Texas. She has made a jolly good companion and wonderful friend on many trips down the years to the meetings of the various organizations to which she belongs. No one can paint a more humorous picture of a visit to Neiman-Marcus than Joyce.

From *Hoein' the Short Rows:* A High Toned Woman

In a song made popular by Tennessee Ernie Ford, the male in "Sixteen Tons" complains that, among other troubles, "ain't no high-toned woman make me walk the line." From one hardworking man's point of view, high-toned women should be avoided. . . . In contrast, and in words from a modern translation of Old Testament sentiment, a good woman of Jack County was laid to rest with these words, "She is a worthy woman, high toned, more valuable than rubies and her husband and family rise up and call her blessed. . . ."

Who or what were High Toned Women? They were those women in every small community who counted themselves as the authorities in matters both temporal and spiritual, but mostly spiritual. They could organize, direct, conduct, and orchestrate feminine matters; could fine-tune, refine, regulate, and monopolize the female psyche; and could judge, draw, and quarter unworthy opponents. They were looked up to, respected, and emulated for their clear judgment, their unerring fortitude, their dogged pursuit of truth as they saw it, their unflagging dedication to showing the rest of us how to live. They were the nearest thing a community had to folk heroines, and they strutted in a hen yard just big enough to accommodate them. . . .

There may have been High Toned Women in cities. We often speculated that there might be some in Dallas, but we never knew for sure. We knew Fort Worth was a big town, but still a country town and their ways were not the stranger's ways. But Dallas! Dallas was such a dangerous place and we didn't go—hardly ever. All the women there were Quality, which is not the same as High Toned or the same as Choice or Prime. I had Quality explained to me once in Dallas, by my grandmother. Mama Hartman took me once, when I was a small girl, inside the very walls of Neiman-Marcus. We kept to the sides of the store, never venturing into the aisles except to get to another wall. She allowed me to look swiftly at whatever goods were on eye level, but she kept a firm grip on my hand. The ladies who were shopping paid no attention to us, and so I got to look at them all I wanted. What I saw was Quality.

"We are going to hunt the bathroom."

"But, Mama, you told me never to go to the bathroom in a strange house and never, never in a department store 'cause you never knew who'd been usin' the pot. You said, if you were desperate, never to sit on the seat—never—but to hunker above it. And then when you do go, it leaves the seat all wet all over it and you either have to clean up or else not let anybody see you leave because they'd know you were the one who did it on the seat. You said it was better to hold in no matter what; and to always go to the bathroom the last thing before you left the house. Mama, I don't need to use Neiman-Marcus' bathroom." I was pulling back now and whispering so she wouldn't shush me.

"I know all that, Joyce Ann." Now she was whispering so I wouldn't shush her. There was enough rush of noisy air coming from our mouths to have launched a hot-air balloon. "I want you to see something."

We pushed open the door and there was only one Quality woman in the place. She was washing her hands and tucking her hair up. She licked one finger and pushed up her eyebrow. Then she licked another finger and pushed up the other one. Anyone could tell that she was a good, clean woman since she didn't lick the same finger to do the other brow. She was certainly a lesson in Quality. Watching Quality at her toilette was not, however, what Mama had in mind. When the lady left, after giving a good tug to her girdle, we went to the first booth. The toilet seat was dry! We made every stall, eight of them, and—they were all dry!

Mama said, "See, Joyce Ann." I shook my head in amazement and agreement, but never till the day she died did I ever have the courage to ask an explanation about the dry toilet seats. The only logical conclusion was that Quality women took a better aim. ★

Unsung Writers of the Great Depression

Written in the late 1930s and the early 1940s by Dallas workers of the Writers Program of the Works Projects Administration, the *WPA Dallas Guide and History* covers everything from local aviation to the city's zoo. It is one of the most comprehensive histories of Dallas ever written.

When World War II prevented the publication of the *WPA Dallas Guide and History* in the 1940s, the manuscript was placed in the collections of the Dallas Public Library. The *WPA Dallas Guide and History* includes many of the original photographs collected by the WPA staff. It includes the original drawings and the design by the WPA staff.

A. C. Greene suggested that the University of North Texas Press publish the book, which it did, copublishing with the Dallas Public Library. Gerald Saxon of the University of Texas at Arlington and Maxine Holmes of the Dallas Public Library edited the *WPA Dallas Guide and History* for publication. It was a labor of love by all concerned in the project.

From *WPA Dallas Guide and History:* Literature: Voices of the Southwest

As one of the last American frontiers Dallas and its region repeated in its literature the pattern of all frontiers, modified by the former environment of its Anglo-American settlers and the spirit of the era. In its first decade of settlement it produced neither such purposeful chroniclers as the New England Puritans nor such glorifiers of colorful pioneer existence as those who painted the California of the gold rush. The majority of the settlers came from the South, where expression in that day centered on oratory rather than writing.

Unwitting heroes of an American epic, there was little of the consciously poetic in the Dallas settlers, if their latter-day memoirs are to be taken as criteria. It was long after the rigors of establishing a community were over that a later generation pictured in song, poetry, and prose the trees and flowers, the animal life, and the grandeur of space on the open prairies.

First writings in Dallas other than personal letters were political and editorial articles concerned first with local and then with state affairs. Since the people of Dallas had not participated in Texas's struggle for independence they could contribute little to the heroic chronology of that conquest.

There are few records concerning early exploration in the Dallas area. Historians claim that Luis Moscoso penetrated as far east as Dallas County in 1542. Herbert E. Bolton, who wrote of the wanderings of Athanase de Mézières, mentions places located in Dallas County. Edward Smith, an Englishman who had visited in Dallas, published in 1849 *An Account of a Journey Through Northeastern Texas for Purposes of Emigration* in which he included the story of Dr. W. W. Conover's five-year experience in Dallas, as told to him by the physician. Smith's description of a tree in Dallas County one hundred feet tall inclines the reader to believe he was somewhat given to exaggeration.

In the handwriting of the county clerk on the flyleaf of a criminal docket record for 1848-1852 is a parody on the song "O No, We Never Mention Him." It is a lament on taking the temperance pledge. . . .

Reconstruction was a period of reconciliation of the frontiersman's Jacksonian philosophy of democracy with the violent political upheaval through the South, and neither side was articulate. Men spoke and acted in terms of prejudices without reflection. Power of the victor needed no justification; the vanquished, surrounded by those of like faith and fortune, felt no need of the written word to defend his cause. But when John Henry Brown, well-known Texas journalist, historian, lecturer, and Confederate soldier, took direction of the *Dallas Herald* in 1873, he began a series of editorials dealing with Reconstruction in Texas that has remained one of the most scholarly collections on this era.

Mary Hunt McCaleb moved to Dallas in 1873 when her husband, D. McCaleb, became editor of the *Herald.* Mrs. McCaleb wrote first under the name of "L'Eclair" in 1870 and her poems "Lenare," "The Picture on the Wall," and "Little Relics" were widely read. After Mrs. McCaleb no longer resided in the city her poems were published in book form by G. P. Putman's Sons. Mrs. M. Josephine Williams lived in Dallas and wrote for the press some time during the seventies. "A Home Scene" is recorded in Sam H. Dixon's *Poets and Poetry of Texas* (1883). . . .

Sam Bass, the Indiana youth who in the 1870s came down into the Southwest to become a highwayman and train robber, chose Dallas and its adjacent region for some of his most notorious deeds, and became in legend another Robin Hood, while Jim Murphy, the man who killed him, earned only popular contempt as "a six-gun Judas." Never-confirmed exploits of this bandit persist until today in the stories of the old-timers. *The Life and Adventures of Sam Bass* was published anonymously in 1878 and Charles Lee Martin's *A Sketch of Sam Bass, the Bandit* in 1880.

The concluding paragraph of *The Life and Adventures of Sam Bass* contains this query and answer:

> Sam Bass was true to his friends and his convictions, but what of Jim Murphy? That man hated of all men, despised even by the rangers whom he had served, returned to Denton. Words cannot express the supreme contempt and hatred for the man (used for classification only) who, like a rattlesnake, turned and bit the one who befriended him. . . .

John Henry Brown wrote the first chronological history of the county. His *History of Dallas County, Texas, 1837-1887,* published by Milligan, Cornett & Farnham of Dallas in 1887, deals with records, county officers, and important local events. He quotes from an address he had made on the adventures of Captain M. Eastland's company of about fifty men who went on an expedition against the Indians in 1839:

> Through the shelter of the night they reached the river bottom, and along its serpentine banks they were harassed during the succeeding day, but their unerring rifles finally compelled their pursuers to

> abandon the conflict with a severe loss. For five days they followed the river down its meanders till they reached the junction of the Main and Elm forks, three miles above the city. On the sixth day they crossed to the east side at the mouth of Turtle Creek, and, a mile and a half below, came to the bluff, rising above overflow, where the village of Dallas was founded or first settled four years later. Some suffering with wounds, all well-nigh denuded of clothing and their flesh torn with thorns, they resolved to halt for repose. With mud and oak ooze their wounds were poulticed, buffaloes were killed for meat, their hides converted into moccasins and "leggins" and after three or four days thus spent at the spring near where Jackson Street crosses the town branch, they recrossed the river and traveled south along the prairie, but always near the timber for protection, if attacked, and finally reached the border settlements in the lower country.

In the 1880s, with the growth of reading and study clubs, the women of Dallas began to write verse, some of which occasionally appeared in the local papers. Themes of these efforts usually were the death of a loved one, beautiful love affairs never reaching fruition, tributes to family relationships and friendships, the beauties of nature, and religious resignation. The men wrote to a lesser extent, and for the most part in the James Whitcomb Riley style of homespun sentiment. . . .

The study clubs which began in the 1880s evolved into more specialized groups. Among those clubs which today sponsor contests and definite literary projects are the Barrington Fiction Club, the Dallas Writers' Club, the Dallas Pen Women, and the Dallas Branch League of American Pen Women.

Southwest Review, published in Dallas since 1924 and edited by John H. McGinnis, is issued as a quarterly and gives most of its space to prose, short stories, sketches, and some verse reflecting the regional background. It has influenced research and the growth of indigenous literature and has maintained a high standard for inclusion. *The Bard* (1920-22), established by C. O. Gill, was claimed to be the first all-poetry magazine in the South. *The Kaleidograph,* a monthly poetry magazine established in May 1929, has encouraged Dallas poets; five collections of poetry printed in this magazine have been issued in anthology form.

Many present-day Dallas writers have expressed themselves in verse. Grace Noll (Mrs. Norman H.) Crowell's poems have a strong popular appeal to home lovers, nature lovers, and the religious, in both America and England. Her collection *White Fire* (1925) won the first annual book contest of the Poetry Society of Texas. Other volumes are *Silver in the Sun* (1928), *Miss Humpety Comes to Tea* (1929), *Flame in the Wind* (1930), *Songs for Courage* (1930), and *The Light of Years* (1936). . . .

Hilton Ross Greer, journalist by profession, has been the moving spirit of the Texas Poetry Society. Born in 1878 in Hawkins, Texas, he has written lyrical verse that reflects an unusual ear for word music, three volumes of which have been published: *Sun-Gleams and Gossamers* (1903), *The Spiders and Other Poems* (1906), and *A Prairie Flower and Other Poems* (1912). He edited *Voices of the Southwest* (1924), and in collaboration with Dr. Florence E. Barns edited *New Voices of the Southwest* (1934).

Whitney Montgomery, called the pastoral poet of Texas, published his first poem in 1897, since which time several hundred of his poems have appeared in numerous periodicals. He is the author of *Crown Silks and Cotton Blossoms* (1928), *Brown Fields and Bright Lights* (1930), and (with his wife, Vaida Stewart Montgomery) *Locoed and Other Poems* (1930). He edited *Bright Excalibur* (1933), a collection of poems from *Kaleidograph*. . . .

J. Mason Brewer, Negro born in Goliad, Texas, in 1896 but long a resident in Dallas, has written along several lines. His *Negro Legislators and Their Descendants* (1935) is history and biography. The folkways of his people are in his "Juneteenth" (1932) and "Old Time Negro Proverbs" (1933). His *Negrito* (1933) is a volume of Negro dialect poems of the Southwest. . . .

Dallas has steadily developed as a publishing center, and to a large degree the companies have given favorable consideration to regional writers and writings. Southern Methodist University maintains a noncommercial press, established in 1937. ★

John Mason Brewer

John Mason Brewer (1896–1975) was born in Goliad in 1896, the son of a cowboy. Schooled in Austin, he received a BA from Wiley College in Marshall. He began collecting African American folklore, encouraged to do so by J. Frank Dobie, and became one of the most famous folklorists in his field. Brewer would use black American dialect in his talks, particularly when dealing with folklore. He went on to receive an MA from Indiana University and an honorary doctorate from Paul Quinn College. He served as a French interpreter for the American Expedition Forces in 1918 (he spoke French, Italian, and Spanish), taught creative writing at Tillotson College, Romance languages at Samuel Huston College, and Spanish at Booker T. Washington High School in Dallas, ending his teaching career at what is now Texas A&M University at Commerce. His works include *The Word on the Brazos; Negro Preacher Tales from the Bottoms of Texas*; *Aunt Dicy's Tales: Snuff-Dipping Tales of the Texas Negro*; *Dog Ghosts and Other Negro Folk Tales*; *Negrito*, a book of verse; and *Negro Legislators and Their Descendants*, history and biography. The discussion of him in the *WPA Dallas Guide and History* gave the impetus to include him here.

From *Spur-of-the-Cock:* Old-Time Negro Proverbs

God and Freedom were with many slaves synonymous. *Yuh mought as well die wid de chills ez wid de fever* not only goes back to a common plantation malady but was interpreted for me as meaning that "you might as well get killed trying to escape as to remain a slave and die in slavery."

De quickah death, de quickah heaben, I heard an old woman say, and then she sang a song to enforce the idea of the proverb:

Oh Freedom, Oh Freedom,

Befoh Ah'd be uh slave
Ah'd be buried en mah grave
An' go home tuh mah Jesus an' be saved.

Much of the slave's time was spent in trying to find ways and means of escape. *Don' crow tel yuh git out o' de woods; dey mought be uh beah behin' de las' tree* meant "Don't be careless about talking to people you see, until you get to the Underground Railway. You might get caught and returned to your owner."

Don' say no mo' wid yo' mouf dan yo' back kin stan' is an admonition to slaves to speak briefly and seldom, not only to the master but to other slaves. Frequently the slaves would discuss the possibilities of escape among themselves, and be overheard by the overseer, some tattling slave, or the master himself; then his back paid for what his mouth had said. . . .

Don't let no chickens die in yo' han' implies the proverbial connection of the Negro with chickens. The idea is that when the dead chicken is on the ground instead of in his hand evidence against the darkey who has killed it is less incriminating.

As inevitable as chickens is cotton. The obvious meaning of *Dirt show up de quickes' on de cleanes' cotton* is that a bad deed shows up more distinctly on a person of good character than on a person of already bad repute.

Distant stovewood am good stovewood meant that the biggest trees don't grow on the edge of the woods and that if a man wanted big back logs for his fireplace, he would have to go to extra trouble to get them. . . .

Whut yuh don' hab in yo' haid yuh got ter hab in yo' feet. "Dat me'ns lak dis," said Uncle George McKay. "Lak ef yuh goes to de sto' fer some grub an' yuh fergits ter git it all, den yo' feet hab ter take yuh back anudder time fer whut yuh didn' git de fus' trip."

Dere's uh fambly coolness twixt de mule an' de singletree does not so much say that a mule sometimes kicks the singletree to which his traces are hooked as that two factors bound together, as man and wife, do not always work in harmony.

Although the ex-slave was grateful to God for his freedom and "God's chillun" were not supposed to dance, among the first of the freedman's free acts was a surrender to the rhythmic nature inherited from his African ancestors.

He had, as a slave, developed into an excellent clog and tap dancer but had not been free to cultivate the social dance. The "platform dance" and the "cakewalk" came with Emancipation and the freedman revelled as much in dance and song as he had formerly revelled in church worship. Certain proverbs seem to date from this era of dancing and the freer courtship that came with it.

Don' take no mo' tuh yo' heaht dan yuh kin kick off en yo' heels meant, "Don't worry so much about jilts in love that you can't go to a dance and dance your troubles away."

Evahbody say "goodnight" ain't gone home may have evolved as a result of this social freedom enjoyed by the freed slave, especially by courting couples. . . .

Crude sayings of a crude people, humble, optimistic, good-humored. They have not all been collected.

Dey's jes' ez good uh fish in de creek ez evah been caught;
Dey's jes' ez good uh timber in de woods ez evah been bought. ★

From *Tone the Bell Easy:* Juneteenth, section entitled Squirming Out, 'Possum in the Pot

SILAS JONES WAS THE SHREWDEST SLAVE ON the Crockett plantation. Not only that, he was the best 'possum cook on the plantation, and 'possum dinners and 'possum suppers at his cabin were regular fare. Silas's reputation as a 'possum cook spread so far that it reached the ears of the master. So one evening the master decided to go down and taste some of Silas's 'possum.

"Good evening, Silas," said Master John. "What are you cooking that smells so good ?"

" 'Possum, Massa John," answered Silas.

"It certainly smells good," repeated the master. "I have been hearing about your reputation as a 'possum baker; so I thought I would come down and try a piece."

"Sho', Massa, sho'," said Silas. "Yuh's mighty welcome. I jes' put 'im on. We'll have to wait fo' 'im to cook."

The master sat there about an hour and waited, but Silas did not take the lid off the pot.

"Isn't that 'possum done yet?" finally asked the master.

"No, sah, not yit, Massa," said Silas. "Takes 'im uh long time to git done."

The master waited another hour; still Silas did not take the 'possum off.

"Silas," said the master, "it certainly takes that 'possum a long time to cook. I believe I'll take a look at him myself. I think it ought to be done." The master walked over and took the lid off the pan. He found two chickens instead of a 'possum. "These are chickens, Silas," said the master. "I thought you said they were 'possums."

"Sez dey is, Massa! Wal, dey wuz 'possums when Ah put 'em in dar. Ef dey's chickens now, Ah's gwine th'ow 'em away." ★

From *Mexican Border Ballads:* John Tales, section entitled John and the Two White Men In Court

One year the boll-weevils got into the cotton crop on Colonel Clemons's plantation and destroyed most of it. This made times very hard for the colonel, and since he did not make any money, he did not provide sufficient food and clothing for the hands. So naturally they stole anything they could get away with.

Never a week passed that some of the hands were not arrested and carried to jail.

One day the 'sheriff came out to Colonel Clemons' farm and arrested John. With him were two white hands he had arrested on a neighboring plantation. John and the two white hands were all charged with stealing and they were to be tried on the same day at the same hour.

When John and the two white men were brought in to the courtroom and arraigned for trial, John was very nervous and was trembling. This was the first time in his life that he had not been able to think of an excuse. He knew, however, that they were going to try the white men first; so he decided to listen to their answers and imitate them when his turn came.

The first case called was that of one of the white hands who was accused of stealing a horse.

"Guilty, or not guilty," said the judge.

"Not guilty," replied the man. "I've owned that horse ever since he was a colt." The case was dismissed.

Then the judge called the second white man to the stand. He was accused of stealing a cow. "Guilty, or not guilty," asked the judge.

"Not guilty," replied the defendant; "I've owned that cow ever since she was a calf." The case was dismissed.

Then John was called to the stand. He was accused of stealing a wagon.

"Guilty, or not guilty," demanded the judge.

"Not guilty," replied John. "Ah's owned dat wagon ever since it was a wheelbarrow." ★

Margaret Bell Houston

Margaret Bell Houston (1877–1966), poet and novelist, was the daughter of Sam Houston Jr. and granddaughter of "The Hero of San Jacinto." Houston studied at Columbia University and became a member of the Texas Institute of Letters, the Dallas Shakespeare Club and the Poetry Society of Texas. She made her home in Dallas and in New York. Besides five volumes of fiction, *The Little Straw Wife* (1914); *The Witch Man* (1923); *Moon of Delight* (1931); *Hurdy Gurdy* (1933); and *Magic Valley* (1934); she has also published her poems in *Prairie Flowers* (1907); *The Singing Heart* (1926); and *Lanterns in the Dusk* (1930). Her poetry was anthologized in *Voices of the Southwest; New Voices of the Southwest; Signature of the Sun; The Southwest in Literature;* and elsewhere. In the first half of the century, Margaret Houston's poetry and prose works for children became nationally popular.This Dallas poet shows the pull between Dallas and New York.

Song from the Traffic

The black haw is in flower again,
The redbud's rosy tide
Splashes the wood and stains the shade
Where dog-tooth violets hide.
(Manhattan—Manhattan—I walk your streets today.
But I see the Texas prairies bloom a thousand miles away!)

Primroses burn their yellow fired
Where grass and roadway meet.
Feathered and tasseled like a queen,

Is every old mesquite.
(It's raining in the barren parks, but on the prairie-side,
The road is shining in the sun for him who cares to ride!)

The plum tree's arms are burdened white,
And where the shrubs are few
Bluebonnets fold the windy way—
Is any blue so blue?
(Clouds of them, crowds of them, shining through the gray,
Bluebonnets blossoming a thousand miles away!)

How could I live my life so far
From where March plains are green,
But that my gallivanting heart
Knows all the road between?
(Manhattan—Manhattan—when you jostled me today,
You jostled one a-galloping a thousand miles away!) ★

Vaida Stewart Montgomery

Vaida Stewart Montgomery (1888–1959) was copublisher and coeditor of Kaleidograph Press of Dallas, with her husband Whitney Maxwell Montgomery. They published many of the poets of that era out of this press. Vaida Montgomery was a major Texas poet, publishing her first poem, "Stampede" in 1924. Her poetry collections were *Locoed and Other Poems* and *Hail for Rain*, which won the Texas Institute of Letters poetry award. Her poetry appeared in *West*; *Sunset*; *Holland's*; *Parents* magazine; and *The Dallas Morning News*. She was a major contributor to the Poetry Society of Texas yearbooks and was awarded the Old South Prize by that group in 1939 and 1944. She also served as recording secretary of the Poetry Society of Texas. She, Whitney Maxwell Montgomery and Grace Noll Crowell, who follow, were major players in the Poetry Society of Texas, which had been founded in Dallas. The poetry of these three are examples of what those early Dallas poets were writing about—the frontier and rural Texas.

Cattle Brands

The pioneer artists had a canvas as wide
As the hairy surface of a steer's hide.

They worked with a red-hot saddle-ring,
An end-gate rod, or any old thing,
But they drew their lines and they curved them well,
From the Tumbling Crutch to the Dinner Bell.

The Old Timer fumbled and muttered a damn
When they handed him an iron with a monogram.

"Just give me a gaucho, every time—
Them new-fangled curlicues ain't worth a dime."

The Old Timer's Brand was I C U;
The rustler changed it to I C U 2

The hard-riding cowhands played just as hard,
Nor batted an eye at the turn of a card.

There was a cowboy, Burk Burnett by name,
Who held four sixes in a poker game.

"I wager my ranch," the ranchman bawled—
He had three aces—and Burk said, "Called!"

So Burk won the ranch on a poker hand,
And henceforth used the Four Six (6666) brand.

The pioneer women like to see
The Laurel Leaf and the Fleur de Lis.

The pioneer men liked Spade, and Star,
Pig Pen, Pitchfork, and Bar V Bar;

Hog Eye, Mule Shoe, Lazy J,
Buzzard on a Rail, and Anchor K;

Buckle, Broad Axe, Straddlebug,
Bow and Arrow, and Little Brown Jug.

The pioneer artists had a canvas as wide
As the hairy surface of a steer's hide;

And they drew their lines and they curved them true,
From the Turkey Track to the Flying U. ★

Whitney Maxwell Montgomery

Whitney Maxwell Montgomery (1877–1966), married to poet Vaida Montgomery, was born on a farm and resided there until his marriage to Vaida when he moved to Dallas. The two of them began the Kaleidograph Press there, publishing more than 500 books of poetry in addition to the magazine out of the press. He received numerous prizes, including the ballad contest from the Poetry Society of Texas in 1941, 1942, 1943, and 1945. He won the Texas Institute of Letters Poetry Award in 1946 for *Joseph's Coat* and he also served as president of that organization. His other books of poetry are *Corn Silks and Cotton Blossoms*; *Brown Fields and Bright Lights;* and *Hounds in the Hills.* He was one of the organizers of the Poetry Society of Texas.

Death Rode a Pinto Pony

Death rode a pinto pony
    Along the Rio Grande,
Beside the trail his shadow
    Was riding on the sand.

The look upon his youthful face
    Was sinister and dark,
And the pistol in his scabbard
    Had never missed its mark.

The moonlight on the river
    Was bright as molten ore,
The ripples broke in whispers
    Along the sandy shore.

The breath of prairie flowers
    Had made the night-wind sweet,
And a mocking bird made merry
    In a lacy-leafed mesquite.

Death looked toward the river,
    He looked toward the land,
He took his broad sombrero off
    And held it in his hand,

And Death felt something touch him
    He could not understand.
The lights at Madden's ranch-house
    Were brighter than the moon,
The girls came tripping in like deer,
    The fiddles were in tune,

And Death saw through the window
    The man he came to kill,
And he that did not hesitate
    Sat hesitating still.

A cloud came over the moon,
    The moon came out and smiled,
A coyote howled upon the hill,
    The mocking bird went wild.

Death drew his hand across his brow,
    As if to move a stain,
Then slowly turned his pinto horse
    And rode away again. ★

Grace Noll Crowell

Grace Noll Crowell (1877–1969) was a poet of considerable stature in the United States and abroad. *White Fire* was her first book of poetry and won the Poetry Society of Texas award in 1925. She was the Poet Laureate of Texas in 1935 and on into the Centennial year. Her poetry appeared throughout the country in *Holland's; McCall's; Scribner's; The Southwest in Literature; The Best Poems of 1924;* and in other publications both here and abroad. She published twenty-one books of poetry, and in addition she published stories for children and poem and prose devotions. She was so popular that it was necessary for her husband to quit his job to help manage her writing career. He helped answer correspondence and receive visitors from all over the United States and Europe who visited their Dallas home.

Summer Nights in Texas

Days must be hot to make the cotton white,
And have their own peculiar yellow glare,
But when the Gulf wind booms its way at night,
There is no lovelier darkness anywhere.
I lift my face—I turn toward the South,
My hair blows loose—the wind along my path
Is like a drink to any thirsty mouth;
Is like a plunge in some soft-water bath.
I drink the wind! I bathe in it! I dive,
With outstretched arms, a swimmer in my glee!
The wind has made me gloriously alive,
Its waves roll in, and they sweep over me!

No day can be too hot, too long and bright,
If it be followed by a Texas night. ★

Wagons at Dusk

Sometimes when the grass in Texas
Is deep and green and lush,
And the wind dies down at evening,
I can hear through the deepening hush
The sound of covered wagons
Creaking in box and spoke,
I can see them stop at nightfall,
I can smell the supper smoke.
And voices call through the darkness—
Lonely and strange they sound
In the vastness of the prairies
Between the sky and the ground.

And the ones who have chosen Texas
Because of its clean red loam,
Who are forging ahead to claim it
And name it for their home,
Dream awhile in the darkness:
An ancient wonder dream—
They see homes rise on the prairies,
See schools and churches gleam
Against the red of the sunset,
Against the rose of the dawn,
And, although their old homes call them,
Tomorrow they will move on.

Men and women and children,
Facing the arduous toil
Of rearing walls, and of wresting
A living from the soil;
A Texas wind on their faces,
The Texas sun on their backs
Their only link to the old home
The wavering wagon tracks.

Sometimes at twilight I see them,
These strong sturdy pioneers
I call through the dark and hail them
Across the lengthening years:
And I lift a hand to bid them
Godspeed on the way they go.
I have a debt I would pay them,
I have a debt that I owe
To the founders and builders of Texas
Grouped in these shadowy camps,
Who kindled the first home fires
And lighted the first home lamps.
The roots of my home run deeper,
Its walls climb nearer the sun
Because these brave ones finished
The task that they had begun. ★

Evelyn Oppenheimer

Evelyn Oppenheimer's (1907–1998) distinctive voice has been heard all over Texas and even beyond the borders, from her book reviews on radio to her reviews in person. She was born in Dallas in 1907 and died there in September of 1998 at age ninety, lucid and active in the literary world almost to the end. She had given her extensive book collection to the DeGolyer Library at Southern Methodist University. The collection reads that she was a "noted book reviewer who greatly contributed to the literacy of the Dallas community. The collection consists of more than 300 modern first editions and five feet of archival material, including manuscripts and tapes from 1942 to the 1980s." It could be added that she contributed greatly to the literacy of Texas. She edited or authored *Tolbert of Texas; The Articulate Woman; Heroes of Texas; The Book of Dallas; Texas in Color; Red River Dust; Legend and Other Poems; Tilli Comes to Texas; Oral Book Reviewing to Stimulate Reading; Book Reviewing for an Audience;* and *Gilbert Onderdonk: The Nurseryman of Mission Valley, Pioneer Horticulturist.* She was one of a kind and her voice and wise counsel have been greatly missed. Her impact on the literary life in Dallas was enormous.

From *A Book Lover in Texas*

I was an only child, but never lonely. Who could be lonely in that house at 1619 South Ervay Street with its big attic and basement and trees to climb and big backyard for riding my Shetland pony? There was a stable for my pony and my father's horse, and on Sunday mornings we would ride south on Ervay to the woods that were still on Park Row in the First World War days when an army camp was at Fair Park.

At that time South Dallas was locale for as many fine homes of prominent citizens as were those to the north on Ross Avenue and in Munger Place. On Ervay at South Boulevard were the fine old homes of Simon Linz of the jewelry company, and Gerard Dreyfus, owner of one of the quality menswear stores, among others such as E. M. Kahn, Gus Roos, and Hurst Brothers.

Across the street (and streetcar tracks) from our home was that of Morris Liebman, who with his brother Rudolph owned the Texas Paper Company. Next door was the Buell family of Buell Lumber Company. . . . In the next block was the home of one of the few general practitioners, Dr. Emil Aronson. Later I would borrow and read all the classical and medical books in his and his son Howard's library, just as I went through the Rover Boys and Tom Swift series that the Liebmans' sons Walter and Richard had. Variety was the spice of my early literary life, as indeed it has continued to be. . . .

In those World War I days one went with one's mother shopping for delicacies at the grocery and market stores, Craddock's on South Ervay, and Hunt's on North Ervay, . . . and of course for clothes and accessories at Sanger Brothers and A. Harris and Titche-Goettinger and the new Neiman-Marcus and for shoes at Volk Bros.

What fun it was at Sanger's to ride up and down that first escalator and to browse in their book department, presided over by Miss Bertha Prager, or to go to that first lending library of Edna Smith's at A. Harris. For our school books we went to Van Winkle's or the Schmalzried secondhand book store. . . .

Growing out of the frontier days when circuit-riding Methodist preachers carried religious books in their saddlebags to the pioneer farm and ranch homes was the great book store of Dallas, Cokesbury's, so named to combine the names of two early bishops, Coke and Asbury. As managed by J. F. "Bliss" Albright, it developed the biggest sales of books in the country, which was quite a shock to folks visiting this hinterland from the east.

In the later years of the 1920s, 1930s, and 1940s, there would be the literary rendezvous of Elizabeth Ann McMurray's famous book shop on Commerce Street. . . . I remember visits there with Sinclair Lewis, Frances Parkinson Keyes, Paul Wellman, Irving Stone, Harnett Kane, etc. When Mrs. Keyes (she pronounced it Kise), author of the bestsellers *River Road, Dinner at Antoine's,* was entertained at an elitist woman's club and served tea, the grande dame of New Orleans literati bellowed out, "Get me a bottle of bourbon!" Hastily the Dallas ladies appointed a committee to rush to a liquor store in one of their

Cadillacs and rush back with a bottle of whiskey. The guest of honor became more affable, in fact downright sociable. After a couple of slugs, she glowed.

Our class went on to Forest Avenue High School and the wonders of Virgil, Cicero, Caesar, Keats, Longfellow, Wordsworth, Shakespeare, Poe, Shelley, Hawthorne, Emerson, and de Maupassant, as well as chemistry, biology, history, and the challenge of algebra and geometry. . . .

Whatever talent I have as a speaker and broadcaster was nurtured initially by our high school debating society, and the time spent winning the state championship and then the interstate debates held in New Orleans. . . .

In the later years of the 1930s and 1940s, deluxe dating was dining and dancing at the rooftop Baker Hotel's Peacock Terrace, featuring Herbie Kay and Dorothy Lamour, or the Adolphus Hotel Century Room with the Phil Harris Band. Also very popular socially was dining at the downtown restaurants, Town and Country and the Golden Pheasant, the latter famed for its French salad dressing which was bottled and sold regionally for a number of years. I can almost taste it now. . . .

My parents had a very big surprise for me between high school and college. They had met a woman named Della Mohr who was related to their friends the Emil Stern family. Her specialty was taking small groups to Europe for the traditional Grand Tour. Before I knew it, this teenager was on the SS *Rotterdam* sailing out of New York Harbor.

Under the expert guidance of that teacher from Alabama who had spent so much time and study abroad, we traveled all summer in England, Scotland, France, Switzerland, Italy, and Austria. Even then I avoided going into Germany, as memory was still fresh about the barbarism of Kaiser Wilhelm's army in Belgium, a forerunner of what would come a decade later in the horrors of the holocaust. Austria, too, can leave a taste of bitterness which all the whipped cream and chocolate cannot cover, especially in Vienna where some of us can still hear the sound of the locking of ghetto gates at sunset under the melodic flow of Strauss waltzes. . . .

All that mattered was the great experience of actually being where most of our literature had come from originally, especially England and France. To stand at Stratford by those sculptures of Hamlet and Lady Macbeth and

Falstaff and Prince Hal, to stroll beside the swans drifting on the River Avon, just to be in Stratford or in the Lake Country, or to walk along the book stalls by the Seine or to look into the bronze face of the Victor Hugo statue and see all the faces of *Les Misérables,* such an experience is to enter literary heaven.

My generation of high school graduates in Dallas were fully prepared to take college entrance examinations, and in most cases, pass them and qualify for any of the top level colleges or universities.

My first choice was Columbia University, but unfortunately I did not know that it, like too many other eastern educational institutions, enforced a quota system for Jewish students. Accordingly, when I got there I was informed by the head of the admission office that I had met all their standards but could not be admitted because their quota for Jews was filled. Then she went behind her desk and tore up my examination papers to remove evidence.

After the shock of that first personal encounter with anti-Semitic prejudice and discrimination where one as naïve as I was then would least expect it, I immediately shifted to the University of Chicago where scholarship was all that mattered. The midwest was America, like our southwest. The Fates had dealt me a blow but then gave me a rose, one of the finest silver as in *Der Rosenkavalier.*

I soon learned that Chicago in the late 1920s and early 1930s, not New York, was the capitol of literary America.

Editor's note: Evelyn Oppenheimer was introduced to book reviewing and reviewing on the air in Chicago.

When time came for me to return home from Chicago, I remembered that Carl Sandburg had once said that Dallas had the worst newspaper coverage of books in the country. I found that not quite true. Maybe he had based that comment on the page in *The Dallas Morning News* when it was edited by Dr. John McGinnis of Southern Methodist University, who contended that nothing written after 1900 was worth his time. The professor was, of course, entitled to his opinion, but he certainly missed some very good reading.

Fortunately he was succeeded by Lon Tinkle and later Allen Maxwell, both also of Southern Methodist University, and then book reviewing in *The*

Dallas Morning News rose to a level of notable quality and was nationally recognized. Today Robert Compton carries on a consistently high standard.

For too long, however, reviewers continued to project in various ways the conviction that literature in Texas began and ended with the sanctified trinity of Dobie, Webb, and Bedichek. . . . Not that those pioneer literati deserved less respect, but new writers of quality who were then emerging such as Mary Lasswell, John Lomax, George Sessions Perry, J. Evetts Haley, David Westheimer, Benjamin Capps, Loula Grace Erdman, Fred Gipson, and others, merited more attention and recognition. . . .

The evening paper in Dallas, the *Times Herald* had a succession of very interesting and highly qualified book review editors less bound to the old buddy system. They were Kenneth Rockwell, playwright and historian John William Rogers, author Luise Putcamp Jr., Decherd Turner, Jeff Unger, and A. C. Greene. . . .

[Rogers] and I were friends, and . . . as he also was music and theatre critic for the *Times Herald,* it was always of special interest to read his reviews of those events in juxtaposition to the coverage by the brilliant *Morning News* critic, John Rosenfield, famous as the cultural czar of Dallas, who could make or break any celebrity who came to the city.

Rosenfield and I were also friends, as our families had been. His major achievement was in getting the city's moneyed society to back Margo Jones and the initiation of her theatre-in-the-round. He also supported Antal Dorati in bringing the Dallas Symphony to a level of excellence it has never surpassed. . . .

When I had come home in the mid-1930s to be with my parents, I wondered what I would do beside writing book reviews for the local papers. . . . The first organization to engage me for an oral book review was the Dallas Temple Emanu-El chapter of the Council of Jewish Women, and their request was for no less than Eugene O'Neill's *Mourning Becomes Electra.* I prepared what I thought was the way to do it—adapting a professional review into an entertaining lecture form.

The reaction of the audience was most interesting. The ladies either liked it or very much disliked it as something they were not used to hearing. The latter was of most interest to me, and I went to hear some of those other review programs and was appalled at what I heard and saw.

With all too few exceptions, such as Mrs. Roscoe Bates and Mrs. V. Y. Rejebian, they were not reviewers but merely storytellers and amateur actresses of little or no educational background, who in no way stimulated anyone to read the books they reviewed. What I did see was that this held the potential for a new form of oral reviewing, which, if properly and professionally done, could get many more people interested in reading books than the minority who read newspaper reviews. And so I found my métier and my future.

For some time I had been thinking that book review programs so popular with clubs should not be limited to those exclusive memberships. . . . I took my idea of making book review programs available to the general public, and thereby promoting books and reading on a much larger scale, to Mr. E. P. Simmons, president of Sanger's at the time, as I knew they had an upper floor auditorium which could seat a couple of hundred people. The idea appealed to him as a new way to attract people into the store. Sanger's ran several newspaper ads about the new event, and the book I chose to review, . . . *The Last Puritan* by Harvard professor of philosophy George Santayana. We had a capacity audience.

The next month I reviewed the classic Rostand play *Cyrano de Bergerac*, as the following week the great actor Walter Hampden was bringing the play to Dallas. Again we had a full house.

At the upper end of downtown was the Titche-Goettinger department store with a top floor auditorium more than double the capacity of Sanger's. I went there next, and to the great satisfaction of Mr. W. J. Brown, president, and Mr. Milton Pandres, advertising manager, my review programs went on a weekly schedule and filled their auditorium.

Women would drive in from a hundred-or-more-miles radius to attend the program, have lunch, do their shopping and return home. The auditorium was enlarged to a seating capacity of six hundred, and when that became standing room only, we began repeating the programs. That put the schedule on a twice a week basis. Then came requests from business and professional women and men for reviews on Saturday and a weeknight, when the store was open as it was in the war years of 1941–45. . . . Inevitably, Titche-Goettinger developed a book department with Mr. Marvin Steakley as manager. . . .

By 1948 I realized that the popular demand for my book reviews should not be limited to store and school and church auditoriums, nor the confines of clubs and homes. The biggest audience for books was to go on the air—Radio.

The president of the Skillern chain of drugstores agreed with me, and with that sponsor I began broadcasting once a week at night on KRLD Radio in their studio in Dallas, located in 1948 in the Adolphus Hotel building. Response came in from as far westward as New Mexico and Colorado, and it was the southwest that always held my greatest interest. . . . Now books had wings, magic wings across time and space.

Then the McMurray Bookshop became sponsor until it was sold to Ralph Gilliland, who continued to sponsor until selling to Doubleday Bookshops, which syndicated the program from Dallas-Fort Worth to radio stations in Houston, Phoenix, Los Angeles, and San Francisco. That sponsorship through the 1970s was followed by the Southwestern Booksellers Association and then from 1988 to 1993 the Half Price Bookstores. We called my broadcasts *Book Talk*, which freed me to discuss old as well as new books and authors.

Through the more than four decades of my radio book reviewing—a national record—the program moved from KRLD to WFAA to KIXL and then permanently to the municipal station of classical music and arts, WRR-FM. ★

ALAN GOVENAR
(WITH JAY F. BRAKEFIELD)

Alan Govenar is president of Documentary Arts, a nonprofit organization dedicated to broadening public knowledge of multicultural, multimedia arts. He has a BA in American Folklore from Ohio State University, an MA in folklore and anthropology from the University of Texas at Austin, and a PhD in Arts and Humanities from the University of Texas at Dallas. Alan Govenar is a writer of numerous books and articles about Texas music and folk and traditional music nationwide. He has also made several films on Texas music. His books include: *Masters of Traditional Arts: A Biographical Dictionary; African American Frontiers: Slave Narratives and Oral Histories; Osceola: Memories of a Sharecropper's Daughter; Meeting the Blues: The Rise of the Texas Sound;* and *The Early Years of Rhythm and Blues.* Govenar's films include: *The Devil's Swing; The Hard Ride: Black Cowboys at the Circle 6 Ranch;* and *Osceola Mays: Stories, Songs, and Poems.* In recent years, Govenar has conceived and written a musical with Akin Babatunde entitled *Blind Lemon Blues*, which had its world premiere in Europe and was performed in New York's Central Park in 2004. Available audio recordings include *Deep Ellum Blues; Osceola May: Spirituals and Poems; Texas, USA—John Burrus—Cowboy Songs & Country Hymns;* and *Trio Los Olmos Traditional Music of Northern Mexico.* He lives in Dallas. Govenar's coauthor on the piece excerpted here, Jay F. Brakefield, has been a writer and editor of major Texas newspapers for more than three decades, including *The Dallas Morning News.* A longtime Texas journalist, Brakefield is also a freelance writer. The impact of Deep Ellum on the Dallas scene and nationally was large.

From *Deep Ellum and Central Track: Where the Black and White Worlds of Dallas Converged:* Deep Ellum Blues: Song of the Street

THE BEST-KNOWN SONG ABOUT DEEP ELLUM, "Deep Ellum Blues," is still performed more than sixty years after it was first recorded. Though the lyrics may not be factually accurate, they recall a past that is romanticized and distorted, but nonetheless evocative of a time and place where one had to be ready for anything.

When you go down in Deep Ellum
To have a little fun
Have your fifteen dollars ready
When that policeman comes.
(Chorus) Oh, sweet Mama, Daddy's got them Deep
    Ellum blues.
Oh, sweet Mama, Daddy's got them Deep Ellum
    blues.

Once I had a sweetheart
Who meant the world to me,
But she hung around Deep Ellum
Now she's not the girl for me
(Chorus)

When you go down on Deep Ellum,
Keep your money in your shoes
'Cause the women on Deep Ellum
Got them Deep Ellum blues.
(Chorus)

When you go down in Deep Ellum,
Keep your money in your pants
'Cause the redheads in Deep Ellum
Never give a man a chance.
(Chorus)

Once I knew a preacher
Preached the Bible through and through

But he went down in Deep Ellum
Now his preachin' days are through.
(Chorus)

When you go down in Deep Ellum,
Keep your money in your socks
'Cause the women in Deep Ellum
Will throw you on the rocks.
(Chorus)

"Deep Ellum Blues" quickly spread beyond Dallas. Trumpeter Harry James, who had grown up in Beaumont, Texas, persuaded his boss, bandleader Ben Pollack, to record it. Subsequently, it has been performed and recorded by a number of other bands, including the rock group The Grateful Dead. This song, probably more than anything else, has made Deep Ellum one of the best-known and least-understood sections of Dallas. From its origins as a folk song to its popularity on radio and record, "Deep Ellum Blues" embodies the values of a city in transition. Certainly, within the lyrics there is a sense of irony and humor associated with the foibles of those who went there. The allusions to women, preachers, and police cut across cultural boundaries and are reflective of a shared experience among the people of a particular time and place. "Deep Ellum Blues" is a window on music and life in Dallas, from its earliest years as a city through its heyday and its ultimate demise and redevelopment. ★

Blind Lemon Jefferson and Downhome Blues

At least by his teens, [Blind Lemon] Jefferson began spending time in Dallas. In the Deep Ellum area, apparently about 1912, he met Huddie Ledbetter, better known as Leadbelly, one of the most legendary musical figures to travel and live in Texas. . . . His wild and reckless youth in that frontier country foreshadowed the trouble that would keep him in prison for much of his life. His musical talent was evident early, too. Leadbelly first played a small, accordion-like instrument called a windjammer. He soon learned other instruments, including guitar, and played for country dances, or "sukey jumps."

Leadbelly married in Kaufman County, Texas, east of Dallas, in 1908, and it's believed that he and his wife, Lethe, moved to Dallas about two years later. They alternated between doing farmwork in outlying areas and living in the city, where Leadbelly worked as a musician. He said later that in Dallas he heard his first jazz band, and that may also be where he discovered the instrument that became his favorite: the twelve-string guitar, at that time associated mostly with Mexican musicians.

In the extensive interviews he gave later, Leadbelly gave various dates for his initial meeting with Jefferson. . . . The two became musical partners in Dallas and the outlying area. Leadbelly learned much about the blues from Blind Lemon, and he had plenty to contribute as a musician and a showman. Leadbelly was a dancer, too, and he'd often break into a "buck and wing," a kind of flat-footed shuffle, as the two performed on the street and around Union Depot near Central and Elm. . . .

Navasota songster Mance Lipscomb told biographer Glen Myers, "When we got to Dallas, we hung around where we could hear Blind Lemon sing and play. . . . [T]here were hundreds of people up and down that [Central] Track. So, that's where I got acquainted with him, 1917. . . .

Jefferson, like other blues players, relied on a stock of musical figures, or "licks," but also could improvise—brilliantly at times. And his rhythmic sense was fluid, even quirky, making him difficult to emulate. His vocal range was unusual, too, comfortably spanning two octaves. . . .

Many of the songs that Blind Lemon recorded were personalized versions of traditional folk blues from East Texas that utilized proverbs and other elements of African American folk speech. These songs included "Jack O'Diamond Blues," about the perils of gambling; a rendition of "Two Horses Standing in a Line" that he renamed "See That My Grave Is Kept Clean"; "See, See Rider," which he transformed into "Corina Blues"; and "Boll Weevil

Blues," a legendary song about the creature that devastated the cotton fields of his homeland. In his songs, Blind Lemon identified himself with the experiences of his audience's suffering and hope, economic anxiety and failure, the breakup of the family and the desire to escape through wandering, love and sex. In "Shuckin' Sugar Blues," he sang:

> I've got your picture, and I'm goin' to put it in a
> frame.
> I've got your picture and put it in a frame, shuckin'
> sugar,
> Then if you leave town I can find you just the same.

In "Sunshine Special," though, his attitude toward travel was less optimistic:

> Gonna leave on the Sunshine Special,
> gonna leave on the Santa Fe.
> Leave on the Sunshine Special,
> goin' in on the Santa Fe.
> Don't say nothin' about that Katy
> because it's taken my brown from me.

Jefferson's music expressed the emotions many African Americans of his generation must have felt, leaving rural towns of East Texas and moving to the city of Dallas looking for work and a place to live. . . .

In general, the women in Blind Lemon's songs were revered for their sexuality and allure but condemned for manipulative personalities and fickleness in matters of love. In "Pneumonia Blues," he held his women responsible for his illness; in "Deceitful Brownskin Blues," for robbing him; and in "Peach Orchard Mama," for cheating on him. The details of Blind Lemon's actual relationships with women and his family life are sketchy. . . .

By casting women into such a wide range of roles in his songs, Blind Lemon was able to more fully identify with the experiences of his audience, an identification that carried over into other areas of life and suffering. In "Mosquito Moan," he recounted the displeasures caused by a common insect, but retained his sense of humor:

Now I'm sittin' in my kitchen, mosquitoes all around
    my screen.
Now I'm sittin' in my kitchen, mosquitoes all around
    my screen.
If I don't arrange to get a mosquito bomb,
I'll be seldom seen. . . .

In addition to the personal hardships of his audience, Blind Lemon sang about the ravages of natural disaster in "Rising High Water Blues," and about the injustices of the criminal justice system in his songs about prison life, though there's no record that he actually spent time in jail. In "Hangman's Blues," Blind Lemon demonstrated his ability to project himself into another man's fear and anxiety:

Well, mean old hangman is waitin' to tighten up
    that noose.
I have a mean old hangman waitin' to tighten up
    that noose.
Lord, I'm so scared I am tremblin' in my shoes.
Jury heard my case and said my hands was red.
Jury heard my case and said my hands was red.
And judge he sentenced me to be hangin' till I'm
    dead.
The crowd is around the courthouse, and time is
    goin' fast.
And the crowd is around the courthouse and time
    is goin' fast.
Soon a good for nothin' killer is goin' to breathe
    his last. . . .

Blind Lemon Jefferson's death marked the end of the riotous 1920s, a time when the commercial possibilities of African American popular music were first explored, but his art also looked forward. As an early recording artist, he was an influence on other performers and writers. He taught Leadbelly much about the blues and apparently introduced him to slide guitar. The line "I walked all the way from Dallas to Wichita Falls," from Jefferson's "Long Lonesome Blues," has appeared in the repertoire of countless blues singers. A verse of "Black Horse Blues" turned up in slightly altered form in Mississippi singer Charley Patton's "Pony Blues": *Got to get on my black horse and saddle up my gray mare.* His line *Well, the train I ride is eighteen coaches long* became the basis for Little Junior Parker's "Mystery Train," later recorded by Elvis Presley. And there's another Elvis connection, a line from Jefferson's "Teddy Bear Blues": *Say, fair brown, let me be your teddy bear/Tie a string on my neck, I'll follow you everywhere.* Robert Johnson apparently borrowed from Jefferson's "Change My Luck Blues" in his "Walking Blues": *She got Elgin movements from her head down to her toes/And she can break in on a dollar anywhere she goes.* Jefferson's "Jack O'Diamond Blues" became a hit for Lonnie Donnegan during the 1950s skiffle craze in England. And of course "Matchbox Blues" was the basis of hits for both rockabilly pioneer Carl Perkins and the Beatles. Blind Lemon's phrasing, the "suspended time" of his guitar playing, was a harbinger of the swinging Texas style of guitar playing that T-Bone Walker and others would make popular on a much wider scale. They would electrify that sound, put it in front of a full orchestra and take it to California. His use of flatted fifths may even be seen as a harbinger of bebop, which made extensive use of them.★

Buster Smith: Dallas Jazz Goes to Kansas City and New York

Dallas did not play as clear or dramatic a part in the development of jazz as it did in the blues. There is no single towering figure who was the obvious Dallas jazz counterpart to Blind Lemon Jefferson, yet in the mid- to late-1920s, in the words of jazz historian Ross Russell, Dallas was "the most important band town in Texas." The city and the surrounding area produced a number of musicians who went on to play vital roles in swing and bebop: saxophonists Budd Johnson, Herschel Evans, Buddy Tate and Henry "Buster" Smith; trombonist Jack Teagarden; and electric guitar pioneer Charlie Christian, who was born in Bonham, in East Texas, and grew up in Oklahoma, but spent a great deal of time in Dallas. . . .

In addition to street singers such as Jefferson, who performed alone, there were groups such as Coley Jones's Dallas String Band, which included Marco Washington, a versatile musician whose stepson was Aaron "T-Bone" Walker, born in 1910. The whole family, including Walker's mother, was musical, and they organized a band that played for money on the streets on weekends. The instrumentation included bass, guitars, fiddles, mandolins, and homemade instruments. Sometimes Jesse Hooker joined in on sax and clarinet. . . .

Jazz was being played in Dallas as well, indoors and out. Brass bands played in parks and in "colored carnivals." They were even used in funerals to some extent. A 1925 *Dallas Morning News* article recalled a black funeral procession with a brass band coming up South Lamar Street. . . .

Of the Dallas scene, Smith said:

> T-Bone Walker was around; he used to dance where I played down on the Central Track. He wasn't singing much then, just dancing. Sammy Price was down there, too. He was a dancer too, at first. Of course there were a lot of bands around here, too. Alphonso Trent, Jap Alien, T. (Terrence) Holder, George E. Lee. . . . We had two bands here as good as you could find anywhere: Troy Floyd and Alphonso Trent. In 1928, Trent was playing at the Adolphus Hotel. Another band was Fred Cooper's. And then there was Carl Murphy's little seven-piece band. They called themselves the Satisfied Five or something like that when they first started out. They played at the Adolphus Hotel evenings, and Trent played there later in the night. Then there were any number of four- and five-piece bands playing around the roadhouses and after-hours spots. Trent and Floyd were the big bands and did most of the traveling.

Though some black musicians played for white audiences in the big hotels, many played exclusively for black audiences in areas such as Deep Ellum. "Man, Deep Ellum was wide open," Buster Smith said. "You could see everybody you knew in Deep Ellum; they'd hang out by the railroad tracks and listen at the medicine shows, and then go to the Tip Top. It was the most popular place down there. . . .

Smith started his own band, which included a teenage alto player named Charlie Parker. "Well, he used to tell me he wanted to play like me," Smith said. "He used to call me his dad, and I called him my boy. . . ."

It's not hard to see why Charlie Parker regarded Buster Smith as his musical father. As writer Nathan W. Pearson said, Smith "strongly influenced Charlie Parker by stretching the harmonic dimensions of the alto saxophone and using a lightning-fast 'dancing' style that anticipated and influenced Parker's. . . . "

Basie and other old friends visited Smith when they played Dallas, but he never saw Parker again. "Bird" died in 1955, thirty-four years old, ravaged by alcoholism and heroin addiction and other personal demons. "Charlie came down, too, one time, but I missed him," Smith said. "He was here for a couple of days with Stan Kenton. . . . It was just a little while before Charlie died. I didn't even hear about them being here till they were already gone. They told me Charlie was looking for me up on Hall Street. I went on up there, but he was gone. . . ."

Budd Johnson remained musically active almost until his death in 1984. His importance as a jazz figure is often overlooked, possibly because he seldom led his own bands. He was a common thread linking the large bands of the early and mid-1940s that were involved in the transition from swing to bebop: those of Earl Hines, Boyd Raeburn, Billy Eckstine, Woody Herman, and Dizzy Gillespie. Johnson wrote music for all these bands and played tenor sax in live performance or on records with all but Raeburn's. . . .

Eddie Durham became an important arranger for Basie and other bandleaders. According to one story, he received $5 from Glenn Miller for his arrangement of "In the Mood," which became a huge hit for Miller. Durham was also a mentor to Charlie Christian, who became one of the first black musicians with a major white band when Benny Goodman hired him at the urging of his [Goodman's] brother-in-law, John Hammond. Christian, probably the first electric jazz guitarist, took part in late-night jam sessions in the early 1940s that were the leading edge of bebop. Had he not died of pneumonia at age twenty-four in 1942, Christian would have taken part in the postwar jazz revolution with Johnson, Miles Davis, Dizzy Gillespie, Charlie Parker, and others.

Smith remained well-known among Dallas musicians and became a mentor to such figures as David "Fathead" Newman, who played tenor sax with Ray Charles for a number of years. . . . Smith was also featured, along with Basie, Budd Johnson, and others, in the 1977 documentary film *The Last of the Blue Devils.*

By the last phase of Smith's career, the Deep Ellum of his youth was long gone. The building that had housed the Tip Top was torn down in 1968. An article in *The Dallas Morning News* reviewed the building's days as a hotel, but said nothing of its more recent history as a dance hall. In a sense, though, Smith must have felt that he had come full circle. ★

Frank X. Tolbert

From *Legendary Ladies of Texas:* Glamor Girl Called Electra

Electra Waggoner Biggs, the world famous sculptor, should raise a statue in Electra on the town square for her remarkable aunt, Electra Waggoner Wharton Bailey Gilmore. Or perhaps the statue should be in the 4700 block of Preston Road in Dallas where Electra One made life exciting in the early years of this century.

Anyway, Electra town (pop. about 4,000) was named for the first Electra Waggoner. . . . In 1902 the townspeople petitioned to have the post office's title changed to Electra in honor of the beautiful and popular cowgirl.

Electra was well educated—and willful. While on a world tour with her parents, she annoyed them by such an action as having a butterfly design tattooed on one of her shapely legs when they were in China. She was given a big ranch in Wilbarger County for a birthday present. She called the ranch Zacaweista, the Indian name for the tall grass that grew there.

By 1918 the Waggoner cattle kingdom was well planted in producing petroleum wells, as the half million acres in six counties still is today.

The first Electra was one of the first girls in Dallas to have a complete trousseau from Paris, which she bought before she was married to a Philadelphia socialite, A. B. Wharton. She was also Neiman-Marcus's first customer to buy $20,000 worth of clothes in a single day. Mrs. Carrie Neiman told me Electra came back the next day and got about $20,000 worth of other things she'd forgotten. And these were 1907 dollars, real dollars.

If you want to see where Electra lived in Dallas, drive by and take a look at 4700 Preston Road, an estate backing on Turtle Creek. Life then at 4700 Preston Road was just one big exciting party. Guests included socialites such as Ann Morgan, daughter of old J. P. Morgan, and politicians of the likes of Theodore Roosevelt, and New York matinee idols such as Lou Telegen and Carlyle Blackwell.

One of the most successful house parties started at 4700 Preston Road and wound up two hundred miles to the west at Zacaweista. On the ranch, the timing was just right for Electra's guests, mostly from the East, to watch an oil well gush with such savage force that it blew off the crownblock of the derrick.

Carrie Neiman told me that almost every day when Electra was in Dallas, Neiman's had orders to send out a large stock of dresses for the gorgeous cowgirl's selection. The dresses would have to arrive in the original packages from Paris or New York, for she refused to consider a dress that anyone had tried on.

Her dressing room was like a Neiman-Marcus stockroom. One long closet was hung with fur coats. There were usually 350 pairs of shoes in her shoe cabinet, and she had a new pair of shoes delivered daily either from Neiman's or from New York.

Electra One paid only about $200,000 for that great estate on Preston Road. You probably couldn't buy the gatehouse for that now. After buying the house only a year after it was built, she caused $100,000 worth of remodeling. And she furnished the place with $500,000 in art objects collected from throughout the world, including Persian rugs that cost $42,000. . . .

Electra One died Thanksgiving Day, 1925, in New York City. She was only forty-three. Yet no one could say she hadn't lived life to the fullest. ★

Ronald L. Davis

Ronald L. Davis, retired professor of history at Southern Methodist University, grew up in Dallas. He holds three degrees from the University of Texas at Austin and is the author of biographies of John Wayne, Linda Darnell, John Ford, and Van Johnson. He lives in Dallas and Wimberley and devotes himself to writing. His biography of John Rosenfield shows the impact of one man on Dallas culture.

From *John Rosenfield's Dallas: How the Southwest's Leading Critic Shaped a City's Culture, 1925–1966*

Dallas in the early 1920s was more of a cotton town than an oil center, while its leading citizens were mainly merchants and realtors. What music and theater there was in the community was treated lightly and most often reviewed in the local press by some bland reporter more content with recording the event than with evaluating a performance in anything like a critical manner. But such nonchalant commentary on the lively arts became outmoded soon after John Rosenfield took charge of the amusements desk at *The Dallas Morning News* in 1925.

Rosenfield was the city's leading cultural voice for more than forty years, 1925-1966. His reviews covered theater, music, film, dance, popular amusements, and sometimes books, paintings, and politics. His daily column "The Passing Show" won Rosenfield national recognition of sufficient prominence that New York editor Bennett Cerf referred to John as "the Alexander Woollcott of the Southwest." Like Woollcott, Rosenfield came from the era of big personalities in journalism. . . .

Rosenfield, a native Dallasite, was not merely a critic; he became an instructive columnist and an astute editor, yet he also played a leadership role in building the arts structure of his city. "John was the guy who engineered the arts in Dallas," Rosenfield's friend and colleague Charles Cullum said. "He almost created culture in this city." Fund-raisers and management for nascent arts projects sought out Rosenfield for counsel, knowing that his support was essential to their success.

Like his equivalents in other cities, Rosenfield wrote dazzling reviews, but he also made the arts seem important. His style was distinctly journalistic, and he covered practically every area of the performing arts—plays, opera, musical comedy, movies, ballet, concerts, even the circus—with aplomb. While Rosenfield shied away from the term critic, which he saw as a more technical function than that of a reviewer, he nonetheless exerted a monumental influence on professional standards in the Southwest and on Dallas in particular.

Rosenfield wanted the best for his city and exhibited a cosmopolitan view of the arts within a regional setting. He watched Dallas grow from a provincial town into a metropolis and was determined to see that his city become imbued with an appreciation of culture. His approach was erudite, witty, educational, and entertaining, while his enthusiasm seemed as boundless as his vocabulary. No one doubted where John Rosenfield stood on a performance, for John seldom minced words. All of his energy and intelligence were directed toward accomplishing a lifetime goal—to plant the lively arts firmly in Texas soil and teach its citizens lessons in taste. He preferred to operate with tact but wasn't beyond coercion and reproach if necessary. Rosenfield emerged as the czar of Southwestern culture—acknowledged as such everywhere in the country with the possible exception of Houston—and he wielded immense power. Stanley Marcus once called John the "Little Caesar of Show Business," and there is little doubt that Rosenfield traced the dotted line he expected Dallas's leaders to sign.

A Falstaffian character, nearly as wide as he was tall (approximately five foot, six inches), John craved knowledge and food with almost equal voracity. His doctors periodically insisted that he lose weight, which he would do for a time, but soon he would be back to his usual 240 pounds. He loved to sit up late at night talking and drinking with friends, and while the fellowship was stimulating and cordial, the sessions did nothing to lessen his girth. . . .

Rosenfield was an intense man, devoted to his work, his city, his wife, and his home. Along with John McGinnis and Lon Tinkle, successive book reviewers on the staff of *The Dallas Morning News* , John Rosenfield exerted uncommon influence in shaping his region's cultural and intellectual life. McGinnis once commented, "We are all present at the birth of culture in the Southwest but only as midwives." Rosenfield was an assertive and consistent midwife to cultural institutions in Dallas and often played a supporting role in neighboring cities. The arts, he contended, are essential to a community's balance and well-being. "I want Dallas to be as sophisticated, as knowing, as any other place in the world," John told a friend. "The arts are an integral part of urban civilization." To that end he brought the fire of an evangelist. He was prepared to agitate and ramrod on behalf of what he considered a sacred cause. He respected the city fathers, yet he was not afraid of them. He understood their temperament and could couch his plea for quality in terms they understood. "Dallas does not take with equanimity the thought of being second in anything," he wrote in a column in June 1947. "There is a civic psychology that cannot be satisfied with anything short of knowing that some part of any Dallas endeavor is unexcelled. . . ."

Rosenfield had a way of being upbeat even when he was critical. Somehow he always seemed to get at the heart of the matter and did so with a combination of literacy, charm, informality, and punch. His columns glistened with fresh phrases, yet his writing was sprightly enough not to intimidate the average reader. He could be worldly and unashamedly Southwestern at the same time and usually considered the audience as well as the performers in his reviews. In a delightful style free of didacticism, John emerged as an extraordinary teacher, setting high standards in a wide range of art forms, all with the hope that one day Texas would become a haven for distinguished creativity. ★

Selected Reviews:

The Jazz Singer (*The Dallas Morning News*, April 9, 1928)

THE CALL OF THE SYNAGOGUE AGAINST THE tug of the jazz stage is a mighty conflict. The "Kol Nidre" and "Toot, Toot, Tootie, Good-Bye" are strange and dissonant bedfellows in harmony. Such provide dramatic impetus of "The Jazz Singer," a picture with Vitaphone accompaniment that introduces Al Jolson, greatest of ballad singers, to a movie audience and which begins the Melba Theater's new policy of synchronized films and music.

The story was written by one Samson Raphaelson, who gathered his materials in an interview with Jolson himself. Much of the story is, therefore, biographical. The tale was marketed for a while as a short story and then converted into a play. The stage opus was a great success, although not Jolson, but George Jessel played the central role. For the screen version Jolson, himself, was commandeered to portray his own life, and Jessel, a far more experienced screen performer, was overlooked.

Jolson's real name is Asa Yoelson and he is the son of a cantor in an orthodox Jewish synagogue. Cantorhood is a sort of family prerogative, and the scion of the Yoelsons was next in line for the vestments. He had song within him, but not the impulse to wail the woes of Israel. Instead he turned Al Jolson, blacked his face and rouged his lips to chirp serenades to the "Mammy of Alabammy." Likewise does Jakie Rabinowitz of "The Jazz Singer" become Jack Robin to sing "Dirty Hands, Dirty Face" in beer halls. For this the Cantor Rabinowitz grows into a thundering patriarch and locks his door against the sinful son. The boy, nevertheless, progresses from beer hall to vaudeville, from vaudeville to musical comedy, from musical comedy to the summit of song-and-dance achievement, the spectacular Broadway revue. Ballads, comic and heartrending, are his stock in trade, and to these he gives distinction by "A Voice With a Tear." Jack Robin concludes his Odyssey on the eve of the Jewish New Year, where he is to be heard for the first time in New York. His father is stricken and in delirium cries for the son of Rabinowitz to chant the Rosh Hashonah ritual. There ensues a mighty grapple, somewhat needlessly extended, between ambition and duty with the ancient figure of Moses on the sidelines pointing to the fifth commandment. Jack Robin finally yields to race and religion, and there was no performance of the "Follies" that night, as Jakie Rabinowitz sings the "Kol Nidre" to cheer his father's last hours. This defalcation evidently was ignored on Broadway, for shortly after Jack Robin is the rage of the town, and in the chaos of electric lights his name flashes bigger and better than all others.

Without the Vitaphone, "The Jazz Singer" might have been another large dose of treacle with certain exhibitions of ham acting from the novitiate Jolson. With the Vitaphone, it is something else, for the producers have taken advantage of synchronization to work ballads and dialogue in as integral to the plot movement. When Jolson faces his audience to sing a song one is not confronted with the dull pantomime, but actually hears Al Jolson sing a song. And Jolson can sing a song over the Vitaphone with bigger effect than his rivals can realize in person. These sequences become the most appealing of the picture and alone will guarantee this attraction's worthiness for patronage. The mother-father-son phases of the plot are, of course, sure-fire and will wring the emotions of the more impressionable. May McAvoy is in the cast as a delicately attractive and decently behaved heroine. The finest acting performances come from Warner Oland as the elder Rabinowitz and Molsha Yudelson as teetering "Kibitzer." Eugenie Besserer plays the mother in approved matriarchal fashion and shares honors with Jolson in a brief but touching piece of dialogue—the first "talking sequence" in modern motion pictures.

The presentation of "The Jazz Singer" was preceded by three short subjects in sight and sound. The popular screen star, Conrad Nagel, acted as a kind of conferencier in the first of these. He explained the use of the Vitaphone to the audience. This was followed by a one-act comedy, entitled "Papa's Vacation," in which the conversation of the characters was heard over the Vitaphone. Two pianists were presented in a group of popular selections, which found favor with the audience.★

Better Than Shaw (*The Dallas Morning News,* March 14, 1933)

MR. MEREDITH IS SUCH A DEVOUT SHAVIAN that he does not hesitate to apply a Shavian paradox in Shaw. His "Caesar and Cleopatra," which is the most stupendous physical achievement of the Little Theater's thirteen seasons, is the complete repudiation of its author whose relentless logic killed all the joy of Julius Caesar's visit to the Nile. But our Mr. Meredith renders unto Caesar those things that are Caesar's, namely, a Cleopatra with at least the temperament and allure of Clara Bow and an Egypt of poetic nights and architectural rhapsodies. The second of "Three Plays for Puritans" came to Dallas Monday evening as a pagan riot, leaving the audience drunk with the beauty of Alexandre Hogue's settings and the witchery of Margaret Jameson's enactment of the Egyptian queen.

If Mr. Shaw's play made sturdy framework for such ornamentation, it was because Mr. Shaw in 1898 built dynamic plots. There may have been something in the opus to contrast Shaw's sixteen-year-old spitfire with Shakespeare's serpent of the Nile, the Irishman's foxy and nonchalant general with the Bard's pompous fascist; there may have been jibes through the character of Britannus at the British proprieties and possibly a treatise on war and reparations, but the audience of Monday night had no head for such academic matters. They were intoxicated by the opulence of the spectacle, interested throughout a long evening by artful acting of Cleopatra, and amused often enough by the infallible hokum which Shaw never disdains.

However this treatment may have disconcerted the intellectuals, it was the best possible use of the Shaw play for the majority of us groundlings. Mr. Shaw's wit has been made stale by an era of debunking. He himself has bettered it. We were disposed to thank him, not for his message, but for the soundness of his play. It made the three hours and a half something more than a tour through a picture gallery.

The star of the performance was the invisible Mr. Hogue, whose sets represented both his conception and his handiwork. It is perfectly safe to say that nothing like them has been seen in Dallas by either this generation or its ancestors. That probably goes for it descendants also. There was a magnificent sphinx that might have been a wonder of the ancient world. Sacred Ra was an imposing, fearsome idol. Courtyards, throne rooms, ramparts, esplanades rose in magnificent piles and were trimmed with warm and sensuous colors. But we are not done in a discussion of the bigness and brightness of things. Workmanship, proportion, and perspective, scaled to bring grandeur to a tiny playhouse, were masterly exemplification of the scenic art. If the Hogue sets do not win national recognition, somebody is sleeping. You may argue with abundant reason that the investment misplaces the emphasis. But they are quite a show and to miss them is to deprive oneself of a sensation. In sympathetic harmony were the costumes of William Cole, the armor of Claude Yost, and the lighting effects of Roy Lee.

The rest of the cast, which was excellent in many roles, never equaled Miss Jameson in the lively pace of her performance or the brilliant clarity of her characterization. She kept Bernard Shaw on the stage Monday night without forgetting Charles Meredith either. She was entirely the child-woman of the script, showing real terror at the approach of the cannibalistic Romans, making her contest with her brother over the crown of Egypt a delicious nursery fight, subduing her officious nurse with cute outbursts of temper and then exerting her wiles in such a fashion as to make real Caesar's regrets for his age. She underlined the sensuous note by her joyful anticipation of Mark Antony's arrival with his rounded arms. She saw clearly both Shaw's role and Mr. Meredith's amendments and presented the composite as a complete personality.

Jack Hyman's Caesar was drugged with insouciance in the early scenes, but finally came to life when he and his staff were beleaguered in the Pharos lighthouse. Mr. Hyman won the heartiest laughter of the evening by the buffoonery of his feet-first dive into the Mediterranean. After that he quickened his tempo, spoke up so you could hear him, and realized in fair degree the lovingly-limned character of the author. Mr. Hyman was, all told, a good Caesar. Despite his tendency to underplay, he is too sincere and intelligent to miss a role entirely.

The lusty Rufio was well played by Paul Moore and Boris Trapp registered several esoteric points in Shaw's satire on the English. Mae Harvey was an adequate Ftatateeta.

If we could write in detail about the 100 others in this cast, who would read it? May we cite then J. W. M. Crocker's able description of the approach of the Romans, ten-year-old Robert Campion's broken proclamation of the boy-Ptolemy, Toledo Kemendo's patriarchal sorrow at the burning of the library in Alexandria, Harry Buffs duel with Ftatateeta, and R. W. Williamson's grandiloquent reading of Apollodorus's lines as some of the memorable occasions of the evening? And never to be forgotten was the opening tableaux in the courtyard in which the hosts of Egypt, with poised spears, stood silhouetted against the blue and red sky.

"Caesar and Cleopatra" is Mr. Meredith's or any other regisseur's biggest and most impressive accomplishment in Dallas. The noble contributions of others reflect, after all, upon the director's generalship. Manipulation of 102 players, smoothness of the performance, and the consistent aim of the production were his artistry.

The play will be repeated each night this week and at a matinee Saturday to full houses, according to all reports. Because of the length, the evening starting hour has been advanced to eight P.M. The performance Monday night began at 8:20 and closed at 12:05. Speedier handling of the scenery will cut down this time for subsequent performances.

There was a slight disposition of the audience to disperse before the play was over but the auditorium remained well filled until the end and there was a hearty salvo for the cast at the conclusion. Each scenic presentation evoked a demonstration. If the Little Theater had just done "Caesar and Cleopatra," it would have been cause for wonder. That they did it so well is cause for amazement. ★

Betty Holland Wiesepape

Betty Holland Wiesepape teaches creative writing along with Southern and Southwestern literature at the University of Texas at Dallas. More than a dozen of her short stories and creative nonfiction compositions have been published and several have been included in anthologies. She is a member of the Texas Institute of Letters. Her story of the impact of one man on Southern Methodist University gives another view of literature in Dallas.

From *Lone Star Chapters: The Story of Texas Literary Clubs*: The Makers of Dallas

By the first weekend in April, the landscape in North Dallas had turned a vibrant shade of green. All around the newly constructed red brick buildings, plants were putting out tender shoots of new growth, and the night air was fragrant with the scent of blossoms and freshly turned earth, as the group of Southern Methodist University students made their way from the campus to the nearby home of Professor Jay B. Hubbell. They were in high spirits, for they had been invited to the home of one of their favorite professors to participate in the organization of a poetry club.

Just how many students Dr. Hubbell invited to his house that evening is unclear, but seven undergraduates responded to his invitation: George D. Bond, Loia Magnuson, Edyth Renshaw, Jeanne Calfee, Sherwood Gates, Sam Hilburn, and Faye Lemmon. In Hubbell's opinion, these seven students were some of the most talented individuals in his classes, but on that April evening in 1922, they were far from the serious writers they would become under Hubbell's direction. . . .

Dr. Hubbell suggested that the students call themselves "the Makers" . . . a modern English translation of the Saxon word *scop*, the equivalent of a poet or minstrel in the Middle Ages. The students submitted to Hubbell's guidance and named the club the Makers. No one, including Jay Hubbell, could have foreseen then the contribution that this club, started by a group of immature college students, would eventually make to Texas letters. . . .

By the 1920s, Texas colleges began to nurture local residents' interest in verse writing, and literary societies and writers' clubs began to be organized in most towns where colleges and universities were located. The Makers of Southern Methodist University (SMU) quickly emerged as one of the most important of these college groups. This club's importance was due, in part, to its location in the city of Dallas. With a group of talented visual artists in residence and with a rapidly developing little theater movement, Dallas was emerging as an important center of cultural activity in the Southwest. . . .

By all accounts, Hubbell was the key figure in the success of . . . the Makers. . . . John McGinnis recruited Jay Hubbell to the position of assistant professor in the SMU English Department in October 1915. The college had been in operation for only thirty days when a greater-than-expected enrollment precipitated an acute need for additional faculty, and Hubbell, who had not yet completed requirements for his doctoral degree, accepted the position McGinnis offered.

When Hubbell came to SMU, he was one of a small number of young scholars who were determined to make the study of work by American authors respectable, for universities were not offering courses in American literature at that time. While Hubbell and his colleagues were developing a curriculum for the new English Department, they were also experimenting with new methods of teaching literature. Unable to find a suitable text for their sophomore English classes, Jay Hubbell and John Beaty coedited *An Introduction to Poetry.* This textbook, published by the Macmillan Company, included works by contemporary American poets such as Robert Frost, Carl Sandburg, and Vachel Lindsay, along with poems by Henry Wadsworth Longfellow, Edgar Allan Poe, Robert Browning, and Alfred Tennyson. The book soon became a best-selling college text that carried the names of the two young professors and Southern Methodist University into classrooms in prestigious universities all across the country. The name recognition and the contacts that Hubbell made while working on the book enabled him to persuade well-known contemporary writers to come to Dallas to give readings and lectures. Hubbell's reputation as a scholar continued to increase, and while he was on the faculty at SMU, he chaired the first American Literature Group of the Modern Language Association. . . .

Another of Hubbell's accomplishments involved the transfer of the *Texas Review* from the University of Texas at Austin to SMU in 1924. He renamed this publication the *Southwest Review.* With the help of John McGinnis, George Bond, and Herbert Gambrell, Hubbell turned it into an outstanding literary journal that became an important organ for the developing field of Southwestern life and literature. . . . [T]he *Review* [also] carried the names of the journal's editors, Southern Methodist University, and emerging Texas writers into major literary centers. . . ."

The objective of the Makers, as that objective was stated in an article in the SMU college newspaper, the *Campus,* was to stimulate student members' interest in poetry and to improve the quality of their writing through a process of mutual criticism. In reality, Hubbell had an ulterior motive for encouraging the organization of the student club. He needed a venue where he could train promising student poets and then encourage them to submit their compositions to a national poetry contest that was soon to be sponsored by the SMU English Department. Dallas businessman Louis Blaylock Jr. had given an anonymous donation of $175 to SMU, and the staff of the English Department had decided to use this money to sponsor a poetry contest that would be open to undergraduates in colleges and universities all over the country. . . ."

When the winners of the first national student poetry competition sponsored by the SMU English Department were announced, the time and effort Jay Hubbell had invested in the student group did not go unrewarded. In the 1921–22 contest, a cash prize was offered in each of three divisions. The first division, with a prize of one hundred dollars, was open to undergraduates enrolled in American colleges or universities. Entries in this division were submitted by college and university English departments rather than by individual students. The second division, with a prize of fifty dollars, was open to all residents of Texas; and the third division, with a prize of twenty-five dollars, was open only to SMU students. Notices of the contest appeared in national publications such as the *Bookman,* the *New Tork Times,* the *Editor,* and the

Student Writer. In response to these notices, the SMU English Department received 155 entries in the first division. These entries came from some of the most prestigious universities in the country, including Yale, Columbia, Stanford, Radcliffe, Wheaton, Randolph-Macon, William and Mary, Johns Hopkins, Smith, Cornell, Emory, Wesleyan, Mount Holyoke, and the universities of Chicago, Michigan, California, and Nebraska. Tucked inside envelopes with the entry forms came notes from various professors congratulating the faculty for their efforts on behalf of student poets. When winners in the three divisions were announced by three separate panels of judges, a poem by SMU sophomore George Bond won first place in all three categories.

Like many of the poems written by members of the Makers during their college years, George Bond's winning poem reflects the concerns of an agrarian population in a period of advancing industrialization. Today, few scholars know of the existence of the poem that won the first U.S. collegiate poetry competition. The first and last stanzas of the poem are reproduced below:

Sketches of the Texas Prairie (George Bond)

I. In Winter

All winter long the prairie lies remembering;
Old, old, and gray, and blurred with drifting mist,
Silent and listening, hearkening to the rain,
Hearing the wind scream in its desert places.
The cotton rows stretch long and brown and lifeless,
The stubble fields are still and sad as death;
The prairie lies defeated, broken-hearted,
Conquered by winter, brooding in the cold—
Pining for fields where the tall, green grass is waving,
Longing for flowers that the springtime brings,
Brooding on other springs that are long since gone,
Brooding, and thinking of its endless past,
In the rain and the mist.

V. The Gift of the Prairie

I am sick unto death of sin and of talking of sin,
And I long for the cleansing touch of the wholesome
  earth;
O, I want to be clean as the wind-swept prairie is,
Or a rock that is washed by the rain and dried by the
  sun.
I will go lay me down in the sun-drenched field,
With my face to the earth, among the weeds and the
  flowers,
Where the tall dog-daisies wave in the prairie wind.
There I will feel the warm steam rise from the damp
  earth,
And the white-winged moths will flutter about my head,
While the grasshopper's song will throb through the
  Noon-day stillness.
Yes, I will go and lay me down on the prairie,
As a child at a mother's breast: and lo, she will give me
Peace and forgetfulness and care-free strength.

The prize money awarded the young SMU sophomore proved to be a good investment on the part of the university. . . . Dr. Bond taught English, journalism, and creative writing classes, and he served for many years as chair of the SMU English Department. In addition to his academic duties, Bond served as editor of the *Southwest Review* and as associate editor of *The Dallas Morning News* Book Page. . . . Because of George Bond's influence, a number of SMU students pursued literary careers after graduation. William Humphrey, author of the highly acclaimed *Home from the Hill,* and James Hoggard, the poet laureate of Texas in the year 2000, are among the students who studied with Dr. Bond at SMU. . . .

By the time Hubbell left Texas, he had launched some of his most promising students on productive literary careers. He and his associates in the English

Department had brought favorable attention to Southern Methodist University and had established the college as a center for Southwestern life and literature. A 1925 article in the *Semi-Weekly Campus* credits Hubbell with having done "more to put SMU on the literary map" than any other person connected with the university. In "A Tribute to a Giant among Men" former Makers George Bond and Ottys Sanders write: "How could one man do so much in so little time to bring favorable attention to a new, penurious university, struggling to stay alive, out in the hinterlands? We, his former students . . . cannot answer the question. We only know that this man had an abundance of intelligence, good taste, good humor, civilization, and grace and shared those scarce commodities with everyone whose life he touched. . . ."

Members of the Makers served for many years in leadership roles in organizations that promoted statewide literary arts, such as the Poetry Society of Texas, the Texas Institute of Letters, and the Dallas Little Theater Center. As publishers, editors, journalists, and book reviewers, they promoted Texas writing and Texas writers, both inside and outside the state; as teachers and college professors, they served as mentors for succeeding generations of Texas writers. ★

John Neal Phillips (with André L. Gorzell)

John Neal Phillips holds BA, MA, and MFA degrees in art and currently teaches art and film at Tarrant County College in Arlington, Texas. An authority on Texas prison history and Depression-era outlaws, particularly Bonnie and Clyde, he wrote *Running with Bonnie and Clyde: The Ten Fast Years of Ralph Fults.* Phillips edited and annotated the prison memoirs of Blanche Caldwell Barrow, wife of Buck Barrow and sister-in-law to Clyde Barrow—*My Life with Bonnie and Clyde.* Phillips has appeared on radio and television programs and documentaries about Bonnie and Clyde and the Texas Rangers on PBS, A&E, Discovery, the History Channel, and the Learning Channel. Phillips's coauthor, André L. Gorzell, was born in Galveston, Texas, in 1955. She holds a BFA degree in literature and art from Stephen F. Austin State University. She is a mother, volunteer, Girl Scout troop leader, and bookseller. The Texas Folklore Society Publications included the following piece from *Legendary Ladies of Texas,* of one of Dallas's most legendary ladies.

From *Legendary Ladies of Texas:* 'Tell Them I Don't Smoke Cigars': The Story of Bonnie Parker

THEY REMEMBERED IT AS THE COURTHOUSE Café, the place where she worked. It was on South Jefferson, just a half-block or so from the old red courthouse in downtown Dallas, Texas. It was the young waitress everyone really remembered. She was petite, tiny really, standing just under five feet and weighing less than one hundred pounds. A stylish arrangement of reddish-gold hair complemented her friendly blue eyes. Her skin had a porcelain glow, prompting another customer to describe her appearance as china doll-like. Possessing a quick wit and attractive personality, she was easily one of the most refreshing features the café had to offer. Attorneys, businessmen, and law enforcement officials frequented the café, and many of the men liked to flirt with her.

Hinton, at the time a young postal employee, was a café regular. He liked to watch the young waitress rushing orders from table to table, chatting, joking, and cajoling with the clientele. He liked it when she did so with him. He grew extremely fond of her. But then she suddenly quit the café, and left Dallas altogether, only returning sporadically, secretly, and for short periods of time. It was nearly two years before Hinton met her again.

The reunion took place on the morning of May 23,1934, when Hinton, by then a Dallas County deputy sheriff, and five other officers unleashed the contents of nearly a dozen automatic rifles, shotguns, and pistols into a nearby grey 1934 Ford V-8 Sedan. The car lurched forward, rolling down the Louisiana country road and against an embankment. Hinton rushed to the passenger side of the car, still firing his .45 automatic. He threw open the door and there, falling into his arms, was the delicate, bullet-riddled body of the popular waitress he had grown so fond of, twenty-three-year-old Bonnie Parker. Slumped over the steering wheel to her left was her constant companion of the previous two years, the reason for her abrupt exit from the café and Dallas, Clyde Barrow. As he caught her body in his arms, Hinton held Bonnie close, trying to stand her up, then laying her gently back into the car. Her red dress was blotched with a darker red. Her stylish hat, apparently shot away, lay on the backseat. A blackened, gaping hole marked the spot where the left side of her face had once been. Hinton turned away, sickened. But at the same time he was relieved to have helped bring about the end of one of the most frightening crime sprees in the history of the Southwest.

Nine lawmen and several civilians had died in the two years since Hinton last met Bonnie Parker. They died either at the hands of Clyde Barrow, or his brother, or some other man in Barrow's circle. There's no hard evidence that Bonnie Parker ever shot anyone. And yet the image of her as a cigar smoking gun moll persists. . . .

"I never understood Bonnie's attraction to the outlaw life," gang member Ralph Fults once commented. . . . She identified with Barrow's notorious battles with law and authority. "I'm just a loser, like Clyde," she told Fults. And she understood the only outcome was death. "They knew they would be killed," Fults stated. "There was no other way."

"Clyde's name is up," Parker told her mother. "He'll be killed sooner or later because he's never going to give up. I love him and I'm going to be with him 'til the end. When he dies I want to die anyway."

The concept of Bonnie Parker as a gun-toting outlaw with stogies poked in her face emerged in the aftermath of a particularly deadly gunfight in Joplin, Missouri, on April 13, 1933, in which two Missouri officers were killed. Among the items recovered from the outlaws' garage apartment were a camera and several rolls of unprocessed film. The film was handed over to a local photographer who processed and printed the images. The photos, some of the best-known images of Parker, Barrow, his brother Buck, and W. D. Jones, were distributed around the country to law enforcement agencies. Many were printed in newspapers and magazines nationwide.

In one picture, Bonnie is posed in front of a Ford V-8 with one foot propped up on the bumper, hips thrust out to support the weight of a large pistol gripped in her hand. Her face is frozen in a scowl, bright sunlight causing her to squint. In her mouth is a large black cigar. The picture quickly made it onto the front pages of newspapers across the country. Above all else, this one photograph caught the public's fancy. Indeed it remains one of the most famous American photographs of the twentieth century.

The photograph was probably snapped by W. D. Jones on a road between Marshall and Tyler in north Texas. He said he took the picture. He also said the cigar was his. There are similar shots in the same series showing both Jones and Barrow with the same cigar, mugging for the camera just like Parker. But it's the picture of Bonnie Parker that is most remembered. She hated it.

But perhaps the events of April 1, 1934, did the most to color the public's opinion of Bonnie Parker. . . . It was supposed to be an Easter Sunday family gathering. Nevertheless, by mid-afternoon Parker and Barrow had been parked on East Dove Road nearly six hours. With them was a cohort named Henry Methvin. A fourth outlaw, Joe Palmer, had been sent to Dallas to gather the families and escort them back to the meeting place. A white rabbit was also present, a gift for Bonnie Parker's mother.

At three in the afternoon, a trio of motorcycle officers from the Texas Highway Patrol passed East Dove Road, traveling on Highway 114. Apparently, all three patrolmen spotted the Ford V–8. Officer Polk Ivy had noticed it earlier when he and his fellow officers were patrolling in the opposite direction that morning, but thought nothing of it. Twenty-six-year-old Ed Wheeler, however, was curious and motioned for twenty-two-year-old rookie Holloway Daniel Murphy to follow as he turned up the road to investigate. It was Murphy's first day on the job.

Driving behind the patrolmen were Fred and Mary Giggal, a Dallas couple out for a drive. They had been following the officers for several minutes and noticed two of them turn off onto a side road. As they drove past East Dove Road, they saw that the officers had already dismounted and racked their bikes. The Dallas couple joked about how terrible it would be to get a ticket on such a beautiful Easter Sunday afternoon. Then they heard several loud explosions—backfires they thought at first. Then, with growing concern, they slowed down, turned their car around, and drove back to the intersection. When they arrived, they saw "the taller of two men" firing into the prone bodies of the patrolmen. That describes Henry Methvin. Then the "smaller man," Barrow, noticed the Giggals and started hurrying back to his car. The Giggals turned around and sped away in search of the third patrolman.

By this time, Ivy had noticed his colleagues were not behind him and had turned around to search for them. He soon encountered the Giggals who flagged him down and told him what they had seen. Ivy continued on to East Dove Road where he found Wheeler and Murphy alone, lying in the dirt, their motorcycles still racked. Wheeler was dead. Murphy died minutes later en route to a hospital in Grapevine, Texas. . . .

The murders shocked Texas and the nation. Sizable rewards were offered for the apprehension of the killers. . . . The image of Parker as a bloodthirsty killer was solidified. Prior to that, her name was rarely mentioned in news accounts of Barrow's activities. But she never fired a shot on East Dove Road. Methvin did. Oddly, his name is almost completely omitted in the resulting media frenzy.

Odder still, Methvin was issued a pardon from the State of Texas just four and a half months later for his part in the ambush of Parker and Barrow.

Six days after the Easter Sunday murders, Parker, Barrow, and Methvin were sleeping in their car on a dirt road in northeast Oklahoma, between Commerce and Miami. Commerce City marshall Percy Boyd received word from a citizen that a car had been parked all night long just off of Highway 66 in the mining district between Commerce and Miami. Boyd asked Campbell to accompany him as he went to investigate. Campbell agreed, apparently expecting to find nothing more than a carload of drunks sleeping it off, the same thing Boyd expected to find.

Turning off Highway 66, they pulled to a stop in front of the strange car and got out. Suddenly the car took off in reverse, moving fast. Approximately one hundred yards down the road, however, the driver lost control of the car and it veered into a ditch—miring its rear wheels in mud up to the axle. Boyd and Campbell were still standing in the road, apparently dumbstruck by what they had just seen. Suddenly someone from the car was shooting. The officers pulled their weapons and returned fire. Boyd was struck in the head and knocked unconscious. Campbell, still firing, was struck in the abdomen and killed instantly—a bullet severing his spinal cord.

When Boyd regained consciousness, the taller of the two gunmen was standing over him, coaxing him to get up. Once on his feet, Boyd was hustled over to the distant car, which was still stuck, its windshield punctured with bullet holes. A crowd began to gather as the shorter man began to order bystanders and even Boyd to try and push the car out of the ditch. Eventually a vehicle happened along and the assailants used it to pull the car free. Boyd was loaded into the car. Besides the gunmen, the car was also occupied by a petite young woman, who sat in the front on the passenger side. The shorter man took the wheel. The larger man got in the back with Boyd. The car lurched forward and Cal Campbell was left behind, dead in the road.

Not having bothered with introductions, Boyd at first didn't realize who his fast shooting, hard driving assailants were. Finally he recognized them and said, "I don't mean to be nosey but aren't you Clyde Barrow and Bonnie Parker?"

"Yes," they replied. . . .

Boyd warmed to Bonnie, and she to him. Interestingly, he came to like Barrow as well, later referring to him as the coolest operator he had ever seen. Boyd remembered seeing the white rabbit that Parker was going to give to her mother. Parker told Boyd all about her family and the two exchanged family photos. For fourteen hours the bandits and the peace officer laughed, joked, and acted like a bunch of buddies out for a drive. Parker asked Boyd if he would deliver the rabbit to her mother if anything happened to her while he was in the car. He agreed. Bonnie dressed Boyd's wound and gave him a new shirt. When he was released in Kansas, Clyde gave him bus fare to get home. Boyd asked Bonnie if there was anything she would like him to tell the newspapers.

"Tell them I don't smoke cigars." ★

Bryan Woolley

Bryan Woolley left Fort Davis to pursue his schooling at Texas Western, now the University of Texas at El Paso. He worked his way through school by stringing for the *El Paso Times* and thus started on a long and illustrious journalism career. He earned a Master of Theology degree from Harvard University and then was a journalist in Oklahoma and Kentucky before finding his way back to Texas and work at the *Dallas Times Herald.* He later moved to *The Dallas Morning News* where he retired in 2006. He won a Spur Award from the Western Writers of America for his novel *Sam Bass*, a PEN Western Literary Award for Journalism and the Texas Institute of Letters O. Henry Award for magazine journalism. His other books include *Edge of the West; Where Texas Meets the Sea; Some Sweet Day; Texas Road Trip; Where I Come From;* and *Mythic Texas.* Bryan served as president of the Texas Institute of Letters and has remained active with the group. He and his wife, Isabel Nathaniel, make their home in Dallas. His story of Toy Woolley is a story of love, sex, money and violence in the Dallas of the Depression days.

From *The Bride Wore Crimson and Other Stories:* The Bride Wore Crimson

You get a strange feeling when you discover—even half a century after the fact—that your uncle once stood trial for murder, and that the victim was his wife. Such knowledge becomes a burden, and you feel compelled to do something about it. So I'm telling the story.

Dorothy Marie Woolley, a bride of two months and six days, was lounging on her bed in her new honeymoon cottage on Ellsworth Avenue, trying to solve the puzzle posed by "Ripley's Believe It or Not" in the comics section of the Sunday paper:

"There are two volumes of a novel, each two inches thick, with covers one-fourth of an inch thick. If the volumes are upright side by side and a bookworm starts eating on the first page of the first volume and eats straight through to the last page of the second volume, how far will he go?"

It was 9:30 A.M. The breakfast dishes were washed, the garbage had been carried out, the beds had been made. November 5, 1933, was drizzly in Dallas, a good morning to be at home and reading the paper.

Dorothy was a pretty young woman, blond, slender, blue-eyed, just twenty years old. She was dressed as a woman might dress on a Sunday morning when her marriage was still new—a pink teddy, silk stockings, slippers, a delicate pink smock. She was lying on her side, propped on her left elbow, her left hand against her face. Her head was near the foot of the bed. Her feet were resting against the arm of a rocking chair close beside the bed.

Dorothy's sister-in-law, Mina Woolley, also twenty years old, also pretty, was sitting in the rocker, reading another section of the paper. On the other side of the bed, near its foot, Dorothy's husband, Toy Woolley, sat on the vanity bench that had come with their new dresser. He was handsome, blond, blue-eyed and slender, too, and eight years older than his wife and his sister.

Toy was facing away from the bed, holding a shotgun across his lap. It was a new Browning automatic, given to him only the day before by his wife. Dorothy had bought it as a Christmas gift, but she had presented it to him early so he could go hunting with it before the duck season ended.

On the floor beside the bench lay a Remington .22 rifle, Toy's own early Christmas gift to his wife. Near the rifle were a cleaning ramrod, an oil can, and some rags.

The way Toy was holding the shotgun, its barrel protruded back toward the bed under his left arm. Its muzzle was only a couple of feet from Dorothy. With his right hand, Toy was rubbing the gun with a rag.

"It went off," Mina would testify later. "Toy threw the gun down and jumped. As he did this, the back of his knees sent the bench across the room several feet. At first I thought he had shot himself."

But it was Dorothy who had been hit. All the shot and even the wadding of the shotgun shell entered her body just above her heart. The arm that had been propping her collapsed, her head dropped, her blood poured over "Ripley's Believe It or Not. . . ."

Mina ran to the home of William Hidell, a neighbor. "My brother was cleaning his gun," she said. "I think he has killed his wife." Mr. Hidell and his wife returned with her. They found Dorothy lying in her blood on the bed. Toy was holding her head.

"Let's take her to a doctor," Toy said. He laid Dorothy down and went to get his car out of the garage. When he returned, Mr. Hidell met him at the door.

"Dorothy is dead," he said.

Toy collapsed. Mr. Hidell carried him into the house. "Did his grief seem real to you?" the defense lawyer later would ask him.

"Yes, it was real. He couldn't have been that good an actor."

"Did they get along well with each other?"

"Like a newly married couple. They showed the utmost consideration for each other."

Mina telephoned Dorothy's mother, Esta Joynes, and broke the news. When Mrs. Joynes arrived at the house, Mina and the neighbors begged her not to go into the room where Dorothy lay. But she insisted.

"She was alone there . . . dead . . . lying on the bed," Mrs. Joynes would testify. "It looked to me like she had been shot while she was asleep. Her eyes were closed, and there was a faint smile on her lips. Toy was in the front room. He was raving, but he never shed a tear. He told me it was an accident."

Mrs. Joynes went back to the living room and sat down. Toy knelt in front of her and put his head in her lap. "What am I going to do without Dorothy?" he asked. Mrs. Joynes stroked his hair.

The police had arrived. Toy told them he had been duck hunting in East Texas the day before, and didn't know he had left a shell in the gun. Dr. D. P. Laugenour pronounced Dorothy dead and shot a quarter grain of morphine into Toy's arm to calm him. Justice of the Peace John Baldwin returned a verdict of accidental homicide. An ambulance carried Dorothy away.

Monday morning, Toy went to the funeral home with Mrs. Joynes and her son, Ralph. They chose a casket, and Mrs. Joynes and Ralph signed the note for the funeral bill of $1,037.50. Toy didn't. "He just sat there," the funeral director would testify.

Later that morning, two of Toy's brothers, Lynn and Ray, and James Godfrey, their brother-in-law, accompanied Toy to a florist shop to buy flowers for the funeral, which was to be at two P.M. in the living room of the honeymoon cottage. James would say later that he and the brothers took turns watching over the distraught widower all day Monday. "We were afraid he might try to commit suicide because of the accident," he said.

The clerk at the florist shop remembered that one of the brothers had to support Toy while he was in her store, that he was too grief-stricken to choose the flowers he wanted. He left the choice to her.

The men returned to the cottage on Ellsworth Avenue, and Toy's brothers put him to bed. When the hearse brought Dorothy's corpse to the house, about one-thirty, Toy got up to look at her.

"He collapsed twice," James said. "We put him back to bed."

He remained there while Dr. L. N. D. Wells, pastor of East Dallas Christian Church, said the last words over Dorothy in the living room, and while the hearse carried her to her grave in Restland Memorial Park.

Mrs. Joynes would testify that on Tuesday, two days after the shooting, Toy was "anxious" about a $1,000 life insurance policy that he recently had taken out on Dorothy.

On Wednesday, during a meeting with Mrs. Joynes and Ralph and his own lawyer, Toy declared that he wouldn't waive any of his legal rights to Dorothy's estate. "He claimed all her cash and estate and an interest in my property," Mrs. Joynes said.

Later that day, she met with her own lawyer and learned to her dismay that since Dorothy had left no will, Toy was entitled to her entire estate, possibly including an interest in Mrs. Joynes's own home.

For a twenty-year-old woman in the midst of the Great Depression, Dorothy had been well-fixed. A year before her own death, her father had committed suicide, leaving a note addressed only to her. He also left her a $14,000 life insurance policy and several pieces of real estate, including an interest in the family home. He left his widow less than $3,000. Ralph inherited nothing.

Dorothy had put her money in a trust fund with the insurance company.

A week after she and Toy married, they bought their new house on Ellsworth Avenue for $5,650. They paid $3,150 in cash, and signed a note, payable in thirty days, for $2,500. Both the cash and the note were paid from Dorothy's trust fund.

Dorothy also had paid for the car that Toy drove, most of the food they ate, and the shotgun with which Toy killed her. When she died, about $6,000 remained in her trust fund. Her checking account had a balance of about $300.

On Wednesday, Toy met with Mrs. Joynes again. This time he offered to relinquish his interest in two pieces of real estate and give Mrs. Joynes $2,000 if she would give up any claim to the rest of Dorothy's estate.

"I told him I would accept the settlement," Mrs. Joynes said. "The next day, he kissed me and told me he had decided to give me $2,500 in cash instead of $2,000."

But at one P.M. that day, when Toy was walking on South Akard Street, a pair of Dallas police detectives approached him, flashed their badges, and arrested him. They took him to a room in the Jefferson Hotel, where they and investigators from the district attorney's office questioned him for six hours.

At seven P.M., they took him to the Dallas County Jail, and at nine P.M., they charged him with deliberately planning the murder of his wife. District Attorney Bob Hurt wouldn't agree to bond. Toy was locked up.

Two nights earlier, J. J. Cantrell, described in the newspapers as "a wealthy landowner from Comanche County," had telephoned the Dallas police. He said the shooting of Dorothy Marie Woolley "might have some unpleasant angles" that they should investigate. The police asked him to come to Dallas.

Mr. Cantrell and his daughter, Mae, had arrived Wednesday by bus. He handed over to the police a packet of letters that Toy had written to Mae. . . .

Mae Cantrell was born on a farm three miles from the farm where Toy was born, near the tiny community of Lamkin in Comanche County. She was two years younger than Toy. As they grew up, they knew each other well. Indeed, they were first cousins once removed. Toy's grandfather was Mae's uncle. . . .

In 1926, when he was twenty-one, Toy moved to Dallas. He studied accounting at a business college, then got a job as an auditor with Trinity

Universal Insurance Co. During his first three years in Dallas, he lived with James and Georgia Godfrey, his brother-in-law and his half-sister, on Madera Street. Then he rented a place of his own.

In 1924, when she was seventeen, Mae finished high school and enrolled at what was then John Tarleton State College in Stephenville, where she was very popular. When she finished Tarleton—it was a junior college then—she enrolled at Texas Tech and earned a degree in psychology. In the fall of 1930, she moved to Dallas, too. She took a teaching job at Winnetka School in Oak Cliff for $40 a month and registered for graduate work at Southern Methodist University.

She hadn't seen Toy for eight years. But when she was settled, she wrote a note inviting him to call on her. He did.

Sometime that fall, Toy brought Mae to the Godfrey home and introduced her to James and Georgia, and they would get together from time to time to play bridge. About a year later, the Godfreys learned that Toy and Mae were living together, and that Toy's teenage sister, Mina, was living with them.

Both James and Georgia would testify that they assumed Toy and Mae were married. . . . Then one day, during a conversation with Georgia, Mae revealed that she and Toy were living together out of wedlock.

Georgia was upset. She knew that if Gatewood Lafayette Woolley, the patriarch of the large Woolley clan . . . were to find out that young Mina had been living in such an unrespectable domestic environment, there would be hell to pay. She urged Mae to marry Toy before that happened.

Mae wasn't interested. It was a policy of the Dallas school board at that time that female teachers must be single. If she were to marry Toy, she would lose her job. Besides, she said, Toy wasn't the first man with whom she had had an affair. And, she said, he might not be the last. She wasn't ready to marry.

If Mae would marry Toy, the Godfreys told her, she could file for a divorce immediately. They just wanted the couple to appear to have been married during the time that Mina lived with them.

Finally, Mae acquiesced. On March 11, 1933, she and Toy drove to Hugo, Oklahoma, and got married. It was a "courtesy affair," Mae would testify, meant only "to save his name with his family." She said Toy had promised to divorce her immediately.

On the same day—apparently only a few hours after his wedding—Toy applied to rent a room that Mrs. Joynes had advertised at her home on Elliott Street. He told her he was single. Mae moved into a room of her own on Belmont Street. But when the school term ended in June, Mae and Toy rented an apartment and moved back in together.

Their marital bliss, if they enjoyed any, didn't last. Within a week, Mae was demanding a divorce. Toy resisted, but finally said he would grant her one if he could be the one to file for it. Mae agreed, packed her bags, and went home to Comanche County. Shortly, Toy drove to the Cantrell farm and begged her to return to Dallas with him. Instead, they took a trip to Galveston to talk over the possibility of making a success of their marriage.

"I decided we could never be happy," Mae said. She went back to her parents, and Toy returned to Dallas. On July 12, he filed for divorce. In his petition, he charged that soon after their wedding, Mae had begun "a course of cruel treatment, disagreed with him continuously and that he could not please her at all. . . ."

Meanwhile, at the house on Elliott Street, Mrs. Joynes had learned that Toy was courting Dorothy. "If I had known he was married at the time, he could not have gone with my daughter except over my dead body," she would testify.

Then, on the afternoon of August 26—two days before his divorce was final—Toy, carrying a suitcase, was starting out the door with Dorothy. "Well, Mrs. Joynes," he said, "Dorothy and I are going to Oklahoma to be married."

"I told him I didn't think that a very honorable thing to do—start off like that without telling me before," Mrs. Joynes said. "I asked him to put the marriage off for a while. . . . I suggested they could have a nice home wedding later on. But he walked off with Dorothy. . . . They returned the next day. They said they had been married. But "Dorothy had no wedding ring on her finger."

The newlyweds lived with Mrs. Joynes for a week, then bought the cottage on Ellsworth. For the first two days of their marriage, Toy was a bigamist.

The prosecutor asked Mrs. Joynes: "Did you know that four days after this marriage, while he was living under your roof, accepting your hospitality and living with your daughter, that he had written his first wife and told her he had married again, but did not love the girl he married?"

"No, sir."

"Or that he told his first wife he soon expected to make enough money to gain her back again?"

"Oh, no!"

The prosecutor already had placed into evidence a letter that Mae had received from Toy four days after he married Dorothy. It was one of the letters that J. J. Cantrell had turned over to the police. It told of the divorce being granted, and continued:

"I am married again, and am here to say I do not love her and never will. Words will not express my feeling about it, but I intend to take care of you, all the time. You are before anyone in the world to me.

"Yes, it was a radical thing to do. . . . I did it, you know why and I expect to make enough money to gain you back again soon, Darling. Please stay close to me, for I love you above anything else on this earth. I want to marry you again as soon as I can and I expect to have some money, too.

"Sweet, please stay with me for I am lower than I will ever be anymore in my life. . . . I need your help, as I always have. I hope and pray for you to come back every day that passes. I hope you will write me and tell me you will marry me again, if I will build myself up and make some money. Will you, Darling, *please.*

"Write me by return mail, Darling. I love you and need you every hour. Always and forever. TGW."

According to the newspapers, Dallas had never seen a trial to compare with the one that began on Monday, December 4, 1933, in Criminal District Court No. 2, Judge Noland G. Williams presiding.

From the moment District Attorney Bob Hurt rose to read the indictment, through ten days of testimony by 113 witnesses and almost five hours of final arguments, the city would be transfixed by the sad and sordid drama unfolding in the courthouse.

"The courtroom, by the time a session opens, is so packed that the spectators cannot move a hand," a *Dallas Morning News* reporter, wrote. "The doors into the corridor were opened . . . but the crowd in the hall became so boisterous that Judge Williams ordered the doors closed and the hall cleared. Instead of leaving, the overflow crowd went into the courtroom across the hall and sat chatting about the trial. . . . Some of the spectators who arrived before eight o'clock in the morning did not leave their seats until the night session closed. . . . Persons who were forced to leave the courtroom because they had to go and prepare dinner for hubby or go feed the baby, sold their seats. Two front row seats were reported to have sold for $1 each."

They brought lunches in brown bags and threw their bread crusts and fruit rinds on the floor. They paid tips to people who brought them water and soft drinks. Souvenir hunters stole buttons off the coats of the court bailiffs.

Five women fainted. Several were hurt in the press of the crowd against doors, windows, and walls. Dr. Horace Duncan, the county health officer, was called upon twice to give medical aid to persons overcome. A man who suffered a heart attack groaned so loudly as he was being carried from the courtroom that Judge Williams sent the jury upstairs until the commotion had ended.

Through it all, the papers said, "Woolley sat as if he had no great concern with the case, remaining calm throughout the day while attorneys repeatedly referred to the tragic death only a month ago of his young wife. He wore a navy blue suit, light blue shirt and darker blue tie. His shoes were freshly polished, and his blond hair parted in the middle. At one time in the proceedings . . . Woolley smiled, and his eyes sparkled with good humor."

Aligned behind the defendant, in the front row of the audience, were three of Toy's brothers, the Godfreys, and Gatewood Lafayette Woolley, the fifty-nine-year-old patriarch. "Woolley's father . . . a heavy man in comparison with his slender son, sat stolidly throughout the day," a reporter wrote. "He wore dark trousers, upheld by suspenders, a blue shirt with white stripes, a collar open and no tie. In his shirt pocket was a cigar case. . . ."

Indeed, the case provided all that an entertainment-hungry public could desire: a bloody killing; a young, beautiful victim; a young, passionate slayer; a *femme fatale;* sex; money; a touch of bigamy; a prosecutor demanding the electric chair. And almost as fascinating as the case itself and the tangled life of its defendant were the lawyers who were arguing it. . . .

But there's another, last story about the gun.

Not long ago, a friend mentioned an old newspaper page to me. It was framed and hanging on a wall of the Bonnie and Clyde Suite—Room 305—of the Stockyards Hotel in Fort Worth, he said. . . . [T]here are newspaper clippings about the Louisiana ambush that six officers set for Bonnie and Clyde on May 23, 1934, about five months after Uncle Toy's trial.

I drove to Fort Worth and read the old page, published the day after the ambush. Spread across it is a story that Bob Alcorn and Ted Hinton, Dallas County deputy sheriffs, told a reporter from the *Dallas Dispatch.* They're describing how they and the others killed Bonnie and Clyde.

"You couldn't hear any one shot," Deputy Alcorn is saying. "It was just a roar, a continuous roar, and it kept up for several minutes. We emptied our guns, reloaded and kept shooting. . . .

"Each of us six officers had a shotgun and an automatic rifle and pistols. We opened fire with the automatic rifles. They were emptied before the car got even with us. Then we used shotguns.

"Ted's was the shotgun given to him by Toy Woolley after his trial in Dallas for the death of his wife. It was the gun Woolley was cleaning when the thing went off and killed the girl. . . ." ★

Donald Vogel

Donald Vogel (1917–2004) was born in Milwaukee, Wisconsin, and began his formal art training at the Witte Memorial Museum in San Antonio under Eleanor Onderdonk when he was seventeen. He studied at The School of the Art Institute of Chicago in 1936 and was accepted in the WPA program, giving him more freedom to work at his art. In 1942 he came to Dallas where the Dallas Museum of Fine Arts gave him a one-man show. He worked as a set designer for the Dallas Little Theater and after establishing himself as a painter, later began promoting the work of other artists. In 1954 he opened the Valley House Gallery where he continued to paint and promote other artists as well. His paintings reside in collections around the world. Valley House Gallery was the first gallery of importance in the South and Southwest that dealt with major twentieth-century art. He was also a writer and his works include *Aunt Clara: The Paintings of Clara McDonald Williamson* for the Amon Carter Museum; *Drawing for Paintings*; *Charcoal and Cadmium Red*; and *The Boardinghouse*, among others. This excerpt is from his autobiography and gives a view of his place in the art scene in Dallas during the 1940s.

From *Memories and Images:* Dallas: A Home at Last

In 1942 Dallas's train station in no way resembled Grand Central or Union Station, where I had done most of my boarding or stepping off trains. Nonetheless, it appeared just the right size to a twenty-five-year-old youth who was allowing himself another five years to reach his goal as a painter. The city held the promise of growth, and I hoped to be a part of it.

At the information booth I received directions to the YMCA, several blocks away. As I walked up Main Street, however, I passed a small hotel, and my body yelled, "Stop!" Turning in, I rented a cheap room on the fourth floor. Thoroughly exhausted, I undressed and flopped on the bed and closed my eyes. . . .

The next morning, after a long, hot, soapy shower, I found a coffee shop to refuel my stomach and my spirits. I then called my father's office, which was located at 2421 Commerce Street, about fifteen blocks from my hotel. His secretary told me that he was out of town for a few days, but that if I would come by, she might be able to help me find an apartment. It was a long walk, but I welcomed the opportunity to see the city. . . .

My father's secretary was very kind and helpful. The first thing I needed was a place to live, so she gave me addresses and directions, explaining that a streetcar would take me within a block and a half of one place. I thanked her, boarded a streetcar, and headed for 5705 Reiger Street. There I rented a small apartment in a dreadful firetrap of a three-story frame building that looked like a disaster waiting to happen. The next day I would look for a job. I used the rest of that day to call about the crate I had shipped, send out cards with my new address, find a store and lay in a few supplies, cook a simple dinner, and retire early. I needed more sleep.

Over coffee and toast the next morning, I read the want ads and circled every prospect I could find. Then, well rested, I set off to find a job. Walking down Reiger Street, I heard the streetcar approaching and started to run to reach the corner in time. The conductor saw me and held up his hand to slow me down as he stopped the car and opened the door to wait for me. When I stepped in, he said, "Good morning," and smiled. To my amazement, looking down the car, I saw welcoming nods and smiles from the other passengers.

Tears came to my eyes. I remembered that not long before in Chicago I had stood in a foot of snow in the middle of the tracks, waving my hands above my head and yelling at an approaching streetcar, "Stop, or run over me!" The motorman tried to wave me aside, but when I held my ground, he had to stop. (Another motorman had told me once that most of them felt it wasn't worthwhile stopping for just one passenger, especially in bad weather.) I ran to the back to get on board, but the car started to move even before I could jump on. The conductor growled, "What the hell's the matter with you, you damned fool?. . ."

Oh, Dallas, I thought, I am so happy to be here.

My rent was paid for one month, and I needed to find work soon. Each day I ran down the hill to the streetcar and went from one defense plant to another, applying for jobs. I went to the Arlington aircraft plants and to the Murray Cotton Gin people, who manufactured bombs and such things, but there were no jobs left. It was too late.

In my apartment I sat on the floor, painting. I had no easel, so I turned a chair upside down and leaned my canvas against it. It must have looked odd, and it certainly felt odd to paint a forty by thirty-inch canvas sitting on the floor. My first floor-painting was of a young girl in a large black hat.

I looked in the Yellow Pages under "picture framers" and noted a few names and addresses. The first was John Douglass, who had his frame shop on Brown Street at Fairmount in a large, old house. He used the entire first floor for his shop. The living room in the front of the house served as a gallery, where he hung framed work waiting to be picked up. The dining room held sample moldings. A bedroom served as the storage room, and the kitchen was the workshop.

John Douglass was warm and kind, a true gentleman who created the finest frames in the city. I called on him in the hope of finding a job. He had no job for me, but I found something much more important there, my first friend in Dallas. He welcomed me as an old friend, and I felt like one before I left. . . . He had a man working for him named Bill Casey, who eventually became one of my closest friends.

Bill was a misfit. His many interests and his kindness always got in the way of his financial success. His love for books led to his opening a bookstore, which failed, as did his hardware store, his goldfish business, his worm farm, and many other interesting enterprises. He was a fine craftsman with a knowledge of chemistry that led him to become the first local conservator to restore paintings. Knowing him and being his friend were among the best privileges life in Dallas offered me. He painted only three paintings that I'm aware of, and they were all exceptional. . . .

So there I was. I had to look for work again. My rent was due that day, and I had no job prospects, but I had a can of beans and a can of soup in the larder and sixty-three cents in my pocket. No use to panic, I told myself.

I knew a job was waiting for me; all I had to do was find it. As I was about to leave my apartment, I glanced at my mailbox and saw a white envelope. I would read it on the streetcar, I thought, but then I noticed the return address in the upper left corner said, "American Academy in Rome." I opened it to find a check and a letter stating that I had won a place in their competition. The letter went on to say that later I would receive a bronze medal with my name inscribed on the edge. That check provided the breathing room I needed for a while.

John Douglass had talked to me about the Dallas Little Theater, and I went by to see what it was all about. I met the director, Talbot Pearson, and suggested to him that the theater could save money on its insurance if I lived there and worked as the custodian and night watchman. He thought it was a good idea and got approval from the Board of Directors. Within the week I moved into a spacious room backstage in the theater, across from the costume storage. At last I had a studio to work and live in. With dreams of masterworks to come, I immediately set to work to build an easel.

The theater had a great reputation. Prior to my arrival on the scene, it had won the Belasco Cup for three or four years running, but it still had only a fair following. When I arrived, they were about to produce *The Women,* by Clare Boothe Luce, a play requiring several set changes. I made the mistake of offering a few suggestions and soon found myself designing, building, and painting sets, as well as lighting and working the show. For this, Mr. Pearson paid me five dollars a week.

I also served as the theater's delivery service. One day Pearson handed me some photos and typed press releases with instructions to take them to the newspapers. He ordered me to go to *The Dallas Morning News* first and hand them in person to John Rosenfield, and then to go to the *Daily Times Herald.*

John Rosenfield, amusements editor for *The Dallas Morning News,* was almost as round as he was tall. When I entered his office, he extended his hand and took the package from me.

"Sit down while I look to see what I want of these photos," he said. "Now let me tell you the rules if you're working at the theater: all press material comes to me first, or we won't use it. Anything I don't want you can take to the other paper. Understand?" Clearly, he was in the habit of calling the shots.

He welcomed me to Dallas and asked about my background. When we had finished talking he invited me to keep in touch, then called a staff photographer and sent me to the photo studio so they could have a picture of me on file.

At the *Herald* it was quite different. The editor took the package from me, dropped it on his desk, said, "Thanks," and waved me away. . . .

[S]igns of a limited view of art appeared in the city's museum administration. The annual Dallas Museum of Fine Arts No Jury Show was coming, and I thought it might be fun to submit a large painting I had done as a background for the play *The Women.* It was fourteen by eighteen feet. I brought it out and worked some more on it, then delivered it to the museum, to the horror of the museum's acting director, Mrs. Louise McGraw. She had replaced the director, Richard Howard, when he went into the armed services. The lady had little humor or interest in art and was just filling in during the war period.

Mrs. McGraw called me at the theater and asked if I was serious or just pulling her leg. No Dallas painter had ever submitted such a large painting or one done in such a free and splashy style as this before. The more contentious and demanding she became, the more determined I was. I reminded her that no size limits had been stated and that this *was* a no-jury show. My main aim was to show that painting need not be so serious. I was even so bold as to suggest, "Let's enjoy it!"

As she hung up, her parting words were, "I will call some of the board members and get back with you."

The painting stayed. The museum staff had set out a box to collect the public's votes for the favorite painting, with a cash award for the painter receiving the most votes. Afterwards, the museum workman and guard, Jimmy Garrett, told me that I had more votes than all the other painters combined, but McGraw had thrown out my votes. It was good sport.

My first opportunity to create a complete set came when John Anderson's play, *The Eve of St. Mark,* was released simultaneously to little theaters throughout the country. A new play with eight set changes; what a challenge it posed! Pearson gave me a budget of forty dollars to build the sets. "You've got to be kidding," I said, half-laughingly.

"Just do it. That's it," he growled. For a farm kitchen scene, I wanted to rent an old lamp to hang over the checkered oil-cloth-covered table. The lamp cost twenty-five dollars. I had no resources other than my budget, so that left me fifteen dollars. I designed the set largely as a light show, using old flats and battens to create silhouettes and moods. It was a success. I've often wondered how sets for that play were designed elsewhere. I feel certain none were done with a budget to equal mine. . . .

We produced a play titled *Three Men on a Horse* and were asked to present it at the army camps. Mr. Pearson was paying me five dollars a week, but offered me an extra five dollars to change the set to make it portable and to work the show at the camps. At the camps I had to set it up, light it, work it, and afterwards break it down and stack it in the truck while the cast and the rest of them enjoyed the hospitality of the Officer's Club. I didn't mind it too much, though, because I met and made friends with several young, interesting, and talented soldiers whose interest brought them to help me.

I discovered the main advantage of being in the theater, whether on the road or in Dallas, was the large number of friendships I gained. Now and then in Dallas, when all was quiet and Pearson wasn't around, I invited all my new friends to bring their dates or friends and join me for a party. They supplied the food and drinks, I supplied the place. And what a place it was for a party! Those parties became quite famous because of the freedom and good fun the stage and costume rooms offered us. They gave us all an opportunity to perform and express ourselves through pantomime and inventive performances. I set different moods by adjusting the lighting, and the costumes helped to release all inhibitions.

The thought of seeing John Douglass in a tutu, tiptoeing onto the stage, still makes me smile. How he ever squeezed that hulk into the tutu remains a mystery. What a spectacular sight it was when he slid down the banister in all that pink net!

We could get the parties together with little advance notice. Two hours and the word spread like wildfire. Pearson never found out; God knows he never would have permitted it. ★

Kent Biffle

Kent Biffle, a columnist for *The Dallas Morning News,* has received awards from the Associated Press, United Press International, the Society of Professional Journalists, Sigma Delta Chi, and the Southwest Journalists Forum. He is a Distinguished Alumnus of East Texas State University and a member of the Texas Institute of Letters. His "Kent Biffle's Texana," takes him across the state in search of the unique, the picturesque, and the bizarre. Biffle's columns offer a personal, witty, and humorous perspective of Texas history, heritage, and folklore. In the following piece, Biffle tells the story of a Dallas hero.

From *A Month of Sundays: Kent Biffle's Texana:* Old Salts Remember Sam Dealey's Valor

Sam Dealey was a Dallas boy who smiled easily when he wasn't studying math. At the U.S. Naval Academy, he bilged out—as midshipmen say—in his first year. But he bounced back, trying harder. He mastered Annapolis math, won a commission, and became one of the most decorated U.S. submarine heroes of World War II.

Hearing old salts talk about Commander Dealey, I concluded that, math aside, he was a flawless hero and well-liked by everyone he encountered—except the crewmen of enemy warships and merchantmen. He was the first and only skipper of the *Harder,* a U.S. submarine generally credited with sinking more than a score of Japanese vessels. Sixteen kills were officially documented.

After combat patrols that sent more than 54,000 tons of enemy shipping to the bottom, *Harder*'s bold career ended in 1944 when Japanese depth charges blasted the boat, killing Commander Dealey, age thirty-seven, and all hands.

Harder, with her crew of seventy-nine, was lost August 24, 1944, south of Lingayen Gulf on the west coast of the island of Luzon in the Philippines.

The skipper earned the nation's highest award for valor, the Medal of Honor, and too many other medals and citations to count here. But among them were four prized Navy Crosses and even an Army Distinguished Service Cross. The Navy named a destroyer escort for him, the Naval Academy named a room for him in Memorial Hall. Unexplainably, Dallas has no real monument to Sam Dealey.

Landlocked Dallas was an unlikely hometown for a deep-diving torpedo marksman. But similarly landlocked was the high, dry hometown of his boss in the Pacific, the nation's last five-star admiral, Chester W. Nimitz of Fredericksburg. Inland origins of blue water heroes are among the mysteries of the deep.

Fredericksburg's old Steamboat Hotel, with its simulated seaworthy facade, built by the Nimitz family, is now the flagship of the Admiral Nimitz State Historical Park and Museum of the Pacific War. About 600 historians, military buffs, and members of Sub Vets groups gathered in rocky, arid Gillespie County in May 1989 for "Up Periscope," a symposium on submarine warfare in the Pacific, 1941–1945.

The program was dedicated to Sam Dealey. But adventures were recounted of all seven WWII submariners who won Medals of Honor. Remarkably, four were aboard. USN retired, yes, but walking on their own sea legs, were Vice Admiral Lawson P. Ramage, Rear Admiral Richard H. O'Kane, Rear Admiral Eugene B. Fluckey, and Captain George L. Street.

An exhibition was installed to recall Commander Dealey's sea battles that included his photos, citations, saber, and medals. In addition, a plaque on the museum's wall of honor was unveiled at a ceremony for U.S. crews of fifty-two subs lost in World WarII.

The events drew more than fifty kinfolks of the skipper, who was the son of the late Samuel David Dealey and Virgie Downing Dealey of Dallas. Young Sam was the nephew of George Bannerman Dealey, the late publisher of *The Dallas Morning News*. . . .

Commander Dealey's widow, Edwina, survived her husband several years but never really recovered from his loss, Joan Ewen told me. "My mother was a casualty of the war."

Rousing cheers greeted another submarine hero, a visitor from Boca Grande, Florida, retired Rear Admiral Chester W. Nimitz Jr., son of the sailor who gave his name to the museum. Chester Jr. was a buddy of Sam Dealey and skipper of the *Haddo,* one of the subs in Commander Dealey's last wolf pack.

"I'm the last living person to have talked with Sam Dealey," revealed Rear Admiral Nimitz, who's credited with sinking more than five enemy ships.

Of his old friend, Rear Admiral Nimitz said, "Peacetime prediction of who would or would not become an aggressive wartime commander is still, in my opinion, a highly uncertain gamble. I submit Sam Dealey's case as an example. He was one of the greatest skippers of our initial submarine officer pool, although he was certainly not so recognized before the war."

Sam Dealey proved a brilliant fighter. In one patrol, the Texan killed five enemy destroyers in about as many days, his comrade said. "I last spoke to Sam about eleven P.M. on August 23, 1944. We lay to [surfaced] side by side, my *Haddo* and his *Harder,* about five miles off the west coast of Luzon, some twenty miles north of Manila.

"I pointed out the lights and activity in a small coastal indentation directly inboard from us, where the Japs had tried to tow and beach the remains of a destroyer whose bow I had blown off early that morning. I, being out of torpedoes, Sam said, 'Leave it to me.' He sent me off to an advance base to get more torpedoes. *Harder* was lost the next morning as she approached the beach submerged. Subsequent intelligence information indicated that *Harder* was depth-charged repeatedly, at successively greater depths, by Japanese Patrol Boat No. 102, which . . . destroyed one of our greatest submarine skippers and his crew."

The two-star son of a five-star father talked about the Pacific war: "U.S. submarine operations in the Pacific in WWII can quickly be put in dramatic perspective. Some 15,000 submariners, a minute fraction of the U.S. Naval personnel in the Pacific Theater, with 288 submarines, sank two-thirds of Japan's merchant fleet and a third of its navy.

"And they did it with losses of only an approximate fifth of their people and submarines—a remarkably favorable comparison to the horrendous losses incurred by German WWII submariners, who waged a similar campaign in the

Atlantic. They lost 28,000 of the 41,000 men they sent to sea—a 68 percent casualty rate. . . .”

Rear Admiral Nimitz said: “The war with Japan was the perfect opportunity for unrestricted submarine warfare—an island enemy, poor in natural resources, with widely scattered bases and supply sources, not to speak of a vulnerable code.”

U.S. cryptographers became so fluent in the codes of the Imperial Japanese Navy that U.S. submariners sometimes complained when an enemy convoy was late for a date.

The retired admiral told Texas Sub Vets and others: “Submarines weren't very useful when or where they were denied the element of surprise. In the presence of determined enemy forces, concentrating on a specific objective, such as a landing at Balikpapan (Indonesia) or Lingayan Gulf, submarines cannot stand and oppose to keep the enemy from achieving his objective. Sink a few ships, yes. But drive them off, no.

“Nor could they defend Midway against a carrier strike force and landing attack group. Nor could they force a fanatical Japanese government to throw in the towel. But I will aver that in the performance of their primary mission, interdiction of supplies to Japan, U.S. submariners accomplished their important assignment in a manner that has to be rated outstanding. In short, although you didn't win the war singlehandedly, you almost certainly eliminated any Japanese chance to win, and contributed greatly to their predisposition to quit.”

Ancient submariners talked tactics for hours and told war stories into the night. A favorite among his peers of the periscope, Captain Slade Cutter of San Antonio, credited with sinking more than twenty enemy ships, paid concise professional tribute to his friend, Sam Dealey:

“He was damn good.” ★

Lee Cullum

Lee Cullum is a journalist who contributes columns to *The Dallas Morning News* and commentaries to National Public Radio. She has done regular commentary on *The NewsHour with Jim Lehrer* on PBS and for *All Things Considered* on NPR. In addition she has appeared on ABC's *Nightline*, MSNBC, CNN, and television news programs in Europe. She also has done political analysis for the CBS affiliate in Dallas-Fort Worth. Cullum hosted *Conversations*, a series of biographical interviews for the DFW public television stations and is currently the moderator of *CEO* on KERA-TV. She has also conducted workshops on journalism in central and eastern Europe. She is author of *Genius Came Early: Creativity in the Twentieth Century.* Lee Cullum is former editor of the op-ed page of the *Dallas Times Herald.* She also edited *D Magazine,* which won a National Magazine Award during her tenure. She comes from the legendary Cullum family, one branch of which founded Tom Thumb food stores. They were important builders of Dallas.

Mac and Charlie

Mac and Charlie, Charlie and Mac—to think of them now is to plunge into a reverie of dazzling recollection. I prop up pictures, and search, for what? Surely their secrets belong to them now and would not shock me even if they suddenly revealed themselves. I eavesdropped on them often enough as a child, standing outside their door, absorbing the tension of their temperaments—her anger, his calm. And yet it was more than a marriage. It was a love match. He was fascinated by her. She believed utterly in him, to the end.

But the pictures. There she is, undeniably a beauty, twenty perhaps, in a dress cut low, trailing off into abstraction, making clear nonetheless the loveliness of her neck and shoulders; hair short and soft with no reference to time; a smile that seems to radiate a natural perfection. It's the eyes, however, that are riveting. The gaze is steady, without artifice, unguarded. Those eyes expect a lot of life, and they never blink, not when it counts.

And him? Here before me is a photograph of a young man thirty or so, handsome, with a reassuring symmetry; forehead high, brows that mean business; demeanor disciplined, composed, committed to a competitive world; not reserving judgment, just not expressing it; pleasant but sensibly silent, waiting for the moment to be heard. The thing I notice mainly, though, is the hands: strong, capable, and sure, never fidgety, hands on which a woman could rely.

Charlie was not always as responsible as he appeared in that picture. At Southern Methodist University he had a capacity for trouble and a gift for getting away with it. Trouble was not hard to find at SMU of the 1930s. Definitely drinking was against the rules. And dancing? Even worse. This gave Charlie and his friend, Raymond Tate, a great idea. They would stage a dance in the campus gymnasium. The problem was the gym was locked at night. How to get in? The answer they found in a nice but naive freshman named Charlie Sprague. Though Sprague one day would be president of Southwestern Medical School and build it into an institution of high distinction, he then was easy prey for a couple of swaggering seniors like Cullum and Tate.

What they did was entice Charlie Sprague to slink into the gym in the afternoon and wait there, for long hours, until the fall of night. Then, at the appointed hour, he threw open the doors, and in poured a horde of students plus fantastic musicians hired for the evening. They waltzed round the floor with the ones they adored and the band played on. Until the dean got wind of the extravaganza and extinguished the lights.

This, however, was nothing but a momentary bother. Everybody who had a car drove those Fords and Chevies right up to the gymnasium entrance and shone their headlights directly inside. Once again the music blared—"It Had To Be You," "Alexander's Ragtime Band"—and bodies beat time in a way rarely seen in the bosom of Methodism, until in rushed the dean with the University Park police and shut the whole thing down with thorough finality.

Charlie collided with authority that night, but did it faze him? Not a bit. He was editor of the campus newspaper, after all. He had more shots to fire.

Nor did he lose any time taking aim. It wasn't long before he published a provocative editorial accusing the administration of sloppy management. Charlie believed the president, always a Methodist minister in those days, was angling to be a bishop and bending everything to that endeavor. The president did become a bishop, later, but at that moment he was wracked by fury. He summoned Charlie to his house one night, and left the dinner table for a dressing down in the living room, demanding an immediate apology, in print.

Charlie said he couldn't agree to anything without consulting first his parents. He did, and they said, "No, we see no reason for you to apologize. You had every right to say what you did."

The president waited another day, then the next, watching anxiously for the *SMU Daily Campus.* No apology. Nothing. So he telephoned Charlie's father, A. W. Cullum, a mild-mannered man in the wholesale grocery business who also was lay supervisor of Christian education at a church founded by *his* father, a Methodist circuit rider of stern character when he brought his family to Dallas from Tennessee after the Civil War.

SMU's president was in for a surprise. Mild-mannered A. W. may have been, but he knew his own mind and didn't hesitate to express it: "I don't think he should apologize," he said. "I wouldn't apologize myself under the circumstances."

Filled with frustrated consternation, the president turned the matter over to the dean, still smarting from the shock of the dance, Charlie assumed he was going to be kicked out of SMU, and his mother, Eloise—a relentless doer, quick to make plans—arranged right away for Charlie to go to school in London and live with his half-sister Alice and her husband, Joe Warford.

This turned out to be unnecessary. The dean, evidently a meticulous man, cautious at the center, had thought things over carefully, noticing that Charlie's uncle, T. M. Cullum (another of Reverend Marcus Hiram's sons to turn to business—his was sporting goods) was on the City Council. More importantly, he was on the board of SMU and that worried the dean. Would T. M. join forces with his brother A. W. and that no-account son Charles and make trouble for the university? It was possible. So the dean told Charlie he would be willing to let the matter go, but issued this warning: "I know who was responsible for that dance, and don't you forget it."

Charlie did forget it. He had other things on his mind. He had met Mac Chapman, a reporter for the *Daily Campus,* and they were dating. Summer came and he repaired to Ruidoso for a little holiday. Mac was in Kerens, her hometown, stewing, stewing, stewing. What was Charlie up to in Ruidoso? She decided to check it out for herself. Taking a bus to Dallas (who knows what she told her parents, strict Methodists and not used to this level of aggression), she collected her Kappa friend, Teddy Taylor, and off they rode, on another bus, to New Mexico.

What did Charlie think when they showed up, unannounced, unexpected? He was delighted and immediately arranged a horseback ride, up a fine mountain with a view of deep-green trees plus a melon-colored sunset coming down. The ride grew steep, and it wasn't long before Teddy—intrepid enough in time to join the navy as a WAVE—felt a wave of fearful rebellion. "I just can't take this," she said. "You all go ahead. I'll stay here till you come back." She tied her horse to a tree and settled herself on a rock, happy to wait.

Mac was amazingly game, sticking to the saddle, no matter what the cost. The cost, apparently, was quite a lot. After they were married, Charlie took her on vacation to a Texas dude ranch. Of course, he set up a horseback ride. "I'm not getting on that horse," she barked. "Do you think I'm crazy?" She had nabbed Charlie Cullum. It was no longer necessary to go riding. She already had proved how determined, how gutsy, she could be when she saw something she wanted.

This is the way Charlie saw the story of New Mexico, the way he related it to me, many years later, in the ten months between her death and his. But he had typed a letter that long-ago summer of 1937 to his cousin, Marvin (Hookus) Brooks, suggesting that the bus ride to Ruidoso was not entirely Mac's idea.

> Well, Mr. Brooks,
>
> Thanks for the long and interesting letter about Mr. Kipling. I note with awe that you're becoming quite an astute movie critic. Your views on "Captains" were the first cinema comments I have read since departing. Refreshing, for a change.

Well, Kid, futile would be the attempt to describe my days and ways in these mountains. For the most part, it's been an orgy of sleeping, eating, riding horses, walking up mountains and looking. I've seen so many strange scenes and met so many strange people that I now and then think strange thoughts. But, hellfire, most of one's thoughts up here evolve into the constant stream of appreciation for the clean, cool air, the fires at night, the smell of pine trees. Watch out. I'll be waxing lyrical at any moment. . . .

I met a girl who can ride horses better than anybody I have ever seen, and is pretty and definitely a lady besides. I still take Mac. If you see the latter, tell her please to get hell on up here before I lose my temper.

God, it's wonderful to loaf, M. J. I hate to say, but it's really wonderful. With this thought I close, and return to my loafing. Write me about everything.

Chas.

P.S. No dead soldiers. None even wounded.

There would be dead soldiers soon enough, but not before Charlie had done a stint as nightclub editor of *The Dallas Morning News,* working for the great critic, John Rosenfield, who, it once was said, wanted to make Dallas a city where he could live, with arts worthy of his imagination. The best thing about this job was Charlie could take Mac out for fabulous dinners with terrific entertainers.

The high moment came after he switched to public relations for the Adolphus Hotel. Glenn Miller, soon to be a fabled trombonist, was booked into the Century Room, and Charlie could see what a hit his band was bound to be. With a maximum effort Charlie built a big audience in Dallas for the smooth Glenn Miller sound—"Moonlight Serenade," "Tuxedo Junction," and the others—and, in those brief days, came to like him tremendously.

On December 15, 1944, he went down with a single-engine plane—a C-64 Norseman—that never made it to Paris, where Miller was heading to do a broadcast for Christmas. By then, there were dead soldiers, everywhere, too many of them.

By then, also, Mac and Charlie had accomplished a hasty marriage. This came about when she was seen with someone else—he gave her a ride, all very innocent—and Charlie, unwilling to put up with that, decided to go to London, ever at the back of his mind, and bicycle across the British Isles. Mac told him when he came back, she would not be there. The only answer was a wedding.

With his mother in tow, they drove to Garland (that was Mac's first name, after her father, hence the choice) and found a Methodist preacher out mowing his lawn. Would he marry them? Yes, he would. Come on into the parsonage.

The date was May 6, 1938—"Apple Blossom Time," as the Andrews Sisters liked to sing, Mac and Charlie's time, Mac and Charlie's song. *The Dallas Morning News* ran a photo of them, both in hats and light-colored suits, she wearing a corsage of five blooms—baby gardenias perhaps—and carrying a proper stiff-sided handbag with black gloves, her other hand entwined in his, both smiling, immensely pleased that their spat had ended so happily. They showed up that night at the Kappa dance (surely not on the SMU campus), then it was off to Galveston by train for a honeymoon. Charlie's old boss at the *News* sent flowers with a card reading, "Roses from the Field."

When they returned from Galveston, Mac still had a few weeks to go before graduation, also a paper to write and no time to do it. Charlie volunteered for the assignment, but the professor refused to be fooled. "You didn't write this," he admonished Mac, "so I'm giving you a B." It was the only time in the whole of her college career she didn't make an A.

They moved into an apartment near the corner of Cedar Springs and Inwood where Charlie's parents had built a farmhouse and where, by the late 1930s, Eloise had developed a neighborhood known as "Cullumville." There she settled all her children when they married. There Mac lived in uneasy proximity to a mother-in-law who liked to dominate the world around her and was good at it. An unspoken respect developed between the two of them, however. This became clear one day after A. W. had died, when Eloise showed up at our house and asked Mac to type her will. (She didn't believe in lawyers.)

Mac sat on the couch, with me at her side, typewriter on her lap which was the way she liked to work, while Eloise dictated the following from a chair nearby: My stock in A. W. Cullum & Company to Robert, James, Charles and Eloise (Charlie's sister and two brothers); my interest in Mary Nash dress shop to Mary (another sister); the house to Mary and Eloise; and please send the *Dallas Times Herald* to my brother, Elbert Brooks (a patient at Terrell State Hospital for the mentally ill, which is where people went before the age of miracle medications).

"Why," I asked my mother, "would she come to you for this?" "Because" said Mac, "she knew I would not tell a living soul."

That was the late forties. Earlier, in 1942, Charlie joined the navy and looked fantastic in his dress whites. Mac used to say, "If a man doesn't look good in dress whites, he's never going to." They spent some time in Boston while he went to Officer Candidate School at Harvard. . . . Charlie finished second in his class at Harvard. Amazed, he pondered what it might mean for him: "I'm as good as they are," he realized, those brainy boys of privilege and caste on the Eastern side of the American equation. It gave him a special confidence that was evident in a photo from those years, sitting on a step of our front porch, this time in navy blues with one stripe on the sleeves, white cap at a jaunty angle on his head.

At age twenty-six, bright but not worldly, Charlie shipped off to Hawaii. Immediately, some older guys on board spotted him as a likely target and to the poker table they lured him. They would clean him out with no trouble at all. But they misjudged him, as would happen over and over through the years. *He* cleaned *them.* He won $200, which was a lot of money in 1943. He sent it home to Mac, with no explanation.

By then she had bloomed beyond anything that might have been predicted at SMU. A photograph from the war years shows her no longer to be a quiet beauty. With dark hair piled atop her head and a white flower nestled in the curls, lipstick more pronounced, brows also accentuated, she had acquired a new kind of flair and verve. Not tentative now, she had discovered who she was. The eyes, however, remained the same, direct and sure, just more dramatic, more intense. I'm in that picture too, with a tiny arm around her neck, and we both look solemn, vigilant in our loyalty to the one who was missing.

Mac and Charlie had another song for the war years, "For All We Know," and it carried them through to August 1945, or some weeks thereafter, when Charlie headed home on an old broken down cruiser that had been hit by a kamikaze and could barely stay afloat. It took thirteen days to reach San Francisco instead of the usual six, so he had abundant hours to read a writer who was new to him—Thomas Wolfe. Entranced by *Look Homeward, Angel,* he rushed on to *Of Time and the River* and *You Can't Go Home Again* and embraced Wolfe as his favorite novelist.

He docked in San Francisco, and right away, there on the street, was Teddy Taylor, the one who had refused to ride the horse in New Mexico, now in the WAVES and home from the war, just as he was. They rushed to call Mac in Dallas, the phone lines crackling with excitement and relief. Immediately Mac set about to get to Denver, where she and Charlie would have some time together before the deluge at home. Her best chance was a free pass on Braniff, where her younger sister, Dolly, was a flight attendant. . . . Dolly delivered, but it took a while, with Mac chasing to Love Field, day after day, waiting to see if she could get aboard, then returning home when she could not, to put her hair in pin curls and try again tomorrow.

Finally they did connect in Denver, Mac and Charlie, then took a train to Dallas, arriving on Christmas Eve, 1945. Even his father, A. W., not one to veer from his usual routine, turned out to meet them. Charlie found, to his shock, that I had no front teeth.

It wasn't long before they took off for New Orleans and a few last months in the navy. Charlie always said that the Officers' Club in the Crescent City was the center of the world. You could see there everyone you knew.

Sometime, during or after the years on Maui, Charlie wrote a short story, called "A Longing in My Heart." I found it, I don't remember when, with a rejection slip. That was the end of his writing, except for the excellent Sunday School lessons he delivered every week. (For a time they were published in *The Dallas Morning News,* and later, in a book. He also wrote a history of the church founded by his grandfather, Oak Lawn Methodist.) Then there were management letters for Annual Reports put out by the company he started with his brother, Bob.

In time there emerged another Charlie Cullum—corporate leader, civic leader, religious leader, a man of deep integrity and much accomplishment. Mac wrote columns herself, for the *News* and also for the *Dallas Times Herald.* She once was offered a television show, but said no because she felt he wouldn't like it. She gave that up for him just as he had given up London to marry her. They sacrificed something of themselves for each other.

But they went to London, many times, flying through the night to meet the dawn. They played records on New Year's Eve, and danced in the kitchen. And in the last months of his life, Charlie talked of the navy, and SMU, and the early years with Mac. Always, he spoke of Mac. Always, it was Mac. ★

Goldie Capers Smith

Goldie Capers Smith was educated in the public schools of Dallas and attended Southern Methodist University. Smith worked as a Dallas journalist and was an active member of the Poetry Society of Texas. Her books include an annotated bibliography of regional literature, *Creative Arts in Texas,* and her six poetry books, among them *Swords of Laughter* and *Deep in the Furrow.* The Dallas poets are still praising rural life, even in war from far away paces.

Ballad of a Bombardier from Texas

Travis Brown saw the light of day
In a weathered cottage down Texas way;

His father chuckled and swelled with pride,
The happiest man on the prairie-side.

"Doc," he grinned, "Here's my last red cent
Says you fetched us a future President."

Travis grew up astride of a pony,
Free as a norther, hating a phony,

As clean a guy as you'd ever meet,
Six-foot-three in his stocking feet.

Then a war came along in his nineteenth year
And turned him into a bombardier.

Before he could blink he was overseas,
Wading in history up to his knees.

He wrote home, "Me and a guy from Dallas
Just went to tea at Buckingham Palace.

"The Queen, she passed us bread and jam;
I remembered my 'Please' and 'Thank-you-ma'am.'"

Then over the channel quick as a rocket
To drop a bomb in Hitler's pocket.

He pulled the lever for "Bombs away,"
Spit through his teeth and crooned this lay:

"We're over the top—so let 'em drop:
One for Mother and one for Pop;

"One for the Army, one for the Navy,
One for pork-chops, cornbread and gravy;

"One for the day when the war is over
And I'm back in Texas living in clover,

"Where a spade's a spade, and a man's a man,
And the prairie spreads like a palm-leaf fan.

"I'll marry a gal with a freckled face
And raise little dogies all over the place.

"We'll teach 'em to cuss and rope and ride,
To skin a steer and stretch its hide,

"To pass a football over the goal
For A&M in the Cotton Bowl.

"The world's too small—as you've got to know—
Hitler, for *you* and the *Alamo*.

"So junk your medals, and hold your hats:
The name of this ship is *Rough-on-Rats*." ★

G. William Jones

G. William Jones (1931–1993) was professor of cinema and video in the Center for Communication Arts of the Meadows School of the Arts at Southern Methodist University and founder/director of the Southwest Film/Video Archives there. The archives were established with twenty-one 35-millimeter feature films given by Ginger Rogers. Jones grew the archives to more than 9,500 films and extensive tapes on the history of the Southwest. He organized a festival in 1970, starting with the film, *M*A*S*H* and its director Robert Altman. That festival became the USA Film Festival, bringing major leaders in cinema to the university and to Dallas. The collection was renamed in 1995 in memory of Jones, who had two degrees from SMU and a PhD from Syracuse University. He was author of many books on film, including *Talking with Ingmar Bergman*. In this excerpt, Jones gives the background of the finding of the Spencer Williams films and his Dallas benefactor and the filming done in Dallas. Jones also gives the synopsis of one of Williams's best comedies, "Juke Joint."

From *Black Cinema Treasures Lost and Found*

In August of 1983, the offices of the Southwest Film/Video Archives at Southern Methodist University in Dallas received a call from Mr. Roy Larsen, who managed several warehouses for the Roosth and Genecov Corporation in Tyler, Texas.

"Would your archives be interested in taking a look at what appear to be some old films which have been sitting in one of our warehouses for a long time? Nobody here wants them, they're taking up a lot of space, and we're getting ready to dispose of them unless you want them."

As director of the archives, my principle of collection has always been the same as that of the late Henri Langlois of the Cinematheque Francais in Paris:

"If it's on celluloid, we want it." So I said I would come to Tyler, a city some eighty-five miles east of Dallas, as soon as I could.

That weekend in their warehouse, I saw a stack of octagonal steel film cans ten feet high, ten feet deep and ten feet wide sitting in a corner. It was obvious that these were films indeed, of the 35-millimeter size which are shown in theaters. My heart sank when I opened the first can I could get to, because a yellow-brown cloud of nitrate dust billowed out at me, signifying that at least some of these films were on pre-1950 nitrate stock, and were already in a state of decomposition. Mr. Larsen helped me pull a few more cans down off the stack. Opening them, I saw that, so far, all of the films were on the old nitrate stock, but some of them seemed to be still in good shape. What began to excite me, however, was a few of the titles which I recognized: *Murder in Harlem, The Blood of Jesus,* and *Souls of Sin.* If the films were actually what their reel-wrappers said they were, these were perhaps the last—or the best—remaining prints of a little-known but important group of films made from the twenties through the early fifties strictly for black audiences! ★

Spencer Williams

The 1940s were Spencer Williams's real heyday behind the camera. Teaming up with a Jewish film entrepreneur named Alfred Sack who operated Sack Amusement Enterprises out of Dallas, Williams was able to find in Sack a hands-off backer who enabled him to do what few other black artists other than Oscar Micheaux had been able to do—to direct a large number of his own screenplays as he saw fit. If Sack had any doubts at first about letting Williams have his own way on the set, the success that greeted *The Blood of Jesus,* Spencer Williams's first true experiment as a writer-director-actor, must have convinced the Dallas producer-distributor that it was just plain good business for Williams to call the shots. Thus began a ten-year association that produced three religious features *(The Blood of Jesus; Brother Martin;* and *Go Down, Death!),* three comedies *(Dirty Gertie from Harlem, U.S.A.; Beale Street Mama;* and *Juke Joint),* and three dramas *(Marchin' On; Of One Blood;* and *The Girl in Room 20).*

The Spencer Williams comedies still play well to audiences today, but especially those that feature the comedy team of Williams as "Bad News Johnson" and July Jones as his mugging sidekick. *Juke Joint* and *Beale Street Mama* exhibit a kind of black Laurel and Hardy team that leave viewers wishing the two had made more comic films together.

Although all of Williams's directorial efforts suffer from the usual technical problems characteristic of any extremely low-budget films (his entire budgets were usually around $12,000 to $15,000, amounts insufficient to produce even the trailers to most Hollywood studio features of the time), at least one modern black film critic, Thomas Cripps, calls *The Blood of Jesus* "an unrivalled example of black control of the medium, with untrammelled expression of black religious sensitivity. . . ."

For Spencer Williams, the 1950s were to be a decade devoted to the new medium of television, but the time available for such devotion turned out to be all too short. In 1950, the Columbia Broadcasting System decided to experiment with turning the fantastically popular old radio series of "Amos 'n Andy" into a television series. . . . By 1950, CBS programmers were wise enough to know that blackface would no longer go down well with large numbers of American viewers, but why not shoot it with black actors and actresses in the roles? Spencer Williams was chosen to play the role of Andy Brown, which he did to the best of his considerable ability until the show was cancelled after the 1952–1953 season because of the vocal protests of, among others, the NAACP.

Although the early fifties established him as a familiar face in the homes of America, in terms of a black artist enabled to practice the fullest range of his talents, the forties were the Golden Age for Spencer Williams. ★

Juke Joint

CREDITS: *Director: Spencer Williams; Producer: Alfred Sack; Cinematographer: George Sanderson; Screenwriter: Spencer Williams; Original Story: True T. Thompson; Technical Advisor: True T. Thompson; Music: Red Calhoun and His Orchestra; Year of Release: 1947; Running Time: 60 minutes (5,378 ft.)*

CAST: *Bad News Johnson: Spencer Williams; July Jones: R. Orr; "Mama Lou" Holiday: Inez Newell; "Papa Sam" Holiday: Leonard Duncan; Honeydew Holiday: Melody Duncan; Florida Holiday: Katherine Moore; Jefferson Lee: Tilford Patterson; "Highlife" Harris: Albert Smith; "Juke Joint" Johnny: Howard Galloway; Bartender: Clifford Beamon; Waitress: Frances McHugh; Master of Ceremonies: Don Gilbert; Specialties by: Mac and Ace, Kit and Kat, The Jitterbug Johnnies, and Duncan's Beauty Show Girls*

SYNOPSIS: *Dusty and hungry, Bad News Johnson and July Jones arrive by truck-bed in The Great Southwest—South Dallas.*

"We are now following the advice of one of the finest men in American history," Johnson orates to Jones, "Mr. Horace Greeley, who said, 'Go west, young man, and do your best; then come back east and spend your grease.'"

"Say, News," Jones counters, "how come I couldn't go back east and get my grease, then come down South and shut my mouth?"

Although they are down to their last twenty-five-cent piece ("the last button on Gabriel's coat"), they need a place to room and board, so they have to think of a strategy. Jones approaches a young man in front of a store, spends the last quarter grandly on an astrology magazine, and asks where they might find accommodations. The young man, who introduces himself as "Jefferson Lee," directs the gentlemen to his girlfriend's house, where a Mrs. Holiday may be willing to take them as boarders.

At the Holiday house, Papa Sam is asleep on the porch, dreaming of his soldiering days in World War I. Mama Lou disturbs his reverie with a straight pin.

"All you ever do is dream!" she berates him. "Samuel Holiday! That name fits you to a tee—you've been on a holiday ever since the eleventh day of November 1918. If you don't get outta here and get a job, I'm gonna give you back your rib and get me another Adam before it's too late!"

She gives him a dollar to go to the butchers and buy some meat for dinner.

Inside, Honeydew is trying on her beauty contest gown. Mama Lou fawns over her, comparing her intelligence and good taste with that of her sister Florida, who only thinks about "men, men, and more men, instead of the higher things."

Mama Lou goes to answer a knock on the front door and finds Johnson and Jones. She assumes they are salesmen.

"No, no, dear madame," Johnson says grandly, "we are gentlemen of the first order!"

He introduces himself as "Mr. Vanderbilt Whitney," and Jones as "Mr. Green."

She is doubtful about taking in boarders, although she has a spare room. She says she will ask Jefferson Lee what he thinks about it when he comes this evening to take her daughter to the theater.

At the mention of the word "theater," Johnson gets his inspiration. He tells Mama Lou that both he and Jones are "not actors—the word is a vulgar name—but thespians!"

Mama Lou is impressed. She offers to give the theatrical gentlemen free room and board if they will consent to give her Honeydew some lessons about how to behave on the stage tonight.

"Mrs. Holiday, the gods of luck have frowned most favorably upon you." Johnson says, swelling. "Watch this."

He goes into his own rendition of Shakespeare's *Julius Caesar,* then follows rapidly with a bit from *Romeo and Juliet,* which winds up with him kissing Jones's hand—much to the latter's amazed disgust.

"If you could only show my daughter how to act like that," Mama Lou says, "I could offer you and Mr. Jones free room and board for as long as you want it!"

Needless to say, they accept, and retire upstairs to rest before supper.

Instead of going to the butcher shop, Papa Sam has gone to Johnny's Juke Joint and is playing poker with his young friend, Highlife. When he gets "busted out" by a hand that he calls "really contributary," he heads for home and his punishment. He leaves behind his daughter, Florida, who is enjoying the flattery of Johnny, owner of the establishment.

Johnny offers to take Florida to Chicago that night, because "a beautiful girl like you ain't got no business going to seed in a town like this—you're too pretty!"

While Florida thinks over his offer, Johnny is called to the telephone. He tells his wife that he may be "a little late tonight, on account of business."

At the Holiday home, Mama Lou wonders what is keeping Sam and Florida, "two chips from the same block." But she comforts herself with the amazing good fortune of getting two theatrical gentlemen to tutor Honeydew into a winning performance.

Upstairs, "Mr. Green" wonders why they had to change their names.

"Hollywood is a big place, and folks from there have to have big names," "Mr. Whitney" tells him.

"But suppose we meet somebody here from Memphis?"

"In that case, you're just plain old July Jones and I'm Bad News Johnson—and maybe in jail if whoever we meet's a policeman!"

Unsatisfied at the explanation, Jones wonders why Johnson gave himself such a big-sounding name but gave him the name "Green?"

"It was all I could think of at the time," Johnson admits, but he has left the first name for Jones to pick.

"Only thing I know goes good with greens is cornbread," Jones says.

"Cornbread Green! That's a good name for the stage—like 'Butter-beans and Susie' or 'Spareribs and Hambone,'" Johnson assures him.

Downstairs, Papa Sam is trying to sneak in without the meat or the dollar. When he is captured by Mama Lou, he tells her a sob story about meeting a poor old widow lady with little starving children and no money to buy something to eat. After he gave her the money, she went to stand on the railroad track. The train was coming, but the old lady didn't move. It was coming closer, but the old lady didn't move. Then, finally, the train ran right into her.

"Then what?" Mama Lou asks.

"The poor old lady moved!" Sam answers.

It's too much. Mama Lou starts throwing everything in the kitchen at Papa Sam, until Honeydew intervenes.

Hearing the racket, Johnson and Jones just hope that it does not mean that supper will be late. Jones hopes it will be pork. Johnson tells him the Bible says people should not eat any animal with a split hoof.

"But I was weaned on pork!" Jones insists.

Johnson looks closely at him.

"The Bible was right!" Johnson says.

Honeydew is sent for supper meat so the guests upstairs can have a proper meal before going to the theater.

Around the table before dinner, Mama Lou warns her family to be on their best behavior that night. When Johnson and Jones come down to take their seats, Mama Lou asks Jones if he will "give thanks."

"Thank you, lady," Jones promptly replies. "And if we able, we gonna eat everything that's on this table. And if there's any left in the pot, bring it now while it's good and hot."

Johnson saves the day by intoning a proper blessing, then everyone at the table says a Bible verse. Florida chooses the briefest verse in the Bible, "Jesus wept," and little Melody prays, "I thank the Lord for this meal—and for some more meal!"

"Amen!" is Jones's heartfelt response.

After dinner, "Vanderbilt Whitney" is showing Honeydew how to walk by the numbers while "Cornbread Green" is nodding off by the same numbers. Finally, they announce that Honeydew is fully trained and ready for the beauty contest. Johnson and Jones retire to their rooms "to change."

"Why'd you tell them we was gonna change?" Jones asks upstairs, "when the only thing you can change is a pair of socks, and you can't do that but once? If you could button up that coat you got on, your trunk would be completely locked!"

Jones turns philosopher momentarily as he gives Johnson his wisdom that "a man's got two eyes, two ears, two hands, and two feet, but only one mouth—which means that he should see, hear, work, and walk twice as much as he talks."

Ready to go, Papa Sam asks Mama Lou how he looks in his suit.

"Like a bale of hay with the middle band busted off," she tells him.

Although Mama Lou warns Florida to finish the dishes and not leave the house as the rest of them leave for the theater, Florida is immediately on the telephone to Johnny, telling him she has decided to take him up on that offer of a trip to Chicago.

There is a full house in the theater for the beauty contest. The master of ceremonies has the girls come onstage, then holds his hand over each one's head, letting the audience applause determine the winner. First prize goes to Honeydew Holiday, "the rage tomorrow and choice of Hollywood and Broadway!"

Backstage, Papa Sam and Highlife congratulate Honeydew as Mama Lou and the others hurry home to prepare the lemonade and cake for the celebration. Highlife insists that lemonade is too weak for a girl who just won a beauty contest, and that they should take her to the Juke Joint for a proper celebration. Papa Sam is too weak to refuse.

As they enter the Juke Joint, the jukebox is playing and the jitterbugs are dancing. Papa Sam makes eyes at the waitress, who ogles him back. None of them see Florida, who is there with Johnny, packed bag and all.

At home, Mama Lou is worried at the delay. Johnson and Jones volunteer to go find them.

Back at the Juke Joint, Papa Sam has wandered off to find that waitress, while Florida asks Johnny to keep Honeydew and Highlife distracted so she can sneak into the ladies' room to change for the train. It is at this moment when Johnson and Jones arrive, spotting Florida. They tell Honeydew she had better go in there and get Florida out so they can all get back to Mama Lou's party.

Florida proudly tells Honeydew that she is done with this kind of life forever and is going to Chicago with Johnny. Honeydew gets on the telephone and calls Mama Lou, who tells her to keep everyone just where they are—she is coming.

Mama Lou dashes through the front doors of the Juke Joint, waving her umbrella like a sword. When Florida sassily tells her mother that she is going to Chicago "and can't nobody stop me!" Mama Lou starts beating on Johnny and Highlife with her umbrella. The audience loves the floor show!

As Mama Lou leads them all outside, she spots Papa Sam on a bench with the waitress, smooching. She swats them so hard with her umbrella that the bench overturns.

At home finally, Florida is screeching and screaming that she will not stay there.

"You will stay here!" Mama Lou promises her. "When I get through with you, you won't be able to sit down for six months!"

She takes Florida into the bedroom. Soon, we hear Florida howling from within. Jones goes to look through the keyhole.

"Hey, boy," Johnson remonstrates with him, "don't you know the Good Book says 'He that looks will go blind?'"

"Yeah," Jones says, "but for something like this, I can afford to trust one eye!"

This sounds right to Johnson, so he joins Jones at the keyhole. ★

Stanley Walker

Stanley Walker, *New York Herald Tribune* city editor, began collecting the fabric of the Dallas story a long time ago, as far back as 1918 when he was a Dallas reporter. In the intervening years, he became a national sensation as the driving, refreshing city editor of the *New York Herald Tribune.* After retirement to the family ranch overlooking the Lampasas River, he continued to write for the *New Yorker; Harpers;* and *Saturday Evening Post* and wrote such books as *City Editor; Night Club Era;* and *Mrs. Astor's Horse.* During his twenty-six years in the East, Walker read the Dallas newspapers and made frequent trips back to Dallas, kept up with its people and its progress, and thus was ready to write the following story. "Dallas moves faster than New York," he said. "In fact, it moves so fast it frightens me." The Texas Institute of Letters each year gives the Stanley Walker Award for Best Work of Newspaper Journalism Appearing in a Newspaper or Sunday Supplement, honoring a venerable newspaperman and writer.

From *The Dallas Story*: The Flavor of a City

Dallas as an incorporated municipality became officially 100 years old February 2, 1956. The end of the first century was marked not with fanfare and skyrockets but by the turning of a page of the calendar. For Dallas understands that centuries do not turn. Centuries slide, gently and almost imperceptibly, one into the other, so that the variations between today and the immediate yesterdays exist, true enough, but the difference is one of evolution, not convulsion.

Throughout much of its existence, certainly since 1872, when a commentator wrote (whether in alarm or admiration is beside the point) that Dallas was "putting on the airs of a city," it has been the habit of strangers and residents alike to ask, "Why?" They mean "Why Dallas?" Why any city at all at the three forks of the dismal Trinity? The question was not foolish in other days. It is not foolish now. Indeed, it goes to the very heart of the matter.

But a thoroughly satisfying, simple answer is not easy. . . . Many sound authorities, sighting down the long and sometimes wobbly gun-barrel of history, have come up with a variety of deductions, many of which make perfectly good sense and are by no means as contradictory as they may seem on the surface.

Some contend that the old "pluck and luck" formula explains the growth of Dallas. The wide diversification of business and industry, which appeared early, is another favorite reason. Others say "great, unselfish leaders," "Men of Genuine Vision," while still others say no, it wasn't so much the leaders as an almost unbroken tradition of teamwork. The most material-minded (who may be close to the true nugget) point to such definite matters as railroads, airlines, flood control, city planning, the State Fair, and so on.

And there is still another favorite explanation, from the school of municipal psychoanalysis, which to strangers borders very close upon a sort of Texas racism—that is, the engaging theory that from the very beginning Dallas attracted somewhat superior folks, that these folks (coming from everywhere but with rather extraordinary genes) in turn bred superior folks, and that still other superior ones were naturally attracted to join (or "homologate with" as the old phrase had it) the Trinity colony. This is a snowballing process which is supposed to be in full operation to this good day. It is easy to smile at this theory of city development, but is it altogether bunk? Don't be too sure. Many wise men say it comes pretty close to being the real answer.

Whatever the reasons for the growth, it is clear enough that even at the beginning Dallas had none of the advantages of resources or geography which traditionally have appealed to the Founding Fathers of great cities.

When the rains came in the spring the first settlers watched the sluggish Trinity come to life, inspiring the old dream of navigation to the Gulf of Mexico. But this was, and still is, an unrealized dream. The place was well enough wooded, with cedar, bois d'arc, cottonwood, hack-berry and many other trees, but it could not be compared with the great pine forests farther east. Cattle were raised, but the bulk of this business clearly belonged to the west and north. The soil was rich (quite as good as that of the Nile Valley, said some of the boosters) but no better than the soil of many other towns already established throughout the black waxy belt.

All the obvious factors which built New York and Chicago, San Francisco and New Orleans, Pittsburgh and St. Louis, and all the others, were clearly lacking in Dallas. It could be a trading post, perhaps. And that, after a fashion, is what it became. People smile today when the old-fashioned term trading post is used, but that is exactly what Dallas is—the briskest, most variegated, most confident, most high-toned, and by all odds the cleanest trading post in all America.

The natural disadvantages of Dallas (that is to say, the things that weren't there) worked in the end to the good of the community. Balance and diversification, which provide the surest cushions against economic shock, became the distinguishing features of Dallas. If the great heavy industries avoided Dallas for obvious reasons, then what of it? Dallas in the end was the winner. . . .

Looking backward, the Dallas leaders of today can be thankful that it was impossible for the young city to emulate either Birmingham, Alabama, or Gary, Indiana, just as they can be thankful that the life and death of the city is not today wholly dependent upon the caprices of King Cotton. . . .

The history of Dallas, of course, shows many errors of judgment. Many things were allowed to happen that could be corrected only at considerable cost, and the mopping up is by no means finished. The city booster, carried away by the gleam of today's city and marveling at the upsurge of the last decade, sometimes forgets that the story of Dallas is not at all a story of continuous success—an uninterrupted march onward and upward. There were dark times. Many men living today remember them soberly and sometimes sadly. . . .

Some ten years ago, Dr. Herbert Gambrell, the lively but sound historian at Southern Methodist University, a man who has done more than most to preserve and interpret the stuff of Dallas's history, wrote a short article in which he attempted, with considerable success, to explain the things that gave Dallas its personality. The facile doctor listed aggressiveness, metropolitanism, promotionalism, opportunism, investmentism, self-appreciation, and competitive determination of civic objectives. And he also pulled off the rack an odd bit of goods which he called "superiority complex." He defined this as "an unexpressed but not carefully concealed feeling of superiority over other Texas cities, which would have made it difficult in 1872 (or 1946) for Dallas to win a popularity contest."

Did Dr. Gambrell have a sound idea by the tail here, or was he merely tossing jocose Freudian balloons? Opinions may differ, but his contention is surely not without much merit. Dallas has many times listened to the half-concealed slurs and catty innuendoes, born of envy, from other Southwestern cities. Many Texans regard Dallas as a mite "uppity." Well, they are not far wrong. It is uppity. It is when the extremists intimate that Dallas, after all, "is not really a Texas city—it's more Yankee," that, my countrymen (to borrow from the incandescent lexicon of the late Joseph Weldon Bailey), go[es] too far. Dallas is as Texan as Jefferson, Waxahachie, or Muleshoe, and in some ways more so. It is not merely 100 percent Texan. It is, to revive a word that unfortunately has fallen into disuse in recent decades, truly Texanic. . . .

Dallas, as noted, lacks spectacular landmarks. No Golden Gate. No Pike's Peak. No romantic ruins such as the French Quarter of New Orleans, and no picaroon to match Jean Lafitte. The Trinity falls somewhat short of the majesty of the Hudson. No desert, and, therefore, nothing to compare with Phoenix or Palm Springs.

Poor old Dallas! The blue blizzards bite in the winter, and the summer heat is murderous. The Indians who once lived at the Three Forks were simple agriculturists, pleasant dullards, far removed from the history-making Sioux. Few desperadoes except such as the repellent Clyde Barrow and Bonnie Parker. Frank James once worked as a clerk in a Dallas store, but his fangs had long since been removed. Even the Dallas poets, doing their best, were under an almost insuperable handicap because bluebonnets do not flourish in the Dallas countryside.

No Alamo. No San Jacinto. No Hornsby's Bend. Even the founder of Dallas, John Neely Bryan, although he had many excellent qualities and was in part at least a spiritual brother of the dynamic Men of Vision who were to come later, fell somewhat short of greatness and was sadly deficient in flamboyant qualities.

All these considerations, among others, weighed heavily upon the minds of the delegation which journeyed to Austin to make a bid for Dallas in the competition for the Texas Centennial celebration of 1936. Ridden by an inferiority complex, gnawed by vague feelings of guilt, apologetic for their presumption—they did their best. You don't say! They won, and it was one of the finest and most characteristically audacious things any group ever did for Dallas.

Among other things, this event resulted in a healthy quickening of interest in the history of Dallas and Dallas County. There is considerable philosophical justification, mentioned by more than one great thinker of the past, to the effect (variously phrased) that the happiest people are those who have no history. Therefore, it was argued by some, Dallas ought to be superbly happy.

But a few perspicacious souls were ready to disagree. Like the man who discovered that for years he had been writing prose without knowing it, Dallas began to learn that it had been innocently making history all along. Or, for another simile, Dallas was in the position of the poor fellow who had been so busy living that he didn't know he had formed what is called "a way of life. . . ."

The 1930s formed a sort of Renaissance period for Dallas.

Culture and fashion boomed amid the pulling and hauling over the great national experiments. The commercial interests called everybody's bluff and began going ahead. And, for the first time, the joys of good old nostalgia were discovered, and Dallas rejoiced that it was not a bloodless, accidental waif after all, but a proud personality with a pedigree and all the other trappings.

From that time forward Dallas would begin reaching toward the heavens, then spreading out over the fields of Johnson grass, and then spreading some more. The time soon came when the words "of Dallas" after the name of a business firm, or a manufacturer of some beautiful or useful article, meant something special. It was a brand, a hallmark, and its connotation was not lost on the world—it meant something like "sterling. . . ."

At the beginning of what we have tentatively referred to as the Dallas Renaissance, it was the habit of the editors of the large popular magazines to think of Texas, including Dallas, in the terms of trail drivers, bad men, sharecroppers, new-rich oil men, and rambunctious politicians who would rather be spectacular than right. Indeed, in the early 1930s a well-known writer suggested to one of these editors (a man of fairly large brain content, and properly bulging forehead) that a great deal was happening in Texas, some of it under the surface, which might well be brought to the attention of the country at large, for its entertainment and edification. . . . They sent out scouts to the Southwestern wilderness, then advance guards of nimble-footed spies, then platoons of shock troops and photographers, and then a steady trickle of interpreters. Dallas began to get publicity. For the most part this publicity was not merely highly readable stuff, but of incalculable value.

Its principal effect, for practical purposes, was to disseminate the idea—long familiar to the citizens of the Southwest—that Dallas was a retail center of unusually high character. It had, for want of a better word, Class—that hard to define air which Colonel J. T. Trezevant had when he was impressing the ladies or which Ty Cobb had when he was sliding into second base.

A few of the more perspicacious outriders for the Eastern magazines and book publishing firms also noted, with mixed awe and relief, that there were persons in Dallas who could, and did, read without moving their lips, that the food and other appurtenances in the better homes and clubs were exceptional, that there was actually a strain of something known as Culture, and that the leading men and women, far from trying to impress anyone, were well-spoken, self-confident persons who wore the mantle of good manners and urbanity as easily as they might wear an old shoe.

This line of interpretation, without question, was good for Dallas, and it was much appreciated. But as time went on a new note crept in. The magazine anthropologists, seeking yet deeper interpretations, hit upon two new lines and played them for all they were worth. These lines were:

1. Here is great wealth, massive, unprecedented wealth, wealth to make the mind reel, carrying with it an arrogance which sought to regiment the minds of the masses and to bring on something resembling a fascist civilization.
2. Here is vulgarity, boasting, tactlessness, eccentric display, rude wit, and a brawling tendency reminiscent of a young and highly prosperous mining camp.

Now, distill and combine these two interpretations, and what do we have? Simply this: A picture of a civilization in which the dominant theme is the gaucheries of the rich. The gentlemen who produced this portrait had keen eyes for the sharp line and the deep shadow. They knew good copy when they saw it. But, perhaps without meaning to do so, they started a train of belly laughs—on the stage, over the radio, and now on television—at the expense of Texas.

This is not in any way to charge fabrication. The evidence was there. It is no news to the thoughtful citizens of Dallas that the jackass in human form, in full bray, is by no means extinct, even in the more high-toned sections of the city; worse, this creature reproduces his kind, and the spirit, like love's old sweet song, goes on and on and on. The trouble is that, as in most such situations, the innocent suffer with the guilty. And nothing much can be done about it. Time will heal the wounds and subdue the guffaws.

As a matter of fact, it is probable that Dallas has not been greatly injured by this sort of thing. One of the more serious complaints is that hurried, perspiring, history-at-a-glance Yankee interpreters do not tarry long enough to find out much. They attend a big cocktail party, they visit a fancy ranch, they talk to a gabby and misinformed taxicab driver, they see a girl in a tight sweater working in a bank—then they put this all together and it doesn't spell mother, but Dallas.

Some of these men work with almost mathematical precision, seeming to argue that if they can "cover" and "interpret" a whole continent in a month, then a city such as Dallas should require about thirty-six hours.

The late William Silas Henson, head of a large printing business and an indefatigable doer of good (when he died he was compared with Ben Franklin, and he would have laughed at that, but it was not too far-fetched a notion), was a man who almost always exuded good humor. He resembled Teddy Roosevelt somewhat, with one important difference—when Bill Henson laughed you could be sure he wasn't doing it for political effect. He also had a deadly serious side, and a penetrating mind. Once, discussing the fly-by-night disciples of Herodotus who have at one time and another given their freehand pictures of Dallas, he said:

"The trouble with these boys is that the good Lord, for some reason I cannot fathom, gave them several extra sets of glands—especially the adrenal glands. They seem strange to us. No use getting sore. They can't help it."

It was also Bill Henson who had a word on the Gambrellian Theory—the idea of the "superiority complex" of Dallas.

"Listen, son," said Henson. "That's not a superiority complex. It's just that simple, old-fashioned thing we grew up with—ordinary self-respect. . . ."

Students of Dallas history have a pleasant pastime in their off moments. They speculate on what John Neely Bryan, the founder, would think and say if he could visit Dallas today. And more important, they wonder what he actually said, if anything, when he alighted from his famous pony, Neshoba Tenva (Walking Wolf), and decided that some day a city would be built where Dallas is today.

The record, of course, is clear enough in the case of Salt Lake City—Brigham Young liked what he saw—"the lay of the land"—and said without hesitation, "This is the place." But neither Frank Cockrell nor John Henry Brown nor Sam Acheson nor Wayne Gard nor John William Rogers nor any other soul, living or dead, knows what John Neely Bryan said.

Mr. Rogers suggests, admittedly without the slightest shred of evidence, that Bryan said, "This is it."

The late William S. Henson had perhaps the neatest guess of all. One night in his home he was talking with a small group of rankly amateur historians when the question of John Neely Bryan came up. Mr. Henson suggested that Bryan probably looked eastward, then out over the Trinity bottoms, and then addressed Neshoba Tenva, saying:

"Well, old hoss, it ain't much, but it'll have to do."

It did pretty well, considering. ★

PART TWO

The Kennedy Assassination and Its Aftermath

Lawrence Wright

Lawrence Wright (1947-) graduated from Tulane University and spent two years teaching at the American University in Cairo, Egypt. A member of the Texas Institute of Letters, he is a staff writer for *The New Yorker* and a fellow at the Center on Law and Security at New York University School of Law. The author of five works of nonfiction—*City Children, Country Summer; In the New World; Saints and Sinners; Remembering Satan;* and *Twins*—he has also written a novel, *God's Favorite*, and was cowriter of the movie *The Siege*. His latest book, *The Looming Tower: Al-Qaeda and the Road to 9/11*, garnered a Pulitzer Prize for Wright. He had just received the Carr P. Collins Award for the Best Book of Nonfiction for the year from the Texas Institute of Letters for the same title. Wright brilliantly sets the stage for the temper of the times in Dallas.

From *In The New World: Growing Up with America from the Sixties to the Eighties*

My first sighting of the new world came from the back of the family station wagon, in the late afternoon as the slanting sun behind us lit up the city skyline with fierce and brilliant color. Now, of course, the vista of skyscrapers that awed me as a child is buried in the shadows of modern Dallas; the buildings that seemed so monumental then against the flat horizon were the pale blue Southland Center, the Mobil Building with the neon winged horse atop, the Republic Bank, largest bank in the Southwest. When I come upon these structures today they seem petite and almost historical. Foremost, as we approached the city, was an unpretentious cubical edifice with a large billboard on the roof advertising Hertz rental cars and blinking the time and the temperature. The building itself was anonymous, and afterward, when the world knew it as the Texas School Book Depository, people in Dallas identified it by the Hertz sign and said, "Oh, *that* one."

We were moving from Abilene, Texas, where my father was vice president of the largest bank in town. My sisters and I had been in mourning for weeks, since Daddy returned from his mysterious trip to announce that he had gotten a new job—at last he would be president of his own bank. It was small, he warned us, but it was in Dallas, and Dallas was growing, and as the city grew so would his bank. Dallas was a place where dreamers like my father would be given a chance.

As in all boomtowns, tension in Dallas was high. . . . And yet this was only a prelude to the sixties, when the new world that was arising in the South and the West erupted like Atlantis, a civilization that seemed to pop up overnight.

What distinguished Dallas from the other cities of the new world (this was the legend we told ourselves) was that there was no reason for its existence. . . .

And because there was finally no reason for Dallas, there was anxiety among its citizens. It might all disappear tomorrow: the customers would go elsewhere, the companies would relocate, the train wouldn't stop here anymore. Dallas was a fire that might go out at any time. To keep it alive the citizens advertised it far and wide, and even to ourselves; it was "Big D, my oh yes!," the city that works, *et cetera*. We were blowing on the coals.

My father, John Donald Wright, was typical of the men who made that new world. . . . [H]e had learned the frustration of small-town banks with sleepy family management, so when he was finally offered the presidency of the Lakewood State Bank in Dallas he accepted at once. In 1960 it was a small and troubled storefront bank on Gaston Avenue, between Doc Harrell's drugstore and Kirk's Beauty Salon. To see it now—three entire city blocks of land, a tower, a parking garage, fountains, expensive art on the walls, and a modern, amalgamated name, Allied Bank of Dallas—is to realize my father's aspirations in their most tangible form. He built this bank, with the help of people like him, people who came out of nowhere with nothing, who came to Dallas because Dallas would give them a chance. . . .

By comparison with Abilene, Dallas seemed wide open, but it wasn't, as we soon learned. Politically, it was shut up tight. Hungry newcomers like my father found the leadership of the city distant and mysterious. You had to prove yourself, endure probation. If you did, you'd be noticed; you'd be brought along slowly, like a colt being trained to a bridle. One day someone would approach you. You'd be asked to "do something for Dallas." You'd get an assignment. For my father it was to head up a bond election to air-condition the public schools. People were surprised when the bond passed; the secret circle opened and admitted Don Wright.

The cabal he entered was the Dallas Citizens Council, which was once defined as "a collection of dollars represented by men." There was not a doctor or a practicing lawyer on the council, and not a single woman. These were the board chairmen, men who could commit money without consulting anyone else, the "yes-or-no men," as Mayor R. L. Thornton Sr., who founded the council, called them. The men on the council chose the candidates for local office and made decisions for the good of the city, without consulting the voters or the elected representatives. When, for instance, Chance Vought Aircraft was considering relocating in Dallas, the head of the company announced that the runways at Dallas's Love Field were two thousand feet too short for its purposes. Three hours and forty minutes later a council member called him and said that the city had approved an emergency bond and that work would start on the runways Monday morning. That's the way Dallas operated. As a political model the city was ruled from the top down, by corporate junta, but by and large it was well ruled. . . .

Dallas was a city of believers, a city of eight hundred churches, among them the largest Methodist, the largest Baptist, and one of the largest Presbyterian congregations in the world. While every one was religious, some were superreligious, and they thought of themselves as a spiritual vanguard. They were contemptuous of the rest of us; we might as well have been agents of the devil. In the face of so much belief, honest doubt hid itself; skeptics and heretics were one and the same.

My family was conventionally religious—Methodists—although my father was devout. God had spared his life several times on the battlefield, and he repaid Him by living righteously and teaching Sunday school. But even my father was scared off by the fanaticism of the first church we joined. . . .

We later moved downtown to the First Methodist Church, and when we were brought into the congregation we knelt before the choir as they sang the final verse of "The Battle Hymn of the Republic." They began in a melodic whisper—"In the beauty of the lilies Christ was born across the sea"—but the sound swelled and grew thunderous, and I felt my skin turn to gooseflesh as the refrain "Glory, glory hallelujah!" nearly levitated me above the organ pipes. I asked God to bless me and keep me, and save me from my evil nature.

Dallas was filled with suspicious Protestants. In 1960, when John Kennedy had not yet secured the Democratic presidential nomination, the Reverend W. A. Criswell of the First Baptist Church declared in a sermon that "the election of a Catholic as president would mean the end of religious freedom in America." One of Criswell's 18,500 parishioners was billionaire H. L. Hunt, who took the trouble to have 200,000 copies of Criswell's sermon mailed to Protestant ministers all over the country. . . .

The richest man in the world lived only a few blocks from us, in a reproduction of Mount Vernon on the shore of White Rock Lake. You could see H. L. Hunt in the morning raising the flag in his front yard, or sitting on the porch in the late afternoon, in a white shirt and a clip-on bow tie, playing checkers. . . .

In his front yard he posted a billboard advertising his superpatriotic radio show called "Life Line." He hired a former FBI agent named Dan Smoot as his commentator, who later founded his own conservative newsletter and opened an account in my father's bank. The Dallas extremist fringe found its voice and radio ambassador to the rest of the nation in Smoot. He talked about the enemies within, and their names were Eleanor Roosevelt, Walter Reuther, Edward R. Murrow, Earl Warren. . . .

Hunt never really fit in to the city; he loathed charity and all civic functions—you would never see him at a symphony ball, mingling with the sophisticates, but you might catch him at the state fair, personally hawking his HLH Gastro-Majic indigestion pills. Despite his wealth and radically conservative politics, he was essentially bohemian and wildly out of place in a city where pretense mattered. . . .

We fought school desegregation with the same cleverness as the rest of the South. In 1954 the Supreme Court had ruled in *Brown v. Board of Education of Topeka* that public schools should be desegregated "with all deliberate speed";

eleven years later, I graduated from high school without ever having had a black classmate. . . .

Understanding that integration of public facilities was inevitable, the Citizens Council arranged a coup. One day a black couple was seated for lunch at the Neiman-Marcus Zodiac Room. That was it—a signal to the entire city that desegregation had arrived. It was typical of Dallas that social change would be accomplished in the parlors of power, and not at the lunch counters of Walgreen's. . . .

Dallas was as publicly anti-sex as it was anti-Communist. In fact there seemed to be a subliminal link between the two, having to do with -verting, either per- or sub-. There was a high level of hypocrisy in sexual affairs, which was not surprising, given the go-go egos of the big winners in this sanctimonious city and the idle and pampered status of its women. The city fathers, publicly pious, were in private a rough and jaunty bunch, with thick knuckles and heavy appetites, men who were used to grabbing what they wanted. There was a tacit understanding, in those tall buildings, that the flesh was weak. . . .

The city never, in my memory, went to the trouble of formally banning a work of art or literature, as we heard had been done in Boston, although in the fifties the local art museum removed from display some of its collection of "Communist" art, including paintings by Picasso and Rivera. In 1962, after Henry Miller's erotic novel *Tropic of Cancer* was published, the Dallas police swept through the city's bookstores and the book simply disappeared. We were sexually sanitized. . . .

Dallas was so straitlaced it got a national reputation as a lousy spot for conventions. Outsiders couldn't get over the way pedestrians froze into place in front of a don't walk sign on an empty street. Edna Ferber once went to jail for jaywalking in Dallas, and many people suspect she wrote *Giant* in revenge—a theory I endorse, having received two jaywalking tickets myself during a teen-aged crime spree. . . .

The superheated political climate in the city brought ordinary life to a rolling boil. . . . The brakes were off in Dallas. We had the giddy feeling that we were careening toward some majestic crack-up, but it was a thrilling ride, and who had the nerve to say slow down?

Once again—it wasn't just Dallas. But we who lived there began to feel that we were in the middle of a political caldera, a grumbling, reawakening fascist urge that was too hot to contain itself. I wonder what might have happened in Dallas if Kennedy hadn't died there. . . .

Soon after we moved to Dallas my mother set out to become a "Dallas Woman." The phrase carried freight in Texas, where it signified a stylishness and sophistication that were uncommon in the rest of the state. Women advanced themselves in the city through a network of clubs and auxiliaries, such as the Bankers Wives, which Mother joined as a matter of course, and bridge clubs, which were her passion. She loved society and bright talk. . . .

In Dallas she joined the Jane Douglas chapter of the Daughters of the American Revolution, which was the largest DAR chapter in the country. There she learned about the politics of the Dallas Woman. It was a politics of paranoia. The female patriots of the DAR were obsessed with "Communist plots"—which, decoded, meant fluoridation of the drinking water and desegregation of the public schools. Once a week Mother attended the Public Affairs Club, a woman's group sponsored by H. L. Hunt, which concentrated on bringing conservative speakers to town. George Wallace came, and Ronald Reagan, and Dr. Fred Schwartz, the right-wing California educator, and Barry Goldwater, who spoke so frequently in Dallas that he got to be known as the "third senator from Texas." But the most popular speaker was the only elected Republican in Texas, Dallas congressman Bruce Alger.

Alger was a Princeton man, a bomber pilot in World War II, and the handsomest man in town. Even in his own party he was ridiculed as a hopeless extremist. In the ten years he represented Dallas in the House of Representatives there was never an important piece of legislation with his name on it. He was the only man in Congress to vote against giving free milk to schoolchildren. Pork barrel projects that might have gone to Dallas went to Fort Worth instead. . . . In the last four years of Alger's congressional reign, Dallas lost eight federal agencies. Despite his record, Alger survived political challenges by two of the most popular Democrats in the city, first by District Attorney Henry Wade, and then by Barefoot Sanders, a state legislator who became a federal district judge.

In all of his contests, Alger was carried along by a formidable cadre of angry right-wing women. . . . Alger was their prince. He was an extraordinary sexual presence, and he found power through the fears and the sublimated desires of the right-wing Dallas Woman. . . .

Dallas liked Nixon because he stood up to Khrushchev in the kitchen debates. He had brought down Alger Hiss, the exemplar of the Eastern Establishment. Kennedy talked tough—a lot tougher than Nixon—but in Dallas the national Democratic party was thought to be weak on Communism. . . . The enemy was Walter Reuther, head of the auto workers union, who had spent time in Russia during his youth. "The campaign for President in 1960 is not the usual contest between old-time political parties. It is a life and death struggle between Vice President Richard Nixon on the one hand, upholding American principles, and the candidate of the Walter Reuther party, on the other hand, with what this plainly implies."

The Democratic candidate made an obligatory visit to Dallas, drawing a surprisingly large crowd, estimated at 175,000 people (Nixon, the day before, attracted only 100,000). Kennedy had just come from Houston, where he had spoken to a large group of Protestant ministers about the issue of his Catholicism. There was a widespread fear that Kennedy's election would be tantamount to letting the Pope rule America. Since Catholics believe the Pope to be infallible (the argument went), Kennedy would have to do whatever he instructed. Dr. Norman Vincent Peale, the apostle of positive thinking, gloomily wondered if American culture could survive a Kennedy presidency. There was some irony in this, since Kennedy was, as his wife privately admitted, an awfully poor Catholic. In Houston Kennedy had given a fine, important speech that seemed to have settled the matter. He won over House Speaker Sam Rayburn, who was escorting the candidate through his native state. However, the Protestants in Dallas weren't so easily persuaded. "The more I listen to him, the more I 'ha-ha,'" said Dr. Criswell.

No Democratic candidate had ever won the White House without carrying Texas; Kennedy knew that—that's why he picked Lyndon Johnson as his running mate, to the outraged dismay of the Eastern press and many of Kennedy's advisers, who regarded Johnson as a hard-shell Southern conservative, a native racist, a drawling, backslapping political whore with no guiding lights other than the oil-depletion allowance. They despised Johnson in the East because he represented the insurgent Southwest. They had no idea how much more we hated Johnson in Dallas. Here he was called a closet socialist, a leftover New Dealer, a bleeding heart in domestic matters and a weak sister when it came to standing up against Communist aggression. Was there ever a man in public life with such a divided image?

Four days before the general election, Lyndon Johnson came to town. It was November 4, 1960, Republican Tag Day in Dallas, and the downtown lunch crowd was being canvassed by three hundred women in red, white, and blue. They were Bruce Alger's women. Many of them were in the Junior League, and they looked disarmingly girlish in their patriotic outfits and their red coif hats with ribbons streaming down the back. They were passing out literature for the Nixon-Lodge campaign. It was chilly, and some of them wore their minks. . . .

Several women spotted the Johnsons arriving and rushed over to surround their car. As Lady Bird was stepping out, one of the pickets impulsively snatched Mrs. Johnson's gloves from her hands and threw them in the gutter. Lady Bird went white. It was still a time when incivility was rare in politics, when public figures felt safe in crowds. No one, perhaps not even the tag girls themselves, was prepared to understand the ferocity and the anger of these apparently happy and well-cared-for women. . . .

Johnson was expected to speak at a luncheon across the street in the Adolphus Hotel. Congressman Jim Wright of Fort Worth accompanied the Johnsons, and he forayed ahead. As he passed through the mink-coated rabble in the street, he encountered his colleague Bruce Alger grinning hugely and holding a sign saying LBJ SOLD OUT TO YANKEE SOCIALISTS. Wright told him that it was inappropriate for a United States congressman to be standing in the middle of a mob, and that no matter what Alger might think of a man's politics, Johnson was the Senate majority leader and was due the respect of his office. "I went to hear your man [Nixon] in my city this morning," Wright said. "I listened with courtesy. I wouldn't do what you're doing even if I felt that way."

“We’re gonna show Johnson he’s not wanted in Dallas,” Alger replied, and the tag girls cheered.

As the Johnsons made their way through the Baker lobby, the crowd closed ranks behind them, becoming bolder. There were more of them waiting in the street, and beyond that, in the lobby of the Adolphus. This was an odd political gauntlet to pass through. It recalled the stoning of Vice President Nixon’s motorcade by Communist students in Caracas, Venezuela. But this wasn’t South America; this was Lyndon’s own state.

The demonstrators in Commerce Street waited with placards and catcalls. . . . The Johnsons moved inside a small capsule of personal distance that grew smaller and threatened to collapse entirely under the crush of protesters. In retrospect it was that violation of private space that heralded our new, tragic political era. Years later, as president, Johnson would become accustomed to seeing hateful signs with his name on them; indeed, he would know the fury of the public as few men ever have, but in 1960 it was something new, something unheard of.

What was more surprising was that the sign carriers and catcallers were well-groomed women from the finest homes in the city. And yet, as the Johnsons waded into Commerce Street, the women in red, white, and blue began to curse them, and to spit. . . .

Why? What accounted for the hostility—or to use her word, indignation—of the fashionable and affluent Dallas Woman? In part she was simply a prisoner of her age: a woman of unfocused ambition, intensely competitive but unemployed (the working wife was still a signal of economic desperation), lonely at home and given to causes. She may have been financially secure, but she was deeply troubled by some unfathomable fear that her castle was built of sand and the coming tide would wash her away. She named the tide International Communism or Creeping Socialism. She worried about the “missile gap” and the spread of Communism. Moreover, people in her own country were talking enthusiastically about social change—Kennedy was already speaking of “the revolutionary sixties”—and the Dallas Woman knew those changes would come at her expense. . . . The Dallas Woman felt herself to be under attack at home and abroad. Now she was striking back.

Johnson made his way through the placards with his wife practically buried under his arm. Lyndon, of course, loomed over the tag girls, his huge hound-dog face visible even at the farthest reaches of the crowd, but Lady Bird was on their level, and she could see the rage in their faces. She started to answer one of the insults, but Johnson put his hand over her mouth and guided her into the lobby of the Adolphus. "Let's just let them do all the hollerin'," he said.

They were waiting there, the tag girls and the hangers-on, but also press photographers and television cameras. John Tower, Johnson's senatorial opponent, was lurking in the stairwell, waiting for a chance to spring into Johnson's path with a list of political charges; but Tower, despite his name, is a diminutive man and was easily shoved aside by the crush of women.

Even in that mob it would have been a short walk to the elevators if Johnson had bulled his way through. But instead of pressing ahead, Johnson did something quite surprising. He slowed down. He moved with excruciating slowness through the chanting mob and the rain of spit. For thirty minutes Johnson and his wife withstood the harangue of the crowd, as the senator stared into the television cameras with a martyr's embarrassed smile.

It was the most triumphant half hour of Johnson's career, because that evening on the television news millions of Americans met the new Lyndon Johnson. They suddenly understood him exactly as he understood himself. He was a liberal—in the Southern context. Overnight he became an acceptable candidate to big-city Northern Democrats who had automatically hated him and to traditional Democrats everywhere who had not (they now admitted) seen past the corn-pone mannerisms of LBJ to the winking FDR inside him.

That evening, watching the news, thousands of Texans and millions of Americans decided how to vote. Although Nixon carried Dallas by a larger margin than any other city in the country, Texas went for Kennedy-Johnson. . . . It was the closest election in history, and it was decided that day in the lobby of the Adolphus Hotel. People said afterward that they were not voting for Kennedy so much as they were voting against Dallas.

Against us. Until then, Dallas had had very little national identity, but now we found ourselves with a new municipal image: a city of angry parvenus, smug, doctrinaire, belligerent—a city with a taste for political violence.

We were shocked to see ourselves portrayed this way, but it had little effect on the way we thought of ourselves.

Until the Adolphus incident, my mother had been coy about how she was going to vote. . . . She and I watched the news together that night—she with horror, because the faces in the mob were familiar to her. They were the same faces she saw at her luncheons and bridge clubs. These were the women she aspired to know and emulate, for they were all Dallas Women, all fashionable, sophisticated, and financially well off; but they were also, Mother saw now, terrified, uncertain, and filled with hate. I remember her cry as we watched the humiliation at the Adolphus: "Shame! Shame!" ★

Darwin Payne

Darwin Payne (1937-), former professor of journalism at Southern Methodist University, and secretary of the Texas Institute of Letters, holds a PhD in American Civilization from the University of Texas at Austin. His books include *Owen Wister: Chronicler of the West, Gentleman of the East*, winner of a TIL award; *The Man of Only Yesterday: Frederick Lewis Allen; Dallas: An Illustrated History; Big D: Triumphs and Troubles of an American Supercity in the 20th Century;* and *Indomitable Sarah: The Life of Judge Sarah T. Hughes*, winner of the Texas State Historical Association Women in History award. Darwin is also a publisher, his press being Three Forks Press. The excerpts chosen here, including a bird's eye view of the swearing in of Lyndon Johnson, give another view of the controversy that surrounded Dallas before and after the assassination.

From *Big D: Triumphs and Troubles of an American Supercity in the 20th Century*

> *November 22, 1963*
> *I sure wish to hell you'd persuade Kennedy not to come. It is a grave mistake to come to Dallas.*
>
> —*Stanley Marcus to Lyndon B. Johnson*

In an era when fanatical right-wing extremism was gaining strength throughout the nation, few if any cities seemed more receptive than Dallas. When army general Edwin A. Walker resigned his commission in 1961 after heavy criticism for indoctrinating his troops with a "pro-blue" John Birch Society political program, he chose to settle in Dallas, where he instantly became the darling of the far right. Walker, a bachelor, moved into a large two-story house on Turtle Creek Boulevard where he regularly flew his American flag upside down as a distress signal that the nation was in danger from being taken over by the Communists. . . .

Another far-right spokesman in the city was Dr. Robert B. Morris, president of a new Catholic university, the University of Dallas. Morris's fulminations brought doubts as to just what was the purpose of this new institution, although in the future it would overcome any negative assessments and become a highly respected university.

More far right activity came through the founding and meteoric rise of the National Indignation Convention (later renamed Conference). A thirty-two-year-old Dallas man named Frank McGehee began the group in outrageous indignation when he learned that Communist Yugoslavian pilots were being trained at Perrin Air Force Base in Texas. Chapters of the Dallas-based organization sprang up all across the nation as a move to force Congress to cease granting military aid to any Communist regime anywhere and to seek the dismissal of all government officials responsible for such actions.

Especially strong in Dallas was the John Birch Society. Its membership included some of the city's oil-rich, notably H. L. Hunt's son, Nelson Bunker Hunt, who also supported many other conservative political and religious causes. The society put its regional headquarters in Dallas under the leadership of Rex Westerfield. Independent oilman Joseph P. Grinnan was the local coordinator. The society operated in the city its own American Opinion Book Store, where a large collection of right-wing material was sold to the public. Robert Welch of Massachusetts, the organization's founder, made periodic visits to the city to make speeches and to give seminars to receptive audiences. . . .

Any mention of arch-conservatives in Dallas would have to include the pastor of the powerful First Baptist Church of Dallas, the Reverend W. A. Criswell . . . who believed in the inerrancy of the Bible in every respect and who preached against the evils of school integration as contrary to biblical command, endorsed Nixon over Kennedy in a sermon.

Overall, Dallas was undeniably out-of-step with the rest of the state in the depths of its conservatism. The *News* had grown especially adamant in its crusades against what it perceived to be Kennedy's socialistic tendencies and also the civil rights movement. . . . Publisher E. M. (Ted) Dealey, son of the late George B. Dealey, raised eyebrows across the nation when at a White House luncheon he shocked fellow publishers in attendance with a display of bad manners. He pointedly told his host, President Kennedy, that the people in Texas and the Southwest needed and wanted a strong president who would get off Caroline's tricycle and lead the nation from horseback. Kennedy was quietly furious, especially at the use of his daughter's name. The incident prompted a *Times Herald* vice president to apologize for his colleague's bad behavior. Kennedy replied that he was certain the people of Dallas were glad when afternoon (and the *Times Herald*) came.

There were organizations in the city that were at least mildly liberal in their outlook. One such organization was Dallas's Council on World Affairs, which began planning a public event to honor United Nations Day in Dallas. The special day, set for October 26, would feature an address from the U.S. ambassador to the United Nations Adlai E. Stevenson. . . .

Edwin A. Walker and the National Indignation Convention announced a counter-event they called "U.S. Day" to be held one night before the UN event and in the same downtown Memorial Auditorium. At first glance, "U.S. Day," seemed innocuous enough, so much so that Texas governor John Connally, who had been Kennedy's secretary of the navy, officially sanctioned it as a matter of routine. What it actually became was an occasion for the gathering of some 1,400 die-hard extremists to make fierce attacks against the United Nations and President Kennedy, including reckless accusations of treason. (One of those who attended that evening's speech-making was definitely not a right-winger. He was a young Marxist named Lee Harvey Oswald, who six months earlier had attempted to assassinate the former general with a rifle from an alley behind Walker's house. The shot had barely missed Walker. . . .) Historian and rancher J. Evetts Haley won loud applause when he announced that *he* didn't want to impeach Chief Justice Earl Warren, as the Birch Society was urging, he wanted to hang him. Messages of support were read at the meeting from Bruce Alger, Dr. Morris of the University of Dallas, political commentator Dan Smoot and Senator Strom Thurmond.

Next day, on the morning of Stevenson's address, handbills were circulated on the city's streets bearing pictures of Kennedy with the words: "Wanted for Treason. This Man is wanted for treasonous activities against the United States."

There followed a listing of such charges as permitting "known Communists" to abound in federal offices.

On the evening of UN Day in Dallas a capacity crowd filled Memorial Auditorium. Stanley Marcus gave a glowing introduction to Ambassador Stevenson, but as Stevenson came to the podium to speak a man with a bullhorn stood up in front of the auditorium and demanded answers to specific questions. He was Frank McGehee, founder of the National Indignation Convention. . . . He persisted until finally police officers had to remove him from the auditorium.

The traumatic events of the evening had only begun. Right-wing extremists in the auditorium equaled in number those supporters of the United Nations, and they consistently sought to humiliate and disrupt Stevenson as he spoke by waving placards, booing, shouting interjections, laughing derisively, coughing incessantly, displaying miniature American flags upside down, and walking up and down the aisles clicking "cricket" noisemakers. "How about Cuber?" was a frequent shout, imitative of Kennedy's accent. "How about Hungary?" "How about Katanga?" The evening became a struggle of wills between the two groups, one determined to cheer on Stevenson and the other intent on disrupting him. . . .

The city's leaders were aghast at the incident and its immediate injury to the city's reputation. Mayor Cabell, Citizens Council president J. Erik Jonsson, Chamber of Commerce president Robert B. Cullum, and a hundred other leading citizens sent a telegram of apology to the ambassador. "The City of Dallas is outraged and abjectly ashamed of the disgraceful discourtesies you suffered at the hands of a small group of extremists." Mayor Cabell . . . now urged Dallas residents to reject the radical right just as it ultimately had rejected the Klan.

"Dallas has been disgraced," read a front-page *Times Herald* editorial. "There is no other way to view the stormtrooper actions of last night's frightening attack on Adlai Stevenson" which amounted to a "senseless inability of some of the residents of Dallas to tolerate those with whom they disagree. . . ." The *Times Herald* asked: "What has happened to Dallas?" The display of malevolence "has brought sensible Dallas to the sickening realization that 'harmless extremists' can not only cause physical harm but create destructive havoc. . . . We must quit preaching hate. We must stop spreading and believing the ridiculous stories of suspicion and distrust of our fellow citizens from the seeds of uncontrolled frenzy." In contrast to the *Times Herald's* fulsome editorial laments, the *News* apologized conditionally: "If the time has come when a distinguished gentleman in his position cannot express his beliefs without abuse, then this city should examine itself."

The most immediate and critical aspect of the Stevenson affair was obvious. President Kennedy himself, the primary target of the extreme right, was due in Dallas within weeks. When Kennedy had his aide, Arthur Schlesinger Jr., convey to Stevenson his congratulations for maintaining his presence of mind and coolness under such extreme circumstances, Stevenson joked about it, then added seriously, "But, you know, there was something ugly and frightening about the atmosphere." He had talked with some of the leading people in Dallas afterwards, he said, and they "wondered whether the President should go to Dallas, and so do I. . . ."

The White House announced on the day after the Stevenson melee that the president's plans to visit Dallas would not be cancelled. The trip seemed important, not just for raising political funds but also to mend the Texas Democratic Party feud between the conservative John Connally forces and the liberal Senator Ralph Yarborough element. . . .

To ensure success at this critical juncture, the Citizens Council once again stepped forward. The organization announced that it would assume sponsorship of the luncheon at which the president would speak. Certain members of the Citizens Council, despite the fact that many of them were Republicans, already had been involved in a preliminary strategy session. . . . The Dallas session, held in the Adolphus Hotel, included J. Erik Jonsson, president of the Citizens Council and a staunch Republican; Robert Cullum, president of the Chamber of Commerce and an influential Citizens Council member; the venerable R. L. Thornton; Joe Dealey, son of Ted Dealey; and Albert Jackson of the *Times Herald*. Connally . . . wanted a nonpolitical body—such as these men represented—to sponsor the visit. The impact of this decision was to place authority for the presidential visit to Dallas in the hands of men who were predominantly Republicans and conservatives. Loyalist Democrats protested loudly to no avail about their exclusion from a luncheon for a president whom they had helped elect. Stanley Marcus, a Citizens Council member and a prominent Kennedy supporter, complained that Dallas's business leadership "froze" even him out of the preparation plans. . . .

Through its powerful membership, the Citizens Council caused the city to be saturated with a series of newspaper articles and television reports emphasizing the need for a cordial reception. The message, also carried forth from the city's pulpits and civic clubs, reached a peak during the six days preceding Kennedy's visit. . . . On November 18, the City Council adopted an ordinance which prohibited individuals from interfering with lawful assemblies. Even former Vice President Richard M. Nixon . . . joined police in "urging Dallas to give President and Mrs. Kennedy a courteous reception."

On the morning prior to the president's November 22 arrival, crude handbills accusing him of treason were spread about the downtown area. A close associate of Walker's had printed 5,000 of the leaflets for distribution about town. The handbills had "mug shots" of Kennedy under the headline, "WANTED FOR TREASON." Beneath were a series of irrational, treasonous charges. . . .

To help pay for the advertisement, they approached oilman Joseph P. Grinnan, local coordinator for the Birch Society. Grinnan raised money to pay for the advertisement and helped polish the final draft in his office. Two of those who contributed money and helped solicit other donations were Nelson Bunker Hunt and H. R. "Bum" Bright, chairman of the board of a trucking company who later would become owner of the Dallas Cowboys and a director of First Republic Bank. The advertisement was approved for publication by *News* publisher Ted Dealey. Afterwards, he defended his decision to his irritated son Joe, now the newspaper's president. . . .

After a short hop that morning from Fort Worth on Air Force One, President John F. Kennedy and his wife arrived at Love Field at 11:40 A.M. on a crisp, sunshiny day. Traveling with them were the eyes and ears of the world—sixty-eight journalists. (*Dallas Times Herald* executive editor Felix McKnight had stepped out of his role as newsman to handle press arrangements for the visit.) A welcoming crowd of several thousand spectators roared their approval at the sight of the presidential couple. Mayor Cabell's wife, Dearie, handed the first lady a huge bouquet of red roses as she stepped from the airplane. The president and his wife approached an exuberant throng of spectators behind a chain-link fence and greeted them. Ten minutes later the presidential motorcade departed along a route planned for maximum exposure to the public en route to the luncheon at the Trade Mart. Some 250,000 spectators were estimated to have gathered along the route, cheering and holding up signs of greeting. Their enthusiasm and displays of affection for the president, all agreed, were exceptional.

The open-topped presidential limousine, surrounded by police motorcycles and followed by cars and buses bearing the other political dignitaries, journalists, and communications equipment, passed slowly down Main Street amidst the biggest crowds of all through the center of downtown. Just beyond the shadows of the downtown buildings at Dealey Plaza, at the very site where John Neely Bryan had founded the town, the motorcade turned from Main to Houston Street for one short block and then turned sharply again in front of the Texas Schoolbook Depository building so that it could head directly to Stemmons Freeway and the Trade Mart.

Now occurred the most horrendous event in the city's history. Shots rang out. Few were certain as to how many. Some mistook them for firecrackers. A handful of people close to the presidential limousine could see the dreadful impact of a rifle shot hitting the president's head. Abraham Zapruder, a dress manufacturer whose business was across the street from the Schoolbook Depository, saw the president's head explode "like a firecracker" as he recorded the event with his 8-mm camera. The driver of the presidential limousine, escorted by police chief Curry and others, sped away to Parkland Hospital, carrying the stricken president, the wounded governor, and their horrified wives. . . .

Minutes after the shots had been fired at Dealey Plaza, an order-filler in the Texas Schoolbook Depository, twenty-four-year-old Lee Harvey Oswald, walked out of the building, caught a bus, and then transferred to a taxi heading across the Houston Street viaduct to his room on North Beckley Street in Oak Cliff. There, he picked up a jacket, grabbed a pistol which he concealed on his person, and began walking toward Jefferson Boulevard. Confronted after a few blocks for some unknown reason by police officer J. D. Tippit, Oswald shot and killed him, then hurried down Jefferson Boulevard, slipped into the Texas Theater without paying, and sat quietly in the audience as the movie played. Officers, summoned there by spectators who had seen Oswald hurrying down the street and appearing to hide at the sound of police sirens, entered the theater at 1:45 P.M. and arrested him. In the brief ensuing scuffle, Oswald once more pulled his pistol and tried to shoot the nearest officer.

At Parkland Hospital, twelve minutes before Oswald's arrest, presidential aide Malcolm Kilduff announced to reporters that President John F. Kennedy was dead, victim of an assassin's gunfire. . . .

By Friday afternoon, the astonishing revelation had come that Oswald once had defected from the United States as a Marxist to live in the Soviet Union. During the rest of the afternoon and evening and throughout Saturday, law enforcement officers at the Dallas police station interrogated him for a total of some twelve hours over several sessions. The suspect resisted his questioners with surprising force and dexterity, denying any involvement with the deaths of the president or Officer Tippit. . . .

[At] 11:20 A.M. on Sunday, officers escorted Oswald from his cell into the basement toward a waiting car for the trip to the county jail at the other end of downtown. . . . As Oswald came through a basement doorway, handcuffed to a detective for security, a local nightclub owner named Jack Ruby stepped from the front of the crowd with his .38 caliber Colt revolver and fired once into the abdomen of the suspect. Oswald lapsed into unconsciousness. The unbelievable event was seen live on nationwide television.

Once again, a shooting victim was rushed to Parkland Hospital, and once again, the wound proved to be fatal. Oswald was pronounced dead at 1:07 P.M. He died without regaining consciousness, carrying secrets of the assassination with him.

The city, the nation, and the world again were plunged into despair. The murder of the suspected assassin while in police custody in the police station was an event almost as shocking as the president's death. No three days in Dallas's history, probably no three days in the nation's history, had been so startling, so surprising, so devastating, so jolting to the public psyche. Certainly no other event had possessed such immediacy or had been assimilated so quickly. ★

From *Indomitable Sarah: The Life of Judge Sarah T. Hughes*

EAGERLY AWAITING THE PRESIDENT'S ARRIVAL at the Trade Mart among the well-dressed and well-heeled crowd was Sarah T. Hughes, her dress with huge white polka dots adorned with a large corsage. As she entered the building, the women's editor for the *Dallas Times Herald,* Vivian Castleberry, intercepted her for a quick interview. Hughes's comments reemphasized the apprehension of the moment. As Castleberry later said, "I recall vividly that she said three things. One, that it was a great day for Dallas. Second, that she had been gravely concerned about the president visiting Dallas. And third that she would be glad when he left Dallas."

Hughes had received one of a hundred or so tickets designated for Kennedy's Democratic admirers. Hers had come from Barefoot Sanders, who at the last minute had been given the tickets for distribution among the Democratic faithful. They had been sent to him only after his personal plea to Vice President Johnson on his trip to Dallas three days before the event. . . .

Sitting next to Hughes at one of the many long and resplendent tables on the first floor was Jan Sanders. Barefoot Sanders would join them when he arrived on the VIP bus in the presidential motorcade. Hughes's court reporter, Odell Oliver, and Hughes's secretary and friend, Gwen Graul . . . had less desirable seats on one of the three upstairs balconies overlooking the central court. After lunch, Hughes planned to ride with the Sanderses to Austin, where they would continue to be with the presidential party.

A few people in the balconies or standing around the fringes of the seated diners were monitoring the progress of the motorcade with small transistor radios. At 12:30 P.M. shots rang out at Dealey Plaza, and moments later those people with radios heard unconfirmed reports of the shots, not knowing at first whether anyone had been hit. "You could just see the news as it seeped into the crowd," Jan Sanders said later. Sanders, Hughes, and virtually everyone became alarmed and agitated. No one knew yet that President Kennedy had been shot just as the motorcade was leaving the downtown area; that Governor Connally had been seriously wounded; and that the presidential limousine with its stricken passengers had bypassed the Trade Mart to go directly to Parkland Hospital. The motorcade buses, trailing much farther behind, stopped at the Trade Mart as planned and discharged their passengers, largely journalists, who themselves were bewildered but understood that something terribly wrong had happened at Dealey Plaza. The frantic newsmen scurried to find telephones and to interview one another about what they might have seen when their buses passed by the horrified witnesses and confused scene at Dealey Plaza.

"The press came in and we kept on waiting, and Jan began to get worried," Hughes recalled. "She [Jan] says 'Something has happened,' and I said, 'Oh, no, no, it can't be.'" But Mrs. Sanders was certain. She began to cry even before a shaken Erik Jonsson . . . came to the podium at 1:01 P.M. to make a cautious announcement.

Speaking slowly, Jonsson said: "There has been a delay in the arrival of the motorcade. There has been a mishap. We do not know the extent of it or the exact nature. We believe from our report we have just received that it is not serious. We hope you will keep your seats. As soon as we have something to tell you, believe me, we'll do it."

Nine minutes after his first announcement, Jonsson, obviously more shaken than before, returned to the podium. He told the crowd he felt a "little bit like the fella on Pearl Harbor day." The president and Governor Connally had been shot, he confirmed. "We do not know how seriously. Our reports are scant, they are difficult to get. We shall tell you as much as we know as soon as we know anything."

Someone in the audience shouted. "Those damn fanatics, why do we have to have them in Dallas?" The shock of the moment was overpowering. It assumed instantly that right-wingers had carried their protests to the ultimate extreme. . . .

There was nothing for Hughes to do but leave. With Sanders, she walked to the parking lot to their separate cars. A television cameraman from KDFW-TV in Dallas focused his lens on Hughes outside the Trade Mart as she stepped in her car outside the building and listened carefully as a blond-headed woman, evidently Gwen Graul, bent over at her window to tell her something. Instantly, Hughes was transformed by a shocked, pained expression in which her eyes widened and her mouth opened. It appears to be the moment she learned of the president's mortal injury. The woman—Graul—then walked around the car to take the front passenger seat. Graul and Oliver had ridden to the Trade Mart with Hughes, intending to drive her car back to her house, since she planned to depart for Austin from the Trade Mart with the Sanderses.

"Numbly and hardly realizing what had happened, I drove home," Hughes wrote immediately after the assassination in recalling the traumatic day for the *Washington Post.* "There was no reason to go to court. In the face of the tragedy that had befallen us, all else seemed of little consequence."

Graul and Oliver rode with Hughes to her house, about fifteen minutes away, where they had parked a car for their return to the courthouse. On the way the three women speculated about where the vice president would be sworn in. One of them—Hughes later couldn't recall who—thought rather foolishly in these moments of complete uncertainty that the planned journey and the LBJ Ranch in the Hill Country might be completed and that Johnson could take the oath of office there. On reflection they agreed it was likely that he would go on to Washington and be sworn in immediately. "No one even thought that he'd be sworn in in Dallas," she said. When they reached Hughes's home, shortly before two P.M., Graul and Oliver departed. Hughes, inside the house, immediately called her court to advise that she was home. She was told that Barefoot Sanders was in the office looking for her. He wanted to speak to her.

"Immediately I heard his familiar voice," Hughes recalled. The vice president wanted her to swear him in. Could she? How soon could she get to Love Field?. . .

Johnson, already inside Air Force One, was pondering the matter of proper accession to the office. Should he take his oath of office in Dallas, or should it be delayed until the return to the nation's capital? He began working the telephone. He called the attorney general, the slain president's brother. "A lot of people down here think I should be sworn in right away," he told Robert Kennedy. "Who could swear me in?" Kennedy, still in shock and disbelief, said he would check it out and get back to him. Johnson made other phone calls to Walter Jenkins and McGeorge Bundy. Then Kennedy was back on the line. Nicholas Katzenbach, the deputy attorney general, had advised him that anyone, even a justice of the peace, could administer the oath. Katzenbach had told Kennedy, "I imagine he'll want Sarah Hughes."

Johnson asked Kennedy about the oath. "You can get the oath," Kennedy said. "There's no problem about the oath, they can locate the oath."

Johnson, who had retreated inside Air Force One to a bed in the state room, dictated brief notes of these telephone conversations to his secretary Marie Fehmer. . . . "Get Sarah Hughes," Johnson now told Fehmer. Hughes's law clerk, John Spinuzzi, picked up the telephone to hear an unidentified voice asking for Sarah Hughes. The judge, he said, was not there; she was at the Trade Mart. After he hung up the telephone immediately rang again. "This is Lyndon Johnson. Find her." And when he located her, she was to contact him immediately at Air Force One. . . .

Having gotten a ride to his office from the Trade Mart, Sanders was attempting to find a statute under which the president's alleged murderer, already arrested by Dallas police, could be charged. There was no such statute—the assassin was guilty only of a Texas felony. Murder of a president was a state crime, not a federal one. . . . Sanders, who already had been alerted to find Judge Hughes, agreed that she was the best person to swear Johnson in. Now with the need to find her paramount, he dashed upstairs to her courtroom thinking she might be there. He arrived just at the moment Hughes called there to advise her office staff that she was home. Sanders took the phone.

"This is Barefoot. The vice president wants you to swear him in as president. Can you do it?". . .

Yes, she could, she said, immediately. "Where do I go?"

"Love Field," Sanders said. "I'll clear you with the secret service. How soon do you think you can get there?"

"Ten minutes," she said, "but what about the oath?"

"I'll have it at the airport when you get there," he replied, still uncertain as to where he would find it.

"Don't worry about it. I'll make it up," the judge replied. She got into her car and drove to Love Field.

Hughes later explained her seeming lack of concern about finding the oath. "The essentials of every oath are the same. You have to swear to perform the duties of the office of President of the United States, and to preserve and defend the Constitution of the United States. I was not afraid. I could do it without a formal oath. . . ."

Later, Hughes would say, everybody wanted to know what she was thinking about on that short and solitary drive. . . . "I was thinking first of all that I must not think about Kennedy," she told historian Joe B. Frantz. "I must think about the country going on. . . . And another thing I was thinking about was that I must get there in a hurry because Vice President Johnson is always in a hurry and wants things done right now and I shouldn't delay. And the other thing that I was thinking about was what the oath of office was in case Barefoot couldn't find it. I was brash enough to think that I could give the oath without having looked it up."

Johnson had had the presence of mind to tell Malcolm Kilduff, assistant press secretary to Kennedy, to make arrangements for the swearing-in ceremony. Kilduff, who had startled some when he made the first reference to Johnson as "Mr. President," had done as directed. Kilduff forestalled an effort by an anguished brigadier general Godfrey McHugh, Kennedy's air force aide, to have Air Force One depart immediately; he arranged for the reporters (Charles Roberts of *Newsweek*, Merriman Smith of United Press International, and Sid Davis of Westinghouse) to come inside the airplane to witness the event and to serve as a pool for the other journalists; he directed White House photographer Cecil Stoughton, a captain in the Signal Corp to take pictures; and he followed Stoughton's suggestion to grab a stenographer's Dictograph—the only recording device available—to make an audio recording of the event.

Jacqueline Kennedy was in the small bedroom, seated on a bed around the corner from her husband's coffin, still wearing the blood-stained pink suit that had been so striking that day. Johnson, comforting her, had advised her a few minutes earlier that the swearing-in would be held on the airplane before departure. "I've arranged for a judge—an old friend of mine, Judge Hughes to come. She'll be here in about an hour. So why don't you lie down and freshen up and everything? We'll leave you alone."

Judge Hughes, en route alone to Love Field, was intercepted by Dallas police officer James Jennings, who had been sent to find and escort her. "We now have information that Judge Sarah Hughes is en route from Parkland to Love to swear President Johnson in," the police dispatcher announced at two P.M. . . . Dallas police chief Jesse Curry, secret service agent John Ready, and Vernon Oneal, the funeral home owner whose hearse had taken the president's body to Love Field from Parkland, were watching for her. It was Oneal who first spotted her, seeing her when her two-door hardtop automobile rounded the *Spirit of Flight* statue at the terminal. "There she is!" he shouted.

A motorcycle officer took up as escort and accompanied Hughes as she drove her own car closer to the airplane parked near Gate 27. She was struck by its magnificent appearance. "It was a beautiful sight, the presidential plane, long and sleek, a blue and two white stripes running the length of the plane with the words, 'The United States of America,' on the blue stripe," she later recalled. "It seemed to exemplify the strength and courage of our country. . . . "

Someone told her Barefoot Sanders wanted her to call him. "I knew that Barefoot had the oath by then," Hughes recalled later, "but I said, 'Well, I know what the oath is!'" As she proceeded up the ramp someone else mentioned the oath. She replied, "I don't need the oath of office, I know what to say." But the exact wording had been found. Nicholas Katzenbach in Washington had realized that the oath appeared in the U.S. Constitution. He had called Air Force One and dictated it to Marie Fehmer. Now someone presented Hughes with the oath, typed neatly by Fehmer on a small piece of stationery.

Hughes, still in the dress with the huge polka dots she had worn to the luncheon, followed Clifton through the airplane's fore sections—communications, forward galley, crews' quarters, and the press and staff area—before entering the state room at the midpoint of the airplane. There, the ceremony awaited her.

Sarah T. Hughes stepped inside the crowded, hot, stuffy, and uncomfortable room—packed because Johnson had wanted as many people as possible to witness the event. Hughes, seeing Johnson and Lady Bird, embraced each of them without saying anything. An embrace seemed to her the "best way to give expression to my feeling of grief for them, and for all of us," she said later. Johnson said, "Mrs. Kennedy wants to be here. We'll wait for her. . . ."

"We'll get as many people in here as possible," Johnson said, sending Jack Valenti, Rufus Youngblood, Emory Roberts, and Lem Johns into the staff area to summon others. Johnson followed just behind them and announced, "If anybody wants to join in the swearing-in ceremony, I would be happy and proud to have you."

Finally, twenty-seven individuals squeezed inside a space designed for ten. Kennedy's traumatized aides, knowing only that their president had been slain on the streets of Dallas, generally assumed he had been the victim of right-wing extremists. Many were reluctant to be included in the swearing-in ceremony, even as spectators. Their feelings of revulsion included not only the city and the state of Texas but also Lyndon B. Johnson as the foremost representative of the state. Some of them were irritated that Lyndon B. Johnson already had taken charge of the situation, delaying the departure for Washington at a time when they were eager to leave. Some were not pleased that Johnson had ordered his and Lady Bird Johnson's luggage removed from the adjacent backup airplane and placed in Air Force One for the return flight.

Nevertheless, several Kennedy aides were in the room to witness the ceremony—Larry O'Brien, Evelyn Lincoln, Pamela Tenure, and Kilduff. Many of Johnson's own aides were now aboard and in the state rooms, too, including Liz Carpenter and the newly appointed Bill Moyers and Jack Valenti. Texas congressman Albert Thomas was there, as was police chief Curry.

"We'll wait for Mrs. Kennedy. I want her here," Johnson told Hughes, then asked that someone bring her. "Just a minute. I'm going to get her," he said, and at that moment Jacqueline Kennedy walked in.

To Hughes, the bereaved widow, whom she had never met, exhibited clear evidence of her great grief but nevertheless was composed and calm. At that moment she exemplified to Hughes the courage the country needed to carry on. Johnson leaned over to the ashen-faced Mrs. Kennedy and introduced Hughes to her as a U.S. judge appointed by her husband. Hughes acknowledged the introduction by quietly saying to Mrs. Kennedy, "I loved him very much."

In these brief moments, Congressman Albert Thomas embraced Mrs. Kennedy. Dallas police chief Curry told her the Dallas Police Department had done everything it could to protect the president. Johnson took her by the hand and said, "This is the saddest moment of my life."

Towering above all others, Johnson asked Lady Bird to stand on his right and Mrs. Kennedy on his left. Stoughton, all too aware of the significance of his photograph, gave quick instructions to the principals to make minor adjustments. He perched on a sofa behind Judge Hughes, who was clutching the presidential oath. Malcolm Kilduff, kneeling low, held the Dictaphone in front of the judge, ready to activate it. Someone asked, "What about a Bible?"

Sergeant Joseph Ayres, the steward on the airplane crew, said President Kennedy kept his personal Bible under a table between the two beds in his cabin. Ayres went to get it (actually a prayer missal) then handed it to Larry O'Brien, special assistant to Kennedy.

"Just a minute, Judge," O'Brien said, interrupting and handing her the book he described as a Catholic Bible. Hughes hesitated. The book was, she saw, a small volume with a soft leather cover. The fact that it was described as a Catholic Bible comforted her, and the pleasant thought entered her mind that President Kennedy might have been reading it on the trip. On the front was a gold cross. On the inside cover were sewn the initials JFK.

Kilduff pressed the record button on the Dictaphone and extended the microphone in front of him; Hughes held the missal in front of her. Johnson placed his large left hand on it, lifted his right hand, and repeated the oath after Hughes, who at this moment became the first woman in the nation's history to swear in a president. "I do solemnly swear that I will perform the duties of President of the United States to the best of my ability and defend, protect, and preserve the Constitution of the United States." Hughes administered the oath in short phrases, consciously thinking that under tense circumstances people do not do well at remembering long ones. Johnson repeated the phrases after her, slowly and reverently. And at the conclusion Hughes added another phrase that did not appear on the oath itself, "So help me God." It seemed to her that the phrase needed to be said. With the twenty-eight-second ceremony over, the president leaned over, kissed Mrs. Kennedy gently, and then kissed his wife. . . .

Immediately afterward, Hughes put her arm around the president. "We're all behind you," she said. Johnson, sinking into a chair, told Lem Johns, "Now let's get this plane back to Washington." Hughes, police chief Curry, Westinghouse reporter Sid Davis, and photographer Stoughton quickly left the aircraft. On her way out, Hughes handed the prayer missal to someone she did not know, who asked her, "Don't you want to keep it?" Hughes replied, "No, it doesn't belong to me. . . ."

At 2:47 P.M. the airplane lifted off the runway. Hughes drove home alone, having in these brief moments performed a service that would render her a historic figure for the ages. ★

Gene Shuford

Gene Shuford graduated from the University of Arkansas. After serving in the air force in World War II, he became an influential member of the Poetry Societies of Texas and America, Texas Poet Laureate alternate, and served for many years as chairman of the department of journalism at what is now the University of North Texas. His poetry won some fifty regional and national awards and appeared in such publications as *Scribner's; Saturday Evening Post; New Republic; Southwest Review; Arlington Quarterly*; and *Southwest Writers Anthology.* Titles of Shuford's collections include *The Red Bull and Other Poems; The Flowering Noose; 1300 Main Street;* and *Selected Poems: 1933-1971*, the latter receiving a Texas Institute of Letters award. As seen in this poem, the poets also reacted to the assassination.

The Visit

One can never tell what November will be in Texas:
it has that delusive warmth of the blood and love,
promising tenderness forever as though death
will never come; it will let lilacs bloom
in the autumn and the great sun shine with a burning
that invites the ultimate passion for living even
while the frost waits in tonight's sleep.
The rain can fall in the night and the sky will wash blue
as a baby's eyes in the morning and the puddles will dry
and the big jet will slip down out of cottony clouds
and the prince and the princess descend and all the banners
will wave above the spirit's shining armor.
Already this is a legend, a myth we only half believe,

saying, surely it must not have happened; surely, it must
have been a dream; surely, it was long ago,
but now is already encrusted with myth and the passion
for forgetting, strong as the passion for remembering,
so that both have woven a golden cloth for the years
of Camelot that were ours, for the greener fields that were ours,
for the tall castle we saw in the clouds, for the knight
and his lady dropped down from the sky who were our king
and the fairest queen we had ever seen walk proudly
across the tapestry of our time, which before
this day was done, all bloody on the stones
would lie and trampled with the blackest death
a man would ever see or bear to dream of.

Edwin A. (Bud) Shrake

Edwin A. (Bud) Shrake (1931-) is a well-known journalist, sportswriter, novelist, biographer and screenwriter. In 1951 Shrake joined the *Fort Worth Press* sports department while he earned a degree in English and Philosophy at Texas Christian University. Shrake moved to the *Dallas Times Herald* as a sportswriter followed by a move to *The Dallas Morning News* to write a daily sports column and became a semi-legendary sports columnist. In 1964 Shrake moved to New York to join the staff of *Sports Illustrated.* Shrake returned to Texas in 1968 and continued his association with *Sports Illustrated* until 1979, while also writing novels and screenplays. Shrake began to write celebrity as-told-to biographies, beginning with his friend, musician Willie Nelson, which was followed by a biography of Barry Switzer, and most notably *Harvey Penick's Little Red Book*, which went on to become the bestselling sports book in American publishing history. He won the prestigious Lon Tinkle Award for Lifetime Achievement from the Texas Institute of Letters.

From *Strange Peaches*

(In the novel, John Lee Wallace is a TV western star who has been traveling around Texas filming a documentary to tell the "real" story of his home state and is in his hometown, Dallas, with his friend Buster, during the Kennedy visit to the city. Shrake gives the novelist's view of the assassination.)

I sat down on the couch and started pulling off a boot, but it would not come off, and the effort made me dizzy. I stamped my foot back down into the boot and put on my hat and ran for the car with the Bolex. I had trouble starting the Morris Minor and feared I might miss the motorcade, but the engine finally caught and the radio came on. Because of the cleared weather that caused me to stop and roll up my sleeves, the bubble top had been removed from the president's black Lincoln, the radio said. Plenty of Dallas cops had been at the airport, where the president had touched hands with admirers, and hundreds more were spotted along the route—a map of which had been printed in the newspapers—where three hundred thousand people were waiting to see the Kennedys ride past in the open car with Governor Connally and his wife, and Lyndon Johnson riding a few cars behind. I drove fast and parked the Morris Minor by the Texas & Pacific Railroad tracks on Pacific Street in a brown-brick warren of warehouses. As I stepped over railroad tracks and around boxcars, I saw a few people sitting on loading platforms eating sandwiches out of paper bags, but most of the workers had gone over a couple of blocks to Dealey Plaza to watch the president. The sidewalks at Elm and Houston beside the School Book Depository building were crowded, and I didn't immediately see an opening in the crowd across Elm in Dealey Plaza, so I trotted on along Houston to Main Street, going past the Criminal Courts building, looking for a view for the Bolex. At the corner where the cars were to turn north off Main onto Houston, I squeezed among people at the curb as I heard cheering and the motorcycles coming amid a roar that boomed toward me along Main like the roar of a football crowd. People flinched back from me, but it didn't matter. I leaned out and saw the motorcade approaching very close, first the motorcycles and then a pilot car of cops, then six more motorcycles and the white lead car with the sheriff and the police chief and the secret service boss, and finally four or five lengths back came the black Lincoln. Through the viewfinder I saw Connally's wavy blue-silver hair. Mrs. Connally was in the other jump seat, hidden from me. Now I found John F. Kennedy. He was on the side of the car nearest the curb, his eyes crinkled and puffy underneath, an arm on the rim of the open car, shirt cuff showing, wearing a dotted necktie, looking at the people along the curb as they applauded and called out to him. Kennedy was smiling a very good smile with very white teeth, and his wife was smiling almost the same way but without as much heart in it. His hair looked thick and healthy, and his face was tanned, and his eyes were clear and seemed to be enjoying what they saw. I was struck by how much like a movie star he looked, what an air of ultimate celebrity there was about him, everything put together exactly right and a good heart showing from that smile and the eyes, with his wife sitting there beside him trying to smile in the same manner. She had the look of celebrity, too, but more distant from the people and from life, a movie star's smile that was like a fence between her and the crowd; where her smile said *keep away I'm doing all right*, his said *we've got it going and I love it all.* They both looked as if they had been made up for the cameras, whites of the eyes sparkling, teeth polished, skin tinted copper, grander than the rest of us, but his face shone with intelligence and humor that broke through the celebrity mask without apology for the mask itself.

As the car pulled abreast, I didn't want to see him through the viewfinder, but the movie might require this vision. I lifted the camera and the president's gray eyes looked directly at me leaning out from the curb, took me all in with an instant's deep gaze, and looked squarely into my lens, and his lips moved a bit, the smile broadening, and he raised a finger and pointed at me, and I took my eye away from the viewfinder and looked straight into his eyes, and a communication flashed from him to me that said *there you are you freak what a time you must have among these people I like you for it don't give up.* At the same second he was sending me that message I was receiving it and thinking as well, with surprise and embarrassment that I would have such a thought, that if I'd wanted to hurt the man, I was so close I could crack his skull with a five-iron or couldn't conceivably miss with a pistol. But I could tell this perverted thought never reached him. He had trained himself to tune out small paranoias. I smiled at him as he looked at me, and his right eye squinted very slightly as if it occurred to him that he had seen me before but could not recall where. Then his eyes left me and held their place in the crowd that was moving past the car, and he said something to his wife, and she looked back, smiling with the flowers in her arms, but our eyes never met, and then the black limousine was going on down the road and I was looking at the back of the president's head.

I didn't wait to film Lyndon Johnson or any of the others. To me they were just politicians, not great men, just part of the crowd the same as me, and I still didn't care for all this big-ass politics, but I knew a great man when I saw one. Reflecting on the sensation of having connected in a mental relay with the President, and repeating to myself *there you are you freak*, I ran and caught up with the car as it turned onto Houston Street. I flipped on the long lens and got the Lincoln in my magnified sight again as the motorcade turned once more onto Elm at the red-brick Depository building and started down toward the triple underpass and the railroad trestle.

I knew it was a rifle shot. The sound is so common as to be quite distinctive. Later, many said they thought it was a firecracker, or the popping of a paper bag, or a backfire, but I knew at once that it was a rifle shot and I heard myself moan as I looked through the viewfinder and saw Kennedy raise his hands toward his throat and Connally starting to turn back toward him.

Pigeons flew up from the Depository building. The car kept moving slowly. I was expecting the car to leap ahead and disappear through the underpass, but it moved so very slowly.

POP

The car had passed an oak tree, and now people were screaming and had begun running around in Dealey Plaza, and the pigeons were circling in the sky, and cops in helmets on motorcycles were looking back and forth, wondering where the shots were coming from. Through the viewfinder I saw Connally sliding down, and Kennedy leaning to the left toward his wife, and the black Lincoln almost seemed to be stopping, edging down from slow motion into stop-frame.

"Go on!" I cried. "Goddamn you, go on before they kill him!"

Someone shouted into my ear. I kept my finger on the button. I was waiting for another shot. The first two shots echoed through the plaza, bounced off the county jail and the Depository, caroming around the plaza, and people were running, falling, dodging, throwing themselves onto the ground as in war movies. On the grassy knoll I saw figures scattering, and Kennedy continued to lean in the creeping Lincoln.

POP

Pieces of skull sailed out of Kennedy's head. A red spray flew out, as if a stone had been thrown into a pot of tomato soup.

"No! They've got him now!" I yelled.

At last the car moved. As the president's wife began scrambling out the back of the car, out of this blood and madness, at last the car moved forward, carrying its passengers too late down into the underpass.

I knew he was dead.

For a moment I kept the camera on the tumult around the plaza, on the stunned and frantic crowd, and then I took the camera away from my eye and began trotting toward the Depository building for no special reason other than that my car was over in that direction.

"He's shot! He's shot!" a voice cried.

Beside me a woman was screaming,

A man with a transistor radio at his ear said, "Well, I'll be damned, they've shot them all."

By then the plaza and the sidewalk in front of the Criminal Courts building were blurred with people running and milling, and voices rose in wails and sobs, and police with riot guns and helmets scurried in the smell of motor oil and exhaust fumes and human breath, and many people were shouting. I didn't look at the rest of the motorcade now passing, at the press buses or the cars of the functionaries. I jogged toward my car, my mouth open, staring straight ahead.

"He's shot!"

I jogged on.

"Grab that long-haired guy! Get him!"

He's shot! Who did it? Where are they now? Jogging along, I looked at the underpass, at the banks of green grass sloping down to the street. I looked up at the windows of the Depository and at the big Hertz sign on top. A weeping woman in a flowered hat looked at me and said, "I didn't want him to die." Jogging, I felt possessed by anger and terror, and the old dread was coming back, the knowledge of the presence of madness and murder as the forces that ruled us. Our truth was lunacy and our destination oblivion, and I had it in the Bolex.

He should not have tuned me out.

"Officer, get that long-haired fellow!"

"What's your name, Buddy?"

"Wallace."

"What's your business here?"

"I came to see the president."

"What kind of work you do?"

"I'm a cowboy."

"Okay, move along."

"Who shot him?"

"How the fuck do I know? Get moving."

I went across the street and passed beside the School Book Depository building. A man came out of the building carrying a Coke, and we looked at each other, and I went on down the narrow street among the warehouses and boxcars and railroad tracks, and the Morris Minor started at once. I put the Bolex on the seat. I didn't want to touch it any more right now. I turned on the radio. There was a report that the president, his wife, John Connally and Lyndon Johnson had all been shot. They were all in Parkland Hospital, the radio said. My God, all of them rolling on slabs down the hall where Ina Mac Leclaire had sat looking at the concrete with foolish attention. Listening to the radio, shivering, with a hot knot in my stomach, I drove out Cedar Springs to the Villa Lopez. Shot!

Hector, his wife, a busboy, and two waiters were sitting with the two club waitresses of Buster's morning bed. They were at a big table, with bottles of beer around a radio.

"He won't die," Hector said.

But I knew he was dead already. I saw his brains fly out.

I got myself a beer and sat down. By now the radio had explained that the president and Connally had been shot, but not the others. We kept sitting there, with our elbows on the table, listening to the radio. No customers came in, and nobody made a move toward the kitchen. Each of us recounted where we had seen the president that noon and how he had looked, as a sort of liturgy to reestablish his presence, a juju against death. In their minds the broken head was healing, the bullets becoming part of a myth, but I knew better. I told them the president had sent me a message, and what he had said, and they smiled, not understanding. Then the radio said Kennedy was dead. One of the club waitresses began to moan, and tears spurted from Hector's eyes. Everybody in the room was crying. We knew we were helpless. We knew what was waiting for us.

And we had a new king.

"That man can't be dead," Hector said with tears pouring down his face.

A new king in the land of death. A new Caesar from the provinces.

"God, he was pretty," said one of the girls.

"He was a good son of a gun," Hector said.

The new king was out there now at Love Field on that airplane waiting for the coffin, to take it back to Rome. ★

Dave Oliphant

Dave Oliphant received his PhD from Northern Illinois University. His prose and poetry have been published in *Southwest; Travois; Texas Stories and Poems; Southern Poetry Review;* and *Southwestern Historical Quarterly*. Under his Prickly Pear imprint, Oliphant edited and published *The Killdeer Crying* and *Washing the Cow's Skull*. His own poetry collections include *Lines and Mounds; Brands; Taking Stock; Footprints; Austin;* and *Maria's Poems*. He is considered an authority on Texas jazz, authoring *Texan Jazz* and *Jazz Mavericks of the Lone Star State*. He has been the editor of *The Library Chronicle*, the quarterly of the Harry Ransom Humanities Research Center at the University of Texas at Austin. Here, a "Cowtown boy" looks at Dallas.

Dallas

encircled by freeway loops,
has wished itself a Roman arena,
styled more after Texas Stadium
where gladiators   this time
Christians from Abilene or SMU
take on Lions Bears Rams
while the lawyer-merchant class
spies down, night & day
from box seats or tinted glass
spots the animals in goal-line stands
or last ditches along skidrow

below
          too are those looking for his-
tory   staring at tobacco stains on

Federal Building walks   visitors in from Boston
wondering
Is this where our hero bled?
buying his souvenirs   windows Xed
in snapshots where Oswald took his aim,
his bullet granting one more wish.

such carpet rides lift powerlines
overpasses skyscrapers high
rises, hopes of masses   recall
how they were raised for
days   driving here as a family when fall
trips to the State Fair were long & hard
where at last in Sears would try
the cowboy boots had wanted so   like Gene's
or Roy's   but with narrow feet
dad said no   they didn't fit
nothing in Dallas ever does.
it's Texas but then it's not
it isn't the West it never was
would have it moved to an eastern spot

partly this comes out as
the talk of a Cowtown boy   Fort Worth-Dallas
called twin cities yet rivals from the start
the real Texas   with cattle & horses
rodeos at Will Rogers Coliseum   versus
the Airport

typical of towns grown near   the closest father & son
are born to carry a rivalry on
Darío's red head sticks
out in any crowd

can be a pain   yet will claim him any time
like all of Texas   or so would rhyme
Big D's a sore thumb too
though giving credit where credit's due
both share winning points,
this city can boast of parks & lakes
are a blue-green sketch
for him to sit & draw   match
with watercolor or tempera paints
outdo this description   make a papa proud

carry him back to creeks shaded
by pecan & peach   running clear & cold
over smooth & green-furred rocks   fresh
by willows   in summer a cool conversing   traded
for memos typed at the Apparel Mart   to baskets sold
beside the bridge   their priceless wrinkled pits
brown-black nuts fallen at feet once bared to ripples   rainbow perch   a movement Darío can better catch,

need for that his art   need his love
needed Love Field too   a where to land
& seek for him athletic fun   a higher flight than had on fleetest jets   a swimming hole for deeper dives than
dips on tollway drives   a where to buy
western boots for the skinny kid
right for walking streets can recover that magic word will trim shed blood
like a genii whisked
back inside an olym-
pic lamp overrubbed. ★

Paul Crume

From *The World of Paul Crume:*
Two Ghosts in a Dallas Plaza, July 27, 1964

One sunny day in 1940, the late John McGinnis, professor of Shakespeare, master of the arts, and book editor of *The Dallas Morning News*, sat lolling at his desk in the old building at Commerce and Lamar.

The McGinnis physical stance was always one of indolence. He customarily sat reared back like this in his swivel chair. Only his roving eye told of a restless mind. The eyes this time lit on a new book on his desk, and he picked it up.

"This is a fine book, a surprisingly fine book," he said. "This young man will stand watching."

I took the book and looked at it. Later I read it, and it was a good book. As I remember it now, it had a red dust jacket.

It was titled *While England Slept*, and the author was a twenty-three-year-old man named John Fitzgerald Kennedy.

McGinnis had an eye for youthful talent, but if he could have looked ahead to the fulfillment of his prophecy, he would have dropped his teeth.

Who would have believed that this young man, known if he was known at all only as one of the sons of old Joe Kennedy, would become president of the United States, that he would be killed in Dallas within three blocks of the office where McGinnis then sat, and that the town would be setting aside there a plaza in his memory?

In the perspective of years, it seems strange. It seems strange, too, that all that history will remember Dallas for up to now—the actual founding of the city and the assassination—took place on the same little knoll overlooking the place where the river used to run.

In the perspective of years, too, Kennedy's book seems a little uncanny, for in it he began to speak for a generation.

The book spoke for all of us who sat by restlessly while the war took root in Europe and began to grow.

The book was more than a book to those who read it. It was a shared experience, and a great many young men felt a quick identification with Kennedy. He was a kind of symbol. In magazines and newssheets, they followed his story in the Pacific even as they fought Japanese, Germans, or boredom in their own small corners of the war. Their lives seemed parallel.

Later they watched the fledgling Kennedy steps in Congress, his surprising victory in the Senate race, and his sudden emergence as a national political figure. When he took office as president, it was as if a small part of each of his followers had gone with him. He spoke eloquently what many felt from afar.

In this, Kennedy must have been unique among all the presidents.

It is the reason that, as the years grow longer, two ghosts will hover in the plaza in Dallas, the ghost of a president and the ghost of old hopes and dead dreams. ★

Thomas Whitbread

Thomas Whitbread received his BA from Amherst College and his PhD from Harvard University before becoming a professor of English at the University of Texas at Austin. His poetry has been published in the collections *Southwest Writers Anthology; Washing the Cow's Skull; From Hide and Horn;* and *The American Literary Anthology* as well as in national journals and magazines, among them *Atlantic Monthly; Harper's; The Kenyon Review;* and *The New Yorker*. His first book of poems, *Four Infinitives*, won the poetry award from the Texas Institute of Letters and his second, *Whomp and Moonshiver*, co-won the poetry award from TIL. Another poet feels the sharpness of the cut.

November 25, 1963

The assassination of the President,
Among its many effects, confers upon
The slightest act of clarity of precision.
The sharpening of a pencil with a knife,
My old Scout knife, twenty years old, today
Sharply reseen as its invented self.
The cutting of my nails with old small scissors,
Trying, as always, not to hurt the quick.
Then encountering, taking up the pencil,
Tooth marks, not mine, and breaking it in half
In the frustration of rage, despair, and grief
At life not being as it ought to be.
She bit it. Our love should be alive, as he
Much more should be, and stupidly is not. ★

Bryan Woolley

[Editor's note: In Woolley's novel covering the 24 hours of November 22, 1963, this excerpt is "The Thirteenth Hour," told from different perspectives of people touched by the event in some way. In this excerpt, the italics indicate what is happening with President and Mrs. Kennedy; J. L. is an elderly oilman; Warner is a Texas legislator; Martha is a volunteer and activist of the right-wing congressman Bruce Alger; Tim is a radio announcer.]

From *November 22:* The Thirteenth Hour

Small children stood on the curb, holding a sign that asked him to stop and shake their hands. "Let's stop," he said. As he stepped into the street, the children charged forward, shrieking, almost sweeping him off his feet. He laughed and shook their hands. The children's parents stood on the curb, smiling, taking pictures.

She watched from the car. The wool suit had been a mistake. They weren't halfway there, and already she was wilting. The sun was so bright.

He returned to the car, still laughing, waving at the children. She put on her sunglasses. "Please don't wear those," he said. "The people have come out to see you." She laid the glasses in her lap, but raised them again whenever there were no crowds.

The car moved under an underpass. Its shadow was cool. The sun made all the difference. . . .

J. L.

He got the can opener and a can of Wolf Brand chili from the stock that he kept in the deep drawer of his desk. He opened the can and poured the chili into the pan on the two-burner electric hot plate on the file cabinet. He opened the top drawer of the cabinet and got the Jim Beam bourbon bottle and a tumbler and set them on the desk beside his bowl and the box of Sunshine Saltines.

It was the meal that he and Buck Pool had eaten just before Buck fell from the derrick, and J. L. thought of it as a sacrament, like the Last Supper of Jesus. He never varied the elements of the meal, not even the brand names, and whenever he ate it his mind dwelt on the details of that day. He remembered the heat of the sun and the sand and the small fire over which he and Buck had warmed the chili, and the flies that swarmed around them while they ate. "Funny thing about flies," Buck had said. "No matter how far out in the desert you get, they find you as soon as you open the chili can." That was about an hour before Buck fell off the derrick, and it was the last thing J. L. remembered him saying.

Anna had forbidden the sacred meal years ago, after a visit to the doctor, but J. L. had continued it at the office. He preferred eating it here, anyway, among the old photographs of him and Buck standing and grinning with some rig or another in the background, in the privacy of his own thoughts. It was easier to relive the details of Buck's last day without Anna whining about his health and Jonathan looking at him as if he were a little boy who had messed his pants.

The chili was still on the burner when J. L. heard the cheering and rolled his chair away from the desk. A sharp pain shot through his hip, but he hobbled to the window. The long cars of the enemy were passing below him, past buildings with faded red-white-and-blue bunting draped at the windows, and the cheers rose like a wind from the street. He could distinguish no words through the glass, but the faces along the sidewalk looked friendly. "They've come after our horses, Buck," he said aloud. He started to turn away, then saw the spot of pink and the roses. The Kennedys themselves. As if by accident, he focused on the couple seated in front of the Kennedys in the big car. Only slowly did J. L. realize who they were. John and Nellie Connally. "Son of a bitch!" he said. He stared at the car until it passed out of view, then hobbled back to the desk. He picked up the phone and dialed Quent Babcock's number. "Is Quent in?" he asked the secretary.

"No, sir. He's not."

"Where the hell is he? This is J. L. Fisher."

"Yes, sir. He's at the Trade Mart, sir. At the luncheon."

"When's he coming back?"

"I don't know, sir."

"Well, when you see him, tell him to get his skinny ass up here. He's got some tall explaining to do."

"Yes, Mr. Fisher. I'll give him your message."

J. L. slammed the phone down and checked the chili. It was almost ready to bubble. He opened the Jim Beam and filled his glass to the brim.

Warner

THE TRADE MART RESEMBLED A PRISON IN which a riot had erupted. Dallas and Texas police, wearing mirrored sunglasses and grim faces, seemed to surround the huge building, standing at parade rest, holding riot sticks ready. They reminded Warner of the Birmingham and Alabama troopers he had seen on TV during the summer, when the dogs and fire hoses were loosed against the Negro demonstrators. As he got out of the cab, two plainclothesmen charged into a group of white pickets who held aloft signs reading HAIL CAESAR and YANKEE GO HOME. After a brief, silent struggle, the plainclothesmen emerged, shoving ahead of them two young men whose hands were handcuffed behind their backs. Their mouths, and the mouths of the other demonstrators, were swathed with adhesive tape. Warner approached a Dallas officer who looked younger and friendlier than the others. "Why the tape?" he asked.

The officer's expression hardened. "You belong here?"

Warner showed his ticket.

"They say it's because they're being muzzled," the officer said.

"They told you that?"

"They wrote it on a piece of paper for a reporter. Dumb nuts. They've been here since seven o'clock this morning, just so they can get tossed in the jug."

"Well, two of them made it," Warner said.

"I hope they all get sunstroke," the officer said. "This ain't good. Somebody could wind up getting shot."

Beyond the doors, Warner found that he had entered a different world. The heat and noise and confusion outside dropped from his mind in the huge hall where layers of balconies rose to a glass roof high above and live trees grew around a clear pond and a fountain spurted almost to the skylight. A blur of yellow fluttered past his face. Other blurs of blue and green were flitting among the trees, above the white-clothed tables set for luncheon. Parakeets, flying free, as if in the wild. Men and women were already seating themselves. Waiters were already serving. Warner ventured uncertainly in the direction of the head table, wondering if he was supposed to sit in a particular place. A man at a table near the front rose and waved at him. Warner waved back, then recognized him as a member of the Dallas County legislative delegation. The man pointed to a chair next to him and motioned for Warner to join him. Warner lurched forward, smiling, his arm extended for the handshake. "Tom! How the hell you doing?"

The legislator caught his hand and pumped it vigorously, simultaneously grasping Warner's elbow with his left hand in the manner of Lyndon Johnson. "Sit with me," he muttered into Warner's ear. "I've hung myself up in a nest of Republicans, including a goddamn Bircher." He led Warner to the table and introduced him around. Warner nodded and shook hands, not bothering to remember the names. "Warner's a colleague of mine in the House. From San Antonio," Tom said.

"Well, we'll let him sit down anyway," one of the Republicans said. The others laughed.

"Nice of you to run interference for me, Tom," Warner said as he sat down. They laughed again. "Quite a place," he said. He scanned the rows of balconies. "What do they sell here?"

"Clothes," one of the Republicans said. "Women's clothes, mostly. This place is going to make Dallas one of the fashion centers of the world."

"Well, I'll remember not to tell my wife about it," Warner said, and they laughed.

"Oh, they won't sell to her, anyway. This place is just for store buyers. They have to mark it all up a few hundred percent before they pass it on to our checkbooks."

"Do these parakeets fly around in here all the time?" Warner asked.

"Not these particular ones," replied a dour man across from Tom. "These are special birds, trained to shit in Kennedy's soup."

The man didn't smile. The Republicans chuckled and glanced nervously at Warner and Tom. The dour man, Warner guessed, was the Bircher.

During the awkward silence that fell, Warner studied the head table. It was adorned with dozens of yellow roses. The presidential seal hung from the rostrum. Near it, a high-backed leather chair awaited Kennedy. Where would Yarborough sit? If he could catch the senator's eye during the luncheon and give him some signal, maybe he could win a handshake with the president. A photograph, even. State Representative Warner Barnhill shaking hands with President Kennedy would look great on his campaign literature.

"Where's Ralph going to sit?" he asked Tom.

"I've been wondering myself. I'm hoping he might invite me up and introduce me."

Warner laughed and slapped Tom on the back.

"Well, you're welcome to him," the dour man said. "And all the rest of his kind."

Anger rose in Warner's cheeks. "If you feel that way, why are you here?" he asked.

The man looked straight at him, unblinking. "To meet the enemy face-to-face," he said.

Martha

When Martha Babcock stepped from the cool of Neiman-Marcus onto the sunny sidewalk, the crowd almost overwhelmed her. Businessmen were dashing across the street against the red light and disappearing into the restaurants and office buildings. Teenagers were running to and fro in packs. A Mexican mother leaned against a wall, trying to shush her infant. An older child clutched her skirt and also cried. Martha thought the motorcade must be nearing the block. Then she noticed that the people were moving in all directions. Some were heading toward the parking lots. She looked at her watch, then held it to her ear. It was running. Cars were moving into Main from the side streets. A policeman stood in the intersection, whistling and waving them by. She went up to a man who was standing on the corner, waiting for the light to change. "Where are the Kennedys?" she asked.

The man looked surprised. "Why, right down the street there."

Martha tried to run, but her high heels and the crowd wouldn't let her. She moved along in a kind of hobbling jump toward the Adolphus, trying to remember whether Quentin had said he was riding in the motorcade or just greeting the Kennedys at the airport. The shopping bag containing her Joy perfume banged against her leg. But slow as her progress was, she was getting closer to the cheering. She scanned the crowd for protest signs, but saw none. At the Adolphus, she paused, panting, while the doorman opened the door for her. She dashed into the lobby. The place was empty. Even the desk clerk was gone. She turned. The doorman saw her coming and opened the door again. "Did any political groups meet here? In the lobby?" she asked.

"No, ma'am. Not that I know of," the doorman said.

"Where is everybody?"

"I guess they're out here, ma'am. Looking at Jackie." The doorman grinned. "I got a glimpse of her myself."

A block or two away, the cheering was getting louder. Martha dashed again, threading through the crowd, bumping people, not stopping to offer apologies or respond to theirs. A huge Negro woman turned from the street. Sidestepping to avoid her, Martha felt her ankle turn, and she went down. Two men in the crowd jumped to help. "Are you hurt, ma'am?" one of them asked.

"No. I don't think so," she said. "Just help me up, please."

The men grabbed her under the arms and lifted her. The heel of her right shoe was lying on the sidewalk. One of the men picked it up and handed it to her. "You sure you're all right?" he asked.

"Yes," she said. "Just embarrassed."

"Can we help you get somewhere?"

"No, thank you. I can manage."

The men released her and watched as she turned and moved slowly in the direction from which she had come. She was sure she looked silly, limping along, holding her heel in her hand. Tears were in her eyes. There were no protest signs anywhere. The Kennedys were getting away with it. . . .

Tim

"MORE COFFEE?"

Tim waved the waitress away. "I'll take the check."

She licked the pencil and totaled his tab and laid it face-down on the table. "Hurry back," she said.

Tim took a swallow of ice water to wash away the black-coffee taste and slid out of the booth. He took a quarter from his pocket and dropped it on the table.

"Everything all right?" the cashier asked him.

"Fine."

The breakfast had refreshed him. There was nothing left but to check at the police station for any arrests connected with the visit and make his routine rounds of the rest of City Hall and the courthouse. He didn't expect much. There was only one real story in Dallas today, and he had already covered his part of it. Maybe he could go by City Hall now, tape a few quotes by the mayor about the visit, check with the cops, drop the stuff off at the station, and knock off early. He checked his watch. No, the mayor would be at the Trade Mart now, probably presenting cowboy hats to Jack and Jackie. He might as well go back to the station and give the boss another opportunity to praise him for the job he had done.

In the Love Field concourse, Tim passed the booth from which he had phoned in his report. On an impulse, he went back to it, dropped in a nickel, and dialed. Lonnie answered.

"Tim! Where the hell are you?"

"Love Field."

"Hold on. The boss want to talk to you."

"Jesus Christ, Higgins!" The station manager's voice was trembling.

“Where the fuck have you been?”

“To breakfast, chief. You told me to.” Tim’s hand was sweating. The receiver was slippery. He switched hands and wiped his palm on his pants leg.

“Well, get your ass to Parkland,” the station manager said. “There’s been a shooting at Dealey Plaza.”

“What kind of shooting?”

“UPI just moved a flash. They say three shots were fired at the motorcade.”

“Holy shit!” Tim’s heart was thumping so hard that he raised his hand to his breast.

“That’s all we know. I hope to hell it’s wrong, but Lonnie’s putting the flash on the air now. Just get your ass to Parkland and find out if anybody’s there. Call as soon as you find out. Got that?”

“Yeah.”

“Well, move!

Tim slung his tape recorder over his shoulder and dashed to the parking lot. He glanced frantically along the rows. In a burst of panic, he was sure his car had been stolen, then spotted the station’s call letters on its door. His hand shook. He couldn’t fit his key into the lock. “Be calm!” he whispered. “For God’s sake, be calm!” He grabbed his right hand with his left and stabbed at the lock. The key slid in. He tried the stabbing motion on the ignition, and it succeeded again. At the exit, he thrust a five-dollar bill at the booth and screamed, “Keep the change! Let me out!” The startled attendant raised the barrier gate, and the car roared to Mockingbird Lane. Its tires squealed as it turned and sped toward Harry Hines Boulevard. Tim’s eyes flickered between the windshield and the two rearview mirrors as he wove among the semis and pickups and delivery vans. “Shit!” he screamed. “Fuck!” Actually, he heard himself saying, I hope there’s a little action. Something like that Stevenson thing, you know? Had he really said it? He had. To Callison and Hayes. Last night. The memory made him feel responsible for whatever he was about to see.

He expected guards at the entrance to Parkland Memorial Hospital, but there were none. A white ambulance stood in the parking bay designated ambulance only by the red neon sign. The big blue convertible was parked diagonally across the two bays marked emergency cases only, its trunk pointing toward the hospital door. Smaller convertibles and motorcycles were arrayed around it at crazy angles. The doors of all the cars were open. People milled and crowded and gestured.

Tim pulled onto the shoulder of Harry Hines and parked illegally. He walked casually up the driveway toward the buff brick hospital, expecting to be challenged and driven away, but no one seemed to notice him. He stopped a few feet from the edge of the crowd, afraid he would attract someone's attention. He could see nothing but the backs of men bending over the cars. "Oh, my God, Mr. President!" someone said. Tim caught a glimpse of Jackie's pink suit and heard her moan. Then the crowd seemed to start moving through the emergency doors.

As Tim was about to follow, more motorcycles roared up the drive, sirens wailing, and more convertibles. Henry Gonzalez alighted from one and joined the crowd. A policeman called Tim by name. "Where do you think you're going?" he asked.

Tim pointed at the hospital door.

"Try it and I'll kill you," the policeman said. ★

Elizabeth Forsythe Hailey

Elizabeth Forsythe Hailey was born in Dallas, Texas, the setting of her first novel, inspired by her grandmother's life, *A Woman of Independent Means*, written for her daughters, Brooke and Kendall. It was a best seller. With the support of her husband, playwright Oliver Hailey, she adapted it for the stage as a one-person play starring Barbara Rush. In 1995 it became a six-hour NBC miniseries starring Sally Field. Betsy and Oliver were not only partners in marriage; they worked as a writing team in film and television, most memorably on the TV soap opera *Mary Hartman, Mary Hartman.* Hailey has subsequently published three more best-selling novels: *Life Sentences; Joanna's Husband and David's Wife* (which she also adapted for the stage as a two-person play); and *Home Free.* Now widowed, Hailey, a member of the Texas Institute of Letters, lives in Studio City, California.

From *A Woman of Independent Means*

November 23, 1963
Dallas
4 a.m.
Dear Mrs. Kennedy,

I hope you will not allow the postmark on this letter to prevent you from reading it. Though I realize I am only one of millions who share your grief, I cannot help feeling a special kinship with you tonight.

You see, like yourself, I lost my husband when I was still young with children to raise, so I know how alone and abandoned you must feel at this moment. But unlike you, I could not direct my anger at an assassin—or at the city that harbored him.

I moved to Dallas as a new bride soon after the turn of the century and watched with pride as it welcomed people from all parts of the world, of every religious persuasion and political conviction. However, only yesterday did I realize we had also become a metropolis large enough to shelter a madman.

Today is my seventy-third birthday. Until now I have regarded every year added to my allotted three score and ten as a personal triumph. But tonight keeping vigil with my radio and television and reliving the horror of the last twelve hours, I feel for the first time that I may have lived too long.

I feel too close to you tonight to call you Mrs. Kennedy—and you are so much more a person than that title implies. Today the nation sees you only as the widow of our fallen leader, but in the weeks and months to come, you must remember what a remarkable woman you can and shall be in your own right.

Courage, *ma chère Jacqueline. Je vous embrasse de tout mon coeur.*

~Elizabeth Steed Garner ★

Nellie Connally and Mickey Herskowitz

Nellie Connally was born in Austin, Texas, met John Connally at the University of Texas, and the college sweethearts married in 1940. Nellie Connally served as the first lady of Texas from 1962 to 1969. At the time of her death in 2006, she was the last surviving occupant of the presidential limousine that carried John F. Kennedy when he was assassinated in Dallas, Texas, on November 22, 1963. Mickey Herskowitz, one of the country's most prolific writers, has written bestselling autobiographies with Dan Rather, Mickey Mantle, Howard Cosell, Nolan Ryan, Bette Davis, and Gene Tierney. His other works include books with or about: Gene Autry; Bear Bryant; Tom Kite; John Connally; Prescott Bush, father of George H. W. Bush and grandfather of George W. Bush. Herskowitz is an award-winning sports columnist for the *Houston Chronicle* and lives in Spring, Texas. He has been a longtime Connally friend. Here Nellie gives her own unique view of the assassination, from the car itself, and then at Parkland Hospital.

From *Love Field: Our Final Hours with President John F. Kennedy*

The President made a great speech in Fort Worth, then out to the cars. This ride, I was put in the car with the Johnsons, since the bubbletop car was not used in Fort Worth and only three could sit in the back seat. Senator Yarborough, who had refused to stay in the president's sitting room on the plane with the governor of Texas, and has twice insulted the vice president of the United States by refusing to ride in the car with him, had been told by the president, in Fort Worth, that he would ride with LBJ or not ride . . . so he was in the car with us.

I chose to ride in the front with the secret service men and did. The crowds to the airport were friendly . . . cheering. There were no inappropriate signs, no unpleasantness with the governor and the Kennedys. We were on our way to Dallas for a luncheon at the Trade Mart and then off to Austin for a reception at the Governor's Mansion that I had been planning and working on for days.

Was everything in readiness at the mansion, I wondered? I felt sure I had everything arranged, even down to what the children would wear, but what hostess doesn't have a qualm or two when she is going to entertain a president and first lady?

The day had changed from gray and rainy to a beautiful, bright, sunshiny day—perfect for a caravan. Before we landed I asked John if I could ride in the car with him in Dallas, he said, "Certainly." When we landed the president's bubble top was being removed and I would have ridden without asking. We got in the jump seats right behind the driver and the secret service man in the front. I was on the driver's side. Mrs. Kennedy got in the backseat directly behind me, and the president sat behind John. The back seat was slightly raised, so that the Kennedys sat a little higher than we did. John and I were in separate seats with a space between us and were not quite as mobile as Jack and Jackie.

We were indeed a happy foursome, that beautiful morning. I had my yellow roses in my arms and Jackie had her red roses in hers. The crowds were the largest yet and the friendliest. I did so hope Dallas would give the Kennedys a warm and very cordial welcome, and I wanted the Kennedys to respond with equal warmth and friendliness. I could not have been more pleased. I felt tingly all over with the pride of a mother whose children are performing just as I had hoped and the relatives were terribly pleased.

We had pleasant banter back and forth between the four of us, but mostly the Kennedys were responding to a rousing ovation, and John and I were just smiling with genuine pleasure that everything was so perfect. We had passed through the downtown area and its great, surging, happy, friendly crowds.

I could resist no longer and turned to the president and said, "Mr. President, you certainly cannot say that Dallas doesn't love you." He smiled in obvious pleasure at the accolades . . . then I heard a loud, terrifying noise. It came from the back. I turned and looked toward the president just in time to see his hands fly up to his neck and see him sink down in the seat. There was a no utterance of any kind from him. There was no grimace and I had no sure knowledge as to what the noise was.

I felt it was a gunshot and I had a horrifying feeling that the president had not only been shot but could be dead. Quickly, there was a second shot. John had turned to the right at the first shot to look back and then whirled to the left to get another look to see if he could see the president. He could not so he realized the president had been shot. John said, "No, No, No," was hit himself by the second shot, and said, "My God, they are going to kill us all," wheeled back to the right, crumpling his shoulders to his knees in the most helpless and pitiful position a tall man could be in.

I reached over and pulled him to me and tried to get us both down in the car. Then came a third shot. With John in my arms, and still trying to stay down, I did not see the third shot hit, but I felt something falling all over me. My sensation was of spent buckshot . . . my eyes saw bloody matter in tiny bits all over the car. John was bleeding badly all over the front of his shirt.

He was not moving in my arms. I thought my husband was dead. Mrs. Kennedy was saying, "Jack, Jack. They have killed my husband. I have his brains in my hand."

The secret service man said to the driver, "pull out of the motorcade," and on his radio phone told the motorcycles preceding us—"to the nearest hospital." We pulled out of the line and drove at a terrific speed toward the nearest hospital. John moved slightly and I knew he was still alive. I started whispering in his ear, "Be still, it's all right, be still, it's all right," all the way to the hospital.

I never looked back after John was shot. But on that terrible, heart-breaking ride I could see the crowds on the right side of the road streaking past, and I couldn't help but think what an awful sight to see, two women holding their lifeless husbands in their arms, streaking down a roadway in utter horror and disbelief. I did not know until later that President and Mrs. Kennedy were in the floor of the car with a secret service man on top of them and that I was the only woman holding her dying husband in her arms for the startled people to see.

We made a sharp turn and I almost lost my balance with the heavy weight of my husband, then, almost miraculously, we were at a hospital. The car screeched to a stop. Secret service men were everywhere. They were crying, "Mr. President," they were begging Mrs. Kennedy to get out of the car. They were crawling all around us, but no one was taking John out of the car. I knew he was alive and, in my heart, I knew the president was dead. I wondered how long I must wait before I could insist that someone tend to my dying husband.

Suddenly, John heaved himself up out of my arms and fell over toward the door. Then some very kind and thoughtful man picked him up in his arms like he was a little baby and put him on a waiting stretcher. They ran off down the strange corridor with him and I ran along behind the stretcher. What I was running from and what I was running to I did not know, but run I must, that much I knew.

The world seemed to be crashing all around me and there was nothing I could do about it. My husband was still living; I knew because he was groaning and saying it hurts as we ran along the short corridor. They took him into a small room on the left and left me standing, as alone as I have ever been, outside a closed door.

There was much confusion behind me, and they were wheeling President Kennedy into the room on the right just across from John. The hall was full of secret service men, nurses, doctors. Someone brought two straight-backed chairs, one for Mrs. Kennedy and one for me. They were placed immediately outside the emergency room doors, the bullet-ridden bodies of our husbands on the other side.

Someone rushed up to me and said I would have to go to the office and fill out an information blank on John. How totally incongruous, I thought. I did not budge.

Mayor Earl Cabell, of Dallas, appeared and asked me if there was anything he could do for me. I was, even at that strangely unreal time, so grateful for a friend. John's assistant, Bill Stinson, traveling with us on the tour, had been a few cars behind and had now reached Emergency Room 2. A masked nurse or doctor brought me one gold cufflink. I looked in the room and saw John pale, but moving on the table.

Mr. Stinson came out and said my husband had said to him, "please take care of Nellie." Could anything nicer happen to a wife than to have her husband, in that pathetic shot-up, half-conscious state, think of her concerns and welfare? He is a remarkable and so very wonderful man. That one statement would sustain me now and could if need be comfort me forever.

The unreal horror of the hallway in Parkland Hospital outside Emergency Room 1 and Emergency Room 2 is indescribable—doctors, nurses, hospital personnel, secret service, machine guns, strange faces and occasionally a familiar face. Mrs. Kennedy, knowing her husband was dead . . . me, wondering, how long could my husband live? Several times I got out of my chair and pushed open the door to Emergency Room 2 to see for myself if John was still with me. A groan, the twitch of a foot would momentarily satisfy me. I wondered too, did they have adequate and good doctors tending John or were they all across the hall with the president?

Suddenly, they wheeled my husband out of the emergency room and someone said they were taking him to surgery. Again, not knowing my destination, I ran after a stretcher bearing the struggling to live body of my husband down strange corridors. Then I waited a lifetime, an eternity for the certain news of life or death. There had been hope up to now in the unknown, actual knowledge was to be so very sure!

An earlier fear was to be alleviated soon. A very kind and excellent thoracic surgeon, Dr. Robert Shaw, was explaining the terrible wound in the chest. Bill Stinson was in the operating room and was sent several times to me by Dr. Shaw with reassuring information during the very long operation. The wound was not as bad as anticipated. Miraculously, the bullet had missed fatal arteries.

The pierced lung was repaired; the sliced out rib would eventually take care of itself. My husband, barring complications and helped by a wonderful physical condition, plus his strong will, would live. We were almost sure. The path of the bullet was explained to me. It entered his right shoulder, took out five inches of his fifth rib, pierced his lung and exited just below the right nipple of his chest. (It passed through his right wrist and lodged in his left leg.) . . .

As soon as I knew that John would live, I called the children. They, of course, wanted to come immediately to Dallas. I asked them to stay in Austin and when their daddy could see and talk to them I would have them brought to us. Mark and Sharon were content enough, with the knowledge that John would be all right, to remain in Austin, but not our oldest, John III, who came that very day to Parkland Hospital and stayed with me to watch for himself the progress of his father. . . .

People were not satisfied with the reports concerning the recuperation of the governor. The doctors, (and two of John's aides) Julian Read and George Christian, were giving medical reports constantly. The press was not satisfied. The people of Texas were not sure. I was asked to make a television statement, knowing everyone would be sure that I was giving them the truth. I had made no statements. I had many requests. I knew I had participated in a tragic moment in history. I had heard and seen so much.

Until the proper authorities had questioned me, I decided to make no statements of any sort. This was different, however, and after first saying, no, I decided maybe I could. I agreed, only if I could read my statement and not be asked questions. . . .

It was perhaps one of the most difficult things I've ever had to do. I could neither hold my paper nor read it. So, I put it on the table before me, put on my glasses and read my prepared statement. I had such a strong feeling about how warmly Dallas had received the Kennedys that I felt the need to tell that to the television audience, not only in Texas, but all over the United States and wherever the telecast might go. I removed my glasses and made my plea for a city that was taking too much abuse for something it did not do:

> "The governor is now apparently out of danger," I began. "He asked me to tell everyone he is going to be all right. John had a very, very close call. We thank God he was spared.
>
> "The governor is in good spirits and we are deeply appreciative of the care he has received at Parkland Hospital from the doctors, the nurses, and the staff.

> "Governor Connally has asked me to convey to the people of Texas, the nation, and the world our deep sorrow over the tragedy which struck at one of President Kennedy's most triumphant hours. Words cannot fully express to Mrs. Kennedy and to the President's family our feelings, which we know all Texans share.
>
> "Our son, John, will be our personal representative at the funeral of the President in Washington on Monday. The governor joins me in asking that all Texans observe the day of mourning in memory of the President."

I asked that well wishers send a donation to the family of Officer J. D. Tippit, who was shot to death trying to arrest Lee Harvey Oswald, rather than continue sending flowers and gifts to the hospital. Then I looked up from my statement and added, quietly:

> "We had been with the President and Mrs. Kennedy during the tour. It had been a wonderful tour and when we arrived in Dallas, and were in the motorcade, the people could not have been friendlier, the crowd more wonderful or more generous in their reaction to the President. The city of Dallas does not deserve to be blamed for this ghastly crime." ★

Bob Huffaker, Bill Mercer, George Phenix, and Wes Wise

Bob Huffaker has been an army officer, policeman, English professor, and editor for *Texas Monthly; Studies in the Novel;* and the *Modern Humanities Research Association Annual Bibliography*. Author of *John Fowles*, he has published in the *Dallas Observer; True West; Texas Parks and Wildlife;* and *Southern Humanities Review*. Bill Mercer, voice of the Dallas Cowboys, Texas Rangers, the University of North Texas, Southwest Conference, and the Chicago White Sox, was also an internationally popular wrestling announcer. Both the Texas Radio Hall of Fame and baseball's All-Pro Hall of Fame honor him. He wrote a history of the LCI, a type of navy combat landing craft on which he served in World War II. He is a professor of broadcast journalism at the University of North Texas. George Phenix, cofounder and publisher of *Texas Weekly* and for twenty years the state's top legislative newsletter, has published several weekly newspapers and served as aide to Senator Lloyd Bentsen and Congressman Jake Pickle. Wes Wise was a pioneer of baseball play-by-play and writer for *Sports Illustrated; Time;* and *Life*, as well as mayor of Dallas for five years and president of the Texas Municipal League. He won three Dallas Press Club "Katie" awards and Southern Methodist University's Southwest Journalism Forum Award. As mayor he guided Dallas through integration, helped save the Texas School Book Depository, and led the city in reclaiming its national reputation.

From *When the News Went Live: Dallas 1963*

Bob Huffaker broadcast the motorcade, then the scenes at Parkland Hospital and police headquarters, from where he narrated Oswald's murder on CBS.

My colleague Jim Underwood, who had been in an open press car close behind the limo bearing LBJ and Yarborough, had vaulted out of the convertible at the sound of three shots from overhead. An alert marine veteran, Jim had been in the thick of the Guadalcanal invasion, and he kept his wits. When JFK's Lincoln braked hard, then screamed away onto Stemmons Freeway, Jim ran with police as they combed railyards above the triple underpass. He joined officers converging on the Texas School Book Depository, then raced to a telephone to make the first report. Underwood, KRLD's assistant news director . . . gasping for breath, made this live report:

"As the car I was in made the turn at Elm and Houston and started down for the triple underpass, I heard three loud shots seemingly from right over my head. There was so much confusion with people running, I thought at first that some of the spectators farther down the street toward the Elm Street underpass had been hit. I saw many of them throw themselves flat on the ground, and the police officers started blowing whistles and running for the scene. I leaped out of the car I was in the parade and ran for the scene also. . . . Evidently police believe that the man who fired the shots is still in the Texas School Book Depository building at the corner of Elm and Houston in downtown Dallas."

Outside Captain Will Fritz's office, Bill Mercer was reporting as our live CBS camera showed the tense and raucous scene in the third-floor hallway. Bill was struggling to keep his balance in the increasingly unruly crowd of reporters who were converging from all over the world. Dick Wheeler was feeding radio reports from the press room down the hall from Captain Fritz's homicide office:

"This rifle is of a six-point-five millimeter size . . . believed to have been manufactured about 1940 in Italy. The rifle was a heavy weapon; it had a bolt action, it had a four-power scope mounted on the top of the rifle, and we understand that there was one live round of ammunition found in the rifle when it was recovered from the sixth floor of the building from which the assassination is believed to have taken place. This weapon has not yet been definitely tied in with the suspect who is being held now in jail here and in Captain Fritz's office. He is being taken back and forth. Our district attorney, Henry Wade, about five minutes ago entered the office of Captain Will Fritz."

Jay Hogan had stuck by the radio desk, and at midnight before he could rest, the old sage ended his last newscast in verse:

It has all been a long dark night since last Friday,
And daylight hours are still needed here.
But Mr. President, may we say one last goodnight,
When there must be perpetual light
In your faraway Valhalla, wherever,
Reserved for souls like yours.
And we can still see your bright smile
And your vigorous stride
Through some mystic Elysian fields.
Good night, Mr. President—good night.

Bob Huffaker writes, Saturday, November 23:

At some point Cronkite spoke of "crank-filled Dallas." We locals regretted that reputation and felt that it was not entirely deserved. . . . Dallas was beset by some mad right-wingers whose brazen demonstrations had hijacked the city's reputation. By that delirious morning, most of the Dallas media had fielded a bomb threat or two, and police were getting edgy about security, as it became apparent that frenzied reporters were getting out of control. Guards stood watching entrances, but in the Police and Courts building, lots of people were coming and going to and from other offices.

Nelson and I were sitting shoulder-to-shoulder on the floor, propped against a wall facing the elevators. We watched their doors sliding open and shut, disgorging loads of people. We were talking about the loose security, noticing how people were roaming the halls without any ID check. . . . I said, "What if somebody stepped out of an elevator and started raking the crowd with a submachine gun?" We watched those sliding doors for a moment, then looked at each other, got up without a word, and moved from the line of fire. From then on, we kept ourselves and our camera crews in the safest positions we could get. We were at the epicenter of a nation rocked by grief and anger, and we began to move with care.

During our vigil at police headquarters that afternoon, Wes Wise was following Oswald's trail through Oak Cliff after a stubby fan of his named

Jack Ruby had delayed him at the assassination site. Bill Mercer reported from among the wreaths accumulating there. And high over Dealey Plaza, George Phenix's pilot popped a window open and slipped the plane sideways into a bank as George filmed the line of cars that seemed to reach the horizon, creeping past JKF's death scene, clogging traffic all the way from Deep Ellum.

Bill Mercer broadcast Oswald's midnight news conference, then the mourning in Dealey Plaza. He writes:

Kneeling in the police basement assembly room after midnight, I looked up directly into the face of the man accused of killing President John F. Kennedy. Here was Lee Harvey Oswald at his peculiar showing before the press. Hundreds of reporters from all over the United States and some from foreign countries were pressed shoulder to shoulder, trying to ask the question of this former U.S. Marine, former resident of Russia, who it was alleged had pulled the trigger on his Mannlicher-Carcano 6.5 rifle three times. He had been hunkered down in his window seat on the sixth floor of the Texas School Book Depository overlooking the presidential motorcade as it was leaving downtown Dallas. . . . Oswald seemed perfectly at ease as questions were fired at him. Had he shot the president? Had he shot Patrolman J. D. Tippit? Who was he working for? Why did he want to kill the president? On and on went the questions for several minutes. I was not concerned about asking any while the media gang hurled theirs at this man with the bruised face. "A policeman hit me" was his answer to how the obvious blow to his face occurred. As police concluded the "press conference" and Oswald started to turn, I stood up with the mike in my hand. When he was again asked, "Did you kill the president?" Oswald looked toward me and said, "No, I have not been charged with that. In fact, nobody has said that to me yet. The first thing I heard about it was when the newspaper reporters in the hall asked me that question." He pronounced it "axed," I looked into his face and said, "You have been charged." Oswald looked a little blank and moved his head backward in a natural reflective response. And then he was taken back to his cell on the fifth floor. Sunday he would be dead.

Wes Wise wrote "Ruby and I" for When the News Went Live:

THE DAY AFTER THE ASSASSINATION, SATURDAY, Eddie Barker had called me into his office. "I want you to take your camera," he said, "and try to trace Oswald's route as close as you can."

I drove one of our Pontiac Catalina wagons with KRLD News lettered on its side along with the CBS eye. My first stop, the already infamous Texas School Book Depository, was only a few blocks away. I angled the shiny mobile unit into the curb across from the building on what is now the extension of Houston Street. At the time it was not a through street, serving as a drive toward the railroad tracks at the rear of the building. I picked up the two-way radio microphone, made contact with the base station, and gave a brief radio report on the scene there.

The "grassy knoll," as early reports had christened it for all time, was already covered with every variety of flowers as well as cards and letters honoring the fallen president. Moving among those flowers and mourners, my colleague Bill Mercer did a memorable piece that day, reading cards on the wreaths and interviewing Dallasites there to pay their respects. Near the gathering banks of flowers, I finished my radio dispatch, placed the mike back in its cradle, and like so many Dallas citizens at those moments, sat in deep reflection.

"Hey, Wes."

The voice came from the direction of the railroad tracks at the rear of the building. I turned to see the portly figure of a man in a dark suit, half-waddling, half-trotting, as he came toward me. He was wearing a fedora-style hat which would later become familiar and famous.

Oh, my goodness, I thought. *This is all I need right now—to stop and take time to talk to Jack Ruby.*

Ruby was the ultimate news reporter groupie of his day. Invariably he would show up at sports events, major automobile accidents, even many funerals and weddings. He was truly a news-hound man-about-town. True to form, he had been at police headquarters the night before when Bill Mercer crouched below the accused assassin, whom police had brought out for the media to see. Jack Ruby was maintaining his reputation for being where the action was.

He leaned into my driver-side window. "Isn't this awful? Where were you when it happened?" he asked.

"I was at the Trade Mart," I said. Then I remarked that I had taken film of the western saddles that were to have been gifts from the City of Dallas to the Kennedy children, Caroline and John-John. Tears welled up in Ruby's eyes.

"I just hope they don't make Jackie come to Dallas for the trial," he said. His voice broke as he added, "That would be terrible for that little lady."

I excused myself and drove on to film Lee Harvey Oswald's rooming house. Reflecting on that conversation, I have wondered whether Ruby was hoping that I might do a radio interview with him. Such a thing would have been a historic part of that sad weekend's coverage. ★

Larry A. Sneed

Larry A. Sneed holds a BS degree from Indiana State University and two graduate degrees from the University of Georgia. He has been a high school history teacher in the Newton and Gwinnett Public School systems in Georgia for thirty years. He and his wife Barbara live in Lawrenceville, Georgia.

From *No More Silence: An Oral History of the Assassination of President Kennedy:* Jim Ewell: News Reporter

The *News*, as I recall, assigned about nine reporters to different areas of Kennedy's appearance in the city. I was assigned to watch his arrival at Dallas Love Field.

That morning, when I arrived at the airport, there was a large turnout of school kids and rank and file people. There had been a light rain, and as we waited for Air Force One to arrive coming over from Fort Worth, it seemed that when he was spotted the crowd stirred when Air Force One approached Love Field, the clouds parted, the light rain quit, and the sun broke out, making it a gorgeous morning. I thought it was most fitting that all this occurred for the arrival of Kennedy. . . .

The crowd was absolutely charmed by the president and the first lady. He was so taken aback, I think, by the reception he got that that's when he broke away from the secret service and went to the fence line and went down the row. I was watching all of that, having a pass to be inside the gate as a member of the press. Once the arrival and the greetings were over, the motorcade got started on the appointed route that would take them to downtown Dallas. Now that was the end of my assignment because all I could tell the rewrite people was what I've already described here. I thought it was a very, very warm reception! They had to be impressed.

So I routinely got back in my vehicle and, instead of trying to follow the route of the motorcade . . . I took the route back on the Stemmons Expressway. My intention was to go back to the pressroom at police headquarters.

Had everything gone routinely I would have simply called in my notes to a rewrite unless they would have wanted a separate story about what I had seen at the airport. That wasn't likely because there were bigger and better things to come ahead in the Kennedys' visit in Dallas. But the setting was absolutely very cordial. In fact, I think the Kennedys were still swept up in this warmth in the motorcade through downtown Dallas. Now that's the real irony of it! At the west end of downtown Dallas was the sniper waiting for the Kennedy motorcade. They were just a jump from getting back on Stemmons. That's where I met the Kennedy motorcade . . . but it was stretched out, speeding, and I knew immediately that something was wrong, although I had no radio communications at the time to tell me what had taken place. I could see the secret service agent hanging on the turtleback. My first thought was that a pedestrian crossing Stemmons had been hit by one of the cars in the motorcade because that was five lanes each way, and pedestrians were crossing that ten lane freeway to get on the side closest to the motorcade. I could not believe that people were risking their lives to cross the freeway in front of my traffic and the northbound traffic. That was the only thing that I could think of that had happened. . . .

I turned on my car radio, and I remember that KLIF, the lead spot-news radio station in those days, owned by Gordon McLendon, had a female telephone clerk in the Dallas Police dispatching office saying that shots had been fired at the Kennedy motorcade. So I just went up Commerce Street and then went down into the basement of police headquarters where two days later Oswald was murdered by Jack Ruby. As I got out of my car, parking it there in the press lot, Sergeant Jerry Hill, who at one time was a former *Dallas Times Herald* crime beat reporter, came running out, and I said, "Jerry, what the hell's going on?"

And his exact words were, "Some son of a bitch just shot Kennedy!" He then ran around and jumped into a black and white squad car; there was a uniform officer behind the wheel already, so I just ran over there and got in the backseat. This officer drove us back from east to west through downtown on the most circuitous route I can recall, and we were back there at the School Book Depository probably in less than two minutes.

When we arrived, the police had their squad cars across the intersection in kind of a circular position. There were officers still standing behind and in front of the squad cars training their shotguns up to the windows of the School Book Depository. We found ourselves standing right out in the middle of the intersection of Houston and Elm. I'm going to say this was probably inside of fifteen minutes from the time that I had seen the swarm of people near the triple underpass and heard on the radio that shots had been fired. It happened that quickly!

I had been a newspaper reporter for about fifteen years, and I thought that I was a seasoned professional. But now that the weight of this was coming down on me, I was beginning to get woozy. I felt light-headed. But I do remember standing there with the police not knowing if they still had somebody trapped upstairs, or if there was going to be an outbreak of gunfire if they exposed somebody. And again, we didn't know how badly hurt Kennedy was, at least I didn't. . . .About that time there was a commotion around one of the squad cars, and we could hear a radio saying that an officer had been shot in Oak Cliff.

Looking back on it, and this is more amazing to me right now, all this time I had never made contact with my city desk. I did not have a walkie-talkie like they do today. They didn't know where in the hell I was! They probably didn't know where the hell a lot of the *Dallas News* reporters were because events were moving so quickly that you had to stay up with it, and you had no time to stop and let them know what you were doing and what they could do to help you.

But, nonetheless, I left the scene of where an attack, a shooting attack, had been staged against the president of the United States to go to investigate, as a reporter, the reported shooting of a Dallas police officer. Now keep in mind, in 1963, you DID NOT shoot policemen! You DID NOT strike policemen! Only in very rare cases did you strike a police officer. Look at what's changed since then! And yet, I left the location at the School Book Depository and jumped into a car driven by Captain Westbrook with Sergeant Stringer. I rode in the backseat as we sped across into Oak Cliff by taking the Houston Street Viaduct right beside the *Dallas News*.

When we arrived in Oak Cliff, I got a chance to go into a convenience store . . . and I did get to make a phone call to the city desk asking them to send me a photographer. They didn't know what I was doing in Oak Cliff. This particular editor was too overpowered by what was going on downtown to pay any attention to what I was trying to tell him, and I know I came out saying, "You know I've got to have a photographer out here!" ★

W. G. 'Bill' Lumpkin, Solo Motorcycle Officer, Dallas Police Department

I HEARD THREE DISTINCT BANGS WITH NONE of them being together or anything like that. . . . The shots came from behind where I was and, as I mentioned, I thought it was a motorcycle backfiring at first, till I turned back and saw the commotion in the president's convertible. I wasn't sure at the time what it was, but it later turned out that it was his wife on the back. There was no problem seeing the car, but at the time, I just saw a figure. Then Chaney rode up to Curry and probably told him that the president had been shot.

We were still stopped at that time, and then Chief Curry comes on and says, "Let's go boys!" I'm not sure that there was anything said other than that and, of course, we headed for Parkland because we knew in case something happened, that was where we were supposed to go.

We went under the triple underpass and took the entrance ramp to Stemmons Freeway. At that time, Sergeant Ellis stopped there at Stemmons. Leon Gray, Chaney, and myself escorted the parade on to Parkland Hospital by way of Stemmons, to Industrial, Industrial to Hines, Hines to the entrance into the back of Parkland.

We were going fast, very fast! I'm going to say we might have hit speeds up to 80-85 MPH on Stemmons. We were going just as fast as we could get the car to go. I saw the limousine behind us, and I noticed this secret service man hanging on the back of it with his coat hanging, and I was amazed that he could hang on. When we got to Hines, there was a railroad track, and I know that I got airborne. I'm sure that I was out front and Gray and Chaney were behind me. More than likely they got airborne, too. You didn't have a lot of space over on the other end, and when you land to turn, I knew that if I went down I'd probably get run over. But you train and you know that you can drag your footstand without going over as long as you don't go over too far. Oh, you're going to get some sparks and some noise when you go over that far, but unless you get on some oil or sand or something like that, you can stay up. But it was a fast ride!

Nothing much goes through your mind at a time like that. You know that you've got a job to do, and you want to do your job well. When we came off of Stemmons, we were supposed to turn into Market Hall. Sergeant Striegel and some other officers were there, including some other jockeys, and he came out into the street waving because we were going too fast and that we were supposed to pull in there. I guess he hadn't heard that the president had been shot, and you have to worry about him not getting too far out into the street. But you're concerned with just doing your job when something like this happens. After it's over, then you have time to think about it.

When we turned into the hospital, there was only a certain amount of parking space back there. Since I was in the lead, I stopped to get off my motor to make sure that cars that didn't belong there didn't come in because I was in a better position to react. So I stopped probably a couple hundred feet from the emergency entrance. When the last cars that I knew and the last jockeys came in, I stopped traffic. We had to get all that secured. I was the only one right then. . . .

I was probably still in the process of just getting off my motor when the limousine came by. I saw the president slumped down, and I saw Lyndon Johnson. Johnson was like a ghost; I thought he was shot. He came by after the president riding in a different vehicle, if I remember right. . . .

I didn't see much of the president other than he was just slumped down and that he had been shot, and that his brains had been blown out. I must have seen that somewhere along the way. I know they kept wanting to know whether Kennedy was going to make his speech at the Market Hall, and finally this three-wheel officer came on and told them that his brains were blown out, and he wasn't going to be there. But nobody would make a decision to tell them that he wouldn't be there, and this kept coming over the radio: "Well, is he going to be able to make the speech?" We knew that he was dead.

We stayed out at Parkland for a long time, and then they sent us downtown to guard Oswald. We were on the third floor where they had him. There were quite a few of us up there and, of course, there were newspaper reporters and cameramen from all over.

The scene up there was wild! Absolutely wild! Forcefully, you had to keep them back. It was hysteria! Just asking them to stay back wouldn't do. They weren't responding! I can remember the cameras back then had big battery packs that looked like they weighed eighty or ninety pounds. I imagine they probably weighed a lot less than that, but they were big things, and their TV cameras were monstrous. Anyway, I can remember this guy that must have weighed over four hundred pounds who wouldn't stay back, and finally, I just had to put my fist into his stomach because I weighed only about 160. Manners were a thing of the past, or courtesy. You could ask our own people to do something and they would try to cooperate with you. In fact, we knew quite a few of them personally. But the national people, a lot of them just didn't want to do what you asked them to do. They decided that they knew how close they could get a lot better than you did. But there was such a rush and, I guess, everybody wanted a story. I've been involved in escorts for Elvis Presley and the Beatles, and those were wild. But the crowds were young. These were adult people that you expect more out of. ★

Bobby Joe Dale, Solo Motorcycle Officer

IT WAS A FAIRLY ROUTINE OPERATION FOR US. We knew to keep the crowd away, that the sooner we could block off the entrance to Parkland up to Harry Hines about half a block away the better off we'd be. The problem was clearing the emergency entrance. Everybody began showing up as the news got out while we were trying to gain control of the scene. It was hectic there for two or three minutes! At that time, some three-wheelers arrived and helped clear it all the way to the street. Meanwhile it was hard to tell somebody that needed to go into the emergency room that was sick or injured that the hospital was closed.

It was so hectic I can't remember everything in sequence. I went over to the limousine and saw a secret service man starting to put the top up. "Help me secure this," he said, since it was heavy and in sections. Blood and matter was everywhere inside the car including a bone fragment which was oblong shaped, probably an inch to an inch and a half long by three-quarters of an inch wide. As I turned it over and looked at it, I determined that it came from some part of the forehead because there was hair on it which appeared to be near the hairline. There were other fragments around, but that was the largest piece that grabbed my attention. What stood out in my mind was that there was makeup up to the hairline. Apparently he had used makeup for the cameras to knock down the glare. It was fairly distinct where it stopped and the wrap of skin took up. Other than that, nobody messed with anything inside the car in any manner, shape, or form. Nobody said, "Clean this up!" We then put the top up and secured it.

After that Chief Curry came back out and said that he wanted me to monitor the radio from my motor sitting right outside the emergency entrance. My job then was to relay information to him and then from him back to the dispatcher's office. Later he told me to advise the people at Market Hall that he would not be there. When they inquired why, I just repeated what he told me. I wouldn't tell them that the president had been hit.

Later on Curry told me that he was going to back his car up and move LBJ back to Love Field and for me to get somebody else to help escort him but not to use sirens. We were to pull the escort at a steady speed, use red lights and whistles and not to attract any more attention than was necessary. He said, "When you see us load, I'll give you a signal and we'll leave. Go through the crowd!" He didn't want to have to stop. So I got Brewer and told him that we were fixing to take some people back to Air Force One and that it was to be a guide escort only, braking at intersections with whistles and no sirens. . . .

As I recall, there were two vehicles that went back to Love Field: Curry's and another. Somewhere in the time between Parkland and Love Field the U.S.

borders had been closed, and then it dawned on me: why have they not said the president was dead? It was obvious; we knew what had happened. But then it all came to me as to why things are done that way. If there had been a conspiracy, the United States was vulnerable to attack and there would be nobody to order retaliation. I guess I didn't realize the magnitude of all this until that time. ★

Vincent Drain, Special Agent, FBI

Vincent Drain attended what is now the University of North Texas in Denton, then took civilian pilot training for the air corps. After being washed out due to imperfect vision, Drain taught school and coached football prior to his joining the FBI in 1941.

"WE HAD NO INDICATION THAT OSWALD WAS dangerous. . . . I didn't consider him a threat then, and it was my responsibility to notify the secret service of any potential problems. I would have gotten the information from Hosty's supervisor but didn't and, of course, that's part of history. . . ."

The last time I had seen the president was when I sat with the Rayburn family at the funeral of Sam Rayburn in 1961. I was with the president at the church, at the cemetery, and then at the Rayburn home before he left for the West Coast.

On November 22nd, 1963, I'd gone down to get a sandwich for lunch and had returned to my office at 1114 Commerce Street after the parade passed to continue doing dictation. As was the usual manner, we monitored the police radio. From that it was flashed that the president had been shot and that they were en route to Parkland Hospital. I knew where they were taking him because I had been privileged to sit in on some meetings with the secret service the previous four or five days in the event that either he or the vice president were shot. Quickly I took my car and went to the basement and arrived there maybe ten minutes after the president had arrived. The secret service had sealed off the area making it somewhat difficult to get in unless you had some assistance.

Knowing the personnel at Parkland, particularly the security chief and the doctors, I was fortunate to have run into the security chief and a doctor, so I was able to go directly into the trauma room without any problem.

When I arrived in the trauma room, the doctors were working with President Kennedy. They were trying to do what they could to stop the gurgling sound he was making by performing a tracheotomy on him. Despite the fact, as I later learned, that he was dead, his body reflexes were still working.

I wasn't up close to the body, but I could still see fairly well the large amount of blood from the head wound. The head was badly damaged from the lower right base across the top extending across the top of the ear. It appeared to me as though the bullet traveled upward and had taken off the right portion of his skull. It may have been the security officer or one of the other officers who gave me a portion of the skull which was about the size of a teacup, much larger than a silver dollar. Apparently the explosion had jerked it because the hair was still on it. I carried that back to Washington later that night and turned it over to the FBI laboratory. . . .

I was able to talk to the doctors the minute I got there. One of them told me that the president was dead and that it was just a matter of time to make the announcement. Maybe I'm assuming something here, but as I recall, a Catholic priest had been sent for, and I was under the impression, or someone told me, that he hadn't been pronounced dead because they wanted to give him the last rites before and after death. At that time, I believe there were three secret service agents, Mrs. Kennedy, and later the priest who were in the trauma room. I left as the priest was administering the last rites. . . .

After I learned that he was dead, I proceeded to leave the area and went outside where I talked with Senator Ralph Yarborough and two friends of mine: Congressmen Jim Wright and Ray Roberts. I'd called the office for some walkie-talkies since I thought that we'd be unable to use the telephones, so as I waited, I talked with them.

It became apparent that they were getting ready to pack the president for transfer to Washington, so I began to leave because in Texas, when a person was shot like that, back then the justice of the peace had jurisdiction and normally there would be an autopsy. But in this case, the secret service said there wasn't going to be any autopsy. As a result, it was a Mexican standoff at the hospital. Finally the secret service prevailed and the body was taken to the airplane where later President Johnson was sworn in. I then followed them in my car.

Johnson hadn't been sworn in yet when I arrived at Love Field. Twenty or twenty-two seats had been taken out of Air Force One to make room for President Kennedy's body for the flight back to Washington. Many people were there, all of them trying to get the best vantage point including reporters and cameramen.

I went to the steps of the plane and no further because it was too crowded inside, and they needed all the area there as they were waiting on the federal judge to arrive to swear in Vice President Johnson, which occurred shortly thereafter. When the body arrived, they had to take the coffin with the end up, straight up, to get it into the plane, which is really a difficult thing to do. Finally, when that was accomplished and Mrs. Kennedy and the Kennedy aides had boarded joining President Johnson and his aides, they took off for Washington.

Earlier in the evening, about 8:00 o'clock, the division chief had talked to me on the telephone and informed me that the FBI in Washington demanded that we bring to them for examination the rifle, the revolver that was used to kill Tippit, as well as the different paraphernalia such as identification cards and other small items that Oswald had on him. I discussed it with the police chief and told him that we'd keep the chain of evidence intact and that I would pick them up there myself and wait for them until they were examined in Washington then bring them back. So it was turned over to us.

By the time we got it all boxed up, it was near midnight. Meanwhile Washington was calling down about every fifteen minutes wanting to know where the material was. All of a sudden I learned that neither American nor Braniff had any flights to Washington out of Dallas after midnight. We were told that the FBI in Washington wanted the material by morning if we had to walk it up there. That's being facetious, but . . .

Fortunately the commanding general over at Carswell in Fort Worth happened to be a good friend of mine and was head of SAC (Strategic Air Command) at that time. So I called him and was told that the president had asked him to give us all the help that we needed. Another agent took me to Fort Worth where they had a C-135 tanker plane and crew ready.

It was a little scary on the way up because I was sitting up on the deck with the pilot, the copilot, and the engineer. This was an empty plane, and they were flying high and really letting her go. During the flight, they let me listen to all the short wave broadcasts about the British, French, and Canadians calling their troops and the submarines going to sea because they were afraid the Russians might attack.

When we landed at Andrews Air Force Base, an unusual thing happened. I had never been in the military service since I had joined the FBI prior to the war and had stayed continuously through then. When I had arrived at Carswell, the commanding general was at the plane with two of his aides. As I got out of the car, they all saluted, so I told myself that I'd better salute back. When I arrived at Andrews, the commanding general there also saluted. I'd gotten used to saluting by that time, so I saluted back.

The commanding general said, "Mr. Drain, we wondered if you would relinquish this airplane for us if we'd furnish you a good airplane to go back in when you're ready to go?"

Of course, I didn't know that it was my airplane to relinquish in the first place, so I said, "Sure, I'll turn it over to you now if that's what you want me to say. But I need one when I get ready to go; I mean really go!"

He said, "We'll give you a good fast airplane," which was an understatement. He gave me his card and I was taken by helicopter over to the Justice building and landed on the White House lawn. During this time, I had an armed guard from the air force until I got safely into the Justice building.

I talked to Mr. Hoover briefly and then watched them do a lot of the experiments such as firing the rifle, looking for prints, ballistics markings, hairs, fibers, blood stains, and anything else that later, down the road, might be relevant to evidence which could be used in the prosecution.

By around midnight on Saturday night, they had the plane ready to go, so I called the commanding general. He sent a helicopter which then flew me to one of those fast F-104s. When we came back, we came back in a hurry! Upon arrival in Dallas, I went directly to the police department and had just turned over the evidence to the police chief on Sunday morning at the time Oswald was killed by Ruby. They then had full custody of it. ★

Hugh Aynesworth (with Stephen G. Michaud)

Hugh Aynesworth has been a sports editor on a small-town daily in Arkansas and a national correspondent for *The Washington Times*, and dozens of stops in between, including *Newsweek* bureau chief and investigative team leader for ABC's *20/20*. Famous among his fellow investigative reporters for his prowess as an interviewer, he's been a Pulitzer Prize finalist four times (once for his Kennedy assassination reporting). He also covered the Martin Luther King Jr. assassination, as well as the Branch Davidian standoff and tragic fire in Waco in 1993 and the 1995 bombing of the Alfred P. Murrah Federal Building in Oklahoma City. Beginning in 1983 Hugh teamed up with Stephen G. Michaud on a series of best-selling books, including *The Only Living Witness*, the definitive study of serial killer Ted Bundy that the *New York Daily News* called one of the "ten best true-crime books ever written." *JFK: Breaking The News* is the sixth collaboration of Aynesworth and Michaud. These are startling views from the people in the trenches and those reporting it. It shows the shock, the professionalism and some shenanigans of the journalists.

From *JFK: Breaking the News*

As Oswald's rapid rifle shots echoed across Dealey Plaza, the scene erupted into chaos. Terrified people ran in every direction, looking for cover, screaming, "Oh no! Oh no!" Some, frozen by fear, stood and wept on the sidewalks. Others tried to shield their children.

I had no idea who was shooting at whom, or why or where, except that it sounded very close. . . .

"The president's been shot!" someone yelled. Sirens blared. "I saw Lyndon get hit too," another man added.

That's when instinct kicked in. I was a reporter and I knew I had to start interviewing people—record the event. I remember three or four persons pointing toward the upper floors of the book depository. Police officers, sidearms drawn, approached the building. Others followed a motorcycle cop who ran his machine up the grassy area to the west of the book depository.

"My God, this is really happening!" I said to myself as I reached in my pockets for paper to start taking notes. The best I could do was a couple of utility payments I hadn't yet mailed, and a third piece of paper, a letter from Empire State Bank thanking me for opening an account.

Next I found I had nothing to write with. In the midst of the pandemonium, I spotted a scared little guy, embraced tightly by his dad—not yet crying, but aware things were more tense than he liked. He forced a half smile and I noted in his hands he gripped a fat jumbo pencil, like the ones kids used to use in early grade school. It had a little American flag on the eraser end.

"Hey, I'll give you fifty cents for that pencil," I said, perhaps a little too eagerly. His father gave me a look of deep suspicion.

"Sure!" said the boy, grabbing my quarters as I clutched the ridiculous-looking pencil and plunged through the panicked crowd toward the book depository, grabbing witnesses and digging willy-nilly into the mass confusion.

Reporters tackle national disasters such as the Kennedy assassination with much the same verve as firefighters rushing to an eight-alarm blaze. The pressure is often immense; sometimes the memories hang around for a long, long time.

You wouldn't want to do it every day.

"It took me a long time to get over the assassination," CBS newsman Bob Schieffer told me. "I was so emotionally spent. Not until 9/11 did I again have that same kind of feeling as I covered a story."

Of all the reportorial skills that come into play when covering a major catastrophe, the abilities to think quickly, act on instinct, and improvise are among the most important.

Bob, then a reporter for the *Star-Telegram*, was handling the rewrite desk telephones on Friday afternoon when a woman called to ask if anyone at the paper could give her a ride to Dallas.

"Lady," Schieffer told her, "you know the president has just been shot, and besides, we're not a taxi service."

"Yes, I heard it on the radio," she replied. "I think the person they've arrested is my son."

Schieffer told Marguerite Oswald to sit tight, he'd be right over. But first he needed appropriate wheels. "I had this little Triumph TR4 sports car then," he said. "I didn't want to drive her over in that."

So he asked the paper's automotive editor, Bill Foster, what kind of car he was reviewing that week. When Foster said he was driving a Cadillac, Schieffer decided that the two of them would chauffeur Mrs. Oswald to Dallas.

Schieffer made sure the *Star-Telegram* received full value for the favor. On the way to Dallas he conducted the first interview with the accused assassin's mother. Then he used her to penetrate the inner offices of the Dallas police department.

"I just walked up to the first uniformed Dallas policeman that I saw," he recalled, "and said, 'I'm the one who brought Oswald's mother over. Is there any place we can put her so these reporters won't talk to her?"

The officer found a cubby hole in the Burglary and Theft Bureau where Schieffer stashed Marguerite and then surreptitiously passed back and forth into the hallway, gathering up *Star-Telegram* reporters' notes, which he then phoned back to the city desk from his hideaway.

Mrs. Oswald had astounded Schieffer with her conversation on the drive from Fort Worth. "It was a great lesson for me," he explained, "because she said such outrageous things. She was already talking about how the wife would get all the money and people would feel sorry for her. Marguerite was the mother and she would be forgotten.

"I just thought, this poor woman is under such strain and such pressure, she can't mean what's she's saying. Some of the stuff I didn't put into the Saturday paper. Well, it turned out that she was obsessed with money. It was all she had on her mind. Even years later she'd call me at CBS and say, 'Is there any way CBS would pay me for an interview?' Oh, she was awful. She really was a villain."

Sunday afternoon, Schieffer was part of another *Star-Telegram* coup.

Over at the *News*, Jack Beers had just developed the extraordinary photo of Ruby about to shoot Oswald that he took in the City Hall basement.

Standing next to him in the dark room was Bob Jarboe, an AP photographer who doubled as a wire photo operator.

Beers seemed transfixed by the image, Jarboe recalls.

"He just sort of fell back against the wall, and told me to make two prints for him." But Jarboe also made two prints for the AP, which sent the stunning photo out over its wires within the hour.

A short while later, Bill Rives, assistant managing editor at the *News*, approached Jarboe with a smug expression. "We've got a picture I bet you'd love to have," Rives smiled.

"You mean this one?" Jarboe replied, holding up a copy of the Beers photo.

"Rives went bananas," Jarboe remembers.

When the Beers picture popped up on the AP machine over at the *Star-Telegram* that Sunday afternoon, managing editor Loren McMullin decided to use the photo to anchor a special Sunday afternoon edition, essentially scooping the *News* with its own picture.

"We were just thrilled to death," said Schieffer, who phoned in copy from Dallas to the newsroom in Fort Worth for the special edition. "We all just worked our asses off. Everybody had no sleep. We were all worn out. But man, when that *Star-Telegram* truck came by, I just grabbed a bundle of those papers and took 'em right down there to Dealey Plaza.

"I don't think journalism is like that anymore."

Eddie Barker, news director at KRLD-TV, gambled big time and came up a winner. Broadcasting from the Dallas Trade Mart on Friday, Eddie got a tip from a doctor at Parkland that Kennedy was dead a few minutes before the official announcement. While the competition over at WFAA-TV was forced to wait for confirmation, Eddie broadcast what he had.

"When I announced this over the air," he told me, "the network panicked. The validity of my source was questioned. However, I knew this man was trustworthy, so I kept repeating that the president was dead."

In a later *Journalism Quarterly* article, Richard K. Van der Karr called Barker's announcement one of the most important events of the weekend. "It will certainly be one of the greatest snap evaluations of a source in the history of broadcast journalism," wrote Van der Karr.

Bert Shipp, assistant news director at WFAA-TV, got the same tip about the same time—from a man all the media trusted, Sheriff Bill Decker. Decker had told Shipp there was no way the president could be alive, that the entire back of his head had been blown off. Shipp told his bosses, vouched for the source, and begged them to broadcast it.

But he was told the news director had provided a recent directive: "No more dead people mentioned without death certificates."

Associated Press reporter Mike Cochran's long weekend started Thursday night in Fort Worth, where he helped host White House staffers, the press corps, and assorted federal agents at the Fort Worth press club bar. They partied until three in the morning, when Mike went home.

However, some secret service agents and reporters weren't quite ready to stop. Several of them went on to The Cellar, a late-late place. Disclosure of this revelry got the group in serious trouble after the assassination next day.

Friday morning, Mike was at Carswell Air Force Base to make sure Air Force One lifted off on time, with the president inside. He filed what was called a floating bulletin, a brief advisory to editors that "President Kennedy left Carswell at 10:45 this morning."

Driving back from the military base, Cochran and his wife, Sondra, were caught in a hopeless traffic jam. So they went to breakfast, and she dropped Mike off at the AP office in the *Star-Telegram* building. Minutes later Cochran heard a copy boy screaming, "The president's been shot!" as he ripped the AP bulletin from the wire machine. Mike tried to reach Dallas by telephone, but the lines were jammed. So he teamed up with *Star-Telegram* reporter Jack Tinsley and some other of the paper's staffers and drove away in Tinsley's car, racing for Parkland Hospital.

"We got within two blocks," Mike recalled, "and couldn't get any closer. Tinsley just abandoned his car in the middle of the street, and we ran on up. When we walked in the front door here came a wave of nurses.

"My memory of this is so vivid. Three or four nurses were just sobbing, almost hysterical. You don't often see nurses get that emotional. I said,

'Kennedy's dead.' We learned later that Malcolm Kilduff had just announced it."

Cochran stayed at Parkland long enough to file an update on Governor Connally's condition, then headed for the AP's Dallas office, where he worked through the night. Sunday morning, he drove home to Fort Worth to shower and change his clothes. He expected to head back for Dallas where he was to relieve fellow reporter Peggy Simpson on the AP's Oswald watch at City Hall.

Instead, Sondra greeted him at the door with news that Oswald had been shot, so Mike hurried back to the Dallas office to man the desk.

"We started getting telephone calls from papers, wanting a story on Jack Beers' 'Pulitzer' photograph," said Cochran. "I hadn't seen it. Then Bob Johnson, the Dallas bureau chief asked, 'Can't we do a story on this thing?' We were just besieged by calls. A couple of hours later people started asking about Bob Jackson's 'Pulitzer picture.' I wrote a piece about the two without ever having seen them. I really can't remember what I said. Of course, I can't remember a lot about that weekend. . . ." ★

John Mark Dempsey

John Mark Dempsey is an associate professor of radio-television at Texas A&M University-Commerce. He has published four books, *The Jack Ruby Trial Revisited: The Diary of Jury Foreman Max Causey; The Light Crust Doughboys Are on the Air!; Eddie Barker's Notebook: Stories That Made the News (and Some Better Ones That Didn't!);* and *Sports Talk Radio in America: Its Context and Culture.* Dr. Dempsey has worked in commercial broadcasting as a radio news anchor and producer for the Texas State Network in Dallas since 1998. He holds bachelor's and master's degrees from East Texas State University and a PhD from Texas A&M University. His wife, Tricia, and children, Jenny and Mike, live in rural Delta County, east of Commerce, with assorted horses, cats, and dogs. He is a nephew of Max Causey, the first juror selected for the Jack Ruby trial. *The Jack Ruby Trial Revisited: The Diary of Jury Foreman Max Causey* includes Causey's diary kept during the trial, a memoir written shortly afterward, excerpts of the questioning of jurors, letters, and selected news articles. The final drama of the assassination was played out in a Dallas courtroom and in one juror's experience.

From *The Jack Ruby Trial Revisited: The Diary of Jury Foreman Max Causey:*
Jim Lehrer, *Dallas Times Herald,* Feb. 21, 1964, Juror Faces Lonely Life Until Joined by Another

Max E. Causey has taken sixteen steps into a world where there are dominoes and playing cards, but no opponents—where there is much to say, but nobody to say it to.

Mr. Causey, the first juror accepted by both sides in the historic Jack Ruby murder trial, is now in virtual seclusion.

And he will remain that way until the second juror joins him. It could be a while.

After Judge Joe B. Brown swore the Garland man into jury service Thursday afternoon, court bailiff Bo Marbra unlocked a door behind the judge's bench.

The door opened to the [sixteen] steps up to the jury deliberation room. Mr. Causey passed through the door and Mr. Mabra followed.

In the room at the top of those stairs the Ling-Temco-Vought electronics man will spend his days—alone. At night, he will sleep upstairs in the special jury quarters.

The only companion Mr. Causey will have will be Mr. Mabra, who, fortunately for the juror, is a warm, friendly man with a likable personality.

But Mr. Mabra will only be around for conversation at meal times and just before both men go to sleep at night.

The rest of the time, the bailiff will be in the courtroom carrying out the other duties for the court and judge. In his pocket will be the key to the door behind which Mr. Causey is lodged.

The deliberation room, a half-floor up and behind the courtroom on the second floor of the Criminal Courts building, is anything but spacious—22 by 12 feet, to be exact.

In the middle is a long table with twelve chairs around it and against one wall are a sofa and two stuffed chairs.

Off to one end is an even smaller room—12 feet by 12 feet—where there are tables for playing games. Domino sets and cards are available. Maybe Mr. Causey plays solitaire.

If Mr. Causey wants to see the outside world from his locked room, he may go over to the east wall to the windows. The view, however, is not the choicest. He will see only the two-yard breezeway between the Criminal Courts building and the Records building next door. Its main inhabitants are pigeons.

Mr. Causey probably will be allowed to read, but only on matters that have nothing to do with the Ruby case or anything remotely connected with it.

The only times he will see outside people—until the second juror joins him—will be those three times a day he goes out for something to eat.

Bailiff Mabra usually takes locked-up jurors out to a nearby restaurant for all meals, rather than having them sent up from the Dallas County jail kitchen.

Unless there is a special change for the Ruby case, this is expected to be the practice for Mr. Causey.

At night, the thirty-five-year-old juror will follow the bailiff to the jury quarters on Floor 7-M in the courts building. Mr. Causey will take one of the fourteen small, clean bedrooms, furnished with a Hollywood bed and a lavatory.

The beds have pink bedspreads. The walls of the room are green.

Mr. Mabra will have a bedroom close by.

If Mr. Causey wants to send messages to his wife or business associates, he will have to do it through the bailiff. Mr. Mabra will have to tell Mrs. Causey, for instance, how many pairs of socks, shirts, and other clothes her husband will need—to begin with.

It will be Mr. Mabra also who will arrange for the delivering and picking up of Mr. Causey's personal effects, including other items he will need to live away from home for a while—razor, toothbrush, etc.

A lonely life is in the offing for Max E. Causey. And how does he feel about it all?

He won't be able to answer this or any other question until he and eleven other persons answer the more vital question of the guilt or innocence of Jack Ruby. ★

From *The Diary*

[Thursday] 20 February 1964 11:25 A.M.

I WAS CALLED TO THE COURTROOM AND WAS seated in the box. DA Wade questioned me on capital punishment in proven 1st-degree murder cases. After approx. 20 min. of questioning, the state accepted me as a juror. At this time (11:45 A.M.) Judge Brown recessed for lunch. I was admonished about discussing the case and released without restraint until 1:45 P.M. I had two hours for lunch but no appetite, so I walked the several blocks from the courthouse to midtown where I entered the Eatwell Restaurant on Main Street and ordered a bowl of tomato soup and a glass of ice tea. By the time I had finished the lunch it was 12:45 P.M., still an hour to kill. . . .

Many thoughts went through my mind, the most recurring one was that I must not allow myself to become confused or mixed up when I face the rapid fire questions of the chief defense counsel, Mr. Melvin Belli. All I intended to do was to state the truth of what I had seen, heard, and read since Nov. 24, 1963, regarding the case. . . . I certainly didn't have any desire to serve on this jury . . . I told myself that on this fact I really need not worry, that the defense would find reason to strike me from qualification as they had the previous 23. . . .

Having reassured myself that I would not really be found qualified (or acceptable) by the defense, I glanced at my watch for probably the hundredth time in the past two hours. It was 1:20 P.M.: twenty-five more minutes. I returned to the courthouse, rode the elevator up to the sixth floor where I used the restroom . . . I checked my appearance in the mirror to make certain my lunch wasn't showing and strolled back to the elevator which carried me back to the first floor. . . .

It was 1:50 P.M.; my three-and-one-half days of waiting were up. If I were lucky in an hour or two at the most, I would certainly be disqualified as a juror and dismissed to return home to my family where I would assume my regular routine. The defense lawyer who questioned me was Mr. M. Belli, but not at all like what I had expected. I was not ill at ease under his questioning. He was courteous, charming and eloquently smooth. The questioning was thorough and deliberate. . . .

My juror qualification questioning by the defense continued for approximately one hour. At about 2:50 P.M., Mr. Belli asked Judge Brown if he (the defense) was to be allowed more than the prescribed 15 inexcusable strikes [peremptory challenges], to which Judge Brown answered something to the effect that he could not foresee this possibility. . . . After a three- or four-minute conference, Mr. Belli rose to his feet and passed the juror qualification acceptance back to Mr. Wade. Mr. Wade rose to his feet and stated that the state would accept me as a juror. He then sat down. Mr. Belli again rose to his feet. He stated that the defense had no real objection to me as a juror and that I was acceptable.

In my thirty-five years on this planet, I have never been exposed to a more devastating shock than at that moment. I suddenly felt as though the ceiling and all the upper seven floors of the building had collapsed on my head. The next thing I remember was Judge Brown speaking to me, to swear me in with the oath of a juror. I remember trying to stand erect but Judge Brown allowed me to remain seated for the oath, and considering my real shock of the moment, this was indeed a kind gesture.

The juror's oath was administered to me and the court bailiff, Mr. Bo Mabra, quickly escorted me through a locked door immediately behind the judge's bench, up a winding flight of stairs to a large suite which was to be used as the jury deliberation room. This was to be my daily habitat during the many days ahead, while downstairs the long, slow deliberate jury qualification continued in the quest for the other eleven jurors. . . . The bailiff made me as comfortable as a man in my present state of mind could be. He hurriedly returned to the courtroom, locking the massive door at the foot of the stairs. The locked door served a dual role; one was to keep anyone from approaching me, the other was to restrain me if need be. . . .

The next hour was spent in familiarizing me with my sleeping quarters. These were far short of the comforts of home but fully adequate for their purpose. The bedroom was about 7 feet by 7 feet with a single built-in, comfortable bunk bed, lavatory, and commode. There was a shaving mirror over the lavatory. A tiled shower was next door to my room. The bailiff slept just across the hall. His room was a carbon copy of mine with the exception of a telephone. This telephone was our emergency link with the outside world. Although I was at no time allowed to talk to anyone over this phone, it was some comfort to know that it was there in the event that an emergency should arise within my family. The bailiff called my wife to inform her that I was to be detained for a while. He gave her his phone number for use in emergency situations.

At about 7 P.M. the bailiff suggested we go out to dinner. I welcomed the thought of getting out in the open but I didn't feel hungry. We stepped out of the courthouse into the cold, damp, and dark night, as a fast-moving cold front had engulfed Dallas since I had been out at lunch. We walked the three blocks to the Dallas-Jefferson Hotel on Houston Street where we ordered dinner. The food, under any other circumstances, I'm sure would have been delicious, but I could only pick at it. I had no desire for food at that time. We returned to our sleeping quarters at about 8 P.M. By this time, my wife had brought the luggage that I required for a prolonged stay. The luggage was left at the sheriff's office where we picked it up.

Bo Mabra (the bailiff) and I talked a while and very soon I found that he was a very friendly, considerate, and likable person, ideally suited for his job. He was to be my nursemaid, den mother, chaplain, doctor, and most important, my only link to the world beyond for the days ahead. . . . Neither of us dared to predict how much longer it would take once the jury was finally picked to hear all the evidence in court and reach a decision as to the innocence or guilt of Mr. Ruby.

I went to bed that first night contemplating what lay ahead. I wondered who might be the 2nd juror, how long would it take to pick him (or her), would it take as long to get the 2nd as it had to get me. . . . I slept fitfully until 3 A.M., at which time I looked at my watch and thought. Would this night never end? For the next 3 hours, I frequently catnapped, waking up each time thinking that it was all a bad dream. At last, I heard Bo in the shower next door to my room. Thank heaven it was morning.

My second day started with my shaving and a quick shower. By the time I had dressed, Bo had brought coffee down from the jail kitchen so we enjoyed a cup before departing outside for our breakfast. As we left the courthouse, the press and spectators had already begun to assemble with still two hours before the court was to reconvene in the jury selection. As we stepped out onto the street, it was bitter cold. Snow had sprinkled the autos that were parked on the street. An occasional snowflake still fluttered from a dark, overcast sky. . . .

With lunch recess over, Bo returned to the courtroom. I tried to kill time by playing solitaire. After numerous failures to beat "sol," I had just given up, when I heard the lock turn on the massive door at the foot of the stairs and the noise of the excitement in the court filtered up the stairs. I heard footsteps. This time it was evidently more noise than Bo had usually made each time he visited me. Excitement swelled within me as I anticipated company. I was really in luck. Not only was Bo bringing me a companion, but I quickly recognized him as one of the prospective jurors whom I had lunched with only two days ago. Mr. Allen W. McCoy was the second acceptable juror. I quickly greeted him with a warm handshake and a hot cup of coffee. My "solitaire" wait was over. I looked at my watch. It was 3:55 P.M. After 25 hours, I now had a companion to share my waiting. . . .

Monday, 2 March 1964

Today starts the 3rd week of jury selection and it is my 11th day to be locked up. I never realized before so completely the meaning of freedom. However, it is not the 11 days just passed that causes me concern. It is the many long days ahead during the selection of the two [remaining] jurors and the trial itself that I fear. Monday, 2 March passes without another juror being selected. This was my worst day since the day I was accepted. The time period to conclude this entire affair may exceed my worst fears. We now have gone through 2 days of questioning since juror number 10 was chosen on Friday.

This group of jurors is outstanding. The intelligence level is well above that of the average jury. So far, everyone has been very congenial, and considerate of each other. We have a good cross-section from all walks of life. The personalities of a couple are such that the morale of the group is kept high through joking and witticisms. We joke about how long the trial will take with what we hope is vast exaggeration, anything for a laugh. For the most part, everyone is holding up as well as could be expected under the circumstances. . . .

Saturday, 14 March 1964

We arose around 7:30 and proceeded to breakfast by about 8:30. By 9:00 A.M., we had finished breakfast and returned to the deliberation room. While I was in the restroom, the rest of the jury elected me foreman. However, I wouldn't accept this election and a new election was held. Again, I was elected foreman. I suppose it was my seniority that drew this honor. After two hours and twenty minutes (11:20 A.M.), we had agreed unanimously on a verdict. I walked down the familiar twenty steps to the foot of the stairs and knocked on the door. Quickly, Bo Mabra opened the door and I told him we had reached a verdict. He told me he would have to call the judge to the courtroom.

It was approximately 45 minutes before the court could assemble to hear our verdict. At approximately 12:15, we were seated in the jury box for the last time. Judge Brown asked if we had reached a verdict, and we answered or nodded affirmatively. Then, Bo came over and I handed him the charge, which had been filled in and signed by me. We all looked at the defendant as the judge read the verdict aloud to the court. "We the jury find the defendant guilty of murder with malice and affix his punishment at death." There was no visible emotional change in the defendant. He was ushered out by the deputies and immediately Mr. Belli was screaming like a wild man. Pandemonium broke loose in the courtroom. The cameramen climbed the walls to get shots and microphones up to Mr. Belli and others to Mr. Wade. Simultaneous with this pandemonium, Judge Brown was dismissing us and thanking us for the service we rendered as jurors. . . . When I called my wife it was the first time in 24 days that I had been allowed to talk directly to her. It was wonderful to hear her voice and be able to speak to her. . . . No matter how historians reflect on the events of the past four months, whether history commends this verdict or condemns it, only time will tell, but as for me, my mark (insignificant as it may be) is niched in history. My "Trial of a Juror" is finished. ★

Part Three

The Rebuilding and Growing—1964 to 2008

Lon Tinkle

Lon Tinkle (1906–1980) was born in Dallas and made his home there with his wife Maria Ofelia Garza. He graduated from Southern Methodist University with bachelor and master's degrees and completed post-graduate work at the Sorbonne, University of Paris, with a diplôme de phonètique, and then Columbia University. He was a literary critic, writer, and teacher, beginning as book editor and critic for *The Dallas Morning News*. He was also the E. A. Lilly Professor of Literature at Southern Methodist University. He is best known for his books *Thirteen Days to Glory: The Siege of the Alamo,* which garnered prizes from the Texas Institute of Letters and the Sons of the Republic of Texas; *The Key to Dallas*; *Mr. De: A Biography of Everette Lee DeGolyer;* and *An American Original: The Life of J. Frank Dobie,* which won a Texas Institute of Letters Award. He was a member of the Philosophical Society of Texas and served as president of the Texas Institute of Letters, which honors him by giving the prestigious Lon Tinkle Award for Lifetime Achievement at its award banquet each year.

From *The Key to Dallas*

DALLAS IS A CITY ON THE GO. THE PEOPLE OF Dallas like to do things; they prefer action to sitting around and talking and thinking about it. The city strikes the eye with all the brightness and freshness of a newly minted silver dollar. Most cities look weathered, like sturdy trees, or like ships at anchor after a long voyage. Dallas, with its aluminum-skin buildings and its gleaming white structures, reminds you more of a jet plane ready to take off.

About a million people live in Dallas and the twenty-eight smaller cities and towns that touch hands with it in the county of Dallas.

Some of the people are rich, very rich—like certain oil millionaires. They live in mansions on big estates. They have their own private airplanes and pilots ready to whisk them at a moment's notice to and from their large Texas ranches, their private islands in the Gulf of Mexico, or even in Canadian waters, their other homes scattered in distant places around the globe.

Some are poor, very poor—like hundreds of Dallas families, white and black, who live in flimsy wooden shacks on dusty streets (or muddy in the rainy season), without city water or sewers to serve them.

But the vast majority are neither rich nor poor. They are ordinary people of average middle income, the same as most other city dwellers in the United States.

But one streak runs like a common thread through all the people of Dallas: a love of brand-new things. They like to erect new homes, stores, schools, factories, office buildings, public structures of all kinds, places where they may work or play. And this leads them impatiently to tear down the buildings of yesterday to make way for new and larger ones. Dallas has trouble keeping intact the few old landmarks it has. A hundred-year-old house in Dallas, for example, is as rare as a buffalo in the streets. A storefront or a bank building half a century old is a source more of shame than of pride.

At the core of their city—the mile-square main business center—Dallas leaders insist on building skyward. Their spirits soar the higher their skyscrapers tower. The favored word for any new building is "Tower"; six or seven of the tallest include that word in the official name. . . .

All this earthbound thrust upward creates a skyline for which Dallas is justly famous. Seen from any of several dramatic approaches, it looks like a magic city as pictured by a storybook artist in some timeless tale of adventure. By day the buildings glisten in the tireless Texas sunlight. Their white surfaces or gaily tinted metallic sheathings are kept spotless by soot-free air, for Dallas burns no coal. Only natural gas or fuel oil or electricity is used to heat and cool its homes and other buildings and to power its factories because these are found nearby in great abundance and are therefore much cheaper than coal, which must be shipped in from long distances. By night the smoke-free skyline sparkles with myriad-colored lights, and huge neon-lighted symbols—such as a flying horse for an oil corporation and an oil derrick for a bank—flash with moving color atop the tallest towers.

Even more revealing, though, of the energy and drive of Dallas as a community is the series of large-scale public works on which the city seems constantly engaged. Citizens have been civic-minded ever since Dallas was started a century and a quarter ago. . . .

Engineers for the city thought nothing a few years ago of physically moving a river flowing past the foot of downtown Dallas. They dug a new ten-mile-long channel for the river, called the Trinity, half a mile to the west. They built levees thick and high enough on each side of the river to keep its waters from overflowing. This cured the menace of costly flood damage in the very heart of the city. It also restored to use thousands of acres of former swampland. On these acres now, hundreds of new business concerns have their homes. Most of these are laid out, parklike real estate developments for business concerns created in the former wasteland. One of these planned industrial parks of Dallas has served as a model for other cities both in this country and also abroad.

Love of the new on the part of Dallas people extends to the latest in inventions and gadgets. Dallas has an enviable record for being among the first to adopt and try out the wonders of applied science. This has long been true, whether it be the last century's newfangled horseless carriage or the electric lamp replacing gaslights, or whether it be today's jet airliner and refrigerated air conditioning to cool both homes and automobiles. . . .

The fashion industry has long been a ruling goddess in Dallas. It is uppermost in the thoughts of the city's daughters. It crops out foremost in the matter of the clothes they wear and in other items of personal adornment. Dallas today is one of the three or four fashion centers of the nation. One store alone, Neiman-Marcus, with its worldwide reputation, has enough weight in that fickle business to help pace the style of a season's manner of dress wherever women of the Western world gather. Dallas has a nourishing garment-making industry, with thousands of skilled workers turning out dresses for the women of America, most notably sports clothes and those to be worn at fashionable seaside and other resort centers.

Homemakers—present or future—find many of the home-furnishing stores and shops of the city to be rewarding, for oil wealth and cattle money have allowed many Dallas homes to be of interest to national magazines, and Dallas women spend as heavily on their homes as they do on their clothes. A number of Dallas's residential areas enjoy high standards of good taste as well as facilities for wholesome family living. On the other hand, recent construction of row upon row of low, rambling so-called "ranch style" houses is deplored by many. Some of the more stately Dallas homes, designed by such internationally famous architects as Frank Lloyd Wright and Edward Stone and William Wilson Wurster, rank among the most notable in the nation.

Beyond fashion, they tell us, lies style—a more abiding way of looking at every phase of human life to find its more artistic satisfactions. Dallas women bring a sure sense of style to the whole range of living, and this spirit of excellence reaches its peak here in the life of the mind and of the spirit. In matters of culture, the leadership of women goes far to explain the important place given in Dallas to the theater, music, painting, dance, and other fine arts.

The spoken drama, musical comedies, opera, concerts, and ballet have their roots running well back into the early days of the city's cultural life. In the heyday of "roadshow" theater in this country, the great stars and the great plays of the nineteenth century were as well known in Dallas as in the larger and older cities of the nation. . . .

Student concerts given by the Dallas Symphony Orchestra are attended by many of the more than one hundred thousand schoolchildren of Dallas. Founded over a half century ago, this orchestra has been led by such noted conductors as Antal Dorati, Paul Kletski, and George Solti. Other concert series have presented great soloists, ranging from Paderewski's first triumphal tour of America to the homecoming acclaim of Texas's own Van Cliburn.

The city has long been visited each spring by the Metropolitan Opera Company of New York (usually performing in the South and Southwest only at Atlanta and at Dallas). These presentations are given in the Music Hall in Fair Park and attract twenty to thirty thousand opera fans each season. The same hall is the home of the summer musicals, which are produced by the State Fair Association from June to September.

The recently born Dallas Civic Opera, giving its performances in the autumn, has been termed by authorities "the most exciting new development in the musical life of America. . . ."

How did Dallas ever grow from a one-room log cabin trading post into one of the key cities of America? ★

Natalie Ornish

From *Pioneer Jewish Texans:* Patsy Rabinowitz Nasher and Raymond D. Nasher

> *The Nasher Sculpture Garden, founded by Raymond D. Nasher, opened October 2003. When Nasher announced the gift of the sculpture center to Dallas, The* New York Times *reported: "For years, museums from the Solomon R. Guggenheim in Manhattan to the National Gallery of Art in Washington to the Fine Arts Museums of San Francisco have courted Raymond D. Nasher and coveted his extensive collection of modern and contemporary sculpture. All but one of the museums have courted in vain." Nasher said his reasoning was that he had spent most of his life in Dallas and his daughters grew up in Dallas. Also, it seemed important to provide a cultural catalyst for downtown development. His action has made the city an international art destination.*

When Patsy and Ray Nasher started collecting art, they didn't envision themselves as creating one of the finest private art collections in the world. Over time, they helped lift Dallas's reputation in art and architecture and shared their art collection with an international audience.

Patsy Rabinowitz was born in Dallas and graduated from Highland Park High School. She attended the Hockaday School's junior college and then Southern Methodist University and Smith College in Massachusetts, where she graduated magna cum laude 1949. That same year, she married Ray Nasher, a Boston-reared real estate developer who held degrees from Duke and Boston universities.

In 1950 they moved to Dallas, where their family grew to include three daughters: Andrea, Joan, and Nancy. Ray became involved in the development of industrial sites, planned residential communities, office parks, and shopping centers. Ray's innovative shopping mall, NorthPark, was one of the first enclosed air-conditioned shopping centers in the nation.

As Ray earned a reputation in building and architecture, Patsy began collecting art objects that held special meaning for her. At first, she gathered driftwood on the beaches in Massachusetts. In Dallas she started buying pre-Colombian artifacts and moved on to paintings by Texas artists, Guatemalan textiles, and Indonesian gold.

Over a period of thirty years Patsy and Ray built an extensive art collection. Patsy helped to build her community as well. She was instrumental in founding the Martin Luther King Jr. Community Center in Dallas. . . . She also served as a board member of the Dallas Museum of Art and the Fort Worth Art Museum.

The Nasher Company received the Business in the Arts Award for sponsoring ballet, symphony, and theater performances in company-owned business developments, and the American Institute of Architects award, "Design of the Decade—1960," for NorthPark. Ray coauthored the National Science Foundation book *Land* and in 1967 served as a US delegate to the General Assembly of the United Nations. An honorary doctorate was conferred upon him by Southern Methodist University. Patsy received an honorary doctorate of humanities from Northwood Institute. While Ray lectured nationally on art, architecture, and land use, Patsy traveled throughout the world collecting.

On April 5, 1987, "A Century of Modern Sculpture: The Patsy and Raymond Nasher Collection" opened at the Dallas Museum of Art and then went to Washington, DC, for exhibition during the last half of 1987 at the National Gallery of Art. The collection then moved to Madrid, Spain; Florence, Italy; and other cities. Although Patsy was in great pain, she traveled to attend the exhibit's openings in Washington and Madrid. After battling cancer for thirteen years, Patsy died July 1, 1988, shortly after the collection began its European tour.

After her death, Ray reminded viewers at the Forte di Belvedere in Florence, "I hope you all feel the spirit of my wife, who was the true curator and developer of this exhibit. She's here with us in spirit." An editorial in a Dallas newspaper called Patsy "a civilizing force in Dallas . . . Patsy and Ray Nasher have meant a lot to this city." ★

Grover Lewis

Grover Lewis (1934–1997) received a BA degree from what is now the University of North Texas and did graduate study at Texas Tech University. His career included stints at *The Fort Worth Star-Telegram; Houston Chronicle; Village Voice; Rolling Stone;* and *New West,* as editor. His works include *Wait for Morning, Child* (one-act play); *I'll Be There in the Morning If I Live* (poetry); *Straight Arrow;* and *Academy All the Way* (reportage). Grover Lewis commented: "All I know about writing is encompassed in the observation of the late Red Smith: 'Hell, writing's easy. All you do is sit down at the typewriter and wait for little drops of blood to appear on your forehead.'" Grover Lewis was one of the defining voices of the New Journalism of the 1960s and 1970s. His essays written for *Rolling Stone* and the *Village Voice* set a standard for other writers of the time. In the catalog touting a reissue of Lewis's writing, the publisher notes: "His articles on Woody Guthrie, the Allman Brothers, the Rolling Stones concert at Altamont, directors Sam Peckinpah and John Huston, and the filming of *The Last Picture Show* and *One Flew over the Cuckoo's Nest* remain some of the finest writing ever done on popular culture." Here Lewis gives his perception of the loss of his old Oak Cliff.

From Farewell to Cracker Eden

History and legend bind us to the past, along with unquenchable memory. Growing up in Dallas's working-class suburb of Oak Cliff in the forties and fifties was the second experience in my life that I never got over. I hadn't been back to those boyhood haunts in thirty years, and I wasn't as calm as I thought I'd be about returning. Under a patchy October overcast, the houses along Marsalis Avenue looked beat, maybe even whipped. I had to slow down to read the sign for my old street because all the landmarks were gone.

When I first saw East Ninth in 1948, the street was a leafy tunnel running past tidy bungalows and well-kept Victorian mansions dating back to the original settlement of the City of Oak Cliff before the turn of the century. Now it was food stamp country—a jungly midden with a Third World flavor. I knew in advance that the house where Spook and I lived had been demolished during the Latino incursion of the seventies, so I eased past its replacement, not ready to look at it yet. I turned south on Patton, and the area changed from merely seedy to wasteland.

At Tenth and Patton, I pulled over in shock. The devastation was total—an entire neighborhood sunk in rot. The surviving houses were vine-choked, boarded up, literally atomizing in a ghastly mockery of the thriving community I recalled. The burned-out hulk of an apartment warren stood on the site where Lee Harvey Oswald allegedly killed Officer Tippit after the Kennedy assassination.

Leaving the car, I passed up and down the broken sidewalks, searching in vain for the duplex where my best school pal had lived. The blasted terrain looked as though war and pestilence had swept through, leaving behind only feral silence.

Turning away, still on foot, I started back toward Ninth. Oak Cliff's soul had changed or maybe died, I couldn't tell which. And what exactly had been lost? Well, a civilization. . . . Growing up on these streets, I had started learning about all the things I was still trying to comprehend—love, sex, money, art, death. But, then, I knew a thing or two about death when I first came to Oak Cliff.

In 1943, my parents—Grover Lewis and Opal Bailey Lewis—shot each other to death with a pawnshop pistol. Big Grover had stalked us for a year, fighting divorce tooth and nail, and when he finally cornered Opal alone and pulled the trigger, she seized the gun and killed him too. They'd started out as Depression kids who had eloped from the Trinity Heights area of Oak Cliff, where they'd both been friends with Bonnie Parker and Clyde Barrow. Like Clyde, my father was an unschooled country jake who fell—or jumped—into low ways in the big city. Opal, like Bonnie, was a bright student who left school early to help support her family—a moral girl with high ideals. Like Bonnie's, Opal's main crime seems to have been picking the wrong guy. In the end, she managed to save my father from everybody but himself.

The fatal events took place in my hometown of San Antonio when I was eight, and I became the ward of a brutish Fort Worth in-law who amused himself by trying to break my body and spirit. By today's standards, he would have been deemed abusive enough to serve jail time. After five years, when I realized that my options were either suicide or homicide, I ran away and refused to return, if I died in the process. Many of my mother's kin considered me unsalvageable because I was "a pure Lewis." They'd give me that look: "Just like his daddy. . . ."

Spook—my great-uncle, C. E. Bailey—saved my life. When he took me in, I was badly damaged—withdrawn, lacking confidence, blind as a bat, smart as fire, dumb as hell. Still, with a friendly home base only a block's walk from my high school classes and the local library also close at hand, I began to mend. My case was extreme but hardly singular in a workingman's district where a lot of families got blown to smithereens.

A sagging condo pile with a "No Drugs" sign out front occupied the lot where our old family boardinghouse had stood. Spook and I had lived upstairs in a bare room with a bare bulb above the iron bedstead. When I started working after school, I bought us reading lamps, feeling grown-up about pitching in.

Spook's insight—his special grace—was to treat me as a younger brother instead of a ward. In his fifties by then, a union machinist and a lifelong bachelor, he kept his mind sharp by studying the Bible and parsing out "the lies in the papers." Half a Wobbly in his secret heart, he taught me a multitude of useful things, one of the germinal ideas being that decency and common sense were most likely to be found in common people. He offered general advice, specific if asked, and never raised his voice or hand to me. In the long haul, I think I was less trouble to him than his batty sisters, both of whom constantly schemed to lure him into their religious cults.

If Spook was our family Samaritan, Matthew Bailey—my mother's father—was our scourge. A Snopesy little jackleg-of-all-trades—he had been Bonnie and Clyde's favorite bootlegger—he worked for thirty-odd years as a maintenance engineer at the Wholesale Merchants building in downtown Dallas, where he routinely slept with maids as a condition of their employment. With a flame of rage perpetually flickering in his head, he once put a black man off a city bus at knifepoint for sitting in front of him. I loved the old devil regardless and helped him out sometimes on weekend plumbing jobs, mostly just handing him his bottle. Matthew approached everything with the maximum violence required for the job, but he never swatted me around, because, as a rule, he only beat on the people who lived under his own roof. . . .

My people, holy and profane, were "pure-dee Oak Cliff," of course. In mind-set, our community on the hard-luck side of the Trinity was a paradise of the deepest redneck dye. The fear of race mixing was a constant topic because the district's communal identity hinged on being white, conservative, "saved," and married with children.

The gabble of bigotry thus became a daily canticle, a sacred text. The ethos of the place—what it promoted—was absolute white supremacy, reinforced by old-time religion and male chauvinist prickism. In our primary-color culture—97 percent white in 1950—the number one rule was, Don't mess up. If you swerved from the True Path, you messed up. Above all, you had to "cut it." Cut the yard, keep your hair cut, cut the mustard . . . "cut the crap, boy," when you spoke out of line. Docility was preferred over intelligence, guaranteeing the whittling down of the individual to fit unvarying social molds. This bred the kind of multi-edged boredom that comes from poverty locked into place by spiritual poverty. As a jumpy adolescent, I was starved for ideas in much the same way that I yearned to sleep with somebody besides Spook—some like-minded, bookish girl, I hoped. But if racism was obligatory, sex without benefit of clergy was out of the question.

Following a zigzag route, I walked to the intersection of Marsalis and Jefferson Boulevard, where the Carnegie branch library had once stood. The building, erected in 1914, had been bulldozed in 1966, when, as someone later told me, "Dallas was tearing down everything old and throwing up junk." It had been an elegant little sanctuary set in a wooded park—one of the community's few true gems. The structure located there now—a Dallas Department of Transportation cubicle—resembled a post-modern pillbox.

The old library had saved my life as much as Spook had. I found my own sacred texts in there, groping for direction in that period when the self doesn't really know what it is yet. A precocious reader by the age of twelve, I read an average of four or five books a week all through high school, including trash, the classics, and everything in between. Above all, I learned how to read and think critically, with no clear sense of vocation yet, but at least the ghost of an ambition forming. Predictably, my hard-shell relatives claimed I was ruining my mind by "thinkin'" too much. Doggedly I read on. Since I worked a night job, I sometimes skipped school to read because reading was as essential as breathing to me.

On my walk through the streets, I passed no one and there was little traffic moving on the boulevard at nine in the morning. Squirrels danced on the power lines. Up the block, a sign over a car lot read, "Kars Fur 'U'—Muchacho Motors." With a sense of sorrow and anger that made my heart race, I realized I still missed the clanking spectral streetcars that had stopped running along Jefferson for good back in 1956. . . .

The shape of things in Oak Cliff was essentially the same, but the lines had run eerily. Nothing—and everything—had changed. The ethnic configuration now stood at 40 percent white, 40 percent black, and 20 percent Hispanic in a district containing roughly one-third of Dallas's area and population. I drove all over the down-fallen suburb, numbed by the decay and patchwork balkanization. Most of the neighborhoods I'd known were now streaked with phantasmagoric blight and filled with desperately poor and sometimes dangerous people—the latest incursion of have-nots from jacales and East Texas slums. Billy Lee Brammer's old boyhood home looked intact in a modest cul-de-sac behind Greiner Junior High, but the block bristled with For Sale signs—not a good sign. My daily forays were depressing, educational, and at times very touching. I found no road back to the cracker Eden of the fifties, but at every turn I encountered Oak Cliff's famous hospitality—and the smell of cooking red beans. Those things hadn't changed.

At the age of seventeen in 1926, Clyde Barrow worked briefly as an usher at Dallas's Palace Theater but soon quit over the paltry $12-a-week salary. Twenty-five years later, I started work as an usher at the Texas Theater for $19 a week—still a pittance but enough to see me through high school. The experience jerked some complex knots in and out of my young life, and I finished growing up very quickly.

In the early fifties, the Texas was the principal seat of allowable public pleasure in Oak Cliff—a spit-and-polish place where Daddy took Mama to the show on Sundays. Already twenty years old by then, it was well kept up, not even close to being run-down. But as Jefferson withered, the once-venerable movie house started falling to pieces too. In 1989, to avert demolition, the nonprofit Texas Theater Historical Society (TTHS), with aid from the Oak Cliff Chamber of Commerce, bought the old landmark, pledging its restoration and development as a cultural arts center. To meet a $3,000 monthly mortgage, TTHS volunteers—many of them teenagers from the area—reopened the theater as a $2 rerun venue. . . .

On a late weekday afternoon before the evening show, Maxine Burroughs, the matronly manager, showed me around. She was a veteran Texas employee, along with her husband, the doorman who had been on duty when Oswald was apprehended. "Butch and I got involved," she explained, "because there's no place left in Oak Cliff for families and kids to go." The lobby looked frayed, sad, smaller than I remembered. We mounted the foyer stairs, passing a mawkish amateur mural of JFK, and climbed to the balcony. . . .

I wandered along the center aisle, glancing by reflex toward the last rows in front of the projection booth where the riffraff of Oak Cliff's hillbilly gene pool had traditionally gathered—the dreaded "balcony rats." In the watery light, I found my old spot by the A stairwell. While I was still a green hand, but a tall one, I was stationed there to keep a lid on the general anarchy. After a couple of grueling break-in shifts, less terrified of the badasses than worried about failing, I bought an oversized flashlight that suggested a club. The bluff worked pretty well for a year, until a beered-up lummox from West Dallas flung himself at me over four rows of seats, and I did the thing that Matthew or Spook would've done—bopped him on the ear. The injured party ran bellowing to the lobby, alerting the manager, who had him hauled off for drunk. As a sort of reward for "cutting it," I was transferred downstairs to the candy case, a choice job compared with standing aisle.

On a fall night in 1952, as I was closing up the candy case, Tess Tyler came out of the auditorium and stopped to shoot the breeze. . . . She was a neighbor, in her mid-twenties, divorced, familiar enough at my boardinghouse to sit down at meals. We had a casual, jokey acquaintance, and we decided to walk home together.

On the way, having our first private conversation, I saw her clearly as a person instead of as a remote adult. She had married a well-off Oak Lawn jerk who bruised her around and then threw her away. Under the blowy elms on East Ninth, slowing down to light one of the Tareytons she chain-smoked when her relatives weren't around, we bumped into each other accidentally and then embraced impulsively. We stood holding each other, kissing, both of us shaken. I was speechless. In the shadows, her face was pale and a little too lean—pure-dee Oak Cliff. "You wouldn't tell anybody, would you?" she asked in a faint voice. "No, I swear." "Wait for fifteen minutes. When you come up, be sure Mama's lights are out."

We met that way for five or six months, fugitives in the dark, risking everything not so much for sex as for deliverance from love-starved isolation—some shared connection to stave off loneliness. Our times together were tender, painful, glorious, wretched, wise, and foolish—but redeemed, I thought, by the solace and comfort we gave each other. Tess taught me to tie a Windsor knot, comb my hair without a part. . . . Sometimes I went to her place to write while she slept with the radio low.

But we were tap dancing on the edge of disaster, and the dread of exposure bore in on us. We both knew that her holy roller mother would shoot us in the name of God if she ever figured things out. After a couple of close calls, we backed off, saw each other less, then not at all. For a while, we took pains to avoid meeting. Then we began exchanging guarded greetings in passing. In the end, we went back full circle to being casual strangers across the boardinghouse table.

Back in the lobby, a crew of young volunteers was busily preparing to open the concession stand for the night's show. Mrs. Burroughs walked me to the main door.

"It's sort of hard to put into words," she said, "but the Texas is still really a special place. To me, it represents entertainment, people having fun—not just Oswald and all that stuff. I hope you enjoyed the visit, hope it brought back pleasant memories for you."

"Yes," I said. "Thank you very much." Outside, the darkness was lowering on Jefferson, and except for the theater sign and the marquee advertising *Naked Gun 2 1/2,* the neighborhood looked abandoned. A DART bus rattled by with no one aboard but the driver. Halfway to my car, I felt a sudden stab of alarm, a prickle at the back of my neck . . . whirled around. Nobody there. ★

Marcella Siegel

Marcella Siegel has lived in the Dallas area for thirty years. After graduating from Western College for Women in Oxford, Ohio, she served as president of Southwest Writers and of the Poetry Society of Texas. Her prose and poetry have been published in *The Christian Science Monitor, Saturday Evening Post, The Dallas Morning News,* and in the yearbooks of the Poetry Society of Texas. Her poetry has been recognized for its excellence by the National Federation of Poets. Siegel's book-length poetry collection is *Swift Season.* Here, she gives a poet's view of a wife waiting for a returning soldier during the Vietnam era.

Waiting Wife

She sped the daytime hours
in a coffee shop on Powell Street
where commuters, tourists and shoppers
streamed in from the cable cars
to have her serve their hurry.
Nights in her flat in an old skinny house
she wrote him letters
that smiled at how the flower stalls
splashed spring on the downtown winter;
how a rock out in the bay
blossomed sometimes like an April tree
with the satin bodies of seals;
and how a rat she had christened Ben
was her kitchen companion at night.

And she was careful not to tell him how alone she was
listening to young laughter passing by on the sidewalk
outside her window
in that city so alien to her East Texas town,
that city by the sea
where she had come, to feel closer to him
while she waited for his return.
She read in his letters of the refugees
on the road from An Loc
turning their tired backs on their smoking huts,
of the old young mothers and their wasting children
walking the napalmed fields,
and of his buddy stilled in the mud at Quang Nghai
And she wondered when he lay in a steaming paddy
waiting for a shadow to move or explode
if her love beside him
would be enough. ★

Paul Crume

Paul Crume's "Big D" columns on page one of *The Dallas Morning News* were a first-thing-in-the-morning tradition for thousands of readers over almost a quarter of a century. Lon Tinkle writes, "Crume's humor comes from a broad, generous understanding of the gap between what people are and what they ought to be, above all of the gap between what dream promises and what reality forks over. For Crume the perception of this gap results in thigh-slapping guffaws far more often than in the melancholy tear." At the University of Texas, Crume trained under J. Frank Dobie and Walter Prescott Webb, being Webb's student grader and assistant. His journalism classmates included Walter Cronkite and Lady Bird Johnson. Marion Crume, editor of Crume's collected writings, recognizes the aid of legendary people at SMU in putting together Paul's book: Lon Tinkle; Allen Maxwell, SMU Press director; Margaret L. Hartley, SMU Press editor; and Charlotte T. Whaley, assistant to the director. Crume's "To Touch an Angel" appears every Christmas Day in *The Dallas Morning News* and has done so since 1967 when it was first written.

From *The World of Paul Crume:* To Touch an Angel

A MAN WROTE ME NOT LONG AGO AND ASKED me what I thought of the theory of angels. I immediately told him that I am highly in favor of angels. As a matter of fact, I am scared to death of them.

Any adult human being with half sense, and some with more, knows that there are angels. If he has ever spent any period in loneliness, when the senses are forced in upon themselves, he has felt the wind from their beating wings and been overwhelmed with the sudden realization of the endless and gigantic dark that exists outside the little candle flame of human knowledge. He has prayed, not in the sense that he asked something, but that he yielded himself.

Angels live daily at our very elbows, and so do demons, and most men at one time or another in their lives have yielded themselves to both and have lived to rejoice and rue their impulses.

> *But the man who has once felt the beat of the angel's wing finds it easy to rejoice at the universe and at his fellow man.*

This sense of cosmos, or angels, or the divine accommodation of a man with the universe, usually happens to a man suddenly. Angels do not take part in work for civic causes or help raise money for the United Fund. A single human heart has to long to touch an angel before it can sense one.

It does not happen to any man often, and too many of us dismiss it when it happens. I remember a time in my final days in college when the chinaberry trees were abloom and the air was sweet with spring blossoms and I stood still on the street, suddenly struck with the feeling of something that was an enormous promise and yet was no tangible promise at all.

And there was another night in a small boat when the moon was full and the distant headlands were dark but beautiful and we were lonely. The pull of a nameless emotion was so strong that it filled the atmosphere. The small boy within me cried.

> *Psychiatrists will say that the angel in all this was really within me, not outside, but it makes no difference. There are angels inside us and angels outside, and the one inside is usually the quickest choked.*

Francis Thompson said it better. He was a late nineteenth-century English poet who would put the current crop of hippies to shame. He was on pot all his life. His pad was always mean and was sometimes a park bench. He was a mental case and a tubercular besides. He carried a fishing creel into which he dropped the poetry that was later to become immortal.

"The angels keep their ancient places," wrote Francis Thompson in protest. "Turn but a stone, and start a wing!"

He was lonely enough to be the constant associate of angels.

There is an angel close to you this day. Merry Christmas, and I wish you well. ★

Hot Nights and Family History
(July 28, 1969)

THE PRESENT HEAT WAVE HAS UNCOVERED SOME defects in modern education as well some weaknesses in the modern degenerate character. All people know to do about the heat now is stay in air-conditioning, which is the worst thing in the world you can do unless you want to be comfortable.

To beat the heat really you have to meet it face to face and eyeball it down. Our ancestors, who were always singing, "If it was good for Paul and Silas, it's good enough for me," knew how to do this. They had various tricks to outwit the sultry antagonist. When I first came to Dallas, for instance, and lived in a rickety apartment on Ross, you made your hot weather bed on a hard mattress with a single tightly drawn sheet.

You directed on this mattress a fan. If you were rich, you owned something called an oscillating fan, but we didn't. You wet and wrung out a couple of large towels, spread them over you under the fan, and settled down, being careful to sleep spread-armed and spraddle-legged so that no part of you would impart its heat to another part. After a night of this, you woke up with a wonderful feeling of having been purged of everything, especially energy.

Air-conditioning robs the ordinary sleeper of the chance of participating in nature.

Air-conditioning, I believe, is also responsible for destroying family history as it used to exist.

Family history used to be kept by word of mouth. On a farm in those days, the hot weather bed was a pallet, a single quilt spread for each sleeper on the big front porch that ran the length of the house. When it was still too hot to sleep, which was anytime before 2:00 A.M., the elders lay there and discussed what had happened to the family. They went into elaborate analyses of motives. What made Cousin Clint quit his wife and move with the children to the remote wildernesses of Mineral Wells? What made Aunt Crecy a witch, though a benevolent one bent mostly on curing erysipelas?

The recurring quotation was, "Nobody will ever know why he done what he did."

Along about dawn, when you could have expected to sleep, you were roused out to get to work. Nobody was worried about the effects of heat on human beings, but working in the full of the day might be hard on the horses.

As a result of these nighttime seminars, I learned very early that there were few saints in our family.

Actually, I do not remember as much of the family history as I might have if I had slept on more pallets. I learned a lot about my uncles that I was too chicken to use against them. Mostly I remember incidents.

There was the time when Uncle Uriah, a pillar of the Baptist church, was mad because the minister, a man contemptibly soft of hands, had asked him to call his go-devil a plowing sled. The preacher thought the correct name smacked of strong language.

"I told him," said Uncle Uriah from the pallet that night, "that no matter what you call it, it's still a go-devil."

And air conditioning or not, heat is still heat. ★

Controlling the Comma
(July 3, 1962)

"That Paul Crume must be a real 'rugged' individualist," writes a North Texas reader. "He leaves commas out of where they are taught to be absolutely required—and puts them in where he damn well pleases."

I thank my North Texas friend for this expression of high admiration.

It took several years to master the comma, but by now I have got it pretty well cowed. A great many people think that all dogs and all commas behave alike. Actually, each comma is an individual and is inclined to do willfully whatever it wants unless it is controlled. Furthermore, you can teach a comma to do a lot of tricks besides those listed in the grammars if you catch it young and train it intelligently.

Most people never learn this, but I learned it early. Now, when I say "frog," a comma better sit up and beg.

This reader's letter indicates that he has allowed himself to be "taught" instead of grabbing control of the comma. It is a common tactical error.

Actually, commas are rather docile, but they are not as docile as most English teachers say. At any moment, one of them is likely to rear up and do something in a sentence that you hadn't expected. You can control them fairly easily.

The semicolon is a different breed of animal. You would be well advised not to get caught in the same sentence with one unless you have a whip. I have occasionally received spectacular results with a semicolon, but they are treacherous and unreliable. Sometimes they won't perform at all for you, and you have to throw them out.

In contrast, people have often said my work with commas has been of circus quality.

Most people never master punctuation because they get scared of these marks the minute they see them. No matter how ferocious punctuation looks, never fear. Wade into the sentence. Throw commas, semicolons, colons, and periods in all directions. Establish your authority.

If you wade right into them, these punctuation marks will never bite.

For the person who has not learned to train punctuation marks to do his bidding, there are a few simple rules of composition which will help him to begin.

When you are writing something and the typewriter stops, put in a period. You are probably going to start off in a different direction or on a new subject entirely, and you don't want to be trailing anything behind you.

If you haven't quite stopped when the typewriter does, put in a comma. It will permit you to turn 360 degrees and still not come unglued.

Never use a semicolon. You'll find yourself rewriting the whole sentence so the semicolon will fit in.

Never use an exclamation mark. It isn't really that important. ★

Stalking the Viable Alternative
(November 17, 1974)

It says here that a Texas senator has been talking with the French about the energy crisis, and he says they are all hunting for Viable Alternatives.

They had better watch out. So many people nowadays are hunting the Viable Alternative that it may become an endangered species.

They should remember what happened to At This Point in Time. Until the Watergate hearings this was an exotic animal known only to the powerful and privileged in Washington. When its existence became known, everybody took after it, and within a few months, it had been shot out of the language.

Before that, there was the Two-horned Dilemma. People were always being caught between its horns. As a result they have bred into existence a polled variety of dilemma. This is a dilemma that doesn't have any horns at all and is the kind of dilemma that faces the world today. You don't know how to dodge it.

It might be wise just to let wild things like the Viable Alternative run at large and not try to harness them to human uses.

The Viable Alternative seems to be a very rare and secretive creature. At least, the people in government have been looking for a Viable Alternative for months, and they haven't found one yet.

A well-traveled friend of mine, Frank X. Tolbert, thinks he knew one once in the Rio Grande Valley. He was a wetback, and his name was José Viable y Alternative, but this is not a definitive sighting. Mr. Tolbert knows a million characters some one-legged, some two-legged, and some centipedes. If this is a member of the family of Alternative, it has to have two legs. It has to be either or. If it had more than two legs, it would have to be just a Plover-dull Possibility. Furthermore, the feet on these two legs have to be pointed in different directions, or you don't have an Alternative. If they were pointed, as normally, in the same direction, you would have a Mandate.

All the clues, as you can see, point to a Viable Alternative that is either ape or bird. I lean toward the bird theory, although it is true that many *Homo sapiens* in the Washington area can run in two directions at once. The bird, however, could probably travel better sidewise, which is the way most Viable Alternatives work.

Great apes like Man have an instinct against progressing sidewise; they had rather go backward.

I believe that this bird not only has feet which run in different directions but also has eyes in the back of its head, because it is always operating from hindsight. If you object that an Alernative that runs off in two directions at once is not very Viable, so be it. That is the nature of Alternatives. That is the way the Good Lord made them.

We can only hope that while hunting down the Viable Alternatives, the Texas senator and his friends hold their fire and do not accidentally shoot down a genuine Prong-horned Dilemma or a lurking Point in Time. Probably we ought just to try to capture some Viable Alternatives. We could study them scientifically and find out how they work. ★

Donald Vogel

From *Memories and Images:* The Meadows Caper: The Art Fraud That Made International News

Much has been written about the "Meadows Caper" throughout the world. Being the first to break the news to Al and set the events into motion, however, I feel it is time to tell it as it was. Before it ended, it was one of the greatest art scandals of the twentieth century. It triggered news stories that reached every corner of the world and inspired investigations by the FBI and police in Los Angeles, New York City, and Palm Beach, as well as Brazil, France, and Switzerland. For me, the "Meadows Caper" was another chapter in my growing-up years as an artist and art dealer in Dallas, a story that seemed to parallel the city's own growth in art: its painters, its museums, its art galleries, and its collectors. . . .

It was a dreary December afternoon in 1966. A cold, damp chill was trapped under heavy clouds that held a threat of snow. I was in the studio drawing, in preparation for the start of a new canvas, when the phone rang.

"Hello, Donald, this is Al Meadows. You are the 'Wildenstein of Texas.' I'd like you to sell some pictures for me."

It had been a long time since I had heard from Al, or even thought of him, but my first reaction was a fervent hope that he wasn't talking about his Spanish paintings, many of which had false attributions. "What paintings do you have in mind?" I asked.

"Oh, I have nine I'd like to sell, including a Gauguin, a Degas, a Manet, five by Raoul Dufy, and a Utrillo. Can you come over?"

"On my way in about twenty minutes," I said, hanging up the phone. I could hear the ring of the cash register, if only the paintings were right. . . . While I was establishing myself as a reputable art dealer, which allowed me to pursue my work as a painter, Al Meadows was building his oil company worth millions of dollars into one of the largest in the United States.

At the time I had three top-quality Renoirs hanging in the viewing room of my gallery and hoped Al might want one of them. They had just arrived from the Vollard estate in France and had not been on the market before, so perhaps. . . . Pleasant images of things to come passed before my eyes.

I remembered a meeting with him nearly three years before in a waiting room just off the elevators in his new office building, where I had assembled about sixty paintings for him to approve for the new offices throughout the floor. Joe Lambert, who owned Lambert Landscaping Company and was a highly regarded businessman, had been responsible for my presence.

When Al appeared, Joe introduced us. Al was a friendly gentleman, with a nice smile and a quiet voice. The two of us started to walk, looking at the paintings. He pointed first at a watercolor by Michael Frary, a painter from Austin.

"How much?" he asked.

"One hundred fifty. That one, an oil by Kelly Fearing, also from Austin, is seven hundred dollars, and the next is six hundred. It's by . . . "

He interrupted, and with a wave of his hand, indicating the whole group, said, "I'll give $12,000 for the lot."

"It's a good offer," I countered, "but I want to sell you only what you can use, at my price, with no discount."

"I understand," he said as we walked on. "You know, I do a lot of business in Spain, and I've acquired a large collection of Spanish masters on which I got a very good buy!"

"How's that?" I asked. He explained that he'd had a free afternoon in Madrid one day and had passed a gallery with an old Spanish painting in the window. There was a sign in the window as well, stating that the gallery had examples of all of the important painters of Spain. Al went in and looked at the paintings that were hanging there, and the proprietor told him that if he wanted assurance of their quality, a book was available in the bookstore across the street that showed reproductions of many of the same paintings. When he left the gallery, he walked away for several blocks, then circled around until he came back to the bookstore from a different direction. He bought the book and returned to the hotel to study it, pleased to find that all the paintings he had seen at the gallery were indeed represented in the book. The next day he went back and bought them all "at a bargain price. . . ." At least that story explained why he was trying to buy all the paintings we were looking at as a "job lot."

But time had passed, and hoping his attitudes toward collecting had changed, I accepted his invitation to see the paintings at his house. When I rang the bell, Al opened the door himself. My optimism lasted only as far as the front hall, where I first saw a picture that disturbed me. It didn't feel right. Al saw me stop and said, "That's a Picasso."

"If that's a Picasso, I'll eat it," I answered.

He shrugged and walked on to the next picture. "Utrillo," he said.

"No way," I said.

"Come on, I'd like you to look at all of them and tell me what you think," he said.

We stopped before two large, handsome canvases, unsigned. I said, "These are very fine Valtats. . . ."

Looking up at the wall beyond the railing of the second floor, I saw several drawings by one of my favorite artists. "Go on up and look at those Modiglianis," Al invited. . . .

In the living room another Modigliani hung over the mantel. "It's bad," I said.

Al challenged me, asking how I knew. . . . "I know and love this artist's work, and there's no way he could have done it."

I glanced into the library and saw a famous Bonnard floral I knew very well. If only this one were good. Oh, let it be good, I thought, as we approached. But it wasn't. This was a disgrace! How could anyone pass this stuff off? It was bad.

Over the fireplace in the library was another Modigliani. "No good," I said.

Al was waiting for me this time. "Ah, I got you! I have a catalog with this on the cover," he beamed. He removed the catalog from a shelf behind a closed door and handed it to me. . . . He had overlooked the very basic fact that the exhibition catalog he showed me had pages missing that would have stated the time, location, and sponsor of the exhibit of the Modigliani in question. Why wouldn't he have seen that, I asked myself as we walked on through the house? Why did he fail to check out the men he was dealing with? If nothing else, the fact that a dealer was selling him a picture alleged to be valued at $80,000 for $40,000 made no sense.

Next, he pulled out six more paintings from a hall closet. "I'd like you to sell these for me. Take them with you and let me know what you can get for them."

I glanced at them and felt they were fakes, but agreed to take them. I made it clear, however, that before I offered them for sale, I would check them further. If, as I suspected, they proved bad, there was no way I would sell them because, from then on, as a dealer, I would be responsible. It was agreed. Before I left, he asked that I take with me the appraisals he'd had done and the photos of the paintings with their provenances so that I could check them out for him.

"One more thing I want to talk to you about, Al," I said, "I have three important Renoirs from the Vollard estate you should see . . ."

He held up his hand to stop me and said, "You sell my pictures, and I'll buy one of your Renoirs."

The day didn't improve. More than ever it looked like snow, but the setting was right for the sad drama of the "Meadows Caper."

Back at the gallery I unloaded the six pictures Meadows had given me and examined the backs for the type and age of the canvas, the stretchers, and the tacks, to see what story they could tell. It all added up; everything was wrong. I read over the appraisals and checked the corresponding photos. If the paintings had been authentic, the values established would have been fair market values. . . .

After going over the information Al had given me, I called and asked his permission to take the material to New York to confirm my findings. He agreed. I had decided to divide the photos and show them to different dealers, those who had the greatest expertise for each particular artist. My first appointment was with Klaus Peris, then president of the Art Dealers Association of America, with whom I had developed a good rapport in past business. I handed him the packet of photos, and he laid them down one at a time, in two piles, as if they were playing cards.

"Good, bad, bad, bad, good," he murmured, saying nothing else until the last photo was on its stack.

I told him my story and said, "I think we should help Meadows. He's a potential collector, and we shouldn't discourage him." I reminded him of the story of Otto Gerson, a dealer highly respected among dealers. Not too many years before, Otto had planned an exhibition of paintings of Modigliani. Several of his clients advanced him sums of money to acquire paintings for them, and he set off to Europe to buy all he could find. He approached Robert de Bolli, who told him that only two Modiglianis were available and where he could locate them. These he bought, but in Switzerland he found a dealer who had several. He bought them all and returned to hang his show.

When it was up, he invited Klaus, whom he respected as the American expert on Modigliani, to view the show before its opening. Klaus pronounced them all bad except for the two that de Bolli had guided him to. What to do? Otto called his investors and suggested a plan. They all approved. He then returned to Switzerland and acquired several good paintings from the same dealer who had sold him the bad Modiglianis, telling the man he would pay after he received the new pictures in New York. When they arrived, however, he returned the bad Modiglianis to him instead. . . .

I suggested that some plan like this might work for Meadows, though I still did not know the source of his purchases. Klaus said, "Let me call Ralph Colin." Ralph was the founder of the Art Dealers Association, a lawyer, and a first-rate collector. He listened as Klaus related my story, then suggested I call Meadows when I returned and get a letter of permission from him for a panel of experts to review his collection and advise him. There would be no cost to Meadows for this, since the dealers already had planned to visit Dallas for the opening of the Picasso show. . . .

Back in Dallas, I dialed Al's number and learned that he was on the golf course in Palm Beach. He returned my call from the ninth tee and agreed to send me the letter I'd requested. He said that he might not be in town at the time the dealers would visit, but his houseman would admit us, and we should make ourselves at home. I called New York and sent a copy of the letter to Ralph Colin. . . .

The plans were set in motion. The panel of experts would consist of Klaus Peris and his wife, Dolly; Klaus's brother, Frank, from Beverly Hills; Stephen Hahn, and Daniel and Eleanor Saidenberg, all from New York; my wife, Peggy, who would take notes; and myself. . . .

When we arrived at the Meadows home, we were surprised that Al Meadows himself opened the door for us. "Gentlemen and ladies, please come in," he said. "I am pleased with your generous offer to help settle the questions about my paintings." He escorted us inside.

After I made the introductions, Klaus took over. "We might as well start with the Picasso," he said looking at Daniel Saidenberg. Saidenberg looked it over and responded, "No way." Klaus explained to Al that, in this country, Saidenberg was the undisputed expert on Picasso.

They moved on to the Utrillo. "Utrillo never painted a tree like that," Klaus said. Glancing back at the Picasso and ahead at the paintings to come, he exclaimed, "Elmyr de Hory painted these. Good God! I remember when I helped that . . . This should be the beginning of the end for him." One by one Peggy wrote down the comments. My first judgment was right on everything but some watercolors by Dufy. . . .

At the conclusion of the inspection, Meadows asked the score. Peggy referred to her notes and totaled the count. She handed it to Peris, who then informed Al that of his collection of fifty-eight paintings, forty-four were forgeries. The count proved wrong only for one of the Dufy watercolors, which was later shown to be genuine by the author of the catalogue raisonné, but only when it was opened in Paris to reveal the estate number.

Afterward, we took part of the group to their hotel. The others followed, with everyone planning to get together that evening at the museum opening. Peggy and I had just returned home when Al called, and not too pleasantly asked me to tell the dealers to put nothing in writing, that he wanted the whole affair kept quiet. He spoke as if he thought I had control of those people. I said I'd do what I could, but that since he had invited the association to his home, it was fairly official. I tried to reassure him that his interest was my interest, and that the dealers wished him no harm. After all, everyone hoped he would continue his interest in art.

That night at the museum opening someone mentioned the events of the day, and it spread like wildfire. It was no longer "quiet" locally. The next day Al, sore as hell, called me and accused me of spreading the story. I told him I wasn't the one and reminded him that I had advised him earlier to buy only from reputable dealers such as Wildenstein or Hahn.

One of the two important dealers Al said he would not mention was Frank Lloyd, who controlled the operations of the large and powerful Marlborough Galleries of New York and London. He had been a member of the ADAA until the famous case that involved the estate of the noted painter, Rothko. The ADAA removed Lloyd from its membership when the courts found him and others guilty of manipulating the price of Rothko's paintings. Lloyd subsequently returned to London. . . .

On February 15, 1967, Ralph Colin documented the results of the examination by our "panel of experts" in the following letter [in part]:

> We regret to inform you that of the 58 items included in the Hogan appraisal which were viewed by our members, it is our members' opinion that eleven of them are or may be by the artists to whom they are attributed, three are probably by established artists but not by the artists to whom they are attributed, and 44 are not by the artists to whom they are attributed.
>
> Since you invited "a panel of experts" consisting of representatives of our membership to view your collection, and write a report of their opinion for your information and guidance, we are reporting to you the opinion which they formed. We deem it of the utmost importance that you have this opinion in mind in the event that you should consider selling, donating or otherwise disposing of any of the items in your collection.

In May, the story broke nationally and internationally. Peris talked to someone with the *New York Times* and all hell broke loose. The phone rang all day at Valley House as reporters called from around the world—London, Paris, New York—from *Newsweek* and *Time;* from NBC, ABC, and CBS; and so on. Television reporters arrived with cameras, and local newsmen buzzed around. What a carnival! Some press people can be dreadful. It's best to give them nothing, for no matter what is said, they can make it sound negative.

Slowly the story behind the story came to the surface. Fernand Legros, a naturalized US citizen of French extraction, later identified by Swiss police as "one of the most successful art forgers of the century," and Raoul Lessard, a French-Canadian and "private secretary" to Legros . . . called on Meadows and told him that Mrs. McDermott had said he should look at the rare paintings they had. Her name was the magic key that opened Al Meadows' door.

After the story of the forgeries became known, Louis Goldenberg, president of Wildenstein, told me that he had advised Al what to say to the press and had written a script for him. Al agreed that the paintings should be sent to Paris to be reviewed by a panel of French experts. Al left Louis with three million dollars for the beginning of a new collection and, by admitting his mistakes, became the new hero of the art world. Authorities eventually jailed Legros, Lessard, and Elmyr de Hory.

The popular version of de Hory's story was written by the novelist Clifford Irving in his book *Fake* which I read and found to be full of errors. . . . Not long after, Irving himself was accused of faking material for the biography of industrialist Howard Hughes. . . .

Nevertheless, much good came from all this. Al's interest in art grew and matured. He began to give support to the Dallas Museum of Art. He built a museum for Spanish art at Southern Methodist University, with the guidance of Dr. William Jordan, replacing the dubious works with good ones. He planned to leave his collection and support to the city. We all benefited from this man who started collecting for all the wrong reasons. Good art once again won the day. ★

Martin Jurow as told to Philip Wuntch

Martin Jurow, producer/agent, had a sixty-year show business career that encompassed a glittering array of celebrities he represented, worked with, and befriended. He was instrumental in casting Frank Sinatra in *From Here to Eternity,* Audrey Hepburn in *Breakfast at Tiffany's,* Peter Sellers in *The Pink Panther,* and Shirley MacLaine in *Terms of Endearment.* During Hollywood's Golden Era, he was executive assistant to legendary producers Jack L. Warner and Hal Wallis. He was behind the scenes and privy to fascinating stories about such cinematic gems as *Casablanca, On the Waterfront,* and *The Fugitive Kind,* and was professionally involved with such Broadway smash hits as *My Fair Lady, Oklahoma!, South Pacific, Guys and Dolls, The King and I,* and *The Music Man.* He helped shape the early careers of legends such as Elvis Presley, Burt Lancaster, and Kirk Douglas. He joined Lucille Ball and Desi Arnaz on their honeymoon, and he was a close personal friend of Katharine Hepburn. Philip Wuntch made his hobby his life's work when he joined the staff of *The Dallas Morning News* as an entertainment writer in 1969. He made his home in Dallas and still loved going to the movies. His name and his presence added a luster to Dallas.

From *Marty Jurow Seein' Stars: A Show Biz Odyssey*

It was the only time I saw Jack Warner smile with real tenderness. . . . He told me he was selling the studio to Seven Arts. Jack had been one of the most tightfisted of executives, but the mellow Jack whom I now encountered gave me sufficient severance. I thanked him for telling me, and my mind flew back a quarter of a century to our nightly ritual when I worked at Warner Bros.

"Let's put out the lights, J. L., let's put out the lights," I said. . . .

I did not seek to give up moviemaking. I just wanted to change bases, and I knew where I was going. Erin-Jo is Texas-born with fond memories of Dallas, where she spent some of her growing-up years. I had read a great deal about the Sunbelt and knew that Dallas was thriving.

The thought of starting over in a new locale was exhilarating. We settled comfortably in our new hometown and found the people warm, friendly, and forthright. Texans truly speak in "terms of endearment."

I became involved in the advancement of Texas filmmaking. There was no movie company in Dallas in the early 1970s, and I spent hours with Governor Preston Smith, nurturing the newly formed Texas Film Commission and advancing the USA Film Festival, which started in Dallas in 1970. . . .

My own first Texas films were inexpensive features, primarily made to test the Dallas talent pool. One film was budgeted at $84,000. Another came in at $102,000. Their titles were *Keep My Grave Open* and *Don't Look Back,* but they were steeped in mythic folklore rather than true horror. My name is not on either of those films. . . .

Sadly, the climate was not favorable for regional film production. Some Hollywood figures had already come to Dallas with lavish plans, only to leave abruptly when immediate funding was not forthcoming. Investors were interested in agriculture, cattle, and chemicals. They were interested in movies, but their interest did not extend to investments.

I was heartsick. I've always loved to keep busy. Retirement did not appeal to me because I've been blessed with an abundance of energy. One evening in Jefferson, Erin-Jo and I were discussing our love of Texas and our understanding of its reluctance to finance film production. Late that night, I felt her hand on my shoulder and her voice in my ear,

"Martin, you have a latent talent that you have not yet used," she said. "The law. . . ." At the age of sixty-five, not having looked at a law book in four decades, I found myself sitting in Southern Methodist University's George Underwood Law Library, studying sixteen courses to pass the Texas bar. I started by studying two hours a day, then four, then eight.

I went to Austin for the bar exam. Looking back, I realize how bold I was. On the bar exam's last question, my answer was simple: "I cannot write anymore. I hope the reader will realize that I know the answer, as I have known other answers. But I cannot write another sentence."

I passed the bar exam. Much to my amazement, the chief justice of the Supreme Court of Texas asked for my autograph. Many times through the years, I had stepped aside as fans begged autographs from their idols. Now I gladly gave mine.

Passing the bar exam after not cracking a law book for forty years gave me vitality and curiosity. I had lived in show business for four decades, and I wanted to expand. It was a great feeling.

I talked my way into the office of legendary district attorney Henry Wade, the noted legal eagle who had convicted Jack Ruby. . . .

I became assistant district attorney and Henry Wade's personal assistant as well.

It was a wonderful period of my life. I had never been a great fan of lawyers, finding some to be insufferably pompous as well as guilty of deeds they would be litigious about. Yet I loved working with a group of 104 district attorneys, most in their early thirties. I was refreshed, and my mind was alert. I had never felt so energized. Walking up the courthouse steps with those young district attorneys was one of the most exciting times of my life.

I had been wise to choose not to grow old in Hollywood.

I was considered something of a curio, and curiosity was heightened when a voice echoed through the corridors of the county courthouse, saying "Mr. Gregory Peck is on the phone, calling for Mr. Martin Jurow. . . ."

One of Erin-Jo's and my dearest friends is Dallas philanthropist and benefactor Ruth Collins Sharp Altshuler. . . . Ruth's daughter Sally, a talented young woman with a strong interest in the arts, was mesmerized by Kate Chopin's haunting early-twentieth-century novel *The Awakening,* which had stoked some of the first fires of American feminism. Sally and Ruth said that if I would produce a film of Chopin's novel, they would help find the funding. Our film version of *The Awakening* was called *The End of August.* It was shot in Mobile, Alabama, with a distinguished cast that included Sally Sharp, Lilia Skala, David Marshall Grant, Kathleen Widdoes, Paul Roebling, Paul Shenar, Mark-Linn Baker, and Saundra Santiago. The movie received strong reviews and was a great success at the Deauville Film Festival. . . .

My next film, *Waltz Across Texas,* starred our goddaughter Anne Archer, daughter of our friend Marjorie Lord, and Anne's husband, golf star Terry Jastrow. The supporting cast included Mary Kay Place and Richard Farnsworth. It was shot entirely in Terry's hometown of Midland, Texas, then a booming oil town. Within one week, we had ample funding. Had we come to Midland even six months later, we would not have been able to raise money. The oil business is that precarious.

And it was in Midland that Erin-Jo had the fateful discussion with Mary Kay Place, which realized my dream of making a movie version of the novel *Terms of Endearment* by Larry McMurtry.

After the adventure of *Terms of Endearment* . . . veteran producer Ray Stark, maker of such films as *Funny Girl*, *The Way We Were*, and *The Night of the Iguana,* called upon me to produce *Sylvester,* a delightful girl-loves-horse movie starring Melissa Gilbert and, once again, the sublime character actor Richard Farnsworth, who would be lauded in 1999 for *The Straight Story.* At the request of Rosemary Benton, wife of Don Benton, minister of the Lovers Lane Methodist Church in Dallas, I helped produce *Papa Was a Preacher.*

I returned to the position of executive producer for a tribute to John F. Kennedy, the film shown in the Sixth Floor Museum in Dallas, the memorial to JFK at the site of the Texas Schoolbook Depository. Dallas documentary filmmakers Allen and Cynthia Mondell were instrumental in its remarkable success. The museum has attracted visitors from around the world.

New opportunities arrived, each one seeming like an early Christmas gift. One day in 1986, Kermit Hunter, dean of the Meadows School of Arts at SMU, came by for a visit.

"You have so much more knowledge about filmmaking than anyone else in the city," he said. "Why not teach a course?"

Just as in my early years I had longed to produce, I now longed to teach. I had been thinking this over before Kermit's visit and suggested a course in business opportunities within the world of entertainment.

I taught the course for ten years. *Goodbye, Mr. Chips* is one of my favorite movies, and now I got the chance to be a Mr. Chips. My students were fascinated by Old Hollywood and respectful of the talent that was involved.

The same year I began my teaching career, I began a radio show at KAAM. I once visited the local ASCAP offices in the Dallas suburb of Plano. In the same building was the KAAM radio station. After a quick meeting of the minds with the station's program director Danny Owen, I began narrating a radio show, *Martin Jurow of Show Business,* which ran for ten years, and was rewarded with many letters and phone calls. . . .

Early in the 1990s, I met one of the brightest men I've ever encountered, Dallas lawyer Stephen P. Jarchow. He came to me with the idea for Regent Entertainment, a mini-studio that finances and produces films. We met regularly for much of the decade, discussing various aspects of the movie industry. I served as senior advisor to Regent, and Steve shepherded the company to great international success with *Gods and Monsters,* with Oscar-nominated performances by Ian McKellen and Lynn Redgrave. . . .

I had the good fortune to be involved in movie production during the studio system's golden era. When I see today's movies, I note the names of Paramount, Warner Bros., Universal, 20th Century Fox, Columbia, and Disney. These corporations function in ways that the old tycoons could not have foreseen. But their names are the same, and I am thrilled to see that their corporate entities still exist after so many years. . . .

My life has been an odyssey in which I used both my law degree and my fascination with the entertainment world, a love that began eighty years ago with those Brooklyn vaudeville shows. I followed my dream and ended up with a wealth of human experience. I was never fired from any job, never prodded to leave. And I made good on a pledge I made to myself many decades ago: I never took the subway to work. . . .

When [Erin-Jo and I] reminisce, I see the faces of Frank, Marlon, Elvis, Sammy, Audrey, Kate, Shirley MacLaine, Gary Cooper, Jack Nicholson, Jack Lemmon, Burt, Kirk, Steve McQueen, Ava, and Lucy and Desi. It has been a remarkable odyssey. ★

John William Rogers

John William Rogers is a native of the city about which he writes. He was for many years associated with *The Dallas Times Herald* as a critic, editor, and columnist, but took time out from his activities as a Dallas journalist to serve as book editor of Marshall Field's *Chicago Sun.* A graduate of Dartmouth College, early in his career he was associated with a number of publishing houses in New York and helped launch the Literary Guild of America. He wrote both short and full-length plays, one of which was produced by the Dallas Little Theatre, *Judge Lynch,* and won the Belasco Cup in the National Little Theatre Tournament held in New York. His wife was the novelist Kenneth Horan. Rogers humorously explains Dallas weather in this piece.

From *The Lusty Texans of Dallas: Their First Hundred and Twenty-five Years*

The lives of Dallasans like people every-where are profoundly affected by their climate, but there is perhaps no place where the climate is so in theory misunderstood. For eight months of the year the weather is mild but brisk enough to be exhilarating and to make men and women dash about as energetically as the inhabitants of any city in the land. For the other four months, however, Dallasans live in practically a tropic region. But the people of the town have never accepted philosophically the reality that a third of their climate is tropic. From the earliest days they have faced the long hot summers somewhat grudgingly as though heat were a kind of imposition on a land that should be temperate. The reason for this anomalous mental attitude is interesting to analyze, for it lies in the racial heritage of the people who settled here. When their pioneer ancestors journeyed from the colder climates of the North to Texas, they brought with them in their covered wagons ideas as well as household goods, and sometimes to their own discomfort, the fixed ideas outlasted the furniture.

One of these ideas that did them a disservice was the notion of the calendar. In the case of weather these emigrants who stemmed from northern Europe accepted the immemorial assumptions of their forbears. Ask any Dallasan today about the seasons of Dallas and very likely he will look at you a little surprised and answer the town has the four seasons found everywhere—spring, summer, autumn, winter, so universally celebrated by the poets of England and the continent as well as the poets of America. And yet this is not true. "What is so rare as a day in June," for Dallas should read "What is so rare as a day in May—or even April?" For it is April and May that affect the Dallasan as June did the poet Lowell, and there are so many "rare days" it would be hard to confine them to a single month.

The conventional minded among Dallas citizens visit England in July and August (which is the time everyone who can tries to be away from Texas). They find things blooming in that glorious profusion which for centuries has inspired its poets to celebrate the summer season. They remember Dallas settled down to a sunbaked two months when no flower less hardy than a zinnia, a petunia, or a periwinkle can flourish and their instinct is to think of Dallas as somehow underprivileged. They have forgotten that in April and May the town had just as glorious a profusion of bloom. It comes at a different time, that's all.

The philosophic appreciation of the Dallas climate is further clouded by two factors from the outside. Strangers from the North arrive in Texas in the heat of summer with clothes unsuited to the weather and quite innocent of the techniques which the inhabitants of tropic lands have evolved for living on the best of terms with the climate. They reach Dallas easily and swiftly without any barriers of borders and customs. They naturally assume that as an integral part of the United States, its life is of the identical pattern with the rest of the land, and on all sides there are superficial proofs of this. There is no quality of drama in arriving and getting settled to remind them that the city is in any way different from the one they have left, and they have left home at what is probably the pleasantest time of their whole year.

The high temperatures appall them, and the contrast with the weather of home makes them fail utterly to appreciate the climate of Dallas in its relation to Dallas. They do not realize that during the two months of slush and mud, melt, and freeze which beset them through February and March, Dallas has weather comparable to the choicest of their year. These things are to be mentioned because the point of view of these visitors tends to affect the outlook of the Dallasans themselves, and makes them accept the idea that they are somewhat put upon by nature. And another aspect of life intensifies this impression for them. The town in its business promotion and cultural activities is magnetized to the great centers of the North, and being in step with these eight months of the year without effort—the general impression is that if keeping step with the other four becomes difficult, the lack is somehow in Dallas. As one of the style centers of the nation, for instance, one observes in Dallas in August the windows of the fashionable stores full of furs, suits, and heavy fall clothes, when the thermometer may be often for days at a time topping a hundred. And a more direct conspiracy on the part of the merchants themselves has also been responsible for this impression. Until recently when men have begun to demand comfortable clothes for summer, if a customer went into one of the better shops and asked for a suit of really light summer material, the clerk very likely raised a supercilious eyebrow and regretted that the store "does not carry that grade of merchandise" (the private theory being that since the larger profits came from suits made of heavier cloth and the human male is a very timid creature where his dress is concerned, he should be bullied to keep on wearing what was most profitable).

Dallas's understanding of itself would be vastly increased if its citizens recognized that the town in fact has five seasons, not four. For here is the way the climate really divides itself:

SPRING—The last of February to the first of May.

SUMMER—The first of May to the first days of July.

SOL—The Latin word *Sol,* sun, is the name which the advocates of the thirteen-month calendar apply to their extra month. Everyone who has experienced a Dallas summer knows that from the first days of July the most striking thing about the world for the next ten or twelve weeks is the glare of the sun.

AUTUMN—The last of September until the end of December.

NORTHER—The fifth and final season ordinarily begins about the first of January and continues well into February. It is designated as Norther and not Winter because Dallas does not have winter as the northern part of this country knows it. Mild sunny weather persists and then icy biting winds sweep straight down from Canada and freeze the marrow of Texans' bones. This sudden blast of cold when the temperature drops as much as twenty or thirty degrees in an hour and slides from balmy air and open windows to a howl of wind and ice overnight is known as "a blue norther." Northers usually blow themselves out in a few days, the wind changes its direction, coming from the south and a Gulf breeze once more brings mildness.

Though the majority of Dallasans are still bound to the idea of the four seasons, here, as is happening elsewhere in America, the community is beginning to be sensitive to its individuality and ingenius in adapting its way of life imaginatively to its particular kind of regionalism. The discovery that its highly keyed atmosphere is ideally suited to bright color is bringing about an effective use of color in decorating homes and shops that only a few years ago would have seemed utterly daring. ★

Jay Dunston Milner

Jay Dunston Milner, from Lubbock, Texas, graduated from Southern Mississippi University with a BA and MA and coached football before becoming a reporter for the Hattiesburg, Mississippi, *American* and the Associated Press. He was the managing editor of Hodding Carter's Greenville, Mississippi, *Delta Democrat-Times* and went to New York as the assistant to the editorial page editor of the *New York Herald Tribune.* He returned to Texas in 1961 and fell in with a rowdy crowd of Texas prose and songwriters to whom much of *Confessions of a Maddog: A Romp through the High-flying Texas Music and Literary Era of the Fifties to the Seventies* is devoted. Milner's adventures in re-establishing the journalism department at SMU, his view of journalism in Dallas at the time, his hiring of legendary writer from Oak Cliff, Billy Lee Brammer, and finally his friendship with newspaperman Stanley Walker give a snapshot of the era.

From *Confessions of a Maddog: A Romp through the High-flying Texas Music and Literary Era of the Fifties to the Seventies:* Literary Giants and William Randolph Hearse

In 1961, Bud Shrake, Gary Cartwright, and Dan Jenkins were still dazzling Dallas with their literate, humorous coverage of college and professional sports (they didn't see athletics as the most important struggle in the world). This was back before there were Mavericks and Rangers, so the Metroplex was essentially a one-professional sports community, not counting soccer and most folks didn't. That one sport was, of course, Dallas Cowboys football. The Texans had moved to Kansas City. Shrake and Cartwright had severed ties with their longtime mentor and editor, Blackie Sherrod at the *Times Herald,* and had gone over to the *Morning News,* where Shrake's daily column now ran down the left-hand side of the sports section page one, in direct competition with Sherrod's popular, prize-winning column in the *Times-Herald.* That rivalry was the topic of conversation at every gathering for a while. Shrake and Cartwright were looked upon by their many hard-core fans as high-spirited rebels with a cause. The exact nature of their rebellious cause was not all that clear, but whatever it was, or wasn't, it seemed to be full of compassion and fun, as all really admirable causes are or ought to be. A few years later, when I was teaching journalism, I was struck by the number of my students who had been lured into the profession as high school kids by the dash and style of the Dallas sportswriters of that era. It is unlikely that any other city has ever enjoyed so much excellent sports writing as Dallas and its environs did when Sherrod, Jenkins, Cartwright, and Shrake were all there at the same time.

Meantime, in Texas letters, J. Frank Dobie was still the king, and people still read Roy Bedichek. Larry L. King was working for a congressman. William A. Owens was on the faculty at Columbia University. A. C. Greene was (depending on the year) putting out the editorial page, book page, and Op-Ed page at the *Times-Herald,* which was the most interesting local daily in Texas at the time, unless it was the *Corpus Christi Caller-Times,* and from time to time Fort Worth's underfinanced *Press.*

Billie Lee's friend Larry McMurtry (they both went to North Texas at different times, or something like that), was around Austin now and then in the 1960s, the early Brammer period. He would show up for a few days, then disappear for months at a time. Somebody said they thought he was teaching English composition at TCU and playing pool against his students on the varsity football team to determine their grades. We found out later that when McMurtry disappeared, he was writing. A few years later, when he was teaching at Rice, he came out with his second novel, *Leaving Cheyenne.* I got a call from Bud Shrake the week I read it. All he said was, "Have you read McMurtry's new one?" I said I had, and Shrake said, "Don't it make you want to cry because you didn't write it?" and I said yes, it did, indeed. . . .

My conclusion about the seventies, when the 1980s threatened to come down on us, was this: a decade that gave us Willie Nelson and Earl Campbell couldn't be all bad. It was in the 1970s that Willie and Waylon and Jerry Jeff and a handful of Texas prose writers managed to create Texas chic even on the isle of Manhattan. And it could get downright crazy in Austin and Dallas and Fort Worth and Luckenbach and, sometimes, Houston and other spots around the state.

McMurtry had kind of exploded upon the literary scene, in his home state and elsewhere, as the seventies opened with the release of the movie made from his novel, *The Last Picture Show.*

I was teaching journalism at SMU then and escorted a small group of my students to Washington, DC, and New York City during the holidays between the fall and spring semesters. The DC stopover featured a night of conversation with Larry L. King, and the next evening's visit was with McMurtry at his home. I had given the students a list of books and magazine articles to read in preparation for the trip. They would be meeting Willie Morris and David Halberstam in New York City. They had been reading the Willie Morris-edited editions of *Harper's* and were duly impressed by the work of King, Morris, and Halberstam. But Larry McMurtry was not yet a name that lit up their eyes. King had fascinated them and kept them up most of the night before, so when we taxied into northwest Washington to McMurtry's home, they were weary and ready to get this assignment over with as soon as possible.

According to my friend Joe Murray, 1970 was almost thirty years ago. That may explain why I don't remember all the specifics about that session in McMurtry's living room, except that it was cozy and chatty, and the students left more awake than when they arrived. But the excitement burst forth concerning McMurtry only after we had returned to Dallas and were into the spring semester. It was then that the movie, *The Last Picture Show,* opened in Big D. For days after that opening, students who had been sleepily impressed by the Texas author's friendliness and willingness to answer all their questions—both the intelligent and the stupid—ran into my office, in pairs and trios and singles, all atwitter, sputtering "You mean, that's the same Larry McMurtry we spent an evening with in Washington?"

During the visit my students and I enjoyed with McMurtry at his home in Washington, DC, Larry and I wandered together into his kitchen, to refill some chip bowls or something, and he said to me, "I apologize for stealing your hearse." As luck would have it, I had not read Larry's latest (at that time) novel *Moving On*, and didn't know what he was talking about. Somehow, however, I sensed he was referring to something in that novel. So, being a straight-forward, honest young man from Lubbock, I said, "Ahh, that's okay." Then Larry said something to the effect that Billie Lee Brammer had told him about my hearse, and it had fit perfectly with a character in *Moving On*, so he stuck it in there. At last, I could tell him the truth. "Don't apologize," I said. "I'm flattered." And I was, and am. At the first opportunity, of course, I grabbed a copy of *Moving On* and read it.

Sure enough, in chapter two, Sonny Shanks, the dashing, handsome, and somewhat rascally rodeo champion, owns a hearse. To quote from page 36: "For years Shanks had driven Cadillac hearses—they were an essential part of his legend. The hearses were white and he always had three sets of bulls' horns painted in gold on each one: A set on each door and one on the top, so people in airplanes would know it was him, he said."

My hearse wasn't white, it was classic black with that buffalo hump over the cab. I had no longhorns painted on it anywhere, but it was a hearse, and I had been traveling about Texas in it in those pre-suburban van times. I naturally dubbed my hearse "William Randolph." ★

Stanley Walker, Baron of Black Sheep's Retreat

Stanley Walker, a Texan, was a legendary editor at the New York Herald Tribune. *The Texas Institute of Letters gives a Stanley Walker Award for an outstanding piece of reporting for the year.*

Stanley wrote that he would like to take a ride in my hearse, since he had never ridden in one.

I arrived about the middle of a Saturday afternoon. Stanley and I sipped hot coffee in a downtown café, waiting until Ruth closed the library, which was in the courthouse. Then she drove out to the ranch about ten miles north of town, and we were to follow immediately in the hearse. But the hearse wouldn't start. After trying the starter so many times the battery began to sound weak, Stanley and I got out, lifted the hood, stared at the engine awhile, fiddled with some wires, kicked the tires, tried the starter again to no avail, and stared at the engine some more. Then he telephoned for help. It was almost dark when the young man arrived in an ancient green pickup truck. He stared, tight-lipped, under the hood awhile, as we had done before him, then announced that he'd have to give us a pull. He said the hearse had fluid drive, so he'd have to pull it pretty fast to start it. It was too heavy to push, he said.

The dilapidated old truck was leading us rapidly through the business district when Stanley noted that our caravan appeared to be attracting an uncommon amount of attention among Saturday evening strollers along the main street. As we rattled by, they were doing double takes that would have done old-time silent movie directors proud.

"You'd think they've never seen a hearse being pulled by a green pickup truck before," Stanley remarked, a twinkle in his eyes.

It was about this time that we first noticed smoke curling up through cracks in the floorboard at our feet. We were whipping along and now folks were shouting at us, although we couldn't understand what they were saying. Stanley opened the door and leaned out. "We're on fire!" he announced solemnly as he slammed the door and lay back against the seat, his eyes closed.

I looked out my side. Sure enough, smoke was blowing up from beneath the hearse as we picked up speed and reached the outskirts of town. Then, the umbilical chain connecting us to the pickup snapped. I tried the horn, but it wasn't working. We both leaned out and bellowed at the young man in the pickup. We were a mile or so past the city limits, and I was stomping on the brakes when he saw the smoke and stopped.

As it turned out, there was more smoke than fire, and we were able to extinguish what little there was with some water we found in a ditch near the road. Then, wonder of wonders, the hearse started easily. We paid the young man and rested there awhile, catching our breath and letting our hearts slow down. Then I drove us, slowly and thoughtfully, back to Black Sheep's Retreat, leaving the young man standing beside his ancient truck scratching his head.

We had gone maybe a mile or two when Stanley started laughing. He said he supposed that was the most excitement they'd had in Lampasas in many a Saturday night. "Must have been some sight," he grinned, "seeing a flaming hearse being pulled down Main Street. Folks'll speculate on that for some time, I expect."

We had turned off the highway, . . . when Stanley said, "That's an experience that would cause any man to ponder—having his hearse catch on fire. It's almost as if the devil were rushing things there a bit." ★

Good Ole Billie Lee

William Lee (Billy) Brammer, journalist and political novelist, was born in Oak Cliff and graduated from North Texas State College (now the University of North Texas). From 1955 to 1959 Brammer worked as press aide in Washington, DC, to Lyndon B. Johnson, when Johnson was Senate majority leader. During that period he wrote a 1950s era novel, The Gay Place, *which is still in print. He is buried in Laurel Land Memorial Park, Dallas.*

Brammer wrote at night, or tried to. He told me he wrote *The Gay Place* while working for *Time* on the White House night shift. Since very little news breaks at the White House at night, he was free to work on his novel. To stay awake he swallowed diet pills. That's the story he told me. I've heard others over the years.

Billie Lee said he wrote what became part three of *The Gay Place* first and sent it to Houghton Mifflin. They liked it, but felt it was too short and asked him to add to it. He then wrote what became part two. When his editor read that, he apparently became excited about what he had and asked Billie Lee to add still more. Brammer then wrote part one, which many consider the best of the three parts.

One morning after somebody's party, Billie Lee and I were watching the sunrise from a hillside overlooking Lake Travis, and he confided that he was afraid he couldn't write a real novel—that he didn't know how. He said that sometimes late at night, when he was alone at his typewriter and the pills were kicking in, he believed he could do it again, but in the cold light of day he was afraid he didn't know how. . . .

As his body became increasingly tolerant to the contents of the ever-present diet pills, Billie Lee's need for more and more grew and grew. Innumerable women felt protective of this quiet little man who had written the book that had moved them so and to demonstrate their dedication, they would volunteer to scavenge pills for him. . . .

Houghton Mifflin looked forward to Billie Lee's second book and paid him several advances for it. His agent was also anxious to see it completed, and for years a number of major East Coast critics kept an eye out for its release. Gore Vidal had called *The Gay Place,* winner of the prestigious Houghton Mifflin fiction prize and several other awards, an "American classic."

Billie Lee's second novel was to be a sequel to *The Gay Place.* The working title was "Fustian Days" and, at one time in 1962, he had written more than a hundred pages. I read them and in my opinion they were vintage Brammer, at his fluid best. . . . Roy Sherwood, Billie Lee's protagonist in part one of *The Gay Place,* was the main character.

I had just been hired as acting chairman of the SMU journalism department, a job that would begin as soon as I got back to the Metroplex. I needed someone with pizazz, who knew what journalism was about, to teach a couple of classes. Not full-time, mind you. Just a couple of classes. Why not, I asked myself, extend the offer to Billie Lee? I recalled what a bang-up impression he made on the student journalists at Texas Tech, and how good the experience had seemed to be for him. His name still had drawing power, at least among people who read books, and I sincerely hoped SMU journalism students read books now and then. Besides, maybe the responsibilities of pedagogy would turn Billie Lee around. I offered him the job. Billie Lee accepted and moved to Dallas within the month.

The journalism program at SMU was at a low ebb when I took over. As a matter of fact, it had been in danger of being discontinued by the liberal arts school when Dean Kermit Hunter of the School of Fine Arts volunteered to take it under his wing. He hired me as interim chairman. To get things rolling, I felt we needed to attract some favorable attention among students, as well as professionals. According to the records I inherited, there were fifteen journalism majors left over from the previous administration. I was able to locate only five of those, and three of the five changed majors that semester. So we were starting from scratch in more ways than one.

My only other faculty member that year was also a part-timer—Peter Gent, who agreed to teach an evening advertising class. Before he became a pass catcher for the Dallas Cowboys, Gent had majored in advertising at Michigan State, where he was an All-America basketball star performer. He had been forced by injuries to retire from pro football and hadn't written *North Dallas Forty* yet. Unlike Billie Lee, Pete was teaching the course strictly as a favor to me. He didn't need the two hundred dollars per month stipend.

For almost the entire school year, Billie Lee (as far as I know) met most of his classes. He was teaching a newswriting lab and a course we had created for upper echelon students wherever we could find them. It was basically a reading and discussion course which attempted to put the students in touch with the responsibilities and rewards of professional journalism. We felt it was inexcusable for a journalism graduate to go into the field without knowing what had been written out there in the real world by the best professionals, and something about the newsmen who were writing the best news media prose, contemporaneously, as well as historically. Later, according to our blueprint, these less than technical aspects of journalism could be incorporated into other courses as they developed. We had to make do with what we had that first year to meet specific student needs the best way we could with limited resources. I had talked with editors at a number of the nation's best newspapers, and they told me they could always teach neophyte journalists to organize a news story and count heads, but news organizations didn't have time to educate them, or to teach them how to write sentences and paragraphs.

As the year got underway, my part-time faculty and I got caught up in the idealism of the job facing us, and the rare opportunity we had to make a difference on the side of the best journalism. I did, anyway, and I think Billie

Lee did too, at least for a time. I was commuting from Fort Worth, and most every evening after work I would stop by at either Billie Lee's apartment or Pete and Jody Gent's Oak Lawn home to let the rush hour traffic subside. We exchanged cosmic resolutions to all the world's problems as we listened to the high-impact music that was coming out at that time—Dylan, Rolling Stones, Kris Kristofferson, John Prine, the Beatles, and the Byrds, as well as Buck Owens and George Jones and others that don't come to mind immediately this far on down the line. Billie Lee's hi-fi system was in hock to the Gents, so we did our listening there. . . .

Perhaps our most productive teaching sessions that year were impromptu, when Larry King, A. C. Greene, Dwight Sargent (my boss at the *New York Herald Tribune),* Bud Shrake, Ken Kesey, and others dropped by to chat informally with my journalism students, in classroom situations or in my living room after hours.

Word of these extraordinary spontaneous appearances began to spread across the campus, and the journalism department entered upon a renaissance that began attracting some of SMU's better students. Some of those students had majored in journalism previously, as undergraduates, but had ultimately transferred to other departments in disillusionment. By the end of that school year, we had 125 majors and minors signed up for the next fall. I would estimate that at least half that number were seriously considering pursuing careers in the news media and had the talent to accomplish some degree of success in the field. I kept up with most of these kids for a number of years after we all left SMU, and they were (and, no longer kids, still are today) performing gratifyingly well at various newspapers and wire services from Boston to Los Angeles to Alaska. I'm proud of them.

During his first few months at SMU, Billie Lee mentioned Dorothy to me only once. "When Darthy comes back from Mexico," he mumbled one evening on the way to the Gents, "I hope she brings me some heart medicine." You could purchase diet pills in Mexico then without a prescription.

It was a very busy year for me. I was teaching four classes and handling all the departmental paper-shuffling, as well as counseling. I don't know exactly when Billie Lee's determination began to unravel. A couple of times I dispatched a husky pair of varsity football players who were taking journalism classes to ensure that Mr. Brammer got to class on time. Many students were telling me how interesting, and even inspiring, his classes were, but others were complaining that Billie Lee wasn't editing their copy in the newswriting lab. "He just glances at my stories and says, 'Looks fine to me,'" one worried coed told me. I checked into the situation, and soon decided to take over the lab myself for the remainder of the spring semester. By the end of the year, Billie Lee was regularly either missing class altogether or bumbling his way through them.

Shortly before school reconvened the next fall, I could see the handwriting on the wall. The new department chairperson was poised to fire Billie Lee, and I figured it would be best to urge my friend to accept the invitation he had from Bowling Green State University to be writer-in-residence there. In his typically passive manner, Billie Lee allowed Pete and Jody to put him on a plane for Kentucky, although he grumbled all the way to the airport that he'd prefer to stay and teach at SMU. He couldn't seem to grasp the undeniable fact that his beautiful bird's nest on Mockingbird Lane was a thing of the past. A couple of months after he left, I received the following letter:

18 October 1970
El Milmoss:

Well sir ah so goddam and hell I am for a fack right here and have been, more often than not, in respectable thrall of good behavior though fearfully strung out at this instant on account of how else muster up the verbiage and vitality to make these here words on them that paper? Why bother? I say (and there are armies of others, nameless for now, eager to join me in saying) why the fuck not? Possibly to demonstrate once and for most that I by god am still fulsomely and tiresomely capable of self expression communication, myriad epiphanies, occasional prophecy and revelation, and sequential nocturnal emissions—all of it channeled toward and into and sometimes out of old discredited print media. Frens and shameless sycophants may claim that one is plainly deranged to abandon stardom as rocky roll equipment manager—yet I say break wind on such provincial tyrannies! It by god does a man a bunch of therapeutic good to at least once or twice a year maybe writing words on yella typish paper. Call me a sentimentalist if you will but I say (and I know somebodies somewheres etc.) a truly full-blooded man can't sang and dance forever without periodically resorting to phonetic alphabets of any color persuasion. And of course it's plain enough is it not? (it is not!) that I'm still possessed of the old magic. Even now, as I compose, frens and strangers wander past remarking of mah prose: "How (oddly) lucid! How cogent! What quaint! Sweet reason! Stupefying imagery! Damn near coherent. Some gonad! Up his vernacular! Praise the Smith Corona composing Machine!" Etc. I have immortal longings and plan to go there at Christmas break.

Enclosed find example of famed BGSU daily J dept fulminations. Very tame, very lame: they could clearly use a reform administration such as El Millmoss and his faithful sherpa guide (whose name, nose and barely recordable height are disclosed only to precious phar out phew). We should real and truly get to some such new assignment as we finish that fancy goddam textbook you forever dawdling over.

This place is pretty, pleasant, seeming safe from hippie peril and riot squad assault. Improbably picturesque, in manner of New England townships: handsome campus, gorgeous under-grads, impressive post-grad programs here and there in evidence (though equally commonplace, an astonishing number of impoverished ones). Enrollment is about 6,000 which is about twice the population of Bowling Green—a still pulsing little microcosm that is (for all its superficial pretties) the spit-niffling image of Anderson's Winesburg, Ohio, grotesques and all.

Most notable aspect at this time is hiatus in cultural apocalypse, abundant evidence elsewhere . . . it seems four or five years behind Berkeley; if SMU seems only now evolved into flower-children, Gentle Thursday concerns but barely activist syndrome of UT in mid-Sixties. . . . well Bowling Green is somewhere there at hootenanny/Kingston Trio stage of. . . . what the fuck was it? The boys look like Pat Boone perhaps, two three weeks overdue at the barber shop. The ladies are rather like Sandra Dee in miniskirt and training bra. My god I'm suffocating in all this interminable wholesomeness. . . .

Was stunned by cultural (lag) shock first week here when, heading home after dark across campus I detected provocative sounds of great masses of people stomping and sanging and raising some sort of radical new left queer commie hell . . . Except I kept hearing ukuleles! How the fuck them anachronistic muzak pickers? Also, loudly and clearly now as I moved closer, these protesting voices seemed directed at one of the larger lady dorms. And so help me Jesus there it was: a genuine pantie raid: mobs of randy crewcut future FBI agents and cybernetic slavies whooping and moaning for lady underwear (pantie girdles accepted). . . .

Still, these nice cleanwashed shorthair nippers are intelligent, reasonably competent as writers, more or less sophisticated (in baroque ways, such as obsessions with modern jazz, V. Nabokov and Wm. Burroughs, little or no interest in Hemingway or A. Ginchburgh) soccer, ice skating, homecoming (homecoming?), such radicalism as has yet been apparent is vaguely anti-establishment (because of Kent State much more than Fred Hampton or Jackson State, etc.) not so much anti-war and anti-draft, not so much pro Democrat (or left of anywhere) as perhaps profoundly disappointed in Nixon, Mitchell, etc. Kunstler provoked an astonishing turnout of the ex-Mickey Mousketeers, and wisely thumped away on the raw nerve of the Administration's all-out war on college students all over. This appeal to their own immediate paranoia was in fact only real responsive emotion apparent in course of his pitch . . . One wonders if they are capable of declaring (not a separate peace) but a separate war on straight old-timer society, clearly distinct from any such dope-crazed guerrilla theater shit or Weatherman terrorism one normally associates with student activism. These kids are going to mount the barricades, win the fucking revolution, then split quickly for hometowns thruout Middle West where they will usurp and seize banks, buildings, stores and Cadillac dealerships once in clutches of their old men.

Booze—Oh Jesus yes: weekends look like fraternity row in Austin at Roundup. But the hippie community, in and out of school, probably couldn't muster sufficient numbers for a Kappa Sig chapter. The local head shop, beautiful little place well stocked with psychedelic posters and Sgt. Pepper field jacks, well, so help me, this place doesn't even stock Zig Zag papers!

Ah but I digress. I had only meant to say hidy and assure anyone who cares that I am unimaginable well-liked here and can't wait to get home to my frens, rocky-roll music, beloved Poodle dog and (reassure me endlessly!) grabass teaching career. I am ever your fawning subordinate and Rotter in Residence.

Billie Lee Rising Gorge, Ont.

I've been involved in a bunch of projects through the years. Some turned out better than others and some were more fun than others, but none was ever quite like the SMU melodrama. When perspective returned, I realized I never had anything turn out as well as that endeavor. Even the idea of getting Billie Lee up there wasn't all bad, nor was it unsuccessful. I personally know of three students who were inspired by Billie Lee to read their first books. That alone is worth a lot, even though Billie Lee's going in and out of focus on me was trying from time to time.

There weren't nearly as many published authors living and working in Texas back then as there are now. New York and California were still a long way from Texas and still held a monopoly on big league success in the letters. Billie Lee was a Texan, living in Texas, who had defined Texas in a unique way, and his prose style had been accepted as engaging and authentic by the biggest of the big leaguers on both coasts. Other Texas writers who were still around were old men who wrote about old times. Or lived somewhere else and probably looked like college professors. Billie Lee was our Norman Mailer. Quiet, yes, but he was out there amongst 'em. In the early-to-middle sixties, if you went anywhere that was anywhere, you ran into Billie Lee Brammer talk. . . .

Billie Lee was one of those folks everybody wanted to meet as soon as they heard about him, one by one, for their own reasons, whatever they might have been. After meeting him, for some reason, most people sooner or later developed an urge to mother Billie Lee. Especially women, but not just womankind. All of his cronies seemed to go out of their way to please him. He had that effect on you. You just felt obliged to indulge him. He was so . . . so civilized.

You had to lean in to hear him, he spoke so softly. And it wasn't always easy to follow Billie Lee's train of thought. But if you tried hard, it was inevitably well worth the trouble. He had always read everything you had read, in addition to everything you intended to read. He was familiar with every album you intended to buy when you got around to it. He had already gotten around to it somehow. . . .

Why did Billie Lee choose being high over fulfilling his potential? Nobody really knows, of course, although the question was pondered endlessly by those who knew him well and many who barely knew him at all. . . . Billie Lee perhaps agreed with Johnny Cash who, when asked if he took diet pills for this or that deep psychological reason, said he took them because he liked the way they made him feel.

Even after he gave up trying to keep up a reasonable front, there was a charismatic aura about Billie Lee. You got the feeling that he knew something you didn't know, and that if you could make friends with him, he might share some of those secrets with you. ★

A. C. Greene

[Editor's note: A. C. Greene writes of the historic and famous Stoneleigh Hotel, a traditional watering hole and place to live temporarily in Dallas for years and now newly reopened after a refurbishing.]

Heartbreak Hotel: Notes on life after divorce at the Stoneleigh

The Stoneleigh Hotel, on Maple Avenue, has a pair of ancient stone lions lying at its front door. Ninety years ago, it is said, these lions guarded the entrance to the commercial center of Dallas, the Cotton Exchange. Perhaps they were fierce when young—a subtle, feral warning to the traders who played dangerous speculations with King Cotton. But time made the lions benign. And now instead of warning, they welcome, their faces and their leonine brows worn down, one thinks, to understanding, after all these years, what an amusing creature a human is, coming and going, going and coming.

The Lions Den is, therefore, the bar at the Stoneleigh; a dark interior with funny little red lights that twinkle dimly near the ceiling, so that you are tempted to sit and look at them for hours, speculating whether they are hooked up to some electrical relay that makes them blink, or if they were improperly installed and merely blink from a poor contact. The Den is a funny sort of place to begin with. The front area of the bar seems to be part of the hotel's entrance hallway, and the back section definitely winds up in the kitchen. A newcomer, walking into the Den, can't tell exactly where bar begins or ends, and he feels awkward, sitting at a table back among diners or drinking a martini near the front while little ladies with blue hair come peeking along the hall, staring quite directly into the drinker's face.

But you get over that rather quickly, finding a table under the funny red lights or sitting stuck out in the dining room and thinking nothing of it. You even find a sort of protection in the way things are strung together. According to how you are feeling, you can take a table close to the bar, with conversation and noise, or disappear into the shadows or around some corner (the Den is full of corners) away from the crowd. The Den becomes, in that beloved phrase used so much by our society which fears domesticity, "a home away from home. . . ."

About five P.M. the really cute people begin coming in: advertising executives and copywriters, East River wetbacks who find something strongly New Yorkish about the bar, semi-young sports on their way to jog or play gentlemen's soccer, a lot of the so-called media crowd and the good-looking women who associate themselves with those types, or are those types themselves. That's the way the Den looks until that most indefinite hour of the restless day: seven o'clock. Then the flacks, the hypes, the gentlemen joggers, and most of the other cute people peel off to go home or somewhere else, and a lull drops over things, and if you happen to be sitting there, nose in your third scotch or your fourth Coors, you begin picking up on another group. Mostly men, men edging into, or in, or past middle age, whatever middle age is. And they're usually nice looking, seeming to be well off, or at least comfortable financially—but if you keep looking, maybe just a little bit melancholy.

"Heartbreak hotel, that's the Stoneleigh," a veteran of the Den, a divorced lawyer, says. "They come here first. It's a halfway house, a therapy center for men leaving home. A certain kind of Dallas man. Maybe they've thought about splitting for a long time. Most of them have been married for ten, twenty, even thirty years. But when they make up their minds, have it out that ultimate time with their wives, or vice versa, they move out of home and into the Stoneleigh.

The hotel manager, at the table, looks around, observing, not counting, and sighs, "I guess we have half a dozen with us right now. Sometimes we get a dozen at the same time. The Stoneleigh's the first stop on the road."

"The road to a new life," someone else at the table says, who's been living at the Stoneleigh for two or three weeks. But the veteran won't buy his remark. "Heartbreak hotel," he says again, "give it a few more days."

After ten years with a woman, even a real bitch, a man misses her, misses marriage: the process, the procedure, the certainty. After twenty years, it nearly kills him to split. A whole life left behind, and a future that wears a zero or a question mark. In the Den you start to look around at that seven o'clock interval. Finding new faces becomes a habit. You see someone you know two, three nights in a row and you get over the shock of thinking, "Why that's the last couple I'd have thought would break up." And sometimes the new face comes over to your table thinking the same thing and asks, himself surprised, "What are *you* doing in here?" thinking that everybody he sees in the Den is like him. "I come here all the time," you tell him, adding, probably to rub it in, "I work around here, you know." He shakes his head as if dazed when he realizes some of the customers are regulars without his particular irregularity. Sometimes the topic doesn't come up that first time you run into a new Stoneleigh man.

Sometimes it waits until the second or third time he comes to your table or you join his. If there are too many others around—particularly if some of them are women—it won't be brought up. But when he gets you alone it surfaces with a rush. He wants to talk, he must talk, to someone who understands, someone who knows him, someone who might, just might, be here in the Den someday for the same reasons:

"She wouldn't accept the fact that I kept moving and she couldn't. We used to fight like hell, then one day we just decided there wasn't any sense in either of us having to take it like that. We fell out of love. The kids are gone so the marriage wasn't needed. We got to be too familiar with one another. I never did love her, I discovered." After ten years? After twenty? Thirty? "Sure, you can live with a woman twenty years and not love her. Don't make me sound like a bastard. Lots of men marry women they don't love. Women marry men they don't love, don't they?" Some admit it was another woman, other women. "I'd been married fifteen years when something in the ol' male genes started me lookin'. I realized I wasn't happy with my wife. I moved out. Of course, it wasn't that quick or easy, but in a few words, that's the way it was."

Not all of them go that way. More than one man, married for years, didn't want the split. He was comfortable with what he had. She insisted they separate, after she got into Women's Lib or Consciousness Raising, or started seeing a shrink. He'd move back home if she would let him. He's begged, too. But she's determined the divorce will go through. She persisted; she won.

"I, I still love her, but," he always says first, smiling; half embarrassed, half defeated, half relieved. "But" is followed by a dozen different reasons, all of them soon familiar. . . .

"Don't let the big talkers fool you," says an older member of the Stoneleigh transients. "We're all hurt. We'd go back if we could. I would." He quits looking at you while he's talking, and you can see he is remembering, or hoping.

But there are big talkers, and they scorn the wistful at the bar—men they do not know, as it often turns out. The Stoneleigh men are not, by any means, acquainted with each other. "She caught me," a better than well-off North Dallas society figure admits. "She caught me by means of my bankbook. Mine, you notice I said. She opened my personal bank statement one month and discovered a couple of checks made out suspiciously. Hell, made out to another woman." He takes a sip of a Bloody Mary and laughs, "Of course, you could say she had some reason to be suspicious, or she wouldn't have opened my bank statement to begin with. She never balanced her own in twenty years. I didn't think she knew there could be anything in it to catch me with. Chalk up one to wifely intuition. And I guess I didn't really care. I wouldn't have sent two big checks like that through if I'd really cared. . . . "

She was the one who threw him out, you are finally told, after a strong marriage, lots of money, and children. But the money didn't matter very much, after a while. And for a switch, age hit him harder than it did her, once they reached their fifties. He came down, she went out. You feel sorry for him. You don't know what to think about her. She's not in the Stoneleigh. "Well, after all, they get it all, you know. They keep the house, the kids, the support money. Why move to the Stoneleigh? Moving out is not a ladies' game."

"See him?" one tells you, one night after the cute crowd has left. "See him? He's a genuine prick. I mean, what he did to her. You know her, don't you? How cute she is? After four kids, yet? Well, he brought this absolute whore home with him and shacked up with her in their bedroom, then made sure she came back from Houston early and found them. The kids all standing in the door watching while Daddy climbed out of bed. He planned every line in the scenario." You find out later that the speaker is now dating the prick's ex-wife.

Years can't be torn off your life the way months are torn off a calendar. Some of the torn-apart couples make it back together once or twice a week. "She helped me decorate my suite," he says. "She's got the best taste of any woman I know." But the marriage isn't about to mend itself. In bed we laugh, in bed we cry, and born in bed, in bed we die. Marriage is like a bed—marriage which is so inextricably rumpled and wrestled with in bed, which cannot survive without bed, and, often as not, within bed. Marriage, ultimately, falls or is sustained by the bedsprings, and the cause of a failed marriage almost invariably is found among the bedclothes. . . .

"You know, I've done pretty well with my life," he starts explaining and defending. But you know all that. You are ready to admit it, and so is anyone else. His name is too well known in Dallas business or professional circles, and he's not lost any of the drive and ability that elevated him in there and up there. But now he's living at the Stoneleigh. This is the slow, terrible realization: that an entire part of life has been lost, has been lived uselessly and in vain, has been deformed, thwarted, killed, missing to everything but recollection. Part of him is destroyed, no matter what he may do hereafter. . . .

The old lions, with their softened stone faces, watch the humans come and go, go and come. The lions, it occurs to you when you study their ninety-year-old features, seem to get sadder and sadder. ★

TRACY DAUGHERTY

Tracy Daugherty is a native of Midland, Texas, with a BA and MA from Southern Methodist University and a PhD from the University of Houston, where he studied with Donald Barthelme. His first novel, *Desire Provoked,* won the Southwestern Booksellers' Texas Literary Award. His second novel, *What Falls Away,* was the 1994 winner of the Associated Writing Programs Award for the novel. Other novels include *It Takes a Worried Man* and *The Boy Orator* from SMU Press. He is professor and chair of English at Oregon State University and a member of the Texas Institute of Letters. Daugherty writes of a Dallas woman who has come here from the oil fields of East Texas and brought old hurts with her.

From *The Woman in the Oil Field: Stories*

ON THE WEST SIDE OF DALLAS MY GRANDmother, no longer beautiful, sits in a wheelchair in a Catholic nursing home. Her room is across the hall from a bathroom and there is one old man—like her, a resident of the place—who forgets to shut the door when he goes to use the john. My grandmother shouts at him and he looks up, startled; the nurses come to clean his urine off the floor. In a rage he steps into my grandmother's room but before he can say anything she raises her voice.

"What are you sleeping with that shanty woman for?" she yells. She's confused him with my grandfather Bill, who (family legend has it) ran off with a prostitute, an "oil field woman," in the thirties.

"She teases me," my grandmother says to the old man. "She comes to me at night and tells me I won't ever sleep with you again. Then she ties my bed to a gelding and he runs me around a field, fast and dizzy, and the whole time she's laughing. In the mornings when the women here bathe me she's outside my window and I try to hide my body but they won't let me. They want to show her what I've become. Do you want her to laugh at me? Am I repulsive to you now?"

The nurses smile because she's mistaken the man, but she has a story to understand and it's the same one I heard in my mother's kitchen twenty years ago. Lately, on these hot summer Friday afternoons, trying to convince Grandma June that her husband Bill is dead, I've remembered the story and learned new ways to tell it. When I'm older and not the same man, I know I'll find another way, then another, until I've resolved it for myself.

I stop in and see June, regular as a city bus, on Monday and Friday mornings, and stay most of the day. Sometimes she knows I'm here, sometimes she doesn't. I've been back in Dallas now, out of work, for eight and a half months, ever since Boeing's Seattle plant laid me off with ninety-nine other machinists. When I called last fall to tell my folks about the pink slip, my mom said I should head back south.

"It'd be a blessing if you could ease June's final days," she said. "I can't go to Dallas each time she gets to feeling blue—Exxon's bringing in a new well near Oklahoma City, and they've got your father looking after it. Mother's asking for me but your daddy needs me here," she said. "Stay with her, Glen. We'll cover your expenses."

I thought it over for a day, then figured what the hell—beats hanging in the Seattle rain looking for jobs. Besides, though we'd never spent much time together, I'd always liked June. She was a straight talker. So I threw a pack of clothes into my Chevy and fastened a set of chains to my tires. I rumbled up the Rockies, dipped into the desert, and wound up in Texas again.

On Monday evenings now, when I leave June asleep, I hit the road and don't turn around until Friday. Six hundred, eight hundred miles a week just to get away from the sickrooms, the musty medicine smells of the Parkview Manor Nursing Home. Tumbleweeds blow across the highways in all the little towns of West Texas. I remember these towns from my childhood, but I can't tell them apart anymore now that the damn franchises've moved in everywhere. Dairy Queens and Motel Sixes. HBO and Showtime blaring in people's houses, through the windows. On Friday afternoons, back in Dallas,

I tell June I've sat with her all week. She doesn't know the difference if I'm here or away.

"You remember yesterday?" I ask. "I read you the newspaper?" She has a favorite daily column, "The Winds of Time," by this local hack historian, Larry Kircheval. His articles always start, "'Whatever happened to—?" and tell the story of some boring old building or once-important citizen. He irritates the hell out of me, really bares his heart when he writes—"Look at me, how much I know, how much I feel about the past"—but June eats it up. I read her his stuff whenever I'm here. On Saturday mornings my folks call from Oklahoma City and say they've tried to reach me all week at my Dallas apartment—an efficiency with only a table and a single bed ("All we can afford for you right now," Dad says). "We must've just missed each other," I tell them. "I go out for ice cream a lot. It's turning hot here now. . . ."

I go to check on June. She's awake now, lying in bed, clutching her box of Kleenex. She's nearly blind; if she pats around on the sheet and can't find her Kleenex she cries. Her hands are tiny and clawlike, tight with arthritis. Sometimes, to exercise or just to pass the hours, she rolls and unrolls a ball of blue yarn.

I ask her if she wants some apple juice.

"Yes," she says.

I turn the crank at the end of the bed to raise her up; hold the cup, guide the straw into her mouth. Her teeth are gone.

"You tell him to talk to me," she says.

"Who?" I ask.

"Stubborn old man." She waves at a chair by the wall. "He's been sitting there all afternoon reading that damn paper and he won't talk to me." Her voice cracks. "Where's your whore today, old man? Off with someone else?"

I stroke the papery skin of her arms, offer more juice. She's ninety-two years old. Since Bill died she's had two other husbands (divorced one, outlived the other), six grandkids, and three careers (store owner, upholsterer, quilt-maker). But now, near the end of her life, it's this one incident—Bill and the oil field woman—that clogs her mind. She's been jealous for sixty years. . . .

I first heard about June's whore late one night in my mother's kitchen. I was twelve. Mother suspected my sixteen-year-old sister was in trouble, smoking dope, driving into dark fields with boys in dirty pants. "When I was her age I could've wound up that way," Mom said. "It would've been easy. Now your sister."

"What way do you mean?" I asked.

She told me the story then: "When she was young, your Grandma June was very beautiful. My father's a fortunate man to've touched her. He was an oil worker in the East Texas fields, and not too smart, not too good or bad. At Christmas he drove home to Dallas bringing us store-wrapped gifts, and slept with us in the house. Your grandmother kept him busy with the vegetables for dinner or the furnace or anything else that needed looking after. At night he combed her blond hair and when he got through his hands seemed to take on her fair color and not the deep black they always seemed to be. But that's me, you know, because I know his hands weren't black. He washed the oil off—I never even saw crude oil—but he worked in the fields and I see him now, dark, in my mind.

"The woman who took him from us wasn't beautiful like your grandmother but she slept in the shanties by the fields and sooner or later he found her, like they all did I suppose, all the men who worked in the East Texas fields. It wasn't uncommon to see women strapping on their shoes at night and heading for the fields because there was money to make and they knew it. So he found her sooner or later. If he came home at Christmas he didn't work around the house anymore. Then he didn't come at all and he was with her, we knew. My brother Bud was old enough to take care of us now so he said, 'Don't worry,' but I knew he'd be lost, like Daddy. The fields were the only place for him to go."

One night, driving home for the weekend, Bud ran his car off the road two miles south of a rig he'd been roughnecking. He never regained consciousness, Mother said.

"Did he ever see your father?" I asked her.

"No, and he didn't meet a woman of his own. He wasn't the type to take up with that sort, and anyway we'd heard the shanty woman was dead by now, killed by some old boy who didn't want to pay for her. They found her half-burned in the Mayberry Field, dress off, doused with gas."

"Whatever happened to Grandfather Bill?" I asked.

"We heard about him, sick and dying, in a Kilgore clinic years later." My mother rubbed her throat; she'd gone dry. As in many family stories, the initial point had been lost in the telling. I never understood her fear about becoming the kind of woman she'd described. Maybe she'd been tempted to follow the oil workers herself when she was young, to raise money for June who'd had to scramble for cash after Bill disappeared. In fact, my mother didn't leave home until she met my father—who also eventually wound up in the fields. (My sister, more levelheaded than Mother ever gave her credit for being, turned out fine. She's married now and living in Houston.)

That night, twenty years ago, sitting with me in her kitchen, my mother laughed sadly. "I don't know what's so damned attractive about the oil fields, but every man in my life has been drawn to them."

I remember thinking, Not me. I won't be trapped by that hard-packed Texas ground.

"Bud was such a good kid," she said. "There was no need for it, no need for it at all . . . when he ran his car off the road, people said the marks looked like he'd swerved to miss something, but there weren't any tracks in the dirt."

At twelve, I was already familiar enough with my mother's grim tales to know they usually ended in guilt or remorse. I knew what Bud had swerved to miss on the road that night. I knew why Mother worried about my father when he worked late. The oil field woman would haunt my family from now on. ★

Elizabeth Forsythe Hailey

From *Her Work: Stories by Texas Women*: His Children

As a child it did not seem strange to me to hear my grandmother speak reverently of her first husband in the presence of her second. I was still at an age when it seemed reasonable that an adult was entitled to more than one of everything, including husbands.

Until I was twelve my favorite story was her description of the day her first husband had come home from work and hugged her so tightly one of her ribs had actually cracked. But during the space of time the term adolescence attempts to dignify, I began to suffer for her second husband—the only grandfather I had ever known. Though my own attitude changed, however, I could detect no difference in my grandfather.

Carefully insuring her comfort by the arrangement of pillows behind her back, my grandmother would delight in recalling the day her first husband celebrated a successful business deal by coming home with a new horse and buggy for her. Then, with a significant look at my grandfather, she would murmur, "He was such a generous man. He gave me everything I wanted."

I would look at my grandfather, hoping somehow her concluding sentence had escaped him. But instead of being offended, my grandfather would add his own confirmation: "He was a dynamo in business. Would have made a fortune if he had lived. Everyone said so." I was the only one who seemed able to imagine what these words cost my grandfather. My grandmother took it for granted that the final seal on this particular story would come from him, as it always had.

I used to search old photograph albums for hours, trying to find what there was about this gentle man that kept him from ever emerging favorably in comparison with my "real grandfather." (This was my grandmother's term for her first husband when talking to her grandchildren. It was a distinction impossible for me to conceive. How could a portrait in her bedroom be more real to me than the man who took movies of my first steps and taught me to play tennis and every Christmas played a faltering flute to accompany the family Christmas carols? No matter how many husbands my grandmother had had, I only had one grandfather, real or otherwise.) After a certain age, when my grandmother spoke to me of my "real grandfather," I would counter by referring to him as "your first husband." She never acknowledged the distinction, but it made me feel better.

There was an undercurrent of feeling among the grandchildren that our grandfather was a victim of discrimination at the hands of our grandmother but, being the oldest grandchild, I was the first to put it into words. One day I approached my mother, "Didn't Granddaddy want children of his own?"

"Howard?" she asked, and hearing the name made me realize that she had never thought of him as her father despite the fact that she was only seven when he married her mother. Her own father had died before she had any memory of him.

My mother hesitated and I insisted, "Well, didn't he? They were still young, weren't they?"

"I don't remember hearing it discussed," she said finally, as if the possibility that my grandfather might have expected more from his marriage had never occurred to her before.

It remained a mystery to me why my grandfather—obviously an eligible bachelor with unlimited prospects—had married a widow with three children who would never call him Father. Finally, about the time I went away to college, I decided the answer had to be a matter of money. My grandmother had been left a substantial amount by her first husband (even my grandfather acknowledged that the man was on his way to being a tycoon). This must have enticed my grandfather to marry her, knowing that he would be her second husband and nothing more—to her or her children.

With this explanation in mind, I called on my grandparents the afternoon I arrived home for Christmas vacation of my freshman year. My grandmother was waiting for me, holding my Christmas check in her hand. She could never endure having to share a holiday with the rest of the civilized world. She presented her gifts and garnered her gratitude several days before the occasion—and usually succeeded in creating the impression that everyone else was a little late.

I took the check—which was generous—and thanked her. My grandfather watched the exchange without comment but my grandmother felt that his silence should be explained: "Your grandfather will be giving his checks Christmas Day," she said, implying that she would have to spend the intervening time coaxing him to his checkbook.

Their checks were always for an equal amount but my grandmother was careful to build the impression that she set a goal my grandfather was obliged to match. Without her check as a guide, she implied that he would settle for a smaller amount—and consequently we would all be a great deal poorer. In this way she assumed the credit not only for what she gave but for a large part of what he gave. And we came away with the vague impression that she was the source of all the money we received. However, I had begun to suspect that her wealth was so much greater than what my grandfather could have accumulated through a life of steady but quiet industry that his gifts came at a much greater cost to him.

And so this year, when she presented her check and commented, as usual, that my grandfather, as usual, had chosen to wait until Christmas Day, I was bold enough to reply, "Why, this check is large enough for both of you. I don't expect anything else."

My reply must have betrayed my attitude more than I realized because this time, instead of accepting the gratitude she was due, my grandmother looked at me sharply and changed the topic. A few moments later when my grandfather left the room, I saw that the conversation had only been momentarily diverted. My grandmother had more to say, and suddenly revealed a startling fact. "Howard has three times as much money as I do. But I never see it. I own this house, and what he gives me each month doesn't even pay for the servants."

What I had assumed to be a marriage of convenience was even less—on either part. Every question of fact had now been answered. My grandfather had not married my grandmother for the children they would have or the fortune he would share. He made no claim on either. What then did he hope to gain?

If I had asked him, he would not have understood the question. As for my grandmother, she clearly felt he was already getting more than he deserved.

Then came the summer I graduated from college and in one afternoon on a road trip my education became complete. I had become a favorite traveling companion for my grandparents from the time I earned my driver's license, and we made frequent weekend trips.

This particular afternoon they were sitting together in the back seat arguing about the mileage to our destination, ignoring maps that might have settled the question. I was driving. I knew the exact mileage but I also knew better than to deny them the pleasure of their argument. Then, not at all in the nature of a confession but rather as a familiar fact, my grandfather referred to his first wife.

The car swerved. I will never know whether my grandfather was aware that this was my initiation into the fact of his first marriage, but it was my grandmother who sensed the need to explain: "She was a very ambitious woman. Her career mattered more to her than anything—her home, her husband."

My grandfather listened in agreement but for once the official version of an event was not to rest wholly with my grandmother. "She was very beautiful," he added in the same way he added details to my grandmother's stories of her first husband, "and she was unfaithful to me."

Though silent, my grandmother made her judgment of this unspeakable act loud in my mind. This was the first time I had seen her give unqualified support to my grandfather on any question and I could sense him drawing comfort from it.

The conversation soon returned to the number of miles saved by the new interstate highway, but now I knew that what my grandmother could give my grandfather was what his first wife had taken from him. In most marriages faithfulness is an obligation. To my grandfather it was a gift and it overshadowed any question of children or money.

In his last years, sitting peacefully in the garden of the nursing home where he had lived since a stroke had left him almost helpless, able to speak only in disconnected words, my grandfather listened while my grandmother spoke my name.

"Nancy has come to see you and she has brought the baby."

I had been living in another state when my first child was born, so this was my grandfather's first look at his first greatgrandchild. My grandfather looked at me without recognition, as if I were at best a concerned stranger, then he turned to the baby and with a delighted smile held out his arms and said, "Come here, Nancy."

I quietly put the baby in his lap. My grandmother adjusted his laprobe and I suddenly knew how wrong I had been ever to think she had denied him children of his own. ★

Jane Roberts Wood

Jane Roberts Wood lived in Dallas for many years before moving to Argyle with her husband Dub. She wrote the trilogy *Train to Estelline, A Place Called Sweet Shrub,* and *Dance a Little Longer.* She is also author of *Grace* and *Roseborough,* from which the following excerpt is taken. She was an editor of *Out of Dallas,* written by the faculty and staff of the Dallas County Community College District where Jane taught for many years, and she has written a children's book, *Mocha, the Real Doctor.* She is a fellow of both the National Endowment for the Arts and the National Endowment for the Humanities and is a board member of the Texas Institute of Letters. Wood was the 1998 recipient of the Texas Institute of Letters Award for Best Short Story and was given the A. C. Greene Literary Award at the West Texas Literary Festival in 2007. She has been a great good friend and source of comfort for many years. You will be able to see something of this in the nurturing of Echo in a Dallas Catholic Church in this piece from her novel. Echo is a fourteen-year-old who has run away from her mother after her Gypsy father's death. She turns up in a Catholic church pregnant and seeking sanctuary.

From *Roseborough*

Father d'Acosta is a solitary priest, but not in the way of most priests. In this great old Dallas church his solitude, although at times a hairshirt, is often simply scratchy, slightly heavy. It is a shirt woven of a simple yet fervent need, a single passionate longing. He yearns to be able, in the manner of other priests, to be given God's grace in order to bestow God's grace. For is not this the office, the deepest office of a priest? And yet he cannot do this. For all the years of his priesthood he has lived with this failure, has become accustomed to the weight of it. Sadly it is a burden that grows with each passing hour of each day. Yet how simple to others is the bestowal of this gift. From the moment Father Keeney enters a grief-filled room, those in his presence feel that he loves them above all others. His tenderness promises God's healing; his compassion offers a future of brighter days. And the joy Father Morris takes in sunsets and birdsong and rain, in good food and brandy, in the religious and the secular, that very joy promises God's grace. Father O'Brien bestows this gift through the easy benevolence of his hearty laughter, his quick wit. The warmth of his embrace. But he himself? How clumsy, how ineffective is his offering. To the deepest needs of his parishioners he is able to offer only a frozen formality. "God moves in mysterious ways. . . ," this to a man who had lost his job, or "His wisdom ordains. . . ," to a woman unable to bear a child. In joy and in sorrow his parishioners turn away from him. And is it any wonder? At times his whole being is slack with regret. But always after the hardness of the day there came the perfection of the evening Mass. This Mass, at once curative and elegiac, is his saving grace.

This evening's prayers begin the long preparation for the season of the Nativity. The clear precise Spanish of his parishioners rises, floats in liquid syllables into the soft air of the church, while from outside comes the cooing and fluttering of pigeons returning to their nesting places.

In the stained-glass window high above his head the sainted Margaret Mary Alacoque of France prays before the Sacred Heart. Just below this window Father Endes's painting of the Virgin of Guadalupe, gorgeously arrayed in a gown of blue like no other, and with golden stars too numerous to count, is hung. Beneath the window and the painting Father d'Acosta kneels and urgently prays, demanding rather than supplicating. He suspects it is the newly hung cross at the back of the church that has engendered this sense of urgency. Primitive, passionate, a Corpus of the eighteenth century from Guatemala, the crucifix reminds him of the sweet promise of his boyhood. As he gazes over the heads of his parishioners towards the crucifix at the back of the church, the plaza, and the Alameda of San Miguel de Allende, its sienna-colored streets and houses, its hungry dogs and laughing children—the entire village of his birth rises before his eyes.

Surrounded by these memories of his childhood and by the perfection of the evening Mass, he fervently prays for all children, for the mendicants who come to the cathedral for its warmth and light, for the old and the young, for the sick in body and mind, for those in despair. And finally, turning again to the altar, he prays fervently for Dolores O'Malley, a woman from his own village; prays that she, who has been given everything, might also be given the grace of God. Then her face would reflect her contentment, her mouth would speak the sweetest of words, and her hands, never still (even at the altar as she waits for the Body and the Blood), would rest quietly in an angle of repose. Thus filled with the contentment that God's grace brings, she would be able to conceive. And blessed with a child, her Irish husband would become the true benefactor of the cathedral for, speaking to Father d'Acosta both as a friend and as his wife's priest, he has promised as much.

"You would bargain with God?" Father d'Acosta had said to him sternly.

"Only if it be His will," John O'Malley had responded soberly and, putting on his hard hat, had hurried off to supervise his crews.

Now the Sanctus bell sounds, heralding that most sacred moment, the elevation of the Host, and Father d'Acosta rises and, turning to the people, lifts his arms. At that moment he sees the face of the girl. In the single shaft of light diffused by the stained-glass windows into a rosy glow, he sees her face framed by hair as black as night, sees her eyes blaze forth like stars. And throughout the service while he kneels and stands and kneels again, he sees the light touch her face again and again. Caught by the innocence and beauty of it, he sees her rise and hold out her hands as if in supplication before she falls, falls softly as a leaf might fall, onto the faded kneeling bench.

After the last worshipers leave Father d'Acosta hurries to his study. There he watches as Sister Mary Celeste holds a glass to the girl's lips. When she has drunk, he asks "Child, are you ill? Hungry?"

"No," she says so softly that he only sees the word on her lips.

"What is it you need?" he asks, hating the useless questioning, for the need is there, welling up from her eyes, over-flowing the room. When she does not answer, "Dear child, I will pray for you," he says, hearing the cold formality of his words.

But she does not turn away from him as others have done. Instead, looking intently at his face, she nods, her gaze steady. The thought comes that in just such a way did the deer that grazed near the monastery in the Colorado mountains look at friendly intruders.

"What is it you want?" he asks again.

"The sanctuary of your church," she whispers.

Disbelieving, he asks, "What? What did you say?"

"Sanctuary. I need this."

Sister Celeste bustles about. "Girl, you need some food," she says. "Hot tea. That'll fix you up. Now, you come with me and I'll see to it."

Taking the girl's hand, she urges her to her feet and it is then that he sees she carries a child. "Wait! Sister, the girl's . . . *embarazada*," he says softly, finding the Spanish easier.

"I know, Father. I see that," she says, ushering the girl from his office toward the small room where she takes her meals. "When she's had a bite we'll come back. Then you can decide what's best to do. Doubtless, Saint Mary Margaret's will take her."

When they have gone he sits at his desk hearing again the whispered plea. Opening his dictionary he finds the word: *sanctuary: a consecrated place, shelter, a refuge for wildlife, protected from predators.* Sister Celeste is probably right. Saint Mary Margaret's would be the best place for the girl. He has been there on numerous occasions. To baptize. To give communion. And always he is surprised at how young these girls are, giggling and whispering through the services, reading paperback romances, weeping over soap operas, as they await the birth of their babies. Sighing, he looks at the definitions once more, reading the last again: *a refuge for wildlife, protected from predators.*

A half hour later, still at his desk, he receives the two of them. Sister Celeste takes the chair on his left while Echo, her face without expression, sits quietly on the black leather sofa. Waiting for him to speak, Sister Celeste seems focused on her hands folded calmly in her lap. He clears his throat. "My name is Father d'Acosta. You know Sister Celeste. What is your name?"

"Echo."

The word startles him. Who would choose such a name for a child?

Unusual, and yet, having heard it, it seems no other would have done.

"Echo, where is the baby's father?"

"I don't know. He had to leave."

Looking at her face he knows she speaks the truth. A social service worker might well have asked more about the father but he'd be damned if he would.

"Do you have a home?"

She shakes her head.

He tries again. "Echo, with whom do you live?"

"Jamie and I were together. Then he left. I don't know where he is. I want to live here until the baby comes. Here. In the church."

Sister Celeste opens her mouth, closes it, opens it again. "Why child, what an idea! That's out of the question. You can't stay here. But we'll find—"

Interrupting, his voice is firm. "Sister Celeste, we'll decide all that in the morning. Tonight Echo will sleep in the bishop's room."

"But father . . ."

"Until morning."

"But Father," again.

"Open up the room. Tomorrow morning the child can walk in the garden, feed the birds, rest. Tomorrow morning's soon enough for decisions."

Bishop Moore's visit on Monday is brief. He sits beside Echo in the garden and watches as she tosses bread crumbs to the sparrows that tumble from the wild pear tree. After no more than twenty minutes he rejoins Father d'Acosta in his study, stirs cream into his coffee, and butters the slice of warm banana bread served by Sister Celeste, who has worn a bright smile all day, presumably in the belief that the bishop's visit will serve, as she has repeatedly said, "to set things right."

When he has finished the bishop delicately wipes his fingers on the worn linen napkin in his lap and carefully places the napkin on the table beside his plate. Then he stands and runs his fingers over the worn fabric of the sofa, the scarred mahogany of the desk, and finally, the badly repaired molding into which the window overlooking the garden is set. Father d'Acosta joins him at the window. Silently they watch the young girl, still graceful under the weight of her pregnancy, attach a hose to a water faucet, turn on the faucet, and add water at the birdbath beneath the small statue, made headless by vandals, of Our Lady of Guadalupe.

Bishop Moore turns to Father d'Acosta, motioning him to his own chair behind his desk. He draws the small chair back and carefully settles his long angular frame into it. Pushing the wire frames of his eyeglasses higher on his nose, he leans forward.

"The girl would not fit into Saint Mary Margaret's," he says. "We are in agreement. But there is much to consider: Our most affluent parishioners, some with quite generous hearts, have moved to the suburbs. The present worshipers are, for the most part, without certain employment; where once we saw men in suits and women in silk dresses, we now see men, those lucky enough to have a job, wearing work shirts and hard hats. If the church is to serve the needs of these people; that is, if the hungry are to be fed, the naked clothed, the homeless sheltered, we must have the munificence of one or two men who, having been given much, can give much in return. One such man spoke to me recently, promised that . . ."

"John O'Malley."

"Yes. And Dolores, his wife. Might not this child be the answer to their prayers?"

"But to ask that the girl give up her baby . . ."

"You yourself said she is not like the others. Talk to her. See what her plans are for the baby's future. If she agrees that her baby needs a good home and loving parents, parents who would give her baby everything a child might need, she can stay here. Of course you will not tell her this is the condition upon which our permission that she stay rests. I want no coercion in this matter. And it might be that the O'Malleys will want to meet her before it's decided. If all should agree, our lawyers will prepare the documents. Father, in a situation so delicate, all needs must be considered: the church's, the parishioners', the O'Malleys', the girl's. A priest's duty is to balance these needs. Appropriate balance. That's the key."

He rises from his chair, places his hands on the small of his back. He smiles briefly, raises his eyebrows. "This interest of yours in the girl," he says.

"What occasioned it?"

After a while Father d'Acosta speaks into the silence. "I have asked that question of myself," he says. "I do not know the answer."

As he leaves the room, the bishop turns his head again to glance once more at the girl in the garden below. Father d'Acosta feels curiously cheated by the ray of sun that, reflecting off his gold wire eyeglasses, obscures the expression in his bishop's eyes.

The papers signifying intent had been drawn up in triplicate and signed early in the morning by Echo. Handing her the document, Father d'Acosta had carefully explained: "The agreement is not binding. But it is a solemn promise that you intend to allow the O'Malleys to take your baby from the hospital, to adopt him or her when the required waiting period is over, and to raise him or her as their own beloved child. Echo, it would be a cruel thing to allow them to believe the baby will be theirs if such is not the case. Do you understand?"

"Yes," she answered, and had carefully written her name on each copy, frowning as she read and explained to him the meaning of each paragraph, so that he might know her understanding was complete.

Then they are signed by the O'Malleys, who have met Echo, spoken with her, and are sure that a child from such a mother, no more than a child herself, would indeed be blessed by the home they could provide. "The child will have our love and all the material advantages he will need," John O'Malley says proudly. When he has finished with the document he turns his wife's face toward the window. "Father do you not see the resemblance? Dolores could be the girl's older sister. Look at her coloring, the shape of her face."

"Why, that's so," Sister Celeste says sturdily, just as the champagne cork pops the bottle.

And indeed the resemblance is pronounced.

When the document has been witnessed the party toasts the baby-to-come and the parents-to-be. That Echo was not present, that none found their way to the window to see Echo in the garden, leaves a somewhat bitter taste in Father d'Acosta's mouth. Or, he thinks later, it might only have been the champagne.

Not since he was a boy has Father d'Acosta felt what it was to be a family. Now day by day his sense of family grows; ill-assorted, oddly shaped, but still, three, almost four generations of a family. By the end of the first week Sister Celeste has taken the girl under her wing: "Child, better get off your feet, rest a little while." Thus clucking over her, remonstrating with her, in her very old age Sister Celeste has become a grandmother. And although he keeps to his usual routines, Father d'Acosta never enters or leaves his study without pausing at the window that overlooks the garden where Echo, more often than not, can be found.

Presided over by Our Lady's headless statue the garden has been long abandoned. Here Echo, with a set of gardening tools . . . digs and weeds and waters. She keeps the water in the birdbath fresh, seeds . . . in the birdfeeder plentiful, and the beds richly cultivated.

"Weed or flowers, it's all the same to her," Sister Celeste tells him. "She works as hard with one as the other. . . ."

"Echo is taking some interest in her appearance," Sister Celeste says one evening. "She asked me for stockings, the kind young girls wear." Leaving him at a loss to know she means pantyhose, she goes on embroidering the pillowcase she is making for the bishop. "And I believe that she's taking up handwork. This morning she asked for embroidery thread," she continues, adding somewhat immodestly, "I suppose she's noticed the fineness of my stitchery."

A week later he looks out the window and sees that, overnight, a head has appeared on the shoulders of Our Lady of Guadalupe. Calling Sister Celeste from the kitchen, he hurries out into the garden and sees that the head, like the heads of rag dolls his sisters had played with as children, is skin-colored, the mouth and eyes clumsily embroidered.

"Why, Father, this isn't right!" Sister Celeste exclaims. "Echo made this head with pantyhose!"

"Wait," he says. Taking her arm he leads her to the bench in the garden. "Sit down. Let's sit here a minute. I don't know that it isn't exactly right. Look at her. Look at Our Lady. She's smiling. And she does seem quite at peace."

It is that very next day, in the early afternoon, that he looks into the garden and sees a thing he will remember the rest of his life . . . when he looks out the window he sees the possum. Surprised by its daytime appearance he watches it making its way heavily across the garden. When it reaches the magnolia tree he sees the babies clinging to her back—five, no, six of them. It is a full minute before he notices Echo sitting on the bench before Our Lady and sees that she, too, watches as the possum makes her laboriously maternal journey across the garden. All at once Father d'Acosta aches to know the girl's thoughts, to be able to read her mind. Since she has signed the letter of intent she has not mentioned the baby. . . what connections does Echo make, he wonders now, between herself and that curious animal? Does she feel regret? Longing? Curiosity? He is powerless to know. But looking into the garden he feels that the slow progress of the possum, the fabricated head of Our Lady, the motionless girl—feels all three have come together for a purpose, and that it is a message, indecipherable, but still a message for him. . . .

As the time for Echo's delivery draws near she no longer appears at breakfast and no longer works in the garden, although she still walks there and, wearing Sister Celeste's heavy cape against the cold, sits on the bench before Our Lady of Guadalupe for long periods of time. Seeing her there Father d'Acosta is reminded of a plant in the garden that, when touched, curls its slender leaves in upon itself as if seeking its own beginning. Her pregnancy has transformed the once slender girl into a woman so enormous that delivery seems impossible. Except for her eyes no traces of girlhood remain.

Time seems suspended as they wait for the birth. Whenever he has to leave the household he hurries back, recognizing his own need to be there and sensing Sister Celeste's deep anxiety for the girl. Still when Sister Celeste taps gently on his door at three o'clock in the morning, saying, "It's time, Father," he feels dismay.

"It's too soon," he tells himself. "She's not ready for this." ★

Ed Garcia

Ed Garcia received a BA from the University of Texas at Austin, MA from Ohio State University, and PhD from the University of Texas at Austin. He is a professor of English at Brookhaven College in Dallas and writes book reviews for *The Dallas Morning News*. He has published numerous articles and poems in *The Texas Observer*. Ed's story is from a collection of writings by the faculty and staff of the Dallas County Community College District and edited by Jane Roberts Wood with Donna Dysart Gormly and Sally Schrup.

From *Out of Dallas—14 Stories*: Here at the Mini-Warehouse

Most of the time you'll find me here at the mini-warehouse, Pilgrim's Mini-warehouse, owned by Mrs. Etta Fontenot. Etta is the main reason I write here: I met her the day after the night my wife, now my ex-wife, suggested I move out and take my back issues of *The New Yorker*, *The New Republic*, and *Show Business Illustrated* (the whole run) among others, including selected numbers of *Sports Illustrated* and the *New York Times Magazine* with me. She could never understand why I kept all those shelves of magazines, cluttering up her closets, she said. We went round and round about that one.

Of course, that wasn't why she finally invited me to leave, that was just a pleasant side-effect for her. I guess I came home late one night too many, and she smelled my breath and could tell I hadn't been drinking and said, very quietly and sort of scary, "That's enough. Get out and take those fucking magazines with you." She didn't usually use the f-word as I call it in discussions with the kids, so I knew she was really hot and, on reflection, it seemed a good idea to take her up on it before she changed her mind.

So the next day I drove to Pilgrim's—the name just appealed to me—and talked to the manager about renting a good-sized mini that I could have access to whenever I wanted to use the magazines for research, which is why, as I told my ex-wife a dozen or so times, I kept them. . . . Something about my request or maybe about me intrigued Etta who was in charge that day and who was wearing a little outfit that several years ago they called "Hot Pants" with some sort of fuschia hose with a pattern in them and little heels.

Etta isn't what you'd call pretty, but she has nice legs and breasts large enough that you notice them because they stick right out even without a bra and you can see the nipple through the little T-shirt she generally wears. I won't go on in that vein because it gives the wrong impression of Etta, but it tells you something about my state of mind when I met her. I had spent the night in the cheapest motel I could find: It had a worn-flat chenille bedspread, clean but a little tattered around the edges, and you had to phone through the switchboard which I think was kind of embarrassing for the kids when they called me. I spent that night full of half-waking fantasies about all the sordid lovemaking that I guessed went on in a motel like that. Surprisingly, there wasn't much coming and going in the night—none at all that I noticed, to my disappointment. But I kept saying to myself, like it was part of a prayer or something, "I'm going to fuck my brains out." If I was going to be divorced, then I was going to f-word my brains out. Over and over again, like a song you find yourself singing, over and over. So when I saw Etta in those little hot pants and the heels and the T-shirt, well you can imagine what I was thinking.

Etta is one of those people you come across who aren't educated—it pretty well shows and they'll tell you every ten minutes, too—but who are so damn competent you've just got to be grateful. She ran those mini-warehouses. She knew what was allowed and what wasn't, where you could get the best locks at the best prices, what size you need for what, what the rates were by the week, by the month, by the year, everything. She just rattled it all off, smiling but not showing too much teeth because she had braces. You don't usually see a woman in her thirties with braces, but that's what she's like. She had hated her teeth for so long and just decided when her daughter's braces were paid for, it would be her turn. As I said she isn't exactly pretty, but she has a pleasant face and the way she talks real fast and smart and smiles, you can't help but like her.

Right off, I was pretty sure Etta liked me even though I wasn't the kind of person Etta had much to do with. College degree, English teacher, even if it's just high school, beard, wire-rimmed glasses, sandals. She liked me, but she didn't make any kind of move, because as it turned out she was still married at the time. With some people, you can't make judgments based on the way they dress. At twenty paces you would have taken her for a hooker, but she turned out, on closer inspection, to be a nice girl who had grown up to be a nice lady, who just didn't have very good taste when it came to clothes. I'm glad I was too afraid to reach over and touch her very nice breast as I thought of doing when we were alone in one of the minis, because that would have been it for us and I might have gotten arrested to boot.

I took the mini and saw her several times while I moved in the magazines and the boxes of *my* books and the few things I had before we got married—some of my mother's old crockery and pots and a little chest of drawers which my folks had at the old house before the one they have now which is pretty old itself. Etta was always helpful and full of good ideas about how to fit things in and if she hung around more than she absolutely had to, well I was trying for bookishly fascinating and she didn't have that much to do. Nothing happened and she probably didn't even know she was flirting which to this day I tell her she was and she refuses to comment on. After that, I seldom went to the mini because, as my ex-wife would love to hear me admit, doing research in old magazines does not come up that often in daily life.

The next school year was my last one teaching and it was awful. If you haven't taught in high school, you don't know just how repulsive young people can be. Not all the time and not all of them, but some of them you want to throw off the auditorium balcony or stuff into a locker—one time I tried to do just that to a senior boy and luckily he was the one who got in trouble. I wasn't doing anybody any good because I went around feeling *alienated* all the time. . . .

That going around alienated and subsequently depressed is probably what convinced my wife that she could do better than a big hairy guy, running to middleage who didn't do squat (as she would have put it) all day and stayed up half the night watching TV. I think it was teaching in a *high* school and being married to her that did it to me but she would disagree. I loved my kids and still do, but when I think back to some of those years I can't even remember the kids being around. So much for quality time. I wasn't drinking, but I probably should have been.

I did have one close buddy up at high school and that was Chuck. Chuck was this extra good-looking history teacher who talked like a Weather Underground-type radical and stayed stoned a lot and wanted to learn to throw pots. Extra good looking, but he never seemed to give any of the high school girls a look to their disappointment and everybody else's surprise, but it was just as well. Chuck seemed to know by instinct—or maybe by past experience—everything that could get him into trouble and he avoided it. . . .

One thing Chuck and I did do when we talked was to make plans. They mostly had to do with quitting teaching and going back to school or getting a potter's wheel or buying a motorcycle and taking out across Mexico. The unspoken part of all our plans was that they didn't include wives, so probably we both knew what was coming at some level. His wife taught with my wife at a junior high—which I've got to admit is even worse than high school. She was a nice girl but a little cold and when you met her mother, you knew where she was going and it was scary. When Chuck finally did get his wheel he managed this one little pot which he didn't even know where he would fire but he was very proud of it because it took him hours to get the clay centered on the wheel. It turns out that this basic thing you have to do if you think you ever want to be a potter is very hard—I tried it for fifteen straight minutes and said to hell with that, I'll paint. So Chuck finally did the little pot and that seduced him into feeling good about it and that was all his mother-in-law needed. She looked at it with a little smile like she thought it was cute and said, "Why don't you make a chicken?" I think that just about did it for that marriage even though the final breakup didn't happen for a couple of years. . . .

Things weren't going that well even though I enjoyed not being married. So I happened to go out one Sunday to my mini and took a chair because I wanted to read some of the back issues and not think about what was going on in other places. Ever since I was a little boy one of my favorite pastimes is to go to the library and look at old magazines. My brother and I used to especially like *Life* because the main thing we were interested in was pictures and ads and *Life* had plenty of them. My brother liked the WWII years, but my favorite thing was to look at the articles about starlets or rising young stars or hot new writers that nobody has ever heard of anymore. I like to imagine that starlet's mom buying twenty copies of *Life* and thinking that now they all had it made.

So there I was, sitting in the doorway of my mini intent on an old *Esquire* with John Kennedy in a rocking chair on the cover and Bobby's head pasted over John's when this woman's voice startled me saying it's against the rules for human beings to live in these warehouses or something like that. I looked up and there was Etta smiling and all fixed up in what I rightly assumed was what she wore to church. She had on this very restrained for her dress which did fit her tight around the hips and bosom but which was dark blue with only the subtlest little shimmer to it and had little puffed sleeves and a modest neckline. She had on white hose with a little pattern in them so as not to look like nurses' I suppose and dark blue and white pumps. She still had her braces I could see because she smiled so broadly. And her hair had grown longer and sort of framed her face in a way that made her look very sweet and young. And she seemed so happy to see me that I wanted to go over and give her a warm hug because I had missed her. Actually, I hadn't thought much at all about her, but when I saw her in that blue dress I missed her retroactively.

Guess what she said holding out her left hand I'm divorced and then she smiled real big and quickly covered up her teeth. But you're still working here I said since I wasn't sure where all this was going. No she said I own it. I got it in the divorce and my husband got the rent houses. She thought she'd make out ok. She wanted to know if I'd had lunch or anything and I said no and she said me neither. So not wanting to be too slow on the uptake, I asked her if she'd like to do something and she said yes and smiled warmly again. I got the feeling that she was interested in me and didn't mind my knowing it, but it hit me sweet instead of cheap and in spite of the fact that I knew it wouldn't work out because she wasn't the kind of woman who my friends would like, I was feeling, well, grateful that someone nice wanted to spend part of Sunday with me. I look down at myself dressed in shorts, sandals, and a button-downed blue Oxford cloth shirt with the sleeves rolled up over my elbows and told her I didn't know where I could take her, but she said don't worry I know a place.

While we drove she gave me directions and talked a blue streak about all kinds of people I didn't know, doing their voices and then her voice and they would all sound real country and she would sound nice and cultured. And she laughed a lot. Finally she stopped for a minute and then she said, looking straight out the window at the road, you can probably tell I'm kinda nervous. You're my first date. I told her we could think of it as two people happening to have lunch together, but she said no she'd rather think of it as a date. The place she picked was named Dwayne's and it was open twenty-four hours. The waitresses all had on blue jeans and Dwayne's T-shirts and they were all real waitresses. I had breakfast and Etta had chicken fried steak, and the hash browns and biscuits were perfect which she told me is how you judge one of these places which I am becoming something of an expert on. There is a big sign next to the clock over the window to the kitchen: it says, "Dwayneburger. Try one. Two not recommended."

Well that day lasted a long time even though I had a couple of weeks of sets of papers to grade and therefore didn't get to. We went to some flea markets and looked at antiques and she seemed to be studying what I liked. She found lots of excuses to get close to me and read something over my shoulder and touch me to get my attention, and I have to admit it felt good and kind of natural. She wanted to know what I read and she told me she had a friend who read two or three of those romances everyday, but she thought they were stupid and wanted to know what I would recommend. There was nothing embarrassed about her asking and I told her one or two things I thought she'd like.

When we finally got back to the mini to pick up her car I wouldn't have thought of touching her breast even though she would probably have let me. It was around six in the evening and we both lingered between the two parked cars. We wrote down each other's phone number and then she turned to her car and turned back real quick and kissed me with her hand on the back of my head. Then she was back in her car and gone smiling and waving. I called her later that night.

That was a year ago and there's been a fair amount of movement in my life you might say. I got a new apartment, smaller but nicer and nearer to Etta's and to the mini where I'm the co-manager and writer-in-residence now. I've got one of the minis all rigged up with an easy chair and a desk with my old typewriter and bookshelves and a reading lamp. I've got my magazines, some in the study as I call it and some in the mini next door and nobody much comes by and bothers me but when they need me I'm there. I'm a good manager. I live ok from some proofreading and index-making work I do and mostly from what the job pays. I quit teaching I guess I forgot to say. The kids come see me here and they love it; they know as much about the place as I do running around and poking their noses in people's business.

My old buddy Chuck comes around pretty often, too. He's still teaching, but he thinks maybe this will be his last year. He rented a mini and keeps his wheel in it and on weekends when it's not too cold he comes by and tries throwing a few pots. He still can't get the clay centered worth a damn, but he claims it's getting easier. . . . He's a lot happier since his divorce but he still makes plans and we talk about that. I tell him I like the way things are going right now.

Of course Etta has a lot to do with that. Most days she'll stop in to check on things in the afternoon and I might suggest we close the doors to my study and put the easy chair to good use, but she says no this is business and besides it's stuffy in there. Sometimes it's hard getting together because of her kid and mine when they are there with me, but we manage and that's not the most of it anyway. My days just fly by now and I don't ever ask who are these people. The few that are here I know why they are and why I am, too. Etta and I have supper some nights and then we'll talk about what she's reading or what I wrote that day, which she tends to be prejudiced in favor of. I admire that in her. Then we'll go for a walk and she fits into the side of me with my arm over her shoulders about perfect. We'll stop from time to time and stand close and kiss.

Like I tell Chuck, things are going just fine right now, and that's as much as I want to say about it. ★

Joyce Meier

Joyce Meier was born in Minnesota and moved to Dallas with her husband, Rodger, in 1949. She has had poems and short stories published in numerous literary magazines, including *descant*, *Amelia*, and *Riversedge.* One of her stories, the following, was published in the collection *Common Bonds,* edited by Suzanne Comer and published by SMU Press. She is the former editor of *Sands,* a literary magazine published in Dallas. The Apparel Mart and its importance to Dallas and the Dallas woman is seen here.

From *Common Bonds*: A Good-looking Woman

I don't mean that I never thought of having an affair. Fantasizing is normal. Then too, knowing someone, even casually, like Ellie Gunderson, I have been exposed to that kind of thing. There was a time when I envied Ellie. She is a good-looking woman . . . one of the chosen few. People have told me we look alike. We do, except her arrangement always seemed to work better.

Every year Robert, Ellie's ex, gives her a two-week trip to the Golden Door spa in California. It was in the settlement. Ellie takes part in the whole program. I have seen her incision scars and it's amazing what a good plastic surgeon can accomplish with a little nip and tuck in the proper places. She wears large Panama straws with bright scarves to keep her hair color from turning brassy (oxidizing, she says) and the wide brims protect the stitches around her eyes, too.

Frank, my husband, saw Ellie at the Tom Thumb in the Village one day early last spring. He was picking up some dill for me so I could finish pickling the cucumbers from my spring garden. She was wearing big rose-tinted glasses, Frank told me. They covered most of her face, he said, and he wondered what she was saving it all for.

When Frank came back with the dill that day, I was sitting out on the porch in the wicker rocker squeaking to the same spring song as the squirrels and enjoying the redbuds flowering along the side of the house. When those redbuds and the jonquils open up, so do my veins. The sap starts running faster. The redbuds were dressed to kill in their pink and white buds and looked so young and fresh against the dried-out March season. It made me ache just to see them showing off like that.

Frank put the dill on the kitchen table along with the receipt and sauntered out the screen door to the backyard. I waited for the door to slam. That man cannot close a door softly.

"I'm going down to the end of the lot to check the crape myrtles," he called back. "Want to make sure the freeze didn't get them."

I wanted to know more about Ellie so I hollered to him, "Come out on the porch when you've finished. You can smell spring and summer all at once today." Those darn crape myrtles, they worry Frank to death. They'll bloom all right. Overnight they'll change. Burst out in their organdy all at once and steal the whole show.

Frank came back up later and sat with me on the porch. He smiled at me. The sun was hitting his bad shoulder just right and he could smell the brisket I had cooking in the kitchen coming through the white curtains at the window over the sink. He was comfortable.

"Saw Ellie Gunderson at the grocery while I was picking up your dill," he reminded me. (As if I needed reminding.)

I waited while he groped for his pipe in his shirt pocket. Wasn't there and he patted his front pockets, both of them. Leaned forward and patted the back ones. Didn't say a word. Looked out across the yard. Got up. Checked the sprinkler. Walked back. Sat down again. Still no word. Started patting his pockets same way as before.

"Well, Frank Jennings," I said, trying to keep too much interest out of my voice, "don't just sit there, tell me how she looks." And I leaned across to his chair and put my hand on the arm of it to prevent him jumping up again.

Frank gave me a long look. He was thinking about Ellie, I could tell. He leaned back, folded his hands across his chest and said, "It's hard to tell, sugar," and he looked at me real seriously before he went on. "'Bout the only thing I could see of her was her navel." Then he laughed. Slapped his knee and laughed. Frank has a way of laughing at things he doesn't understand.

Ellie must have had on her green silk shirt that ties above the waist. That woman really knows how to dress. I've often wished I had her way with style. Frank always wants me in sweaters and skirts or my little beige linen.

"Did you talk to each other?" I asked.

"Said 'hi.' She was racing through the store," he answered. I could just see those long legs of hers on spike heels, of course, and the wide-brimmed hat with the green silk scarf floating through the Tom Thumb. Must have been a sight for sore eyes. Frank stopped laughing. Finally, looked at me. Said, "She did throw over her shoulder, though, for you not to forget Spring Market next week. She said she'd told you to come pick out some clothes and use her discount. Told me to tell you not to forget."

As if I would.

I met Ellie's latest lover that week. She had just come back from California, from her annual sojourn to the Golden Door out there. She was doing some modeling at Market for Mr. Ray's of Dallas and I had taken her up on her discount offer. I spend every extra dollar on my flowers and plants around the yard, or else I'm sending a box off to Marilee, our daughter in Fredericksburg who teaches at a school for deaf children. So the discount Ellie offered sounded like a good idea.

Frank said, "Why not make a day of it? Why don't we have lunch at that new little restaurant by the Apparel Mart?" So that's just what we did. Frank was so happy to get me out of the house for a day. He always acts like he wants me to be a regular "out and about" girl. Like some of our friends whose wives play a little golf at the club and then relax at the 19th Hole with martinis all afternoon. Guess it would make him feel good to have me lounge all day. Men are funny.

The day for our trip to Spring Market, Frank was ready before I was. I had to sew a button on my beige linen dress. I had forgotten it fell off from Marilee hugging me so hard when we went to visit her at Easter. I had saved the button there on the mirrored tray Frank gave me last Christmas. So while he was stacking the clothes boxes that I wanted to mail to Marilee into the car, I was slipping into my pumps (thank goodness for tan legs) and brushing my short hair extra hard. After I fit gold loops into my ears, I was ready. Frank pinched me and said I looked younger than tomorrow.

I was excited about seeing Ellie at Market. I hadn't seen her since her trip to California, and I knew she would have some fascinating tale to tell. One time, she and her roommate at the Golden Door had gone over to Lake Tahoe and gambled at one of the casinos. Ellie made it sound so thrilling that I forgot all about the time Frank and I had been there. It had been hot. Hot and crowded and I told Frank I could hardly wait to get back to Dallas where I could breathe. But Ellie always seems to be at the right places at the right times.

It was dark as a cellar closet when we walked into the Clothesline Restaurant that day. Lattice-covered candles flickered on white tablecloths and a young lady with blonde hair and a black velvet bodice led us through the semi-darkness and soft conversation to a booth against the wall. While I scooted to the middle of the upholstered seat, Frank ordered a vodka tonic for himself and a frozen daiquiri for me. (I am not much for rum, but I love the word "daiquiri.") Our drinks came and we sipped them and ordered lunch from huge menus. We were talking about the addition we planned to make on our farmhouse near Austin and wondering if it would be finished before the mare foaled, when suddenly I just forgot Frank was sitting across from me. For there, coming toward us, was Ellie. Ellie and a very handsome young man. Cherries Jubilee was being prepared at the table next to ours and at the same time the copper pan went "whoosh," there they were. As if they'd emerged from the alcohol vapors. Ellie was smiling at us, her teeth apple white. Head tilted way to the side. One hand played with some beads at her throat, the other clutched the young man's coat sleeve. She tugged him toward our table.

I saw them first because I was facing that way. Frank followed my gaze, saw them and stood up. Ellie introduced the young man as Mr. Ray and then she swooped down and picked up my daiquiri. (All Ellie's movements are exaggerated.) She held my drink to her bright lips, threw back her head and raved, "How divine." Mr. Ray just looked at the stickpin in his Christian Dior pindot scarf and told Frank to please sit down.

"Oh, darlings, the food is divine. Do enjoy," Ellie cooed.

"We didn't expect to see you until later at the Market," I reminded her, all the time appreciating the fine cut of Mr. Ray's sport coat. "How nice that we did, though," I said. I felt Mr. Ray looking at me and before I realized it, I was asking them to join us. "Can you join us for lunch?" I chirped, and suddenly I wanted them to say yes. Yes, of course.

But Ellie answered, "Sorry, loves, just finished. It was delightful."

The waiter came with our lunch and Ellie and Mr. Ray started to leave. Ellie replaced my cocktail glass on the table like it was a bird she had caught. She looked at me. "Don't forget your clothes shopping. Mega bargains, darling." She flicked her tongue across her lips and fluttered beside the fashionable young man for a minute, then they left. Several people turned to watch them make their way through the tables. Frank and I stared after them. Ellie is a good-looking woman.

At the front desk, the young thing in the black bodice handed them a small tray. I saw Ellie sign the check before the heavy quilted doors of the restaurant opened and a streak of sunlight, like an explosion, shone through the darkened room and a hollow "Bye, darlings" floated back to us over the china and silver.

Frank and I went on to the Apparel Mart, as planned, for the shopping spree. We parted company by the guard at the front gate because Frank said he wanted to mosey around the building and maybe find someone who could tell him how they installed the huge wire baskets of greenery that hang from the ceiling five floors down. I went on up to the third floor.

Mr. Ray's of Dallas is just one large room, actually. There is a showroom window on the front that faces the hallway and traffic, and the girls who work for Mr. Ray change the mannequins every time you turn around. The main business, though, is done in the large room with the swatch books and style numbers that Mr. Ray keeps on his desk, which is in the middle of the room. When I came in, he saw me and came right over. He smiled and I offered him my hand. He covered my hand with his own and said it was nice that I came by and to please let him help if he could. His hand was warm.

I told him that I was mainly looking for something for my daughter, Marilee, and that I just might sure enough need some of his expertise. I gave him Marilee's coloring and explained her build—pretty much like mine, sample size. He could not believe I had a daughter teaching school. You look like a schoolgirl yourself he told me. We were interrupted several times with the buyers asking questions about the styles, when would they be available, etcetera, but we did manage to find several things for Marilee. Mr. Ray was most helpful. His eyes are soft blue and when you ask him a question, he has this way of looking straight at you with those blue eyes as if you are the only person for miles around. He really concentrates on you and when he answers, you know that that is the right color, or the right combination or the right length. There is no doubt in your mind that he is right.

The women who work Market are all so attractive. Most of them live in North Dallas and their husbands are in oil or investments, or both, and they work Market because there are all the newest clothes, the latest styles, and also it is a great place for catching up on who is seeing whom. It's all very exciting. I was truly amazed when I found out that Emily Forsythe was having an affair with Robert Gunderson. Why, she'd been married to Bobby John Forsythe for fifteen years and they have two beautiful children. She was Marilee's room mother in the eighth grade.

Mr. Ray and I got along fine right from the start. He seemed to realize that I knew what I was looking for and what I wanted without my ever having been up close to how it all worked before. As I checked fabrics, I could feel Mr. Ray with his eye on me. I knew he was studying me but I wasn't embarrassed. After all the sewing I'd done for Marilee, I was in familiar territory. I knew materials. It reminded me how I had felt twenty years before when I had a date with a good dancer for the prom . . . confident. That is how I had felt. It was like playing a game, a game I enjoyed. While I was holding different colors up to me and looking into the floor-length mirror that hangs on the back side of the entry door, I caught his eye several times. One of the salesgirls came up to him with a question as he sat, knees crossed, on the edge of his desk. I could see the two of them in the mirror. She was wearing one of the new garments, the tags dangling from her wrist, when she sidled up to Mr. Ray. "I can't find the price for this chemise, Mr. Ray," she whined as she hipped her way up to him close enough to touch. She came still nearer and Mr. Ray stood up quickly, eyes over her head; didn't look at her at all, just sort of paddled her away with one hand and moved around her and closer to the mirror where I was standing. He watched me the whole time. He knew then that I knew he was watching me. His face, reflected above mine in the mirror, grinned into the glass—into my face. The creases at his eyes danced. His chin came up.

"I like your style," he said to me, and it was like I was moving into a good dancer's arms at the edge of a dance floor . . . a big band playing and a ballroom all around and saxophone rhythms blending together the colors of the evening. Time was gone before I knew it.

I got so involved with all the hustle and bustle up there on the third floor that I almost forgot about poor Frank waiting for me at the front gate. But there he was just where he said he would be, by the gate, standing there running some soil through his fingers from the large potted ficus in the lobby. Checking the dampness, he said. Wanted to see how watered they keep them.

On the way home all I could talk about was the afternoon at the Apparel Mart. Frank said he bet Marilee would be excited about her new dothes. "You going to call her tonight?" he asked. He was all scrunched down in his seat, concentrating on the downtown traffic, trying to find the best part of his bifocals to see through.

"I will if I'm not too tired. An afternoon like this just wears me out," I answered. Guess I had spent all my energy oohing and ahing over all the pretty clothes at Mr. Ray's, because just then all I wanted to do was just not talk. I wanted to think about the past couple of hours and all the new styles and things I had seen.

But Frank went on. "Yep, I bet Marilee will sure be excited," he said. He was looking straight ahead and waiting for me to ask about the hanging baskets at the Mart and had he found out what he wanted to know. If he had taken time to look at me he would have seen that my eyes were closed and he knows when my eyes are closed that means I don't want any more conversation. He'd want to talk about Marilee, the farmhouse, his flowers, his vegetables, anyway. All the things he always wants to talk about. He looks away when I start talking about anything romantic. Never does have time for what makes the world go round. . . . ★

Pat LittleDog

Pat LittleDog used to be Pat Ellis Taylor. She has worked as a secretary, an actress, and in advertising. She has published stories, poems, and articles in various publications including *Womansight; Sun Magazine; East-West Journal; Cedar Rock;* and *The Dallas Morning News.* She received her BA and her MA from the University of Texas at El Paso. Her first novel, *Border Healing Woman,* won a Southwest Book Award, and her third, *Afoot in a Field of Men and Other Stories from Dallas' East Side,* won a Texas Circuit Book Award. Her books include *The God Chaser,* a collection of fiction and poetry; *Tonics, Teas, Roots, & Remedies,* a selection of poetry; *How it Happened That I Came to Live in the West: Diary of Coyote Pat;* and *In Search of the Holy Mother of Jobs.* The title of this book says it all.

From *Afoot in a Field of Men and Other Stories from Dallas' East Side*

So I have been a secretary these last few weeks, a job I said I'd never take again, a person I believed I wasn't anymore. But it is temporary work, it is Kelly Girl, queen bee of temporaries, offices two dozen floors above the streets with plush carpets, glass tables, and oriental palms. And when I sit down on the waiting room couch my day of testing and application, I remember why the first time, when I was first married, first babied and wanting money, that I had lost myself in the land of the offices so long. It is very quiet, you see, there is Muzak and the clicking away of typewriters, all the women wear little-bitty high-heeled shoes and tiptoe around. The grey desks are isolated in their cubicles, the secretaries turned from the doors fingers playing over the typewriter keys as they dream into the walls above them day after day, the rush of poppy buds unfolding through the earwires of the dictaphones. As I wait for the results of my typing test, the vines twining toward me from an artful planter by the couch, I leaf through old *Vogues* and nibble on a cookie which Kelly Girls set out on a silver tray. A woman tiptoes up to me in her tippy-toe high heels and smiles down. She has gold-blonde hair in a braid looped around her head, Sleeping Beauty's great-granddaughter in a silk suit coat and pearl-drop earrings. She tells me I am a wonderful typist and that I can be a Kelly Girl, too, beginning at five dollars and thirty cents an hour. Money and Muzak and quiet tippy-toeing women to hang around with all day. Better than sitting at home, like I did last year, cooking pots of beans, trying to write the story of everything, waiting for the money to run out, which it always does for me in a quick, quiet, and inevitable way. Besides, it is temporary after all, I am not going to work too long.

So I go to work on January second, all the regular secretaries in Dallas staying late at the New Mexico ski resorts with their lovers, suffering from postholiday depressions, calling in sick with the flu. I am called to work at Henry S. Miller. I suppose Henry Miller was once a man who grew offices and buildings, warehouses and residential homes onto himself like some people grow seed warts, a real estate virus blossoming from his pores, until he became completely encased in a real estate firm which buys and sells huge chunks of Dallas and Houston with a list of overseas offices like a two-week special European tour painted on the front door. I don't know if the original Henry Miller is still alive or if I am delivering memos and typing reports in the halls and spaces of some gigantic sloughed-off outer form, perpetually preserved with cash flow. The men I see are unidentified to me and look the same, slipping in and out of their offices in white shirts and dark suits with prim ties like men have worn for the past forty (sixty? hundred?) years. No doubt they *all* are somewhat Henry Miller. I wait, as I am told to do by the woman in charge of paperwork, until the men are out of their offices to slip in and put fresh-typed letters in their in-files and pick up dictaphone tapes from their out-files, part of an illusion that their words bloom magically into substance on paper formed from air. Then I listen all afternoon to their compositions, copying every word down, my whole body tuned into the little earplugs like the prophets must have listened before writing down the books of the Bible and like the shotgun madmen listen today to the UFO voices from the other side of the moon.

After a week, the errant secretaries drift back in, and I go to work for an architectural firm, housed in the top floor of the tallest building in Dallas. The secretaries are put into little cubicle boxes in the center of the office space and the architects are ranged along the outside walls, each with a window from ceiling to floor, so that the old ones can look out and pat their stomachs at buildings erected from the specifications of their most virile dreams, and the young ones can dream of demolishment of the penile forests to make way for something even taller (taller than the Hyatt-Regency! Domes! Spires! Revolving balls!). The men meet every day in a large conference room with chairbacks as high as thrones around a polished table with inlaid wood, back-clapping, asking about the Dallas Cowboy games, being straightforward with each other ("give it to me straight," they say, and "don't give me that bullshit, Bert"). The secretaries bustle along the sideboard, bringing trays of doughnuts in the mornings, pouring coffee into styrofoam cups, asking that age-old question, cream or sugar? one man at a time. Once the serving is complete, the secretaries tiptoe out, close the doors, nothing to interrupt the masculine convention until noon when the sandwiches come. Then, when the meeting breaks up and the men catch their planes back to New York or Houston, or go to happy hour with each other or do a little desk-work until quitting time, the secretaries divide up the remaining doughnuts and eat them with late afternoon coffee. They are still very good even though the sugar gets crunchy by then. I have just taken to prowling around the closed conference doors in the afternoons, hoping to be first at the leftover doughnuts, hoping to get maybe a peanut crunchy instead of a plain, when the secretary I am replacing comes back to her desk, married and honeymooned in two short weeks, a pleasant enough interlude but ready to be back to work again.

And finally, I find myself in the thick of sales, out of the downtown offices into the new office space complexes along streets called Regal Row, Viceroy Way, Executive Circle, President Avenue, tickling the ambitions of the tenants and adding subliminal content to their letterheads. The president of the firm is not so aloof as the real estate men and architects have been. He has come from a farm in Arkansas to the city where he has learned to sell Muzak sound systems so well that he is now the owner of a sound systems sales company himself and less than forty years old. A bouncy, athletic man with sculptured sideburns, he claps his hand down on his desk periodically and sings out to me through his half-opened door to my outer office, are we making money, Pat, or are we making money? Then I stop typing, turn around in my chair to face him, smile, and say we are certainly making money! He begins to like me very much for my ability to do this so well and keeps me working even after a new secretary is hired.

Now this particular secretary, whom I shall call Betty Lee, a good small-town East Texas name because that is where she is originally from, is in love with a male go-go dancer called Macho Man who strips every Thursday, Friday, and Saturday night at La Bare. I have heard about La Bare before. I know that men dance on the tables for women who tuck dollar bills under the elastic g-strings of the men whose bulges and bumps they approve of. But I have never gone and when Betty hears this, she promises that someday soon, after work, she will take me there. Now it really isn't for me, I don't have to have that kind of vicarious experience after all, I have never even liked bars too much, I am not interested in seeing half-naked men dance on the tables. But Betty brings out in me a feminine archetype that I have only viewed disdainfully before in other women: I begin to giggle, my wrists get limper, my eyes begin to roll around, and I agree with everything she says in exclamation points. So when Betty promises to take me to La Bare, only a small part of me looks on in contempt and mourning for my own integrity, buzzing on about female sin and dissimulation, while the material side of myself claps and whistles, smirks and nods, Betty assures me I'll never recover, of course I agree.

In the meantime I learn some things about Betty. Right now it is February, and it was only last August that she split with a man. And still she isn't quite divorced. The divorce has two or three weeks of paperwork or waiting time or whatever to go. And her husband was a shithead, he was a redneck, unkind, untrue, unkempt, uninteresting. He watched football games and never kept her company. They dated for five years and then they got married and they never were happy. So they were married for two years before they broke up.

The Macho Man, on the other hand, is Dallas while her husband was only small Texas town. The Macho Man has a beard and an all leather outfit. He wears a leather strap around his neck and some leather straps up and down his arms, and Betty points to her own body to show where those straps are. After she does, she wiggles on her chair a little, rolls her eyes up to the ceiling, and putting her top teeth over her bottom lip, makes an inverted whistle. This is a traditionally female signal that means "sensually overwhelmed." I myself say wow wow wow, in order to show that I am no intellectual snob, that I, too, am no slouch when it comes to imagining all of those leather straps on that bearded man. . . . ★

Isabel Nathaniel

Isabel Nathaniel, poet and freelance reviewer, was brought up and educated in New York City. In 1990 she was a winner of the "Discovery"/*The Nation* award, and has won three Poetry Society of America awards. Her work has appeared most recently in *Poetry* and *The Nation.* She is completing a first collection, *Infernal Regions.* A member of the Texas Institute of Letters, Isabel's book *The Dominion of Lights,* won the Texas Institute of Letters award for best book of poetry. This nationally recognized, award-winning poet, sets these two poems on her patio in Dallas.

On the Patio: Dallas

The prickly pear and yucca
dug from a roadside
do fine in pots. Sun,
sunflowers. The August heat.
Petunias, pinks, and even the geranium
probably don't belong. With watering
they hold on. One morning
I fed them Ortho Fertilizer
made entirely of sea-going fish.
I hosed the place till
the hanging baskets dripped
and the fence soaked dark.
There rose the brackish
smell of bays and wharves
and I turned my head
to the distance as if to hear
the regular slapping of the sea. ★

The Dig

Despite a good canvas hat, your mind
burns white like a desert fanatic. Dust
out of the dust scratches your throat.
Slowly, slowly with handpick, trowel,
you are bringing back the dead.
                              I'm dramatizing,
improvising, stealing your adventure.
I'm good at doing you someplace
far—it's an art, it takes
concentration. On the other side
of the world you are kneeling,
you are coaxing small broken pieces
of the ruined city (under ruined cities)
to your hand—
                         Oh to be touched like that
after three thousand years, to be lifted
into light, same light
as before some minor prophet
called down God's wrath on *Moladah.*

I move the dirt slowly, word
by word, on the patio in Dallas
where it's hot as there—sun
same as Cairo's, as Bangkok's,
as Riyadh's, the hot places. Hot
as the flattopped tel in the Negev
where odds and ends of a kingdom's
daily life find your hand.
                                    Into this life
you raise each little potsherd. Lightstruck,
it hears its name in a wrong language

jar, bowl, lamp—word
repeated on cordless phone
$1.45 a minute Holy Land to Dallas.

Give me details, enough words so later
I can work them till your filmy camouflage-tent
casts squiggles of shadow on the diggers'
long breakfast table, transfiguring
cheese, tomatoes, bread.
With words
like globbed paints on a palette
I am ready when the slightest hot breeze
shivers the net, when quick blur of light
and dark transforms the gathered.
I catch them dreamy and complex
at 11 a.m. second breakfast, having
broken their backs since 5. The strong blonde
in starred cap holds a tin of salmon
gently as a pottery-find and the fellow
in the *Just Hafta Run* shirt closes
his eyes, lifts his head to a riddle.

And you in profile, absent beloved,
bend gracefully over plate of cucumber,
hard-boiled egg and onion—listening
beyond words to something in the unalterable
past, unaware how this moment's
tentlight spangles your cheek and beard. ★

Bryan Woolley

[Editor's note: Bryan Woolley shows that Dallas, for all its sophistication, does indeed have its own beer joints.]

Burgers, Beer, and Patsy Cline

I LOVE A GOOD JOINT. BY "JOINT" I MEAN A drinking—and eating—establishment where, whatever else is for sale, the main merchandise is beer. And where the bartender is the owner or his son or a guy who has worked there so long that it's impossible to imagine the place without him. And the waitress calls all customers of both sexes either "Hon" or "Darlin'." Pool and shuffleboard are desirable options, but not essential. Absolutely essential, however, is a good jukebox loaded with genuine country music.

Adair's is such a place.

One neon sign in front says it's Adair's Saloon. Another says it's Adair's Bar & Grill. The T-shirt on the waitress says it's Adair's Beer Joint. The regulars just call it Adair's, and if you're a Dallas-dweller of a certain type, Adair's is heaven.

Looking at some of the customers at lunchtime, you know what has happened. These guys have walked out of some glass office tower, out of some meeting with a boss or a banker, the heat on the street has hit them like a ton of lighted charcoal, their suit coats have begun to fit like straitjackets, and they can't stand the thought of one more person telling them to have a nice day.

And somebody has said, "Hey, this is an Adair's kind of day!" And they've crawled into a car and driven over to that long, narrow, shady room at 2624 Commerce Street in Deep Ellum. They've probably told themselves that they're going to have a quick burger and get back to the office, but they've probably lied.

Ordering lunch is easy at Adair's. You get a hamburger, or you get a cheeseburger. Lettuce, tomato, pickle, and onion. Choice of mustard, catsup, or mayonnaise. The bread is a hamburger bun just like the ones your mother used to buy at the grocery store. The meat is gray and greasy and weighs half a pound. The cheese on the cheeseburger is American. The whole thing is topped with a jalapeño and held together with a toothpick and served in a plastic basket.

It's the kind of burger you used to buy a long time ago in places called Joe's and Louie's and Pancho's, where the burgers were built by Joe or Louie or Pancho in person. Joe's or Louie's or Pancho's might have offered you a few alternatives—ham-and-cheese, say, or egg salad—but Adair's doesn't. If you don't want a burger, you don't eat at Adair's.

On the side, you can get plain potato chips or barbecue potato chips or potato chips with those little grooves in them or Fritos. The side dishes cost extra and come in sacks. To drink, there are your basic American soft drinks and your basic American beers, served with the cans still on them. You can get a drink of the hard stuff, too, if you don't order anything fancy.

For those who liked Joe's or Louie's or Pancho's, Adair's provides the best lunch available in the vicinity of downtown Dallas. But the best thing about Adair's isn't the lunch. It's the place you get to eat it in.

If you grew up in Fort Stockton or Round Rock or Durant or Odessa or some other place that had a real beer joint and you sometimes get homesick, entering Adair's will bring a tear to your eye. The long room is dark and cool, lighted only by the sun through the front plate-glass window and the half-dozen neon beer signs on the walls and cooled by a big air conditioner that hangs from the ceiling and by ceiling fans.

Also on the ceiling are hundreds of gimme caps that somebody nailed up there and hundreds of paper napkins that customers have wadded up, soaked in beer, and thrown up there to stick during the bar's two-and-one-half years on Commerce Street, where it moved after twenty years on Cedar Springs Road.

The walls, adorned with Texas, Confederate, and American flags and portraits of Bob Wills, John Wayne, and Hondo Crouch, also are full of words. Some are rules and information posted by Adair's management:

You Daince With Who Brung You Or No Damn Dancing.
Dress Code Enforced: Clean Clothes.
Yes! We Serve Crabs. Have A Seat.
Bob Wills Lives.
Public Notice: As A Public Service Announcement, This Establishment Will Notify The Next Of Kin Of Any Person Who Dares Drop A Puck On This Damn New Table.

This reference is to the shuffleboard table, which stands along the wall between the two pool tables at the front of the room and the pinball machines farther back, near the patched, vinyl-covered booths and wobbly tables.

There are other signs that used to stand beside Texas highways, identifying or directing motorists to Hondo Creek, Tarpley, Bandera, Orangefield, and, of course, Camp Adair. But most of the words on the walls were written by customers.

The Adair's graffiti collection must be the largest in Dallas, and it covers the entire spectrum of the graffitist's art: classic restroom poetry, insults of all known ethnic groups, praise and abuse of various universities and fraternities, individual brags and lies signed with names or initials, comments on Texas foreign policy *(The Border Patrol is on the wrong river)*, and bits of personal philosophy (*As I look back the only thing I would of saved for my old age is the years between twenty and thirty*). Some very tall customers, including the Secret Service agents who guarded Vice President George Bush during the Republican National Convention in 1984, wrote their remarks on the ceiling.

But the soul of Adair's, the thing that makes Adair's Adair's, is the music. "We have some who come in for lunch and stay all afternoon listening to the jukebox," says Charline Johnston, who hefts the burgers from the cook's window to the tables.

The Adair's jukebox is simply the best country jukebox in Dallas, probably the best in Texas. So in the very shadows of downtown's towers, within earshot of Central Expressway's roar, the good old grown-up country boys take off their suit coats, loosen their neckties, nurse a cool one and sing along with Hank Williams on "Cold, Cold Heart," Hank Thompson on "The Wild Side of

Life," Bob Wills on "Faded Love," Webb Pierce on "There Stands the Glass," Patsy Cline on "I Fall to Pieces," Ernest Tubb on "Walking the Floor Over You." Some even try to imitate Jimmie Rodgers' blue yodel on "Muleskinner Blues," accompanied by the click of pool balls, the ping of pinball, and many fractures of the *No Profanity* rule.

Eyes glaze and minds slide easily into memories of two-stepping thigh to thigh with some long-ago sweetie in some faraway high school gym, of sweaty adolescent grapplings in the backseats of '53 Fords under the bright Southwestern moon, of the first beer drunk—illegally, probably—in a joint much like this.

In Adair's, on such a hot afternoon, it's hard to remember you're really a lawyer or a judge or a cop or a computer programmer or a truck driver or an auto parts salesman who still has work to do. It's even harder to care. ★

Robert Compton

Robert Compton is the former book editor of *The Dallas Morning News.* He has the incredible facility to remember every book he has ever read and the conversations he had with the writers of those books. He was a phenomenal book editor. He has interviewed many authors and he remembered an interview he did with William Humphrey in 1986 and published in 1987. Compton writes, "Humphrey talked for more than two hours, almost a confessional at times, and I culled the best of it for this article. 'By God!' he exclaimed when I showed him the proposed story. 'I didn't realize you were taping it. But that's me, and that's right! By God!' I think it is one of the most revealing interviews with authors I ever did.

"We talked by phone often after he went back to New York, and he kept me informed on the progress of the book he was working on then, *No Resting Place,* his last book, I think. I last talked to him in 1988, when he called and shouted, 'Eureka! It's finished!' when I answered the phone. In the next few years, he had more and more illnesses, and died in 1997."

From On Becoming a Writer: Interview with William Humphrey

Last fall at the University of Dallas, where he had come as a speaker for the university's Texas Writers Lecture Series, William Humphrey sat and talked at length with his friend, William A. Owens, about their Texas heritage and the influences that led them to become writers. . . . Humphrey, sixty-two, overcame a troubled boyhood to gain an education and become an important American writer. His novels include Home from the Hill, The Ordways, Hostage to Fortune, *a number of short stories, and a series of critically praised essays on hunting and fishing.*

Humphrey is a small and wiry man whose speech is still identifiably Texan. His perfectly modulated voice and flair for the dramatic makes him a spellbinding speaker, even in casual conversation. His words that follow were excerpted from a conversation with Owens on the afternoon before his reading at the University of Dallas.

—Robert Compton

On the Fourth of July, 1937, my father was killed in a car crash. In Clarksville. I refused to go to the funeral. I was thirteen years old, just three weeks. I refused to go and look at his body. My father was one of the worst men that ever lived but one of the best fathers. He was a thug and a no-good and an absolute delight and a joy.

The next day he was buried, and that afternoon my mother and I went to Dallas. She got a job at Sears Roebuck—$11 a week and supply your own uniform. There was no way for my mother to earn any money for me and herself in Clarksville because she had only gone to three grades or four grades of school and she couldn't do domestic work because in those days you had to be black to do that.

She married a man she met while she was waiting for a streetcar in Oak Cliff four months after my father's death. They opened a diner on Jackson Street down in the garment district in Dallas. They did well. By their standards. But that was how she did it. She married that man just to raise me up. She married two more after that. She married four. She's still alive and I'm going to be seeing her day after tomorrow. She's eighty-two—at least she admits to eighty-two. She was born about eight miles from where he was born (nodding at Owens). And on the same day.

Writing came about like this. I started drawing pictures and I got a scholarship to the Dallas Institute of Fine Arts. No little boy ever worked harder at a dream than I did because I was awfully lonely in Dallas. . . . I had been transplanted from my lovely little town where I couldn't walk across the square without three men saying, "Billy, let me give you a nickel." Because I was the town's prize boy. My mother kept me so neat and changed my clothes three times a day, even on a school day, and I was so polite and well brought up precisely because we were so low-class and she wanted to climb over shoulders to get into the upper class. So was I a model boy?

Then my father died, and I was brought and plunged into Dallas and terrified—scared to death. And I started drawing like a little demon. An aunt of mine who had lived in Dallas for several years showed them to the Dallas Art Institute, and I got a scholarship.

Well, I worked at that like, oh, like a little slave for five years. I painted and I drew, and at the end of that time my mother and my first stepfather decided to get divorced. Each of them asked me to come and live with him or her. I didn't want to live with either of them, so I left home at eighteen. But before I left home, I went out in the backyard at Number 911 Waverly Place in Oak Cliff and burned every picture I had ever painted because I looked at them—I'm sure I was right—and said, "You'll never be anything but tenth-rate."

Meanwhile, I had started reading. I was not a bookish boy, but an important thing happened. At the age of fourteen, just after I arrived here, I was walking down Elm Street where Field Street used to not run through. And in front of Gene Wagner's book shop there was a bin of books for a nickel. Well, a nickel I had, just about. And I had decided I oughta improve my mind. God knows, it needed improving. And I bought a copy of *Don Quixote*, Part I, from the Harvard Classics for a nickel. I knew I wasn't gonna like it, but I thought that I ought to read it because I knew that this was a self-improving book. I took it home and read it and almost fell out of my skin with laughter. And made the greatest discovery of my life—good books are good.

I went back to that place and said I'd like a job on Saturdays 'cause I could really use the money. And they gave me a job. And there I met a man who was the formative influence on my life.

There will still be in Dallas people who knew this man. His name was Jack Boss—B-O-S-S. He was the littlest—he makes me look big—he was the littlest man I believe I ever saw. He sold insurance for a living. He had a gorgeous wife and the four most beautiful little daughters I've ever seen in my life. He understood that I had been orphaned of my father just the year before.

And he just took me under his wing. One of those formative influences that almost everyone has. And I was lucky to have mine. Mr. Jack Boss. He was then, I suppose, a man of about thirty-five. Tiny, tiny little man. A gust of wind would have . . . he couldn't cast a shadow. He had written five novels, he later confessed to me. And I said, "Let me read them." He said, "No, they're not any good." He had me at fourteen reading James Joyce, Virginia Woolf, *Travels in Arabia Deserta* by Doughty, which nobody can read. He just was everything to me.

Well, when the time came that I decided that I couldn't really be a good painter and burned up all my pictures—I was at SMU then—and I was reading, I wrote a little tiny, tiny short story. I showed it to Lon Tinkle (the late book critic of *The Dallas Morning News* and English professor at Southern Methodist University), who, though he was not a teacher of mine, was a friend of mine. And in fact almost a protector of mine.

He'd occasionally give me two bits to go and get a hamburger. Well, a hamburger only cost a nickel then. He'd give me two bits to go and get a good big meal. I showed it to him, and he said, "This isn't bad." And then he introduced me to George Bond (an English teacher at SMU), and between the two of them they fostered me and it was not easy to do because I was an extremely—by then—rebellious and difficult young boy.

I suppose my father's death had begun to hit me. It hadn't at first, but it had by then. And I was very erratic and difficult. I didn't get into jail, but I did things that ought to have put me in jail. Because I was just rebellious—and unhappy, miserable, lonely. Aaah, I decided one thing I don't want to do is work for a living. So I became a writer. And have never worked so hard in my life as having chosen that career, as this man (Owens) will attest. Not just about me, but about all of us. ★

John Bloom

Joe Bob Briggs, who is in reality John Irving Bloom, was born in Dallas, Texas. He attended Vanderbilt on a sports-writing scholarship and began his writing career at *Texas Monthly*. He also began writing humorous reviews of B-movies and drive-in movies, which is what he calls cult films. He was a host on *Drive-In Theater* on the Movie Channel, a late-night B-movie show, which ran for almost ten years. He then hosted *MonsterVision* on the TNT network. He spent two seasons on *The Daily Show* on Comedy Central. Briggs remained active as a writer, working as a contributing editor on the *National Lampoon* and freelancing for *Rolling Stone*, *Playboy*, the *Village Voice*, and *Interview*. He was the regular humor columnist and theater critic at the *National Review*, and he published five books of satire—*Joe Bob Goes to the Drive-In*; *A Guide to Western Civilization, or My Story*; *Joe Bob Goes Back to the Drive-In*; *The Cosmic Wisdom of Joe Bob Briggs*; and *Iron Joe Bob.* His two syndicated newspaper columns—"Joe Bob Goes to the Drive-In" and "Joe Bob's America"—were picked up by the *New York Times* syndicate. In 2000 he started writing the "Drive-In" column for United Press International, along with a second column, "The Vegas Guy." Bloom was president of the Trinity Foundation of Dallas, Texas, a nondenominational, nonprofit public foundation that serves as a religious watchdog group and publishes *The Door*, a Christian satire magazine, of which Bloom was a regular columnist and investigative reporter. A member of the Texas Institute of Letters, Bloom funds The Joe Bob Briggs Humor Award given by that group. Religion in Dallas is not always the standard or expected brand, as Briggs/Bloom shows in this article.

The God Thing: In which Joe Bob Briggs, America's irreverent drive-in movie critic, gets religion

Ole Anthony was the only preacher I ever met who wanted to talk about getting laid. To be fair, he mostly talked about not getting laid and the crimp it put in his lifestyle. But there were nights in the early eighties when we would hang out at smoky, boozy joints like Arthur's, the notorious upscale pickup bar in North Dallas, and svelte elegant women with bedroom eyes would linger for a long time at Ole's side and then, at some point, click away in their four-inch pumps, bound only for the parking lot. "What happened?" I would ask him.

"Well, I mentioned the God thing."

"You shouldn't mention the God thing."

"I've lost more nookie over that. God is punishing me."

He was only half kidding. Eventually he took a vow of chastity. He said it was either that or get married, and he preferred the simpler form of suffering.

Today, as then, Ole runs the public nonprofit Trinity Foundation, the only organization of its kind, variously functioning as a church, a charitable foundation, a homeless shelter, a job corps for reformed crack addicts, a consortium of muckraking journalists, a private investigative agency, a magazine publisher, a supervisor of criminal parolees and probationers, and the manager of low-income housing projects in places as far flung as Oklahoma City and Dayton, Ohio. There's another school of thought that would say Trinity is a blaspheming parody of Christianity, an ego trip for Ole Anthony, a cult, or a tax shelter for people like me, who have been known to throw a little money in its direction. Most of its members live within a three-square-block area of East Dallas in two-story houses that were built by local *Mafiosi* in the 1930s. Over the years I've asked him on more than one occasion how to describe what he does.

"From what we know," he says, "we're functioning as a first-century A.D. church. This is what existed before denominations, when there was no separation between Christian and Jew, much less Christian and Christian."

I ask him what he does. He tells me what he is. This is the only kind of conversation you can have with Ole.

"Okay, what we do," he says, "is we meet human need."

That's a little vague, I tell him.

"We don't make plans. We do what's put before us each day."

And this Zen-like answer is all you're likely to get. Don't try for more. I've known the man twenty years, and the answer has never changed. Ole (pronounced "OH-lee") is a blue-eyed 6-foot-4 Norwegian-American who, before he became the guru of East Dallas—he hates being called a "guru," which is why I just did it—had a checkered career as an air force intelligence officer, corporate executive for the multinational Teledyne, failed Republican candidate for the Texas legislature, political advisor to former Mayor Wes Wise, owner of an offshore oil exploration company, sports agent, talent manager, political consultant, public relations specialist, and the kind of sexual player who strikes terror into the parents of young girls everywhere. In other words, he was a con man and a hustler—with a great wardrobe. I liked him immediately.

When I first met him, he was homeless. But like many people who have touched millions and then lost it, he had contrived to remain in Highland Park even in the depths of his penury. For a while he lived in a guesthouse on Turtle Creek, then in a garage apartment, and lately he'd taken to sleeping in his office, which was a seedy walk-up over an Oak Lawn carpet store. Three employees of *Texas Monthly,* myself included, had taken space in the same building, and on days when I came in early, Ole would sometimes be sheepishly emerging from the men's room, where he would have performed his ablutions while concealing all evidence from the strait-laced-marriage counselor who functioned as our landlord. Ole had no means of support, either visible or invisible. We were both night owls who liked greasy spoons and lively bars, so I had plenty of chances to question him about this.

"What exactly do you do, Ole?"

"I told you what I do."

"Tell me again."

"I'm the president of the Trinity Foundation. It's the only public religious foundation in America."

"And how much does that pay?"

"Twenty dollars a week."

"So what do you do for money?"

"I'm the president of the Trinity Foundation."

"You live on $20 a week?"

"I live on $20 a week."

"All right, let's change the question. How do you spend your day?"

"I read the Scriptures. I study Torah."

"Do you realize that most people who say their full-time job is reading the Bible are in Terrell State Hospital?"

And then he would go into excruciating detail about just what part of the Torah he was studying at that very moment, and at the time his narratives were so boring to me that I would tune them out. Preston Jones, the Dallas Theater Center playwright, would come into Nick Farley's Lounge, a dart pub better known as the NFL, and razz Ole mercilessly. Jones had invented a complete biography of "Frank Christ, Jesus's older brother," and would hold forth on the superiority of Frank over Jesus by virtue of his prior claim to the virgin birth. Ole would bear up pretty well under these assaults, but secretly he was thinking, "Eventually, Preston will understand what I'm talking about." This is actually Ole's principal virtue as a religious teacher. You can put the man in a rowdy den of nine dozen scoffing atheists, turn a virtual fire hose of abuse on him, and at the end of it, he'll say, "Let me tell you what Paul said in Corinthians." And somebody ends up screaming at him, "Ole! Give it a rest! No more Scripture! The Cowboys are playing the Eagles!"

"Do you know what's occurring spiritually when a man becomes addicted to sports? He's feeding off the flesh of—"

"Ole! Please!"

"No, it's something I was studying the other day."

He was relentless. He was a charging Brahma bull breathing Scripture out of both nostrils. But, unlike most preachers, he didn't limit his exhortations to the church sanctuary, and he didn't stand on a corner with a "Jesus Saves" sign and a bullhorn. He just spouted this stuff off the top of his head, wherever and whenever it occurred to him. And he was studying every day. For a long time, he went to the Perkins School of Theology Library at SMU, but he was kicked out by the spinsterish librarian for spending too much time there and using too many rare books. (I know it doesn't sound like a real reason, but that's basically what happened.) He couldn't use most so-called "Christian" libraries because they were either reserved for members of a particular congregation or limited to preachers with "credentials." (Ole has no college degree.) He finally found a home for his daily researches at Temple Emanu-El, where the rabbis would sometimes come and discuss his studies with him.

This led to speaking invitations, the opening of other collections, and sometimes the actual debate of the Scripture itself, which is a rabbi's highest compliment. One night, after Ole spoke at the Jewish Community Center, a few people asked questions about the Messiah—always uppermost in everyone's minds when Christians and Jews come together—and an elderly man in the rear waved them aside and said, "But he speaks with the faith of Abraham, Isaac, and Jacob. It doesn't matter." Ole got choked up—and he's not a man who cries easily—and found it difficult to tell the story later.

For what was emerging from these studies was his growing conviction that the modern church had gotten it all wrong—that there is no basis for the separation of Christian and Jew. That the apostles, beginning with Paul, had always spoken first in the synagogue and that many early churches were, in fact, synagogues. Increasingly, his readings turned away from Martin Luther and toward the ancient Hebrew authorities. Always at his side were Hebrew dictionaries, Greek dictionaries, and academic word-study books because he felt acutely his inability to read the original languages and was determined not to make a mistake. I watched as he filled up dozens of three-ring binders with his printed notes, painstakingly copied onto yellow legal pads. He became fascinated with the idea of the "three-year cycle," a process in ancient times by which a congregation would read through the entire Torah (the first five books of the Old Testament) in three years, discussing and understanding every verse. He came to believe, with the rabbis, that Torah was the only Scripture and that everything else in the Bible, including all of the New Testament, was merely commentary. He had become, as he was jokingly called at Temple Emanu-El, "our Christian rabbi."

This was the answer to my frequent question, "What exactly do you do?"

Ole had become a Christian by violence. On January 17, 1972, in a mystical flash of understanding, he believed. It's impossible to explain how these things happen. I can state the external facts of the situation. Ole was representing Wes Wise as a political consultant at the dedication of a new television station, KBFI Channel 33, which was one of the first all-Christian stations in the country. The speaker was a Christian teacher named Norman Grubb. In the midst of Grubb's speech, Ole's life changed.

How a person first comes to believe is called, in the Baptist churches of my youth, your "testimony." And anyone who's heard very many of these stories knows that most of them are bull hockey, someone's imaginative reconstruction of what he thinks might have happened or *wished* had happened or, in the case of some of the preaching professionals, an outright falsehood constructed for the benefit of the unwashed. I once tried to describe my own conversion experience at a Baptist Sunday school class in Carrollton, and I didn't hesitate to include the humorous aspects, which included a car wreck, a divorce, and the hysterical assertion of a friend that I had become a cult member and needed to be deprogrammed. My presentation was met with dumbfounded silence, followed by the teacher's suggestion that "I'll bet a lot of our young people would come listen to you. And if they didn't know you were going to talk about Jesus Christ, you might be able to surprise them. They think they're coming to a comedy show, but what they get is Jesus." I resolved, on the spot, never to "give testimony" again.

The process of conversion is mysterious. In Ole's case, it was instantaneous and permanent, a so-called "Damascus Road" flash of understanding. He would later compare it to the moment when, working for the air force, he witnessed a hydrogen bomb explosion that vaporized an entire island. The physical feeling, he said, was similar.

For a time he tried to graft this new life onto his old one. In the fall of 1972, he was part of a small group of Christians who created the Trinity Foundation as the kind of evangelistic enterprise he would later come to hate. (It was named after the first thermonuclear bomb, which had been exploded at Trinity Flats, New Mexico. The members of the group wanted to create the same sort of "explosion of faith.") They tried to buy a television station—Channel 39—but were aced out of it by Pat Robertson. They promoted a benefit Christian concert—Pat Boone and Andrae Crouch singing for two youth charities—but lost $40,000 when Gibson's Discount Stores backed out on its underwriting promise. Ole appeared on the Christian talk show *The 700 Club*—and was permanently banned when he told host Ben Kinchlow that he prayed to God to either send him a wife or stop making him so horny. He hosted a talk show on a Christian radio station in Arlington. He interviewed all the Christian celebrities of the day—Tom Landry, Roger Staubach, Billy Graham, Oral Roberts, Gene Scott, Jim Bakker, Rex Humbard—as well as non-Christian luminaries like Frank Sinatra, Johnny Mathis, football star Jim Brown, several of the astronauts, and frequent guest Madalyn Murray O'Hair, the wacky professional atheist, who became a friend and would always start out saying, "How did an intelligent boy like you become a Christian?" The show was canceled despite achieving an unheard-of-in-Christian-radio six rating. One by one, all of Ole's projects for God came to nothing. By the time I met him, the Trinity Foundation appeared to be comatose. In fact, it was just being born. . . . ★

C. W. Smith

C. W. Smith is the 2006 Dedman Family Distinguished Professor and teaches in the creative writing program at Southern Methodist University. He is the author of the novels *Thin Men of Haddam, Country Music, The Vestal Virgin Room, Buffalo Nickel, Hunter's Trap, Understanding Women, Gabriel's Eye,* and a new novel, *Purple Hearts.* He has also published a collection of short stories, *Letters from the Horse Latitudes.* His short stories have appeared in *Mademoiselle, Vision, Southwest Review, Sunstone Review, Carolina Quarterly, New Mexico Humanities Review, Quartet, Cimarron Review, American Literary Review, American Short Fiction, The Missouri Review,* and other magazines.

He has been a reporter and film critic for *The Dallas Times Herald* and a freelance journalist whose articles have appeared in *Esquire, TV Guide, Texas Monthly, Eastern Review, Atlanta, D, The Texas Humanist,* and *The Utne Reader,* as well as other periodicals and newspapers. His autobiographical book dealing with children after a divorce was *Uncle Dad.*

He has twice received the Jesse H. Jones Novel Award from the Texas Institute of Letters; the Southwestern Library Association Award for Best Novel; the Dobie-Paisano Creative Writing Fellowship from the University of Texas; National Endowment for the Arts Creative Writing Fellowships in 1976 and 1990; the John H. McGinnis Short Story Award from *Southwest Review*; a Pushcart Prize nomination from *Southwest Review*; and the Stanley Walker Award for Journalism from the Texas Institute of Letters.

From *Gabriel's Eye*

We enter their story on a Tuesday at the cusp of nightfall, in a Dallas high school classroom, a dozen students, a teacher. Outside, lightning strobes the canyon of freeway down the hill as taillights glimmer through a rush-hour shower. The air of the classroom is tinted a melancholy, Hopperesque blue. The students sit in gray metal desks, and under them in the foreground—seen from the teacher's perspective—are slashes of black Xs made by the crossed legs of girls in black stockings.

Someone makes a joke. A boy comes through the door while they're laughing; when they swing their heads to look, he blushes, and Susan, the teacher, says, "Can we help you?" She meant to make him feel included, but worries that to him she sounded like a clerk at Neiman's speaking to a wino. He says, squeaking like a damp cloth on glass, "Art club?" then he coughs. She says, "Yes, take a seat," but a chair makes a basso squawk when his hip hits it, so he stands against the back wall, arms folded, buried to his thighs in a nest of empty desks.

Beside him tall windows scumbled by cleanings patina his cheek with northern light. He's handsome enough to model Calvin Klein underwear but looks too shy to show up for the casting call. Susan would like to draw how the boy folds his arms, it's so expressive of insecurity. They're not tightly knotted high on his chest like a surly football coach or someone skeptical of what he's hearing; nor are they laced low and loose with hands dangling from wrists like a woman letting a man know she's listening seriously. No, his elbows press his ribs and his arms cross at the wrists, like the elevator's crowded. Like his stomach hurts. She can tell he's out of place by what he's wearing, as well—rumpled khakis, a tails-out blue Oxford button-down with one cuff rolled to the elbow and the other hanging loose, unbuttoned. Here at this high school for the performing arts most students go for the grunge look, hip-hop fashion, heavy metal; and though some dress like preppies, none of those are here tonight on this second meeting for the new semester and none were expected. Aside from this stunningly handsome lad, the roster comes from last year's bunch and pet students she's snagged from her classes. They're assorted misfits, but they know one another.

The boy interrupted their talk of future projects, and, with him mute but still a vaguely disquieting presence, Matt continues. "I say State Fair, Susan. All that great geeky art on the midway freak show. The Half-Woman, Half-Alligator Man." He's the class clown, the school's cartoonist. "We can take some Polaroids."

"They haven't had the freak show for years and years," says Becki, whose gaze darts toward the silent blushing boy. "Until you show up, Matthew." Susan ascribes this uncharacteristic put-down to Becki's desire to impress the new boy.

Cheryl says, "We did a car wash for art supplies last year, remember?"

"Yeah, you collected the money—Anthony and I did the washing," says Matt. "What about, uh, hey Susan! What about life studies?"

Becki says, with a sneer, "You mean nude modeling, right?"

"Hey!" Matt wails in earnest. "I'm serious. I want to be an artist. Why can't we do that?"

Becki snorts. She and Cheryl roll their eyes at one another. A couple of sophomores are tittering and whispering to one another.

Cracking a wry grin, Susan says, "Well, Matt, it's for the same reason you can't vote yet. Or drink. Legally, I mean."

While they bat about more ideas, Susan glances at the new boy. Is there anything more heart-rending than a kid yearning to join a circle of other kids unknown to him? He's got a cowlick. Nathan had one like that.

From her desk she picks up a questionnaire the others completed at the meeting's outset and hip-swings her way through the broken files of desks to hand it to the standing boy, comes near enough to stretch across a hurdle of chairbacks, and he reaches to meet her, and takes it, eyes averted. She says, "You are?" leaving an inflected blank. He looks up and says, "Jeff," in a voice so richly baritone Susan believes he's been itching to use it again.

"Nice to meet you, Jeff. Why don't you sit up here—" she pats the back rest of a desk behind Cheryl and Becki. "And fill this out?"

She calls for a break so she can load her slide projector. Everyone leaves but the boy bent over the form. He's now seated in a desk that he slid into without moving his feet from where he stood. When her preparations are done, she sits on the bow of her desk, legs swinging, and pretends not to be watching him complete her questionnaire.

She's never seen him before. Transfer? He writes with a blue-capped Bic that tells her he hasn't begun to think of tools the way the others do: Becki writes her name in green and dots her "i" with a red heart, favors the four-color switchable ballpoint. Matt the cartoonist collects Rapidographs; he's been at this since age three and nothing she will do one way or another can make much difference. But maybe that blue-capped Bic says this is the first day in his life the boy has considered doing this, and yes, this is exciting to her, forming the unformed, molding the malleable. Clay. He's got a tall, slender form, lean face, high cheekbones, long lashes, full mouth, just enough dark blonde stubble to undercut the feminine sensuality of those lips and eyes. He needs to be rendered in pencil so that the artist can bring something, a shading, to that unmarked face: age, interest, whatever makes a face look as if it belongs to a body that's been lived in. He doesn't look shallow or empty so much as virginal, as if he's gone this far without a scratch and may not even realize that this is rare, takes it for granted that everyone will give him what he needs when he shines his big blond light at them. Add a mole, a scar? A squint? Why, though? Why not just try to capture what's there? After all, innocence and perfection are rare.

But they also inspire resentment. That face has too much power to lure her gaze. Unearned power. Yet she can sympathize with that, how having that power also leaves you feeling that you do something to people without meaning to, draw them to you before you're ready to have them at you and on you, how you try to nullify the power by looking blank, empty of intent. Men leer at your breasts when you're fourteen and you only want to grow them so you look like your peers and nobody'll mistake you for a child.

So she and the boy share the burdens of beauty; looking at him, her gaze compelled to his face, she is both the viewer and the viewed. . . . ★

Caroline Rose Hunt

Caroline Rose Hunt, creator and honorary chairwoman of Rosewood Hotels & Resorts, was named one of the most powerful women in the travel industry by *Travel Agent* magazine in 1999. An owner of Lady Primrose's Antique Store, she is the creator of Lady Primrose's Royal Bathing Luxuries, a line of products found in exclusive hotels and stores around the world. From 1985 to 1995 she was a presidential appointee to the Board of Trustees of the John F. Kennedy Center for the Performing Arts, and she has been named one of America's 100 Most Influential Women by *Ladies' Home Journal.* She is a graduate of Mary Baldwin College and holds a degree in English literature from The University of Texas at Austin. She was named a Distinguished Alumnus, the most prestigious award given by Texas Exes. She is a Dallas woman who has made her mark all over the world.

From *Primrose Past: The 1848 Journal of Young Lady Primrose:*
Summer of 1991

It was a warm day, even for Dallas. Vivian Young, my partner in Lady Primrose's antique shop and tearoom, and I had just finished lunch: she her favorite chicken salad and fruit and I my usual Bombay chicken sandwich with apple and English walnut salad. We were lingering over a pot of our Secret Garden tea as we discussed our upcoming shopping trip to England.

Vivian was leafing through the accumulated mail when she stopped suddenly. "Here's an announcement of a house sale in Herefordshire," she exclaimed. "It's taking place while we're in England. And the house is named Primrose Hall! Can you believe it?" We were both astonished; neither of us had known there was a country house by that name.

The name was, of course, the reason for our interest. When we had first opened our shop in 1987, we had decided to call it Shopping English

Countryside. To pique the curiosity of our potential customers, on our very first buying trip to England we had sent two thousand hand-penned postcards reading: "Having a wonderful time. Shopping English Countryside. See you in October. Love, Lady Primrose." We knew of no Lady Primrose. It was simply a name we picked out of the blue because it sounded so very British.

To solve the mystery of the postcard, we extended the invitations for the celebration of the opening of our shop in the name of Lady Primrose. And the name stuck. In the end, no one remembered Shopping English Countryside, but they couldn't forget Lady Primrose. A year later we formally changed the name to Lady Primrose's.

Along with the notice of the sale came a copy of an article from the *Times of London* with additional information. The house, it explained, had been built in 1770 by William Henry Primrose, the third Baronet of Chatfield. Since 1866 it had been owned by the family of the current owners, who were being forced to liquidate the estate to satisfy the 70 percent death taxes required by the British government.

The sale was receiving this unusual media attention because letters from several famous literary figures of the nineteenth century had been discovered in a box in the attic. These were being held for an auction to take place later at Sotheby's in London.

The announcement listed period furniture as well as centennial pieces and an extensive selection of decorative and utilitarian objects.

We had never shopped in Herefordshire and were surprised that an auction would be conducted in a location that remote from London. But Primrose Hall compelled us, and we decided the event sounded well worth the travel time required.

Two months later we were in England. The first two days we spent working with a toiletries house, finalizing the formula for the Lady Primrose amenities for The Lanesborough, a new luxury hotel under construction in the old St. George's Hospital. Rosewood Hotels & Resorts, which my children and I had established eleven years prior, had been awarded the management contract.

The toiletries house, in business since 1677, had graciously allowed us access to their archives to aid us in our creation of an old-fashioned, all-natural product whose fragrance would be suitable for both sexes. The formula we selected was an updated version of a honey-based recipe, with the addition of royal jelly, an expensive ingredient known to be restorative to the skin.

The day of the Primrose Hall auction, we rose early for our long drive into the countryside. Traffic on the motorway was bumper to bumper coming into the city, and we were relieved that we were going the opposite direction.

Once we turned off onto the auxiliary two-lane roads, our progress was slowed. We passed through several small towns, and then the roads seemed narrower than ever—especially when passing farm vehicles required us to pull to the side of the road. Gradually the terrain changed: gently rolling hills offered us a vista of golden fields, demarcated with hedgerows or stone fences. After several nervous consultations with our map to be sure we really were on the right road, we were reassured when we came across signs directing the public to the auction.

The imposing entrance gates of the property were of wrought iron centered with a coat of arms topped by a leaping stag. With a sigh of relief, we consulted our watches—the auction had not yet begun.

Inside the estate gates we passed a tiny chapel within a walled churchyard filled with moss-covered gravestones. Our journey had taken longer than anticipated, and we were sorry to find we would have no time to visit the charming site.

We were directed to drive off into a field to park, and to proceed to the marquee to register. A tree-canopied drive led us to the house and to a tent that had been erected outside the house for the purpose of the auction. In the tent large screens were erected to facilitate the bidding; there was still time for a brief viewing, so we completed the registration processing, paid for our catalogs, and hurried on to the house.

Primrose Hall is of classic Palladian design, small but of perfect proportions. It was not one of the massive great houses one can visit in England, and I found it all the more pleasing as a result; I felt I could actually enjoy living there. Above the entrance was a stone carved with the numerals 1770. As I opened the door, with its great iron knocker, I felt a sense of intrigue and wonder, as though I had stepped back into 1770.

We entered a large entry hall where many of the objects brought from the upper floors were being exhibited. On one side of the hall was a large living room, which led to the dining room and kitchen; the latter seemed to have been converted from another use, its appliances circa 1920. On the other side was a book-filled, wood-paneled library and another room, possibly an office, with its own outside entryway. Across the entire back of the house ran a narrow gallery, whose windows looked out on a garden. Though now long neglected, it had once been laid out in a formal design. Remnants of a maze were visible, and its topiary bushes were so overgrown the original shapes were unidentifiable. At the focal point in the middle of the garden was a large obelisk covered with hieroglyphics. The main building was flanked with two wings probably built at a later date, as the architectural detail differed from that in the central portion of the house. I was so busy enjoying the house that I almost forgot to look at the furnishings that filled the entire bottom floor of the home.

Remembering our mission, I turned my attention to the furniture, much of which had been removed from the upper floors to the gallery and large entry hall. Among the items was a small Queen Anne secretary bookcase that caught my eye. I squeezed back between the crowded furniture to look it over carefully, but when I found that the slant top lid was locked, and I was unable to examine the interior, I dismissed any thought of bidding upon it.

The auction had attracted a large crowd. . . . In the distance one group in a festive mood picnicked in the ruins of a pagoda with a sharply pointed roof, its once-shining tiles now covered in moss. I recognized the building as what was called a folly, but quite the most unusual folly I'd ever seen. We had constructed a folly in Lady Primrose's after learning of the popularity of these structures, which the English landscape architects utilized to give perspective to their vistas.

By this time we were quite hungry, but with time pressing we contented ourselves with a cup of tea and scones that were for sale next to the marquee. Vivian returned to the viewing, and I went into the marquee to secure seats.

The auctioneer mounted the dais and tested the microphone; it was time for the auction to commence. A newcomer to British auctions, I bid shyly on some ceramic milk pails decorated with the classical façade of the house, bowing out when I reached the limit I had set for myself. I later learned that the two casually dressed men who had outbid me were in the dairy business and well-known collectors of "dairyana."

I watched quietly as other bidders raised fingers, touched their noses, or simply nodded. Still feeling timid, I successfully reentered the competition when a shoe-shaped copper container was offered. Later research revealed that its original use had been for warming ale; its rarity made it significantly more valuable than my modest bid. When Vivian rejoined me, we successfully bid on a large high-backed settle and three feet of old leather-bound books. Though we had been attracted to them for their beautiful leather bindings, we were pleased to find among them early-nineteenth-century editions of authors such as Shakespeare, Chaucer, Milton, Spenser, Sir Isaac Newton, Sir Thomas Browne, and, of course, the classic Greek and Roman authors in their original texts. As the auction progressed we were successful in acquiring several very interesting decorative objects along with a lovely worktable of many naturally colored woods with intricate inlay design of the type from Tunbridge Wells.

When the items from the children's wing came up, I again felt an attraction—indeed, a curiosity—for the unusually small Queen Anne double bonnet secretary bookcase I had spied earlier. The door mirrors were smoky with age, and the walnut wood had a lovely warm patina. Even though I had not been able to examine the interior, I decided I had to have it—not for our shop, but for my own bedroom! I lost all sense of caution and bid eagerly against several other interested parties. When the gavel came down, it was mine, and I felt like a winner despite the fact that my bid significantly exceeded the estimate.

It was six weeks before our container of purchases was scheduled to arrive in Houston. Knowing that late August is a time for storms in the North Atlantic, we were nervous about its crossing. But finally, only a week late, we received the call from our agent that the ship had docked in Houston and had been cleared by customs. Luckily, only one or two items suffered minor damages, and within ten days our acquisitions were on the floor of our antique shop.

The secretary bookcase, I was thrilled to see, arrived without mishap. Before placing it in my own bedroom, I tried keys from our box of miscellaneous keys at the shop. Miraculously one fit; the ball turned, and for the first time I saw the interior of my delightful purchase. It was a lovely example of late-eighteenth-century or early-nineteenth-century craftsmanship. The fittings were all in beautiful condition. There were small drawers suitable for pens and incidentals, slots for letters and papers, and even two little shelves that could be pulled out for candlesticks. The unfaded interior looked as if it had been locked tight for a hundred years.

Several days later, when I found the time, I took pleasure in cleaning and waxing the desk myself. As I was applying the beeswax polish that I had purchased in London, I noticed that the writing surface seemed loose. Knowing that many of the custom-made eighteenth-century furnishings harbored concealed compartments, I carefully applied a little pressure. The whole surface slid back to reveal a compartment and within I discovered a treasure: a host of personal items, clearly quite old but as fresh as the day they were left behind.

I carefully removed the items hidden within: a small partially filled sketchbook; a handful of letters still bearing fragments of sealing wax; a lovely Victorian-style valentine with a sentimental verse inscribed "To My Moonbeam"; and a book with a coat of arms crested with a leaping stag printed in gilt on the cover—the same coat of arms we had seen on the entrance gates to Primrose Hall. Turning its pages revealed its origins: it was a daily journal written in 1848. I wondered if mine were the first eyes to read these words in nearly a century and a half.

Neat penmanship in purple ink filled both sides of each page. On most of the pages the carefully formed letters made it easy to read, but there were places where the handwriting became less careful and required a magnifying glass to decipher the words. I began to leaf through the book—and was engrossed at once by the heartfelt confidences captured there.

It was a rainy afternoon, so I immediately settled down to enter not just a time long past but the world of an endearing young girl at a turning point in her life.

And what I discovered along the way left me intrigued—no, mesmerized—at the story she told, and the mystery it held. Allow me to acquaint you with the young Lady Primrose. ★

Jack Myers

Jack Myers is the author of seven volumes of poetry, the latest being *OneOnOne*, and five other works about poetry; among them, the reference work *The Longman Dictionary of Poetic Terms* and the anthology *New American Poets of the 90s*.

His work has been widely anthologized and has appeared in hundreds of literary journals, from *Esquire* and *The Nation* to *POETRY* and *The American Poetry Review*. His book of poems, *As Long As You're Happy*, was a National Poetry Series selection for 1985. He has been granted many fellowships and awards for his work: among them, two from the National Endowment For the Arts, and two from the Texas Institute of Letters.

He teaches and directs the creative writing program at Southern Methodist University. He serves on the board of directors of the Dallas literary center, The Writer's Garret, was a past vice president of the 15,000-member Associated Writing Programs, and has also taught creative writing in the low-residency Vermont College MFA Program in Writing. Myers sets these poems in Dallas.

I Already Tried Gardening . . .

I was digging the borderline garden I had conceived of
in a flash and analyzed all winter, clumps of black clay
fastened with grass, which became forced labor so I worked
harder hoping when I looked up it'd all have turned to flowers.

Just as robins migrating from Mexico had reached Dallas,
an old man with a battle-axe cane stopped by and said, "I can't
figure what you're doing," Looking through his glasses I could see
his house clear across the street. "And what denomination are you?"
he asked. So then I knew where I lived and I backed him up with
"God told me to do it. It's artistic."

Then he asked, “What are ya gonna do with them piles of good dirt?”
It was disguised as a craft question, and I thought he could’ve been
one of those Old Masters who can hyperspace when cornered, so I said
“I’m digging a hole in the hill and moving it out back.”

He noticed how the hole was smaller than the hill and said, “Holes
get bigger more slowly than hills. You’re welcome to attend
our church.” I said, “See that cane? I call it your tree-leg.”
He said. “I’m bird-brain and this here dog you don’t see which is
home I call ‘Leave.’” Then I got on my knees and said to my work,

“But don’t make me eat one of those delicious clumps of chocolate-
pudding dirt,” which I mashed with my feet and I did my karate yells
like Shredded Wheat amplified a hundred times and the robins jumped
into the bare plum tree and argued about who’s the boss and who’ll
get the best-looking women while that old man stared at me,

both of us not knowing my denomination, and the question of the birds
in the air: Should we camp here tonight? ★

The Gift

Remember Father’s Day, the banner says.
But I can’t give my father what he wants
much less name it, so I get him a golf machine
that pops the ball right back.

If I can’t give him what he wants
I can get him what seems wrong.
It’s the thought that counts, he’d say,
not having caught the exact misses
I sent past him into interstellar space.

I'm telling my wife how she looks super-good
in this flouncy purple maternity suit,
though in truth it looks like her behind
is in front, when I suddenly think
I'm going to be a father! and I remember
my own two kids who don't live with me anymore
and I get quiet in order to receive their thoughts.

But instead I think about these poor Black kids
I took for a ride through White North Dallas
and how one little six-year-old beauty
leaned over my shoulder and shouted to the wind
"How do you get to live like this?" ★

We Go Away at Home

Oklahoma lies on top of us like a sod quilt
thickened with manure. So we dream we drive all night
into the mouth of boredom, smelling sex,
betting that the long explosions of the stars
have stopped. By dawn the flags of radiation are flying
deep inside New Mexico and I wake you so you can sleep
against me as the ultra-colors pass through rock. It takes off
as the curtain of heat thickens to a lens.
In Louisiana men in bogs are running from tree to tree.
They fall down peacefully and dissolve, then flash out
as green shoots in another life. We are sinking into ourselves
with the inward smile of vegetables as it gets dark.
The night air breathes the black trees like smoke.
Lying here, disappearing, we remember why we stayed at home. ★

Skip Hollandsworth

Skip Hollandsworth was raised in Wichita Falls, Texas, and graduated with a BA in English from Texas Christian University. He has worked as a reporter and columnist for newspapers in Dallas and also as a television producer and documentary filmmaker. Since joining *Texas Monthly* in 1989, Hollandsworth has received several journalism awards, including a National Headliners Award, the national John Hancock Award for Excellence in Business and Financial Journalism, the City and Regional Magazine gold award for feature writing, the Texas Institute of Letters O. Henry award for magazine writing, and the Charles Green award for outstanding magazine writing in Texas, given by the Headliners Club of Austin. He has been a finalist four times for the National Magazine Awards, the magazine industry's equivalent of the Pulitzer Prize, and his work has been been included in such publications as *Best American Crime Writing* and *Best American Magazine Writing*. He is a member of the Texas Institute of Letters. In this piece, which reads like fiction, Skip writes creatively of a crime spree that left the Dallas police puzzled and horrified.

From See No Evil

Charles Albright patiently waited behind an unbreakable glass wall, watching as the prison guard escorted me through three sets of steel-barred doors. "I apologize for not being able to shake your hand and say hello," he said, formally rising as I approached his window in the visiting room. "They do not allow me to have face-to-face visits."

The steel doors clanged shut. Then the man whom the Dallas police had called the coldest, most depraved killer of women in the city's history gave me a long gentle stare, his dark deep-set eyes never wavering, an encouraging half-smile on his lips. At fifty-nine, he had a finely sculpted face and carefully groomed gray hair. Even in his prison uniform, he looked positively distinguished. "Ask me anything you want," he said. "I'm not going to tell you anything that's not true."

Throughout his life, Albright had been described by many who knew him as the portrait of happiness, untroubled and troubling no one. He was, they said, a kind of Renaissance man—fluent in French and Spanish, a masterful painter, able to woo women by playing Chopin preludes on the piano or reciting poetry by Keats. It was simply impossible to believe that he could have viciously murdered three Dallas prostitutes in late 1990 and early 1991. The person who should have been arrested, Albright's friends and lawyers insisted, was Axton Schindler, a paranoid, fast-talking truck driver who lived in one of Albright's rental homes. The evidence pointed to him, they claimed, not to their beloved Charles Albright. Perhaps Albright was a touch eccentric, but he was certainly harmless; he was even squeamish when it came to violence.

"You won't find any woman who'll say anything other than that I was always a perfect gentleman in their presence," he said softly. Behind the glass wall, he wore an almost childlike expression—weak and perplexed and, yes, oddly appealing. "I was always trying to do things for women. I would take their pictures. I would paint their portraits. I would give them little presents. I was always open for a lasting relationship."

In most cases, serial killers are brutal, woefully uneducated young men, lifelong sadists who kill for their own twisted reasons. How, then, could someone so charming, so exceedingly polite, suddenly decide in the later years of his life to become a bloodthirsty sex monster? "Look, I've known Charlie for thirty years," sighed one Albright friend, a retired Baptist minister. "In all that time I think I would have seen his dark side slip out at least once. Believe me, if he really was a psychotic killer, he couldn't have kept it a secret all this time—could he?"

December 1944: Life With Mother

He was known as the most good-natured, eager-to-please of children, a precocious boy who could do just about anything: name all the constellations in the sky, catch snakes without getting bitten, even perform a tap dance routine onstage at the famous Texas Theater. "Charlie was like a Pied Piper to the rest of us kids," a childhood friend recalled. "We always wanted to see what he would do next. He was just so much damn fun."

In 1933, when he was three weeks old, Charles was adopted by a young dark-haired woman, Delle Albright, and her husband, Fred, a Dallas grocer.

The Albrights lived in the all-white middle-class neighborhood of Oak Cliff, then a beautiful residential area across the river from downtown. According to the story Delle would later tell Charles, his birth mother was an exceptional law student. Just sixteen years old, who had secretly married another student and had become pregnant. When the girl's father found out, he demanded that she annul her marriage and give up the baby for adoption; otherwise, he would cut her off from the family.

Delle Albright made sure that Charles knew she would never abandon him. She pampered her boy. She kept goats in the back yard so he could drink goat's milk, which she said was better for him than cow's milk. Yet sometimes her mothering went to extremes. When Charles was a small child, she occasionally put him in a little girl's dress and gave him a doll to hold. Two or three times a day she would change his clothes to keep the dirt off him. Afraid that he might touch dog feces and get polio, she took him to Parkland Hospital to see the polio patients locked in huge iron lungs. "You can spend the rest of your life here," Delle would solemnly tell her son. Delle put him in a dark room as punishment for chewing on her tape measure. When he wouldn't take a nap, she would tie him to his bed. When he wouldn't drink his milk, she would spank him.

Indeed, people around the neighborhood talked about Delle Albright's odd, grim nature. No one could ever remember her buying herself a dress. She kept a scarf over her head and wore clothes from Goodwill. Although she and Fred were far from poor, she usually scrimped at mealtimes, even picking up the old bones the local butcher threw in a box for his dogs. She could use them, she would say, for soup.

Not that Charles ever openly complained. He always appreciated that his mother taught him manners. Delle told him to speak politely about other people or "say nothing at all." She told him to respect women, especially when it came to sex. She lectured him about the way his father acted "greedy" with sex: Whenever Fred saw her in the bedroom in her bra and panties, he tried to grab her. She was going to have none of that, and she was going to make sure Charlie never tried anything like that with his girlfriends either. As he grew older, she insisted on chauffeuring him every time he was on a date. She would even call the girl's parents to let them know that her son would not do anything untoward.

If Delle seemed overprotective, friends said, surely it was because she had never raised a child before. Charles himself recognized how fiercely she wanted him to succeed. Each morning, before the school bus arrived, she had him practice the piano for at least thirty minutes. She taught him so much reading, writing, and arithmetic that he was moved up two grades in elementary school.

Delle also introduced Charles to the world of taxidermy. When he was eleven years old, she enrolled him in a mail-order course—the Northwestern School of Taxidermy, taught by Professor J. W. Elwood. "You are beginning to learn an art that is second only to painting and sculpturing," Professor Elwood wrote in the first book of lessons Charles received. "A true taxidermist must be an artist." As Charles set to work on the dead birds he found, Delle was right beside him. She showed him how to use all the tools: the knife used to cut the skull, the little spoon used to scoop out the brains, the scalpel required to cut away the eyes from their sockets, the forceps that pulled out the eyes. She even skinned the first bird for him, teaching him not to cut too deep.

Dutifully, Charles spent hours on his taxidermy courses, stuffing and mounting his birds, making them look as lifelike as possible. Then he would be ready for the crowning touch—the eyes. He used to go to a taxidermy shop and stare at the boxes and boxes full of gloriously fake eyes: owl eyes, eagle eyes, deer eyes. He loved their iridescent gleam. He wished he could collect them the way other boys collected marbles.

Yet Delle wouldn't let him. Taxidermists' eyes were too expensive, his frugal mother would say; there was a better, cheaper way. She would open her sewing kit, look for exactly what she needed, and get to work. Then she and her son would place the birds in the oak china cabinet in the front of the house.

They were, indeed, Charles Albright's first works of art, just as the mail-order booklet had promised. Everyone who came to the house would peer into the cabinet to see what he had done. And there, peering back, would be his birds, beautiful, lifelike . . . and blind.

The birds had no eyes. Instead, sewn tightly against their delicate feathered faces, were two dark buttons, each shimmering dully in the living room light.

"You never knew a prostitute in Dallas?" I asked.

He shook his head, baffled by the question. "Never! I knew absolutely none of them. At the time I was arrested, I couldn't tell you the names of the motels they stayed in, any of the motels' locations, or anything else. It is a crime that the police never put me on the lie detector to find out what I did know and what I didn't."

"Could the prostitutes possibly have seen you somewhere?"

"None of these girls had ever seen me. They never saw me drive slowly by like I wanted to pick somebody up. Believe me, if I had anything to do with any prostitutes in Dallas, I would tell you."

December 1990: Mary Pratt

The first victim turned up in an undeveloped, almost forgotten lower-class area of far south Dallas. She was a large woman, 156 pounds, naked except for a T-shirt and a bra, which had been pushed up over her breasts. Her eyes were shut; her face and chest were badly bruised. Apparently, the killer had thought it best to beat her before firing a .44-caliber bullet into her brain. A resident of the neighborhood was so horrified by what he saw that he rushed inside his home and brought out a flowered bed sheet to cover the body.

A police officer on the scene immediately recognized the woman as Mary Pratt, age thirty-three, a veteran prostitute who worked the Star Motel in Oak Cliff. While it was not unusual for the "whores of Oak Cliff," as the police called them, to get their share of beatings—almost nightly, a girl would complain about a trick "jumping bad" on her, punching her, kicking her, even trying to run her over with a car—for a whore to be murdered was unusual, especially when it happened to someone as well liked as Mary Pratt. Mary wasn't one of the brazen hookers who stood in the street and nagged down tricks. Because she rarely had any extra spending money—the money she got usually went for drugs—she never bought sexy clothes. Standing quietly on her corner, she wore blue jeans, tennis shoes, and small T-shirts that showed off her breasts. Occasionally, at the end of a night, she asked one of her regulars to drive her to her parents' home in the south Dallas suburb of Lancaster. Mary's parents—older retired people—never knew about her other life. They would call out good night as she climbed into her childhood bed.

Pratt's file was handed to John Westphalen, a short, ruddy-faced homicide detective at the Dallas Police Department. With his thick East Texas accent and a wad of Red Man chewing tobacco permanently packed in his cheek, Westphalen looked more like a rustic county sheriff than a street-smart urban cop. In homicide circles he was something of a character. Defense attorneys loved to complain about his blustery, intimidating interrogation tactics. But Westphalen was also one of the department's most tenacious investigators. He took one look at the Pratt file and realized the case would depend more on good luck than on good detective work. Pratt's killing was a "dumped body" case—one of the hardest types of murders to solve. She had obviously been killed in one location and dumped somewhere else. There were no witnesses to either the killing or the dumping, no murder weapon, little forensic evidence, no fingerprints, and no apparent motive. Considering the kind of felonious characters who nightly swing by the Star Motel, Mary Pratt could have been shot by just about anyone.

Accompanied by his partner, homicide detective Stan McNear, Westphalen drove to the Dallas County medical examiner's office to watch the autopsy of Mary Pratt. It was a routine trip; both men knew the autopsy would show a gunshot wound as the cause of death. As Dr. Elizabeth Peacock, one of the staff's younger pathologists, put down her coffee cup to begin the examination, Westphalen and McNear stood a short distance from the blue plastic cart where Pratt's body lay. Peacock noted the needle tracks on Pratt's arms, the Playboy bunny tattoo on her chest, the bullet hole in her head. She opened Pratt's right eyelid. Then she opened the left.

"My God!" she exclaimed. "They're gone!"

There were no eyeballs, no tissue—nothing. Mary Pratt's eyes had been cut out and removed so carefully that her upper and lower eyelids were left undisturbed. Peacock was dumbfounded. This was not an operation taught in medical school. The killer had to know how to slip a knife around the eyes, making sure not to injure the adjoining skin, and then cut the six major muscles holding each eye in the socket, as well as the rope-tough optical nerve. With the eyelids shut, it was impossible to tell the eyes were missing. Surely, whoever did this had to have had a lot of practice on someone, or something, else.

Quickly Westphalen contacted the FBI's Violent Crimes Apprehension Program unit. Through its computers, the FBI keeps data on the nation's most unusual, depraved mutilations—bodies chopped up, organs removed, even eyes punctured with a knife as a result of a frenzied attack. But an FBI agent told Westphalen that he found no listing anywhere of such a surgically precise cutting.

Longtime Dallas cops take pride in acting utterly unaffected by anything that comes their way. But this time, Westphalen couldn't help it.

"What kind of person," he asked McNear, "would want a girl's eyeballs?" ★

Marshall Terry

Marshall Terry, E. A. Lilly Distinguished Professor of English, has influenced generations of SMU students as a gifted teacher, mentor, and writer. He had major roles in shaping both the English department and SMU's development as an institution. In 1963 he helped President Willis M. Tate write the Master Plan, which articulated the mission and values of SMU and laid the foundation for the Strategic Plan in place today.

Terry earned both a BA and MA from SMU. In addition to chairing the English department twice, he introduced the creative writing specialty into the English major, founded the nationally recognized SMU Litfest, and has directed SMU programs in Madrid, Oxford, and Taos.

Among Marshall Terry's nationally praised novels and short stories are *Old Liberty, Tom Northway, My Father's Hands, Land of Hope and Glory, Angels Prostate Fall,* and *The Memorialist.* He has earned distinction as a critic and essayist and for his history of SMU, *From High on the Hilltop: A Brief History of SMU.* His lifetime achievement was honored when he received the Barbara McCombs/Lon Tinkle Award for a "career of excellence in letters," the highest honor of the Texas Institute of Letters. He has also received TIL's Jesse H. Jones Fiction Award, and the Short Story Award, as well as the PEN Texas Award. Terry was selected three times for the SMU Rotunda Outstanding Professor Award and twice for the SMU Willis Tate Award for Outstanding Faculty. In 2003 he was named as a Distinguished Alumnus of SMU. It would be impossible to have anything about a literary Dallas and not include Marshall Terry. When this piece was read at Arts and Letters Live at the Dallas Museum of Art, the audience was consumed by laughter. It was a lovely evening indeed.

From *Angels Prostate Fall*

All spring and summer Stanley Morris has gone around with odd old tunes in his head that no one else would think of or remember.

Now, in dog day August, it's "Twilight Time" that keeps threading through his mind.

"Heaven-ly da of da da da, day, it's—twi-light time . . ."

Doodle-de da da da . . . The Platters? The Coasters? The Drifters? Ink Spots? Sun Spots? The Plates? Saucers? The Forks? The Spoons?

Stanley lives near his university in a small community set between Dallas and Fort Worth in the ever-burgeoning "Metroplex." He gets in his big old car and drives over to the complex of professional buildings by the hospital off the freeway. With the crazy traffic and drivers on the roads and highways along the way he would drive a semi cab if he could get away with it. He parks and goes into Building A to get his records from Dr. Fishbein so he can take them over to Dr. Miller in Building C.

Stanley's university is forcing the faculty to choose to give up their old doctors to go on a new medical plan with higher premiums and better coverage. Stanley's old friend and internist Dr. Witherspoon is threatening to retire anyway so he has referred him to young Dr. Whittle. Stanley's eye doctor . . . is off the list anyway, so that leaves just the urological base not covered, so to speak. His old buddy Fishbein is off network too so Witherspoon has recommended Miller.

He has had a long, rich relationship with Fishbein, Stanley thinks as he goes into his office. Like twenty years. It's a shame to have to change. Stanley has called Fishbein jokingly "the Man with the Golden Finger." Actually the jolly little man has a finger of steel. Once, in the midst of a digital rectal exam Fishbein is moved to tell Stanley about his only son, Albert, who has flunked out of med school and is now in the submarine service. Stanley has been to see him just two months ago, so he has no worries on that score. "Smooth as a walnut!" Fishbein has barked at him in glee. "You sure don't have cancer!"

Da da da—da da da dah—la da de da . . .

"I called for my records in order that I can transfer them to Dr. Miller," he says to the young woman at the desk. She's a new one from two months ago. Fishbein always seems to have different people out front, as opposed to dear old Witherspoon, whose wife and nurse, who look so much alike they may be sisters, are always sitting in matched chairs smiling placidly at you.

"Mr. Stanley?" she says.

"Mr. Morris," Stanley says.

"Oh. Yeah. That's right. Morris."

"I believe it is."

So much for twenty years.

Humming the Platters or Coasters or Drifters ditty, he walks through the maze of halls and byways between Building A and Building C. He passes doctors and nurses and aides in white smocks and in green caps and smocks and patients moving slowly along the halls shaking, shambling, being helped, or rolled, shuffling with canes, on crutches, or like himself a month ago with patches or bandages on their eyes.

Dr. Miller's office, or the office he seems to share with doctors Martz and Wu, is not bright and jolly like Fishbein's. It is stark, with just a print or two of hunting dogs and a somber tapestry on the walls. He hands the folder to the woman at the desk. She has very large eyes, like fish that swim in a bowl, behind her thick, magnified glasses. She looks startled to receive such an object as this folder.

"What can we do for you?" she says.

"Oh—nothing. Right now, I mean. I called. You said—someone did—that you, actually that Dr. Miller, would accept me as a patient. I'm changing medical plans. I am newly on the Uni-Pro Coalition Network. OK?"

"Mr. Morris?"

"Right," he says. They seem to be able to read the name on a folder.

"Have a seat," she says. "Dr. Miller will want to see you."

"Thanks, but there's no need. I am just delivering the records."

"Have a seat," she says. "I'll tell him. He'll want to see you."

This sounds like an order. He sits.

In a little while she takes him into an examination room and asks for a urine sample.

"Really," he says. He did not come here today to be examined.

It's just been a couple of months. Smooth as a walnut. But he kind of has to go anyway, so he yields on the urine front. A nurse comes and nods at him and collects the cocktail. Then the door opens and a massive, not to say apelike, figure appears. It has a black beard and a thick neck and head and terribly penetrating black eyes and a white coat with *Dr. Miller* written on the pocket. He shifts his feet and seems about to leap up or sideways and holds out his hand.

Stanley takes it. This Miller has a small, strong hand.

"What can we do for you?" he says.

Stanley shrugs. He feels small and out of place, as if he is engaged in a bad joke. He knows he is fine. The last thing he desires or needs is an examination. *Nothing*, he says to himself. *Not a thing. I was just passing by and thought I'd drop the folder off and behold you, and I must say you have surpassed my expectations.*

"Not much," he answers. "I am just checking in, as a new patient. Thought I'd say howdy."

"Take off your pants and shorts," the doctor orders. "We'll see what's what."

"I just had the exam," Stanley says. "Not long ago. Dr. Fishbein—"

"You want to be my patient, I'll say what's what. Take 'em down," Miller says, black eyes glinting with a strange obsidian light, cutting to the chase. Stanley sees that he is not the tapestry. That is Martz or Wu. This one is the hunter.

"You bet," Stanley says.

Dutifully he resigns and aligns himself to what the comedians used to call "the fickle finger of fate."

This guy is gentler than Fishbein, anyway.

As Stanley turns around, reassembling himself. Miller pulls off the white prophylactic glove with a "pop." His dark doctor eyes hold Stanley.

"I think I felt something," he says.

Stanley stares at him.

This mountebank. Charlatan. Pretending to be a doctor! Jesus! This massive black-eyed demon or fool staring back at him. This incredible trickster. Jokesmith—

"Right on the left edge. Just a—tiny—rough spot."

That is impossible, Stanley says, but only to himself. *You are wrong. Perhaps demented. You are a demented person, thank you very much, and I am putting on my trousers and buckling up my belt and leaving here in search of a sane doctor. Kidding around is OK, but—Jesus—*

"Miss Hish will make you an appointment for a biopsy," Dr. Miller says. "Then we'll take a look and see what's what."

He extends again his remarkable small, strong hand.

"Pleasure to meet you, sir," he says.

"Oh my," Stanley says.

Back home, air-conditioning thrumming in the old house, Stanley tells Olive he may have a little problem.

Her green eyes take on a shade of blue in concern.

"There are all kinds of reasons for a rough spot," he says. "The odds are heavily against it being malignant, or anything like that."

"Did he say so or are you saying so?" she says.

"I'm saying so," says Stanley. "It's ridiculous. The semester is about to begin. I have a full teaching load. I have committee duties. I'm supposed to make a talk to the new students. Housman one more time? I don't have time for foolishness. Art Baker had a biopsy, he said it hurts like hell. They shoot a needle into you. *Ka-ping!*"

"Would you like to be sinful and have a steak tonight?" she says. "A little wine?"

He nods. "And a little scotch beforehand," he says.

"'Afore ye go,'" she says.

He shrugs. That's a little more levity than he wishes.

Dr. Miller does the biopsy in his office, with the help of a bland man called Johnny who runs the machine. He laughs that he should be called "Dick" instead of Johnny. "Moby Dick the harpoon guy," he says. Ha ha.

"Moby Dick was the whale, not the harpoon guy," Stanley says. "That was Queequeg."

"Oh no, I wouldn't want to be called that," says Johnny, hands caressing the dials and screens on his smooth machine.

Dr. Miller swings in and without a word hurls six consecutive harpoons through Stanley into his target chestnut. Each arrives with a delicious little blossom of pain.

"I'll call you in four days," the doctor says.

"That wasn't bad, was it?" Johnny says.

"How does it work exactly?" says Stanley.

"The needle goes in, makes the hit, and takes a core that comes back out through the needle for the lab. Pretty slick, eh? Couldn't do it this easy just a couple of years ago."

"Hurray for technology," Stanley says, though he feels ambivalent. . . .

There are a dozen reasons you can have a rough spot, just a tiny spot, on your chestnut, he thinks. (He has come to think of it as his chestnut since he saw the big color picture of the male and his parts on the wall in Dr. Miller's examination room: the prostate there being characterized as the size of a chestnut. Seeing the picture worried Stanley. The chestnut was up there right in the middle of things, it looked pretty inaccessible, and wired up to all the rest.)

Why in the hell didn't Fishbein find it, feel the little rough spot? No wonder he had gotten to be so jolly, he was getting senile. But Stanley had liked old Fishbein. Every time he'd taken him a book or an article—for Fishbein was a reader and a thinker of sorts—the jolly fellow would stick his head out into the hallway and yell up to the desk, "This one's on the house for Stanley!" You had to love old Fishbein.

In five days the doctor's office calls, Stanley wondering if they had forgotten or lost the cores or what, to say the pathologists in Dallas can't tell, they disagree over one of the cores, the one right at the left edge that Miller had felt. Can't tell if it's malignant or not. They are sending it on to Mayo, it will be a few days more.

"They're sending it to Dr. Flimflam, or whatever his name is, the nation's most respected and famous and expert pathologist."

"Hey, don't you feel special?" Olive says. "But, really, doesn't that make you feel like it probably isn't?" Isn't cancer, she means, not even wishing to say the word. Her eyes are kind, but there's a lot of that worried blue in them.

Stanley rolls his own brown eyes, one good, one bad. He would like for it to sound encouraging but somehow it really doesn't. It just sounds even more ridiculous, that in this city full of pathologists and labs and medical expertise they have to send his prostate sample to the Mayo Clinic.

Another three days go by and he is still bleeding a little from the Moby Dicking.

When the call finally comes the nurse says Dr. Miller himself will speak to him.

"It's a malignancy," he says. "Just that one spot. The good news is that it appears to be contained, though we can't be sure it hasn't spread outside the prostate. The bad news, of course, is that you have cancer. It's a Gleason's Five."

Involuntarily Stanley laughs, seeing Jackie Gleason in his mind. Have they named prostate cancers after Jackie Gleason?

"What? Is something funny?" Miller asks.

"Gleason's what?"

"Five. Meaning a mid-level malignancy. Not way up there but requiring attention. Yes?"

Yes. Oh yes.

Dr. Miller suggests he come in and talk about it, the alternatives, which seem to be leave it alone, take it out, or radiate it. He'll send some information. Stanley says he'll be there, with Mrs. Morris.

Dr. Miller's private office, as opposed to his stark reception area and sterile examination rooms, is pleasant. Homey. He seems a different man in here. A person.

Prints of retrieving dogs are on the wall. Hunting and fishing magazines are on the coffee table. Stanley's wingback chair is slipcovered in a pattern of muted colors. Olive sits on a chair beside him. Dr. Lester Miller sits behind his desk wearing small round glasses intensifying the penetrating gaze of his dark eyes. He rolls a Mont Blanc pen in his small hands.

They talk about it.

It's really pretty simple, Stanley gathers from what he says. If you're fifty or sixty and in good shape, go for the fence, go for the cure. If you're seventy, radiate. Some younger men choose to radiate anyway. It can be as effective. If you're eighty, smile and be glad you just got it, right? It's probably not going to kill you sooner than anything else. Every man gets cancer of the prostate sooner or later.

There are hazards to the surgery or to radiation, the doctor proceeds to explain. It's a tricky little operation. Slit you from the belly to the groin. First, you get the lymph nodes in the stomach. If they're OK, go on. Delicado. Take a lot of stuff apart and put it back together. Bleeding is a possibility, so you give two units of your own blood before. . . . Then, if it hasn't spread outside the prostate you can save the veins, maybe avoid impotence. Later, after a successful removal, there can be bad, degrading urinary problems.

"I suppose you have a good success rate with this operation?" Olive says.

The doctor nods, up and down but crossways too. He's honest, not willing to claim perfection. He does it almost every morning, this operation. He always operates with his partner, Dr. Martz. No urological surgeon would ever operate alone.

Reassuring, eh?

"I think I want to go ahead and have it out," says Stanley.

"Think about it," Miller says. But he smiles and nods. This is a good man. His smile is warm and wonderful, really reassuring. Go for it, Stanley, babe, it says. How could Stanley have thought he looked apelike? Actually, he resembles Moses. . . . ★

Clay Reynolds

Native Texan novelist, essayist, scholar, and critic Clay Reynolds is the author of more than nine hundred publications ranging from critical studies to short fiction and poems, essays, reviews, and twelve published volumes. He holds academic degrees from the University of Texas at Austin, Trinity University, and the University of Tulsa. His published novels include *The Vigil, Agatite, Franklin's Crossing, Players, Monuments, The Tentmaker, Ars Poetica,* and *Threading the Needle.* He also has a collection of essays, *Of Snakes and Sex and Playing in the Rain: Random Thoughts on Things Harmful to Your Health*, and a collection of short fiction, *Sandhill County Lines.* His nonfiction books include *Stage Left: The Development of the American Social Drama in the Thirties*; *Taking Stock: A Larry McMurtry Casebook*; and *A Hundred Years of Heroes: A History of the Southwestern Exposition and Livestock Show.* His novels, short fiction, and essays have won numerous awards. He is a National Endowment for the Arts Fellow, a member of the Texas Institute of Letters and serves as professor of Arts and Humanities at the University of Texas at Dallas. This excerpt, set in Dallas, gives a seedy side of Dallas life.

From *Players*

In Eddy Lovell's opinion, Moria Mendle was not an imposing man. He was a short, fat prick. But he was a player. Moria liked to sit in the back of Bishop's Café on Lower Greenville Avenue while he conducted business, eat fried oysters and drink Löwenbräu like he invented the combination. Bob Cole, Mendle's partner, was always there, always on Moria's right: eye sweeping the room like twin electronic scanners, one hand in the pocket of his jacket like it was rooted there. And in the corner, usually in the shadows, there was a steel door with arms, named Hedge.

It was the way he looked.

Hedge was a dark, ugly hulk who wore sleeveless shirts that allowed black, curly body hair to twist out in wiry clumps. The biggest mystery about him was his ethnic origin. He was dark-skinned, his head hair was kinky, cut short, no facial hair, but his eyes were pale green. No one Eddy knew had the guts to ask him about it. In fact, Eddy never heard anyone speak to him. He never heard Hedge speak, either.

Bishop's was one of those places no one went into unless they'd been there before. Even the cops stayed away. It was technically a café, but aside from fried oysters, grilled cheeses Bishop served up from his greasy hot plate behind the bar, no food was consumed in the place. It was a beer joint. No hard liquor, no music, no pool. People who came into Bishop's came in there to drink or to see Moria: business.

Moria's exact business was another mystery to Eddy. He knew it was felony-hot, had to do with easy women, big cash, but it was hard to define, hard to see. He owned a string of mobile home dealerships—the slick, rip-off-the-rednecks kinds of operation lining the interstate approaches to most cities—and he ran four or five tit-and-ass joints out on Harry Hines, Northwest Highway. One was a glitzy spot for high-rolling foreigners in town for a week. . . .

There were other enterprises in Moria's little kingdom: restaurants, gin mills, Adults Only bookstores, a massage parlor pretending to be a whorehouse up in Carrollton, just down from the World of God Tabernacle where the Reverend Will used a more legitimate and more lucrative scam to rip off the same morons who bought trailer houses, watered booze, dirty magazines, and cheap pussy from Moria.

But Eddy decided long ago that it was all a front for whatever it was that Moria really did, whatever it was that kept him in champagne blondes and stretch limos, and whatever it was that made him wary of cops most of the time.

The only thing Eddy felt sure of was that it wasn't dope. Cole set him straight on that: Moria's daughter had had too much crack a few years before, passed out in her father's Beemer on a parking lot down in Arlington. Somebody came by and set fire to the car. Gangbangers, likely. That was what the cops thought, what the press said. Moria thought different. He figured it was a low-ball player named Sanderson from Fort Worth who was trying to edge Moria out of a couple of his boob-and-bounce joints. He wanted to deal, Moria didn't. Sanderson was now someplace in the middle of Lake Worth wearing about a half-ton of Readimix. Or so Cole said. Moria didn't screw around with that kind of thing. And since his girl's death, he didn't screw around with dope. Actually, Cole said, he never had. Neither had Cole.

"We're into bigger things," Cole said.

Eddy didn't care. He didn't do drugs either. And like Moria, he had a personal reason.

Eddy sat in Bishop's, smoking unfiltered Camels and nursing a beer. It was his first, he'd been sipping on it for more than an hour while waiting to be called to the back room. Business was heavy today. Four guys had been in and out, quick and nervous. . . .

A tall, well-dressed man pushed aside the dirty curtain and came out of the backroom. He jerked at the fabric of his shirt, tried to peel it away from his chest while his other hand mopped sweaty film off his face. He wore expensive sunglasses, the haircut said money: New Age Yuppie, Eddy thought. Twelve-banger Jag and five-hundred-dollar shoes.

It was cool in Bishop's, but this guy made it steamy. He straightened his tie and took a good look at Eddy, who flexed his hand around the beer glass. It was a big hand, hairy on the back, full of muscle that ran up into the sleeve of his windbreaker. The guy wiped himself down again and left. Bad news, Eddy thought.

Eddy had met Moria in the joint: Huntsville, Texas Department of Corrections—the TDC. Eddy was in for aggravated robbery: two-to-five, parole in six months if he stayed clean. He was also innocent, but not in the way most of the guys in the joint are innocent. Eddy was away for the wrong gig. He was picked up in a sweep, and he decided to cop a plea rather than face charges for what he had really been doing: selling two crates of virgin M-16s to a bunch of paramilitary nuts from Lufkin. Eddy didn't like to deal guns, but Tommy Bodine came into them cheap: working automatics were worth big money. Tommy was the contact, he needed backup. Eddy was the best backup in Dallas. It was what he did then. In a way, it was all he knew how to do: he was a player.

The buyers were strake, all vets, all former commie crunchers with nobody but the federal government to hate anymore. Eddy thought: retards. One was a deputy sheriff. Another was ex-highway patrol. The rest were strictly from encyclopedia sales. Popped uppers all day, .30-calibers all night. The bumper sticker on their van read: "God packs a Smith and Wesson: No Fear." They planned to overthrow the government, Tommy said: A laugh.

Eddy knew candidates for thorazine when he saw them. Still, if they wanted to run around in the woods and play soldier with hot guns, it was nothing to Eddy. Twenty-five grand, though: that was something to anybody.

Their van was tagged for speeding in Kaufman County, and the local black-and-white found itself in a running firefight across half of East Texas—two dead, four wounded, including the ex-state trooper. Eddy thought: Amateurs. The Alcohol, Tobacco & Firearms suits hadn't yet tied him with them, but he figured they would rat him out soon enough. They had wives, kids, weren't players. Tommy came in on his own and dealt down to accessory: it beat running. He sent word to Eddy that he would be on the hit parade soon. It was easier for Eddy to cop to a bullshit robbery rap, drop out of sight for a while, go to prison.

There's no place better to hide than prison.

He looked like the guy on the convenience store's security tape, anyway. Six-two, two-thirty-five, ponytail and a mustache, body a linebacker works for, but something between the ears. That didn't show up on the tape. Eddy wasn't jerk enough to hit a U-Sak-It in broad daylight. Cops should have known that.

Guy comes in with a Kmart squirt gun and sticks it in the clerk's face. The clerk maybe nineteen, maybe twenty, all Indian, scared shitless pisses his pants and hands over two, three hundred in small bills, hits the alarm. The guy runs down Lower Greenville Avenue and ducks into a bar. Ten minutes later every cop in Dallas is all over the day drinkers, and the sweep brings them all out into the 100°-plus afternoon for a shakedown.

Eddy had just finished stashing the twenty-five big ones he took as his cut from the gun deal, and he walked in with two hundred and change to blow on a beer and a girl—Monica, probably—so he was picked up. Next thing, he was downtown in a cell fighting junkies for a chicken leg. A month later, he was in the piney woods of East Texas wearing prison whites and glad he wasn't looking out onto the plains of Kansas.

Weapons is a federal rap. Leavenworth is hard time. Huntsville can be done on a handstand.

It wasn't Eddy's first time away. One assault and a bullshit breaking-and-entering had introduced him to the Dallas County penal system. More recently, a carrying-a-concealed-weapon beef drew him two-to-five—which was Raul Castillo's fault, that moron, wherever he was. . . .

On the convenience store rap Eddy asked for mercy and got a deuce with deductions. Not bad for a con with a sheet.

The Dallas County DA's office liked confession. It was almost as good for clearing the docket as it was for purging the soul. Especially in an election year.

Eddy first saw Moria in the exercise yard. He was short, not in the wiry way so many cons have when they're trying to be tough: just short. Maybe five-two or three. He was also pudgy, soft. There wasn't any muscle. He walked onto the grass all by himself. His arms stuck out from his body, and even from twenty-five yards, Eddy could see the money: manicured fingernails, high-dollar haircut, used to being taken care of. Eddy thought: Wuss.

But it was all a con. Eddy figured he probably owned strip joints and ran crack and pussy out of the back room. He was right about the joints, right about the pussy, but he was wrong about the cocaine.

Moria squinted into the summer sunlight like it was the first time he'd ever been outside: lost. Eddy figured he'd last about ten minutes in population. The hacks probably brought him right out here from processing, then went up to the tower to make bets. Moria's whites still had their creases: two sizes too big. The cuffs were rolled up, and he could hide a Doberman in the shirt. He looked spongy, just the kind of white meat to attract trouble from the Bloods.

Eddy knew about trouble, he knew about the Bloods. All twenty-to-life, all bad-asses. He'd put three in the hospital already. He didn't like being fooled with, and he didn't need help soaping down in the shower. They bothered him for a week or so, until two broken arms and a set of cracked fingers finally got the word out: Eddy Lovell was nobody's boy. He sure as hell was nobody's girl.

Trouble came quick for Moria. Three of the Bloods who always hung around the bench press stood up and added the short, fat guy in the yard to their inventory. They wore sun-glasses—although it was against regulations—they adjusted them carefully, pumped up their muscles, then rolled over toward Moria.

Moria saw them coming and glanced over at Eddy. There was something in his eyes: not fear, not hope, something else, something compelling, something sure. But Eddy never knew exactly what it was or why it made him move. He had been clean for three months now; didn't even curse out loud. But then, he seldom did. He was out of the action completely, and that was his ticket home. It was stupid to get involved, but Moria gave him that look. It drew him in. It was like the small man had been searching for Eddy. Now that he found him, Eddy had no choice. His feet moved him across the grass.

"Back off," Eddy said to the head Blood, a bull named Judd. "He's taken."

"Says who?" Judd was big. Strong safety for the Packers, two seasons. It was an old story: too much money, too many drugs, too many women. He hadn't broken training, though. He'd found steroids more common than crack in the TDC. And he'd developed a taste for white ass. Moria looked ripe.

Eddy figured his belt wouldn't quite cinch around Judd's biceps. It might not cinch around his cock, if the stories he'd heard were true.

"Jimbo," Eddy said. "He's Jimbo's."

The name worked. Judd looked at Moria for a long moment, then he shrugged, turned, led his two buddies back to the beach press.

"Who's Jimbo?" Moria asked. His voice was soft, like a woman's. Eddy turned.

"Runs the Bloods. Runs what else he wants to. Gang rape, double murder. Bad dude. Lifer, four times nonconcurrent: Don't give a shit."

"And I'm his?"

"He's in the hole. Won't be out for ninety days. Then, you're on your own." Eddy wanted to move away. Moria's eyes held him still.

"I'm out of here in ninety days." Eddy shrugged.

"I owe you," Moria said as he turned away.

They didn't talk after that. But Eddy started getting regular mail: cigarettes, rubbers, shit he could trade. The return address was a box number Eddy didn't recognize. Moria stayed by himself on the yard, in clear view, and he kept to himself in his cell. He was in for jury tampering. He was cooling out, waiting for a new lawyer, new trial. Half the guys in Huntsville were waiting for the same thing. But they weren't Moria. Two months, he was gone. Eddy was out a week later. . . . ★

Harry Hunsicker

Harry Hunsicker is a fourth generation to call Dallas home. *Still River,* his first book, was nominated for a Shamus Award for the Best First Novel by the Private Eye Writers of America. His other novels are *The Next Time You Die* and *Crosshairs.* Hunsicker works as a commercial real estate appraiser and speaks on creative writing when not penning the next Lee Henry Oswald mystery. "The Color of Home" a short story, best described as East Texas noir, was the author's first publishing credit and appeared in the January 2004 issue of the award-winning e-zine, *Plots with Guns.* Hunsicker is an active member of the International Thriller Writers, the Mystery Writers of America, the Private Eye Writers of America, and the Writers League of Texas. Hunsicker uses his Dallas landscape for the setting of his Lee Henry Oswald novels.

From *Still River*

Dallas, the northern portion anyway, owed its appearance to several things. Chief among them was structural engineering and the ability to mold concrete into any design imaginable. Additional factors included a flat, stable terrain and creative mortgage lending. But that's another story.

I made my way up the Dallas North Tollway, the turnpike that split the northern sector of the city. It was before rush hour and the traffic moved well. Since a portion of the highway sat below ground level, you felt like you were in a concrete canyon, swimming in some river of internal combustion engines. Above the walls of the canyon came the jungle. Like the vegetation at a creek bank, the buildings closest to the tollway were bigger, sucking their nourishment from the torrent of cars that passed by every hour. Those farther from the stream of automobiles grew smaller, content to feed on the eddies and tributaries that are the side streets leading off the highway. Beyond those sprawled the dwellings, thousands and thousands of houses and apartments, homes for the workers who toiled in the tall buildings at the edge of the canyon. Nobody kept chickens in their yard up here.

I drove ten miles per hour over the speed limit, in the right-hand lane, and was the slowest moving vehicle. At my exit, a Mercedes swung past me and cut across my lane to make the off-ramp, desperate to save those four or five seconds that would have otherwise been lost. I slid in after him and exited on Belt Line Road, crossing over the tollway and heading west. Traffic flowed heavier here, six lanes between a strip of offices and shopping centers, each disgorging a torrent of cars at one end while taking in an equal amount at the other.

Callahan Commercial Real Estate officed on Lindbergh, a side street in an industrial park near Addison Airport. Addison sits on the far northwest side of Dallas, one of a handful of suburbs bordering the city there. Addison was the only area for miles around to serve liquor by the drink. Consequently it had more restaurants per square mile than any city in America. They were classy places, usually part of some corporate chain, with names like T. J. McFunFuns or Bobblers—A Place to Ogle Teenage Waitresses While You Wait for Your Buffalo Wings.

Lindbergh ran into the airport on the west side, one block north of Belt Line. I turned right on Midway Road, then a quick left and idled down the street. Nothing remarkable, just a strip of dingy one and two story offices and warehouses masquerading as offices. 3912 Lindbergh was a squat, cinderblock building. Gray paint peeled off the sides. A red awning, weathered to the color of three-day-old hamburger meat, proclaimed this the location of "Callahan Real Estate, Your Full Service Property Company." A thin strip of grass and a scrawny pear tree served as landscaping.

I parked in front, next to a late model Cadillac and an elderly Pontiac Sunbird. A new Mercedes, complete with gold wheels and tinted windows, sat on the other side of the parking lot.

A bell sounded when I pushed open the door and walked in. The front room was a small reception area with cheap carpet and cheaper wood paneling. The place smelled of coffee, cigarettes, and copier toner. Sofa and chairs left over from the last Howard Johnson's redecoration clustered to the left; on the right was a receptionist desk.

A woman in her early twenties, a panorama of cleavage, eye shadow, lip gloss, and that big hair that they only do in Texas, looked up from her romance novel and blew a plume of smoke my way. "Yeah?"

"I'm here to see Mr. Callahan. About the office space, the one on Arapaho Road."

She took another hit on the smoke and squinted her eyes. She was marginally pretty, in a fourth string Playboy Playmate kind of way, until she frowned. Then she was ugly. "What office space are you talking about?"

"The one on Arapaho."

"We don't have anything on Arapaho." She pulled a sheet of paper out of the top drawer and studied it. I didn't think she could squint any more but she did. "Nope, nothing on Arapaho. We got hmm, lessee . . . two thousand feet on Spring Valley."

I pulled a piece of paper out of my jacket pocket and looked at it. "My mistake. You're right, it's two thousand and fifty feet on Spring Valley." She smiled, apparently unused to being right about anything.

"I need to see Mr. Callahan about that space. I've got a tenant for it."

"Mr. Callahan?"

"Yes. I need to see Mr. Callahan." I tried not to sound or look exasperated. "About the space on Spring Valley."

She squinted again and I could see the wheels turning underneath all that hair spray. "Mr. Callahan is . . . in a meeting."

I sighed elaborately and put my hands on my hips. "Look, I've got a tenant who needs two thousand square feet, and he needs it yesterday. We've got an appointment in an hour at another building. It's a little farther away than he wants but the agent is willing to deal. Do I take my guy there or can I talk to Callahan?"

She looked scared and I almost felt sorry for her. Almost. "I . . . I'll buzz him." She picked up the phone and punched a button. "I'm sorry . . . I know . . . there's somebody here about some space . . . I know . . . he's got a tenant for the office on Spring Valley . . . Yes. Yes, I will." She put down the phone and pointed to the door behind her desk. "If you'll go right through there sir. First one on your left."

I said thanks and walked through the door. There was a narrow hallway and the first door on my left was open. I walked in. It was a larger and better furnished office than in the front. A middle-aged man sat behind an oak desk, white button-down shirt and tie undone, a stack of files in front of him. He stood when I entered and came around the desk, hand extended. "Howya doing? Tom Callahan. Nice to meet you. What can I do for you?"

I shook his hand and said, "How are you, Tom? My name is Hank Oswald. My client is Charlie Wesson, and he needs to lease some space from you."

He gave me a blank stare, then a frown, then a blank stare again. "What?"

"Miss January, out front, said you were in a meeting. I hope I'm not interrupting, but my client, Charlie Wesson, wants to lease some office space."

Confusion disappeared, replaced by hostility. "Who are you?"

I didn't reply, just stared at him. Silence was an old technique, don't say anything, let the mark get nervous and fill the quietness. Tom Callahan must have seen that episode of *Dragnet* too, either that or he'd been negotiating real estate deals for too long to let a method like that get to him. Five seconds stretched to thirty and then a full minute. Finally he spoke. "There was a man named Charlie Wesson who worked here. He left Monday afternoon and hasn't shown up since."

"Do you know where he is?"

"No."

"Who'd he work with?"

"That really is none of your business. I've got things to do. I think you should leave."

"I was hired by his family to find him. It is my business."

Tom Callahan walked back to his desk and sat down. He began to shuffle papers. "Get out."

I didn't move. "You're pretty nonchalant about this. Do you have employees disappear all the time?"

Callahan put the file down he was holding and looked at me. "Charlie

Wesson was a druggie. I hired him to try and give him a chance at a normal life. But once a doper, always a doper. It's a fucking disease, like epilepsy or herpes. Once you get it, you never get rid of it. Charlie fell off the wagon. He may be dead for all I know. That's what you get when you deal with junkies." His tone was angry and bitter, more so than the situation warranted I thought.

He seemed to read my mind. "My son went through rehab three times. Nothing worked. He died six months ago. Overdose. I thought maybe I could make a difference with Charlie."

I flipped a card on his desk and said, "If he turns back up, or you hear anything, I'd appreciate it if you'd let me know."

At the front, the receptionist was back at the romance novel and sparking up another smoke. She ignored me. I stood in front of her desk and said, "Did you know Charlie Wesson?"

She didn't put down the book this time. "I'm not supposed to talk to you about that. You should leave now."

I left another card on her desk with the same request that I'd given her boss. Her eyes were pleading this time. "Really, for your own good, just leave."

Something was funny here. I couldn't figure out how she had been told not to talk to me. There wasn't time from when I left Callahan's office and got to her for him to have called.

I walked out into the heat of the afternoon sun. A single engine Cessna sputtered in the rubbery tasting air, heading across the horizon towards Addison Airport. Two men stood in the parking lot, leaning against the Mercedes. As I walked down the steps, they came forward, blocking my way to the truck. They were big, obviously strong and well-built even though they were wearing loose-fitting clothes. One was white with a goatee, the other black and clean shaven. The white guy had one hand in the pocket of his oversized jeans. His partner kept both hands hanging loose by his side. They were professionals, hired muscle.

The black one spoke first. "I hear you're asking questions about Charlie Wesson." He smiled as if enjoying the punch line of a joke. "That's not a real smart thing to do." ★

Prudence Mackintosh

Prudence Mackintosh is a contributing editor to *Texas Monthly* magazine where her work has appeared for more than three decades. She gained a loyal following through the years with her observations on social rites of passage for Texas women and her essays on the rearing of three boys. In 1976, she received a Penney-Missouri Award for excellence in lifestyle journalism. Her work has appeared in several national magazines, newspapers, and is frequently anthologized in college writing texts.

Her sons provided much material for her early writing. Her first book *Thundering Sneakers* was followed by *Retreads.* According to Prudence, work on a third book about letting go of her sons stalled briefly when they didn't go. In the interim, she published a collection of essays about being a woman in Texas entitled *Just As We Were: A Narrow Slice of Texas Womanhood.* The boys, now young men, have finally flown the nest allowing her to complete her most recent book, *Sneaking Out.* She is collaborating on a fifth book which will trace the architectural development of the Park Cities, a Dallas suburb.

Born in Texarkana, Texas, in 1944, Prudence grew up in a newspaper office where her father was the editor and her mother, a reporter, women's editor, and a proofreader. She attended Texarkana public schools and graduated from the University of Texas at Austin in 1966. She has participated in the Arts and Letters Live series in Dallas. Prudence lives in Dallas with her attorney husband who is also her favorite editor. Their sons live in New York, Denver, and Houston. She is a member of the Author's Guild, the Texas Institute of Letters, and the Philosophical Society of Texas. She writes here of her experiences as the antithesis of the Dallas woman.

From The Dallas Woman

It is entirely possible to live happily in Dallas for twenty-five years, even in Highland Park, and never own a ball gown.

It is possible to live happily in Dallas and never join a Bible study group; have no exercise regimen beyond living inefficiently in a three-story house; have no yard crew except your husband and sons; plant your own impatiens and caladiums; never join a garden club; see a plastic surgeon only once when, while chasing the departing garbage truck, you tripped over the garden hose and landed cheekbone first on a flowerpot; eat out for lunch alone; never read a diet or self-help book; flunk out of the Junior League; have no gift closet; think new bushings for the old Steinway were a nifty fiftieth birthday gift; get your haircut at the barbershop with your sons; give a speech everywhere but in Dallas called "The Pleasures of Limited Ambition"; believe you had enough money the day you could pay all of your bills and get the washing machine repaired without having to sell your piano; have no sons who made Eagle Scout; have no second home; still cook; drive whatever car is accessible in the driveway, including your father's 1990 Pontiac Bonneville with handicapped plates or your son's '95 Jetta; wonder if Zig Ziglar would meet you in the middle; entertain a negative thought; have great friends; stay married to the guy who graded your papers at UT in '65; laugh at yourself and see all of life in a slightly comic light. It is possible . . . but you will never be mistaken for a Dallas Woman.

In 1996, when the *CBS Morning Show* asked me to say a few words about Dallas on one of their periodic treks through the hinterlands, I told the preproduction interviewer that we had an exquisite symphony hall and the largest and probably best attended churches in the country. For that matter, Fair Park and specifically the Hall of State, their broadcasting location, contained some of the best examples of Art Deco architecture in the country. The interviewer paused, then said, "We want you to talk about Dallas women and, specifically, we were thinking about hair. You know, big blond stuff. We want some footage in a local salon, and we'll probably shoot a shopping mall or two."

I warned them that I was a short brunette who knew nothing about hairstreaking and that I had never aspired to be a Dallas Cowboy cheerleader. With a new book coming out, however, it seemed prudent for me to show up at Fair Park, along with Mayor Kirk and Stanley Marcus, before the crack of dawn and use up two more minutes of my fifteen minutes of fame. My segment followed "Mr. Stanley," who had followed the Dallas Cowboys. The blonde and very lovely CBS anchor, Paula Zahn, asked me why Dallas women wanted to be called ladies. I replied, "They used to say Texas was hell on women and horses. Wouldn't you rather be a lady?" Paula segued to the tape made in the local beauty salon of hair being teased to Madame Pompadour dimensions and asked if big blonde hair was still the order of the day in Dallas. The tape shifted to a local shopping mall, capturing more women with godawful fluffed-out-blonde hairdos, while I tried to make the best of it with "Dallas women have always believed in the restorative qualities of a little lipstick and hairspray."

The tape, which I could see on a monitor, now shifted to a Friday night high school cheerleading squad, while Paula pressed me about the importance of being a cheerleader in our state. I tried to finesse the question by saying that Texas women have always been ready to assume leadership positions wherever they existed. One of our senators, a Dallas "lady," had been a UT cheerleader. I assured her that this was a state where men are men, and women grow up to become governors and senators. After showing some footage of Texans socializing at some fund-raiser, the women garishly made up and costumed in spangled cowgirl suits, Paula moved to the wrap-up by mentioning the time she'd spent with Lady Bird Johnson. I got in a few comments about the strengths of Texas women, but on the whole, I felt that I'd let my Dallas sisters down.

Dallas women today are a heterogeneous and diverse lot, but there is no getting around the fact that they have long been recognized and appreciated for their appearance. Out-of-state people, especially men, often offer up the old saw, "The most beautiful women in the world live in Dallas." A novelist visiting in Dallas for a few days remarked, "There is only one operable verb here—grooming. It applies to the women, the lawns, the houses, the children, the dogs, the cars. Everything." A new resident from Canada, well versed in nautical terms, said of Dallas women: "Looks like a lot of high maintenance bright work to me."

The city's long association with Neiman-Marcus's flagship store probably has a great deal to do with the Dallas preoccupation with appearance. In Vivian

Castleberry's *Daughters of Dallas,* Idella Rabin, then owner of a women's specialty shop, is quoted: "Carrie Neiman (cofounder of Neiman-Marcus) was the epitome of style and class, a fine art in the way she dressed, looked, and acted. She taught me to take the extra seconds to put myself together before I face the world. She never appeared in public without being exquisitely groomed, with every item of her apparel coordinated and fitting exactly the image she wanted the store to convey. It would never enter her head to carry a black bag and wear brown shoes. Sometimes it was tempting to leave the house without being well-put-together. Then, I'd remember Miss Carrie, and I wouldn't dare."

Even women in other Texas cities view the Dallas Woman as a rarified creature. When asked what comes to mind when she thinks of Dallas women, a Houston friend said, "Stockings, even on Saturday when it's 104 degrees." A San Antonio woman said that she never felt comfortable in Dallas because Dallas women actually change purses. "They carry little clutch purses that match their shoes. I just have one big old feed-bag purse that accommodates everything. I never think about how it matches what I'm wearing until I'm landing at Love Field." An Austin woman whose sister lives in Dallas says, "No matter how carefully I dress when I go to visit her, she meets my plane and says, 'Judy, we've got to do something about your shoes.'" Once she took me shopping before my class reunion, and while she was flying all over the store picking out the right bag, shoes, and jewelry to complement the dress, the salesperson in the dressing room with me said, 'I don't know who that woman with you is, but you'd better listen to her. She's got style and knows what she's talking about.'"

"Judy, is your sister in retailing or design?" I asked.

"No. She's a nurse."

The pervasive feeling that there are style police abroad is daunting even to those of us who started their grown-up lives here and have had plenty of time to get with the program. When I was a young mother living in jeans and T-shirts, I remember walking home with a friend from the local Highland Park elementary school after a mothers' meeting at which many women had appeared in casual, but stylish, coordinated cruise wear. "Sue," I said, "sometimes

I just want to hang a sign on my back that says, 'I'm not competing.'" Sue said, "What makes you think you need a sign?" No wonder my boys did not want me working in the cafeteria lunch line when they reached middle school. . . .

Back to bright work. A family who returned to Dallas after several years in suburban New York reports that their daughters were initially blown away by our shiny expensive cars, makeup, and colorful clothes. "We came from a place where everyone either wore L. L. Bean or black. Five days after we arrived, I found my five-year-old in her ballet leotard—wearing red lipstick, bracelets, and earrings—with her hair pulled up in a ponytail on top of her head—running on the scale in my bathroom. 'What in the world are you doing, Elizabeth?' 'Workin' out'. . . ."

Aging in a city like Dallas, especially in a time of such prosperity, is difficult for women. Face lifts, once a shameful sign of excessive vanity, are now no more controversial than orthodontic work for children. Lips are plumped, teeth are bleached, thighs are thinned, and veins disappear. . . . With enough money, there seems to be no need for women to budge beyond a well-rested forty-five. . . .

Hair rarely turns gray here. A Dallas woman, eyeing my salt and pepper hair, once took me aside and said, "You know, Prudence, men here really don't like prematurely gray hair on women." Before she could offer me her colorist, I said, "But mine isn't premature, and the only guy I care about calls me 'Great Beauty.' He also appreciates the low maintenance." Still, when I go to another city for a speaking engagement or a book signing, I have the distinct feeling that my audience is disappointed when I do not show up looking the way they think a Dallas woman should. . . .

A Wellesley woman, transferred here from Boston, tells me she now warns other Eastern transplants. "Just because she's wearing lipstick, don't assume she's stupid." *Morning News* editorial page editor Rena Pederson, originally from San Angelo, says, "Dallas has always been a magnet for overachievers." Scratch most Dallas leaders and you'll find someone who grew up some place else like Stamford, Alpine, Floydada, Archer City, Goldthwaite, or Hereford. Fear that the lint of our humble beginnings clings to our stylish Dallas coattails probably makes earnest strivers of most folks. . . .

The Dallas Woman approaches almost every area of her life competitively. The same careful attention to detail and great intensity that she gives to her house decorating, her children, her parties (especially her daughter's wedding) and her closet, she also gives to her work, her community service, and her church work. The tradition of volunteering is so strong among Dallas women that the title "professional volunteer" has emerged and carries no hint of pejoration. A belief that leaders can be created, usually in "leadership seminars" in the corporate and non-profit sectors, is a tenet of the Dallas credo. . . .

Vast changes have occurred for women in Dallas in the last twenty-five years, but the women's liberation movement never gained much of a foothold here. In 1963, Betty Friedan, promoting her controversial new book *The Feminine Mystique,* spoke to the Temple Emanu-El Sisterhood Donor luncheon. Gerry Cristol's history of Temple Emanu-El, *A Light in the Prairie,* records that there was considerable consternation when the guest of honor showed up in a somewhat dowdy outfit, not well put together at the sellout event. Adding insult to injury, the author proceeded to challenge the room full of Dallas's stalwart volunteers, "What are you doing here? You ought to be out in the work place." She went on to admonish the ladies to "send your kids to school in cabs," if you have to, and to "find someone in the yellow pages to clean your house." Palpable silence reigned as Rabbi Olan quickly closed the meeting without asking for questions. . . .

Flocks of affluent women took refuge in "submissiveness seminars" held in local churches or in Dallas homes (Tim Timmons, Bill Gotherd, and Susan Key's *Eve Reborn).* Fortunately, a handful of Dallas women, most notably lawyer Hermine Tobolowsky, concerned themselves with securing equal legal rights for Texas women to own property and borrow money. Drawing up contracts on who takes out the trash, however, or bashing the men who failed to do it, never quite caught on here. . . .

Some Dallas women's consciousness got raised gently in the early seventies through courses like Explore, begun at the Northhaven Methodist Church, which encouraged women to examine their lives and take control of them. A few years later the Dallas Junior League began a program for its members called Career Development, a title that was quickly changed to Focus when the word *career* was deemed too threatening. "We hit 'em with the three D's—Death, Desertion, and Divorce—which required that married women have a backup plan," recalls Anne Dickson, who pioneered the program. It spawned some careers and paved the way for the enormous changes that the Junior League would face as its once exclusive, sorority-like secret admissions policies were overhauled and its ranks gradually filled with working women from all walks of life. . . .

Dallas women are now entrepreneurs, heads of grocery store chains, engineers, bankers, lawyers, doctors, judges, architects, airline pilots, chefs, clergy, superintendents, principals of high schools, police officers, fire fighters, and city council persons. Two women have served effectively as mayors of the city. The first female city manager, Jan Hart, now heads the Dallas Chamber of Commerce, and Donna Halstead is the president of the original good-old-boy club, the Dallas Citizen's Council. Women artists here, who once had to form their own co-op exhibition gallery to show their work, now seem to receive equal treatment from the Dallas Museum and local galleries. Working women I talked with feel that they are now judged for their competence in the work place without regard to their gender. . . .

Liza Lee, headmistress of the Hockaday School, a product of Eastern girls schools and New York, not surprisingly says, "I love Dallas women." She admits to trying her best to change the media image of women here. "I love their sense of civic responsibility, their resilience, and their willingness to take risks." Imbued with the "can do" spirit that pervades the city, there is no project a school can think up that is too ambitious for a cadre of North Dallas volunteer moms.

What about girls growing up to be Dallas women? Headmistress Lee says, "The colleges certainly love Dallas girls." In his memoir *North Toward Home,* the late Willie Morris said, "People from the South who scratch their way into some sort of intellectual realm always retain a quality of fresh naiveté that their Eastern counterparts discarded in junior high. I think it is an endearing quality."

The same mother from New York whose five-year-old took to the "work out" on the scales says, "I had some concerns about moving back to Dallas. I worried that my daughters would fall into the old male chauvinist patterns I remembered from earlier days." To her surprise, she has watched her daughters embrace the best of Texas womanhood, making them poised, confident, even bold while their counterparts in the East seem to feel the need to sullenly deconstruct and recreate themselves during their high school years. "Bonding in our New York suburb involved a lot of very literate whining," she says. "Here, my girls stay busy. Women's athletics is such a boon. They also do volunteer work. Yes, they conform, they run in a pack, but I think some of their ability to reach beyond themselves comes from the perky confidence gained in knowing that they've got it all together. They are well-groomed. They know the rituals, the manners. No shrinking violets—they have learned to make everyone comfortable, to diffuse unpleasantness, even to deflect sexist remarks with aplomb." Political columnist Molly Ivins once noted that "Texas women are tough in some fundamental ways. Not unfeminine, nor necessarily unladylike, just tough. We can cope with put-downs and come-ons, with preachers and hustlers, with drunks and cowboys. . . . "

In 1996, I was invited to address the Dallas Women's Club (organized 1922), an outgrowth of the venerable Shakespeare Club (1886) and one of the last bastions of old Dallas tradition and propriety. While their very careful attention to rules is somewhat daunting, I found them to be a most gracious and welcoming audience. Since I was speaking to them on Presidential Election Day, in my opening remarks I joked that President Clinton, running for re-election that year, had called me before breakfast to see if I could filibuster all day and keep such a Republican bunch away from the polls. At lunch in the club dining room with the women and their guests after my speech, a diminutive older woman tapped me on the shoulder. "We've been talking about you at our table, and they sent me to ask you a question. You are a Republican, aren't you?"

"No, ma'am, I'm not," I replied. "I grew up in deep East Texas where it's very hard to become a Republican."

"That's not true," she said.

"Well," I continued defensively, "I also worked for Congressman Wright Patman in Washington and later in the White House for President Lyndon Johnson, so I suppose I am beholden to the Democrats for some of the great moments of my early life."

She stepped back from the table, as if I might have something communicable, and said, "You should be incarcerated!"

After more than twenty-five years in Dallas, I guess I'm still on probation. ★

Leon Unruh

Leon Unruh, as a youth in Kansas, dug graves with a shovel and helped maintain three cemeteries. He is a coauthor of *Final Destinations: A Travel Guide for Remarkable Cemeteries in Texas, New Mexico, Oklahoma, Arkansas, and Louisiana.* He is an editor for the *Anchorage Daily News* and previously wrote or edited for the *Larned Tiller and Toiler,* the *Hays Daily News,* and the *Wichita Eagle* in Kansas, the *Minneapolis Tribune* in Minnesota, and the *Austin American-Statesman* and *The Dallas Morning News* in Texas. Under his editorial direction, the travel and geographical Web site Alaska.com received a bronze award from the Society of American Travel Writers and first-place awards from the Alaska Press Club. Unruh has been a freelance editor and proofreader of academic and business books since 1989. He also created and maintains a Web site about his hometown, PawneeRock.org. It seemed fitting to end with the cemeteries of Dallas, and the descriptions of them by Unruh reveal a lot about the inhabitants of Dallas and their mores and culture.

From *Final Destinations*: Graves Reveal Dallas's Parade of History

Dallas has a wealth of notable cemeteries with fascinating stories to tell. At rest under the live oaks are pioneers, politicians, developers, sports heroes, captains of industry, the venal and valiant. Among them:

Oakland

ONCE IT WAS DALLAS'S CROWNING GLORY: Oakland Cemetery, full of pomp and artistry in the city's finest neighborhood south of the Trinity River. J. F. Strickland, who founded the company that became TU Electric, lies under a tall obelisk in the center of the cemetery. John Armstrong, developer of the suburb of Highland Park, is watched over by a towering, gossamer-clad marble angel imported from Venice. The Belo newspaper family is remembered with a pale stone slab and a cross. The Caruths, whose family owned much of what became North Dallas, have a columned monument.

Other families provided a legacy: Kleist, Growler, O'Connor, Ervay, Record, Beall. There are such personages as Confederate General Richard M. Gano, who became a prohibitionist minister and the grandfather of eccentric millionaire Howard Hughes. But their funerals occurred decades ago, before the wealthy left their dead and moved north of the river. Now, these fifty acres seem to be on a Faulknerian slide back to nature, shrubs and wildflowers welcoming the hand-carved works into their grasp.

It is not for lack of effort by the live-in manager, Harold Williams, who works on a bare-bones budget to maintain the lovely old park in the 3900 block of Malcolm X Avenue in South Dallas. His office is an organized mess of records, tools, bronze markers, and the three-foot-tall "Bunny Boy" statue depicting young Joseph Milton Cary, who drowned in 1901. The statue, which originally stood at Joseph's grave, is kept inside for safekeeping from vandals and thieves.

Mr. Williams is a gregarious fellow who gladly provides background on people buried during the cemetery's first century. One of the favorite stories he and Dallas cemetery preservationist Frances James like to tell is about Louis Antonio Pires.

Mr. Pires arrived in this country as an orphan, says Mrs. James, his parents having died on the crossing from Portugal. He amassed a fortune in the utility business, lived in a Salvation Army home, never married, and left $500,000 to Buckner Children's Home. "He was old and sick, and his friends wanted him to go to the hospital, but he didn't want to go because he didn't want to spend the money," she says. In recognition, other families built him a monument for his grave. It has six columns and a dome, with inscriptions inside and out. The floor is inlaid with colored stone.

Oak Cliff

When infant Martha White died in 1844, she was buried in a newly set-aside piece of land on Hord's Ridge, the original name for Oak Cliff. She may not have been the first person buried in what is now known as Oak Cliff Cemetery, which is along Eighth Street a few blocks east of R. L. Thornton Freeway (Interstate 35), but her grave has the distinction of being the oldest in Dallas with a marker.

Although time has made the writing hard to read, the stone is easy to find. Look for a white marker at the base of an enormous slanting oak tree along the western fence where it jogs outward. William Hord, for whom the ridge was named, is buried in Oak Cliff Cemetery, but his grave is unmarked, says David Eisenlohr, a member of the cemetery's board of trustees and relative of pioneer landscape painter Edward Gustav Eisenlohr, who also is here. Sam Houston's brother, William Rogers Houston, rests here, as do Oak Cliff developer Leslie Stemmons, mayors George Sergeant and George Sprague, and drugstore founder J. A. Skillern.

Anthony Boswell has a family plot in the back of the cemetery. A black teamster, he was an important landowner in Oak Cliff's historic Tenth Street area. Anthony and Boswell streets are named for him.

Beeman

John Neely Bryan . . . talked the John Beeman family into moving to the Dallas area (near White Rock Creek south of the present Interstate 30) and marrying their daughter, Margaret. Mr. Bryan eventually became insane and died at an asylum in Austin. The Beemans' graves are in their family cemetery behind a wire fence wrapped in mustang grapevines. The Beeman monument reads: "Mrs. Emily Beeman holding her son Scott and guarding against Indians in Dallas Co. in 1841."

The Beemans, Cumbys, and other neighbors can be visited by turning off Dolphin Road onto Mingo (at the African Methodist Episcopal Church), then Galt and Osage. It is behind Shearith Israel Cemetery.

Greenwood

Genteel old Greenwood Cemetery at 3020 Oak Grove Avenue in central Dallas has a rarity: a new hand-carved marble statue. Ruth Marie Rose was the godmother of State District Judge John M. Marshall's children when she died of cancer in 1987. She was buried in his family plot; as a final gift, Judge Marshall arranged for a statue to be produced in Italy.

"There was some guy over there with a chisel working on this thing for a year," he says.

The angel fits in nicely with the rich statuary of Greenwood, an 1875-vintage graveyard that originally was named Trinity Cemetery. Numerous obelisks and tall monuments were erected during the nineteenth century. Among the Dallas notables buried here are the Cockrells, who owned much of Dallas at one time and are the family for whom the burg of Cockrell Hill is named; developer John Cole; banker W. H. Gaston; and Christopher Columbus Slaughter, cattle king, Texas Ranger, and member of the expedition that took Cynthia Ann Parker back from the Comanches.

The trees and monuments provide such a classic setting that the television series *Walker, Texas Ranger* filmed its cemetery scenes under the tall oaks. . . .

Numerous Civil War veterans are here, too. For soldiers without a military headstone, the white tablet stones of the type found in national cemeteries are requested from the government as details about their federal or Confederate service are confirmed. Despite Greenwood's age, only 40 percent of the grave sites have been sold, Judge Marshall says. Although anybody can apply for a plot here, it helps their cause if the applicants have a family member in place.

Grove Hill

Grove Hill Cemetery at 4118 Samuell Boulevard in East Dallas, is an ornate treasure-trove of post-pioneer Dallasites: Tenison, Stemmons, Murdock, Munger, Genaro, Hubbard, Buckner. The names on the bulky tombstones and mausoleums—this must be one of the grandest collections of granite in Texas—also show up on roads, parks, lakes, and children's homes around town.

But according to people in the cemetery office, the graves most sought by visitors are those of Dallas's star-crossed ring royalty. Professional wrestler Fritz von Erich, born Jack Adkisson Sr., as well as a brother, a six-year-old son, and his four wrestler sons lie in a humble area just east of the cross-shaped hedge marking out the Hilltop area. His four wrestling sons—David, Michael, Chris, and Kerry—all died young, three of suicide, between 1984 and 1993. Fritz von

Erich, who died of brain cancer in 1997, survived them all. He shares a marker with Kerry.

Grove Hill also has at least one Medal of Honor winner: Turney Leonard, a first lieutenant who fought the Germans during World War II.

Laurel Land

Laurel Land Memorial Park has at least two legends. The grave of musician Stephen "Stevie" Ray Vaughan, who died in a Wisconsin helicopter crash in 1990, is on an island at the sprawling cemetery along South R. L. Thornton Freeway in Oak Cliff. It is on an east-west road near the Marsalis Avenue entrance. In the Laurel Land Mausoleum, not too far away from the man with the smokin' guitar, is barbecue king Sonny Bryan. The cemetery also is home to J. D. Tippit, the police office slain in Oak Cliff by Lee Harvey Oswald on November 22, 1963, after President John F. Kennedy was shot.

Pioneer

A stroll through this small cemetery just north of the Dallas Convention Center and adjacent to the longhorn statues reveals the origins of many of the city's street names: Young, Record, Peak, Harwood, Good. The roster also lists Juliette Fowler, who created a home for the elderly and for troubled youths; several judges; members of the Texas Congress; James Week Latimer, the city's first newspaper publisher (of the *Cedar Snag* in 1848); and the Reverend William C. Young, the initial minister of what is now First United Methodist Church of Dallas.

The city's Confederate monument faces south at the edge of the cemetery next to the convention center. The cemetery used to be much larger, but many of the dead were moved to other cemeteries when the meeting hall was expanded in 1959.

Freedman's

Dallas's most historic black cemetery is Freedman's Cemetery, at Lemmon Avenue and Central Expressway north of downtown. Many of the city's early black residents were buried in this five-acre graveyard between 1861 and 1925.

Although the site appears vacant from the street, as many as 10,000 people are thought to be buried there. Highway excavation crews unearthed some graves in the 1980s, and about 1,500 were dug up to make way for construction. They were reinterred nearby, and the city in 1999 dedicated an arch to commemorate the freedmen's lives. A few stones remain, huddled next to a wooded lot along the western fence. The script on one stone reads: "How much of light / How much of joy / Is buried with a darling boy."

Lincoln

Lincoln Memorial Park, a spacious area at 1311 Murdock Road in the Pleasant Grove area of southeast Dallas, is the city's principal black cemetery now. About 75 percent of the city's black burials are held there, *Dallas Morning News* columnist Norma Adams Wade reported in 1990. The cemetery opened in 1924. Listed among the buried are philanthropist Pearl C. Anderson and orator and historian Dr. John Leslie Patton Jr., who four decades ago taught the first black-history courses in Dallas public schools.

Emanu-El and Shearith Israel

Congregations Emanu-El and Shearith Israel organized two of the area's Jewish cemeteries. Founded in 1890 at 3430 Howell Street north of downtown (adjacent to Freedman's Cemetery and Greenwood Cemetery), Emanu-El is the older of the two. Among its neatly kept graves are those of early department store owners Adolph Harris and Philip and Alex Sanger (for whom the town of Sanger was named). There also are several dozen graves of early city residents who were moved here from Pioneer Cemetery when the convention center was expanded in late 1959. Other graves have names that reflect Russian, German, and other European heritages. Many plots are delineated by concrete borders and are covered with gravel or "cribs" planted with ground cover.

Shearith Israel is along Dolphin Road south of Interstate 30 in East Dallas. It is not far from Grove Hill Cemetery and is adjacent to old Beeman Cemetery. Familiar names here include grocer Julius Schepps (his father, Nathan, founded Schepps Dairy; his cousins included philanthropist Julius, for whom Julius Schepps Freeway is named, and George, a Dallas sports entrepreneur). Here, as at Emanu-El, inscriptions are frequently in Hebrew.

Calvary Hill and Hillcrest

Dallas's movers and shakers of recent years often may be found under simple stones in northside cemeteries. In the deep reaches of Calvary Hill Cemetery, a Catholic graveyard on Lombardy Lane, airline founder Thomas Braniff (who died in a private-plane crash in 1954) is just a short hop from hotelier Conrad Hilton, who once was married to Zsa Zsa Gabor.

At Hillcrest Memorial Park Cemetery on Northwest Highway, oilman Haroldson Lafayette Hunt, once one of the world's richest people, lies near 1950s tennis ace Maureen Connolly Brinker and former Texas governor and U.S. Senator W. Lee O'Daniel, who are not far from former Senator and Secretary of Defense nominee John Tower and actress Greer Garson Fogelson. Baseball great Mickey Mantle rests in the Hillcrest Mausoleum; use the North St. Mark Addition entrance.

As with many cemeteries in Texas, Hillcrest began as a family cemetery and was expanded after the passage of a state law restricting the founding of cemeteries near cities, says Frances James, the preservationist. John Bailey, attorney for Greenwood Cemetery in Fort Worth, explains that a 1934 law, in the state Health and Safety Code, forbids the founding of cemeteries within five miles of a city of more than 200,000 population. Smaller cities are allowed to have them closer to town.

Hillcrest was originally a Caruth family cemetery. That section is fenced off near Northwest Highway. (Restland Memorial Park, for another North Dallas example, originally was the Floyd family graveyard, Mrs. James says.) Hillcrest has such a parklike atmosphere that Dallas and Park Cities residents often bring their children to feed the koi in the pond near the entrance. It gives the impression of being the garden spot that Oakland Cemetery used to be.

Hillcrest's self-perception was put on the ropes not long ago when the Vehon family wanted to erect a statue of a nude man atop the family stone. "We decided our families weren't quite ready for that," Barbara Gross,

Hillcrest's office manager, says with a laugh. The statue eventually was allowed, with discreet draping.

Old Letot and Dallas City Cemetery

Old Letot Cemetery and Dallas City Cemetery are neighbors in North Dallas, just south of Walnut Hill Lane and west of Harry Hines Boulevard. Until it was swallowed up by Dallas in the booming 1960s, Letot was a farming village named after Clement Letot, a French immigrant who arrived in 1876 and bought 1,200 acres. (According to *The New Handbook of Texas,* he is also the only Dallas County resident to have fought in the Crimean War.) The cemetery, at 10700 Shady Trail, is up a small rise from the road and surrounded by a fence. Mr. Letot, who died in 1907, is buried two miles away in the Letot family cemetery attached to the north side of Calvary Hill Cemetery.

Dallas City Cemetery provides its inhabitants an almost secluded existence. It is reached by a gravel alley just north of an office park at 10606 Shady Trail. It was founded in the 1930s as a pauper's ground, Mrs. James says. With a few exceptions, graves are marked with a six-by-six-inch block of concrete that holds a small brass plate stamped with the deceased's name, birth date, and death date.

Daniel and Wheatland

Sprinkled across Dallas and Tarrant counties are dozens of family and church cemeteries that hold pioneer residents. Dallas County alone has about 200 such cemeteries. Two of them still in use in the southwestern part of the county are Daniel and Wheatland. The Daniel family graveyard, close to Danieldale Road at Bolton Boone Drive in DeSoto, was set aside for descendants of the Reverend Ellison Daniel. Its earliest known burial was in 1857.

At 8000 Hampton Road in southwest Dallas, the Wheatland Cemetery holds members of the pioneering Nance and Penn ranching families, among many others. It is adjacent to the wonderful wooden Wheatland United Methodist Church, founded in 1847 and reputed to be the oldest Methodist Church west of the Trinity River.

Fish Trap

Fish Trap Cemetery, also known as Old French Colony Cemetery, is tucked into the northwest corner of Singleton Boulevard and Hampton Road, behind L. G. Pinkston High School on Fish Trap Road. The area was settled in 1855 by European immigrants who set up a short-lived Utopian settlement named La Réunion. The small cemetery, all that remains of the colony, is beautified by locust and oak trees and patches of irises. Surrounded by a tall chain-link fence, it has dozens of markers. Among the settlers buried here was naturalist Julien Reverchon (died 1905), for whom Dallas's Reverchon Park is named. The settlement's name was appropriated for a downtown arena and tower.

Western Heights and Crown Hill

Decades after they were shot to death in Louisiana, two of the Southwest's most famous lovers and outlaws are separated by seven miles. Officers of the law ambushed Clyde Barrow and Bonnie Parker in May 1934, ending their (some say his) run of bank robberies. Their bullet-riddled car and belongings have since been sold for thousands of dollars.

Clyde Barrow is buried in his family plot with brother Marvin "Buck" Barrow in Western Heights Cemetery, 1617 Fort Worth Avenue, in West Dallas, just a few miles up the road from where Clyde used to work at Trinity Portland Cement. The Barrows' plot is in the southwest corner beneath some shady crape myrtles.

Bonnie Parker first was buried in Fish Trap Cemetery. But after her headstone was stolen repeatedly, her grave was moved to Crown Hill Cemetery on Webb Chapel Road north of Dallas Love Field airport. People stumbling across Ms. Parker's flat headstone (west of the hedge near the entrance) never would guess her background.

The epitaph: "As the flowers are all made sweeter by the sunshine and the dew, so this old world is made brighter by the lives of folks like you." ★

Selected Bibliography of Books about Dallas—Fiction and Non-fiction—and by Dallas Authors

Acheson, Sam. *Dallas Yesterday*, edited by Lee Milazzo. Dallas, TX: SMU Press, 1977.

———. *35,000 Days in Texas: A History of the Dallas News and Its Forebears* New York: The Macmillan Co., 1938.

Barney, Robert Owen. *The Romantic Story of Dallas: From Buckskins to Top Hat!* Illustrated by Bill McClanahan. Dallas,TX: Robert Owen Barney, 1948.

Barrow, Blanche Caldwell. *My Life With Bonnie & Clyde*. Edited by John Neal Phillips. Norman: University of Oklahoma Press, 2004. Memoir by Blanche Caldwell Barrow who was married to Buck Barrow, Clyde's brother.

Barta, Carolyn. *Bill Clements: Texian to His Toenails*. Austin, TX: Eakin Press, 1996. The author who pens this biography of Dallasite and former governor of Texas has been a political writer, political editor, editor of the op-ed page, and columnist for *The Dallas Morning News*.

——— *Perot and His People: Disrupting the Balance of Political Power.* Fort Worth, TX: Summit Publishing Group, 1993.

Biderman, Rose G. *They Came to Stay: The Story of the Jews Of Dallas 1870–1997*. Austin, TX: Eakin Press, 2001. Chronicles the story of the Jews who settled in Dallas, their lives and contributions.

Beckett, Hazel Williams. *Growing up in Dallas*. Austin, TX: New Hope Press, 1985.

Blow, Steve. *Blow by Blow*. Dallas, TX: Three Forks Press, 2001. A collection of Blow's columns from *The Dallas Morning News*, starting in 1989.

Brown, John Henry. *History of Dallas County, Texas: From 1837 to 1887*. Dallas, TX: John Henry Brown, 1887.

Butler, Steven R. *From Water Supply to Urban Oasis: A History of White Rock Lake Park*. Richardson, TX: Steven R. Butler, 2004.

———. *John Neely Bryan, the Father of Dallas: A Biography*. Richardson, TX: Steven R. Butler, 1991 & 2006.

Castleberry, Vivian Anderson. *Daughters of Dallas: A History of Greater Dallas Through the Voices and Deeds of its Women*. Dallas, TX: Odenwald Press, 1994.

———. *Sarah—the Bridge Builder: Dowager Of A Dallas Dynasty.* Dallas, TX: Odenwald Press, 2004.

Chariton, Wallace Owen. *Texas Centennial: The Parade of an Empire.* Plano, TX: Wallace O. Chariton, 1979.

Cheney, Allison A. *Dallas Spirit: A Political History of the City of Dallas.* Dallas, TX: McMullan Publishing Co., 1991.

Cochran, John H. *Dallas County: A Record of Its Pioneers and Progress.* Dallas, TX: A.S. Mathis, Service Pub. Co., 1928.

Considerant, Victor. *Au Texas*. Paris, France: 1854. See A. C. Greene's excerpt from *A Place Called Dallas* in *Literary Dallas*, p. 13, for more discussion of Considerant.

Cristol, Gerry. *A Light in the Prairie: Temple Emanu-El of Dallas, 1872-1997*. Fort

Worth: TCU Press, 1998. Temple Emanu-El, the first Jewish congregation in North Texas, played a historic role in the growth of Dallas.

Eisenberg, John. *Cotton Bowl Days: Growing Up with Dallas and the Cowboys in the 1960s.* New York: Simon & Schuster, 1997.

Fitzgerald, Ken. *Dallas Then and Now.* San Diego, CA: Thunder Bay Press, 2001.

Gelsanliter, David. *Fresh Ink: Behind the Scenes at a Major Metropolitan Newspaper.* Denton, TX: University of North Texas Press, 1995. A week in the life of *The Dallas Morning News*, the leading newspaper in the southwest, winner of seven Pulitzer Prizes at the time.

Greene, A. C. *Dallas: The Deciding Years—A Historical Portrait.* Austin, TX: Encino Press, 1973.

———. *Dallas, USA.* Austin, TX: Texas Monthly Press, 1984.

Hazel, Michael V. *Dallas: A History of "Big D."* Austin, TX: Texas State Historical Association, 1997. Examines the city's roots as a frontier market town, development as a regional transportation center, entering the twentieth century.

———, ed. *Dallas Reconsidered: Essays in Local History.* Dallas, TX: Three Forks Press, 1995.

———. *The Dallas Historical Society: The Early Years, 1922-1946.* Dallas, TX: Belo Foundation, 2002.

———, ed. *Stanley Marcus A to Z: Viewpoints Volume II.* Denton, TX: University of North Texas Press, 2000. Marcus lets his mind roam through subjects as diverse as dieting, gardening, nonconformists, phobias, sports, toys, and weather.

Hill, Margaret Hunt, Jane Boyer, and Burt Boyer. *H. L. and Lyda.* Little Rock, AR: August House, 1994. Growing up in the H. L. Hunt and Lyda Bunker Hunt family by their eldest daughter.

Hunsicker, Harry. *Crosshairs.* New York: St. Martin's Press Minotaur, 2007. A Lee Henry Oswald detective mystery set in Dallas.

———. *The Next Time You Die.* New York: St. Martin's Press Minotaur, 2006. A Lee Henry Oswald detective mystery set in Dallas.

Jacobs, Mike, *Holocaust Survivor: Mike Jacobs' Triumph Over Tragedy.* Edited by Ginger Jacobs. Austin, TX: Eakin Press, 2001. Memoir by the founder of the Dallas Holocaust Memorial Center.

Jebsen, Harry Jr., Robert M. Newton, and Patricia R. Hogan. *Centennial History of the Dallas, Texas Park System, 1876-1976.* Lubbock, TX: Texas Tech University, 1976.

Jones, Nancy, ed. *Voices From Within.* Denton, TX: University of North Texas Press, 1992. Poetry from the Dallas County Community College District, written by thirty-three members of the DCCCD faculty and staff.

Lavergne, Gary. *Worse than Death: The Dallas Nightclub Murders and the Texas Multiple Murder Law.* Denton, TX: University of North Texas Press, 2003.

Leslie, Warren. *Dallas Public and Private: Aspects of an American City.* Dallas, TX: SMU Press, 1998. An examination of Dallas in the aftermath of the assassination of President John F. Kennedy, probing Dallas's political, cultural, and educational institutions.

MacDonald, Patty Vineyard, ed. *The Best from Helen Corbitt's Kitchens.* Denton, TX: University of North Texas Press, 2000. Biography and recipes from the Director of Food Services for Neiman-Marcus.

Mackintosh, Prudence, Virginia Savage McAlester, Willis Cecil Winters. *Homes of the Park Cities: Dallas, Texas.* New York: Abbeville Press, 2008.

———. *Just As We Were: A Narrow Slice of Texas Womanhood,* Austin, TX: University of Texas Press, 1996.

———. *Retreads.* New York: Doubleday, 1985. This and the following books form a trilogy of her adventures with raising her three sons in Dallas.

———. *Sneaking Out.* Austin, TX: University of Texas Press, 2002.

———. *Thundering Sneakers.* Austin, TX: University of Texas Press, 2002.

Marcus, Stanley. *Minding the Store.* Denton, TX: University of North Texas Press, 1998.

———. *Quest for the Best.* Denton, TX: University of North Texas Press, 2001.

———. *The Viewpoints of Stanley Marcus: A Ten-Year Perspective.* Denton, TX: University of North Texas Press, 1995. A collection of his viewpoints appeared in *The Dallas Morning News* for a decade; an insider's view on the city of Dallas.

Mardis, Jas, ed. *Kente Cloth: Southwest Voices of the African Diaspora.* Denton, TX: University of North Texas Press, 1998. The literary voices offer a varied glimpse into the region's cache of new voices.

McCoy, John Milton. *When Dallas Became a City: Letters of John Milton McCoy, 1870-1881.* Edited by Elizabeth York Enstam. Dallas, TX: Dallas Historical Society, 1982.

McDonald, William L. *Dallas Rediscovered: A Photographic Chronicle of Urban Expansion, 1870-1925.* Dallas, TX: Dallas Historical Society, 1978.

McElhaney, Jacquelyn Masur. *Pauline Periwinkle and Progressive Reform in Dallas.* College Station, TX: Texas A&M Press, 1998. Journalist Isadore Miner Callaway using the pen name Pauline Periwinkle was the first woman's editor of *The Dallas Morning News*; she encouraged women to take part in the reform efforts of the Progressive Era.

McMillan, Priscilla Johnson. *Marina and Lee.* New York: Harper & Row, 1977.

Oppenheimer, Evelyn, and Bill Porterfield. *The Book of Dallas.* Garden City, NY: Doubleday & Company, 1976. A book of essays and photographs of Dallas.

Parker, Emma Krause, Mrs., and Nellie Barrow Cowan. *Fugitives: The True Story of Clyde Barrow and Bonnie Parker.* Edited by Jan Fortune. Dallas, TX: Ranger Press, 1934.

Payne, Darwin. *Dallas: An Illustrated History.* Woodland Hills, CA: Windsor Publications, 1982.

———, ed. *Sketches of a Growing Town: Episodes and People of Dallas from Early Days to Recent Times.* Dallas, TX: Southern Methodist University Press, 1991.

———. *As Old as Dallas Itself: A History of the Lawyers of Dallas, the Dallas Bar Associations, and the City They Helped Build.* Dallas, TX: Three Forks Press, 1999.

——— and Fitzpatrick, Kathy. *From Prairie to Planes: How Dallas and Fort Worth Overcame Politics and Personalities to Build One of the World's Biggest and Busiest Airports.* Dallas, TX: Three Forks Press, 1999.

———. *Big D: Triumphs and Troubles of an American Supercity in the 20th Century.* Dallas, TX: Three Forks Press, 1994.

———. *Dynamic Dallas: An Illustrated History.* Carlsbad, CA: Heritage Media Corp., 2002.

——— and Hlavach, Laura, eds. *Reporting the Kennedy Assassination: Journalists Who Were There Recall Their Experiences.* Dallas, TX: Three Forks Press, 1996.

Phillips, John Neal. *Running with Bonnie and Clyde: The Ten Fast Years of Ralph Fults.* Norman, OK: University of Oklahoma, 2002.

Ragsdale, Kenneth B. *The Year America Discovered Texas: Centennial '36.* College Station, TX: Texas A&M University Press, 1987, 2000.

Rigler, Lewis C., and Judyth W. *In the Line of Duty: Reflections of a Texas Ranger Private.* Denton, TX: University of North Texas Press, 1995. Rigler entered Ranger service as a member of Dallas-based Company B and retired in 1977.

Roberts, Larenda Lyles, and Kay Threadgill. *Dallas Uncovered*, 2nd ed. Carolina Beach, NC: Seaside Press, 1998.

Rosenberg, Leon Joseph. *Sangers': Pioneer Texas Merchants.* Austin, TX: Texas State Historical Association, 1978.

Rumbley, Rose-Mary. *A Century of Class: Public Education in Dallas, 1884-1984.* Austin, TX: Eakin Press, 1984.

———. *Dallas, Too: Stories I'm Telling Again, Because I Want to Hear Them Myself!* Austin, TX: Eakin Press, 1998. Stories about R. L. Thornton, Melvin Kiser, Dr. George W. Truitt, Sheriff Bill Decker, and Dean Imogene.

———. *Strolling Through the Park: The History of the Dallas Park Board.* Austin, TX: Eakin Press, 2006. The history of the Dallas parks begins with City Park, 1876.

———. *The Unauthorized History of Dallas.* Austin, TX: Eakin Press, 1991.

Sanders, Barrot Steven. *The Caruths: Dallas' Landed Gentry.* Dallas, TX: Sanders Press, 1988.

———. *Dallas: Her Golden Years.* Dallas, TX: Sanders Press, 1989.

———. *The Forgotten History of the Four Cabins Built by John Neely Bryan and the True History of the Little Cabin on Our Courthouse Square.* Dallas, TX: Barrot Steven Sanders, 1981.

Santerre, George H. *White Cliffs of Dallas.* Dallas, TX: Book Craft, 1955.

Saxon, Gerald D., ed. *Reminiscences: A Glimpse of Old East Dallas.* Dallas, TX: Dallas Public Library, 1983.

Schiebel, Walter J. E. *Education in Dallas: Ninety-two Years of History.* Dallas, TX: Dallas Independent School District, 1966.

Schiff, William, Rosalie Schiff, and Hanley Craig. *William & Rosalie: A Holocaust Testimony.* Denton, TX: University of North Texas Press, 2007.

Schutze, Jim. *The Accommodation: The Politics of Race in an American City.* Secaucus, NJ: Citadel Press, 1986.

Sharpe, Ernest. *G. B. Dealey of the Dallas News.* New York: Henry Holt and Co., 1955.

Shelmire, Overton. *Secrets Under the Bridge.* Wolfe City, TX: Henington Publishing Company, 1994. A delightful story of boys growing up in the Park Cities in the 1930s and 1940s.

Sherrod, Blackie. *Blackie Sherrod At Large.* Austin, TX: Eakin Press, 2003. A collection of Sherrod's columns from *The Dallas Morning News.*

Simmons, Jerre Graves, ed. *The Orphan Chronicles by Buckner Home Alumni Association.* Austin, TX: Eakin Press, 2004. Called "a beacon on a hill in East Dallas for over 120 years" by the orphans who gathered there for homecomings.

St. John, Bob. *Postscripts in a Rearview Mirror.* Austin, TX: Eakin Press, 2004. A collection of columns written for *The Dallas Morning News.*

Starling, Susanne. *Land is the Cry! Warren Angus Ferris, Pioneer Texas Surveyor and Founder of Dallas County.* Austin, TX: Texas State Historical Association, 1998.

Stimpson, Eddie, Jr. *My Remembers: A Black Sharecropper's Recollections of the Depression.* Denton, TX: University of North Texas Press, 1995. The *School Library Journal* says: "The author intersperses description with rhymes and dialect in their original spelling and syntax, lending an authenticity of voice. Always, his strong conviction that 'tough times never last, but tough people all way do' rings true, carrying its own eloquence of spirit."

Switzer, David S. *It's Our Dallas County: The Story of Self-Government Since 1846.* Dallas, TX: David S. Switzer, 1954.

Tinkle, Lon. *Mr. De: A Biography of Everette Lee DeGolyer.* Boston: Little, Brown and Co., 1970.

Trent, Lucy C. *John Neely Bryan: Founder of Dallas.* Dallas, TX: Tardy Publishing Co., 1936.

Whitson, Kathleen Krebbs. *Bill Jason Priest, Community College Pioneer.* Denton, TX: University of North Texas Press, 2004. Priest developed the award-winning Dallas County Community College District, transforming the junior college program into a seven-campus district, performing major roles in the evolution of nursing education, televised courses, vocational education, and noncredit courses.

Widener, Ralph W., Jr. *William Henry Gaston: A Builder of Dallas.* Dallas, TX: Historical Publishing Co., 1977.

Wiley, Nancy. *The Great State Fair of Texas: An Illustrated History.* Dallas, TX: Taylor Publishing Company, 1985.

Wood, Jane Roberts, editor. *Out of Dallas: 14 Stories.* Denton, TX: University of North Texas Press, 1989. Stories written by the faculty and staff of the Dallas County Community College District.

———. *Train to Estelline*, *A Place Called Sweet Shrub*, and *Dance A Little Longer*, a trilogy. Denton, TX: University of North Texas Press, 2000. The award-winning Lucinda "Lucy" Richards trilogy, spanning the years from 1911 to the 1930s.

Woolley, Bryan, ed. *Where I Come From.* Denton, TX: University of North Texas Press, 2003. Stories of ordinary people in North Texas published in *The Dallas Morning News* from May 1999 to December 2000.

Permissions

Adams, Faye Carr. "La Réunion," from *Hide and Horn*, Peggy Zuleika Lynch and Edmund C. Lynch, eds., Austin, Eakin Press.

Aynesworth, Hugh with Stephen G. Michaud. *JFK: Breaking the News,* published by International Focus Press, printed with permission of Hugh Aynesworth.

Bauman, Jon R. From *Santa Fe Passage*, published by Truman Talley Books, St. Martin's Press, printed with permission of Jon R. Bauman.

Biffle, Kent. From *A Month of Sundays*, published by University of North Texas Press, reprinted with permission of Kent Biffle, Texana Columnist, *The Dallas Morning News.*

Bloom, John Irving (Joe Bob Briggs). "The God Thing: In which Joe Bob Briggs, America's irreverent drive-in movie critic, gets religion," published by *D Magazine's Dallas: The 30 Greatest Stories Ever Told*, printed by permission of John Bloom.

Capps, Benjamin. From *The Brothers of Uterica*, published by Meredith Press, printed by permission of M. Marie Capps, credit to the author Benjamin Capps.

Compton, Robert. "On Becoming a Writer," *The Dallas Morning News*, February, 8, 1987. Reprinted with the permission of *The Dallas Morning News.*

Connally, Nellie and Mickey Herskowitz. From *Love Field: Our Final Hours with President John F. Kennedy*, printed courtesy of Rugged Land Books.

Crowell, Grace Noll. "Summer Nights in Texas," from *Flame in the Wind*, Southwest Press; "Wagons at Dusk" from *Texas in Poetry 2*, Billy Bob Hill, ed. Reprinted with permission.

Crume, Paul. "Two Ghosts in a Dallas Plaza, July 27, 1964;" "Hot Nights and Family History," July 28, 1969; "Controlling the Comma," July 3, 1962; "Stalking the Viable Alternative," November 17, 1974. From *The World of Paul Crume*, edited by Marion Crume, printed by permission of Marion Crume.

Cullum, Lee. "Mac and Charlie," reprinted with permission of Lee Cullum.

Daugherty, Tracy. From *The Woman in the Oil Field*, published by Southern Methodist University Press, printed with permission of Tracy Daugherty.

Davis, Ronald L. From *John Rosenfield's Dallas: How the Southwest's Leading Critic Shaped a City's Culture, 1925–1966*, published by Three Forks Press, printed with permission of Ronald L. Davis.

Dealey, Ted. "Colonel Bill," printed from the October 1, 1935, Golden Jubilee Edition of *The Dallas Morning News* for private distribution to friends and associates of the writer.

Dempsey, John Mark, editor. From *The Jack Ruby Trial Revisited: The Diary of Jury Foreman Max Causey*, published by University of North Texas Press and printed with its permission, © 2000 John Mark Dempsey.

Gard, Wayne. From *The Chisholm Trail*, published by the University of Oklahoma Press and printed with its permission.

Garcia, Ed. "Here at the Mini-Warehouse," From *Out of Dallas: 14 Stories*, published by University of North Texas Press, printed with permission of Ed Garcia. Edward H. Garcia teaches writing and literature at Brookhaven College, Dallas.

Govenar, Alan & Jay Brakefield. From *Deep Ellum and Central Track: Where the Black and White Worlds of Dallas Converged*, published by University of North Texas Press, printed with permission of Alan Govenar & Jay Brakefield.

Greene, A. C. from *Texas Sketches*: "John Neely Bryan: Father of Dallas"; "The Name of Dallas"; "Cedar Springs in Dallas," published by Taylor Publishing Company. Reprinted by permission of Meredith Greene, credit the Estate of A. C. Greene. "Heartbreak Hotel: Notes on life after divorce at the Stoneleigh," from *D Magazine's Dallas: The 30 Greatest Stories Ever Told*. Printed by permission of Meredith Greene, credit the Estate of A. C. Greene.

Hailey, Elizabeth Forsythe. "His Children," from *Her Work: Stories by Texas Women*, edited by Lou Halsell Rodenberger, published by Shearer Publishing, printed by permission of Elizabeth Forsythe Hailey; from *A Woman of Independent Means*, published by Penguin Books, printed by permission of Elizabeth Forsythe Hailey.

Hazel, Michael. From *The Dallas Public Library: Celebrating a Century of Service 1901–2001*, published by the University of North Texas Press, printed with permission of Michael V. Hazel.

Hollandsworth, Skip. From "See No Evil," printed with permission from the May 1993 issue of *Texas Monthly*.

Houston, Margaret Belle. "Song from the Traffic" (poem), from *The Singing Heart and Other Poems*, Cokesbury Press.

Huffaker, Bob, Bill Mercer, George Phenix, Wes Wise. From *When the News Went Live: Dallas 1963*. Published by Taylor Trade Publishing, printed with permission of Rowman & Littlefield Publishing Group.

Hunt, Caroline Rose. From *Primrose Past: The 1848 Journal of Young Lady Primrose*, published by Regan Books, an imprint of HarperCollins Publishers, printed with permission of Caroline Rose Hunt. The author is the Honorary Chairman of

Rosewood Hotels and Resorts.

Jones, G. William. From *Black Cinema Treasures, Lost and Found*, published by University of North Texas Press, printed with permission of Leigh Miller.

Jurow, Martin. From *Marty Jurow Seein' Stars: a Show Biz Odyssey*, as told to Philip Wuntch, published by Southern Methodist University Press, printed by permission of Erin Jo Jurow and Philip Wuntch.

Lewis, Grover. From "Farewell to Cracker Eden," reprinted with permission from the September 1992 issue of *Texas Monthly*. All rights reserved.

Lewis, Willie. From *Willie, A Girl from a Town Called Dallas*, published by Texas A&M University Press and printed with its permission.

LittleDog, Pat. Pat LittleDog was once Pat Ellis Taylor.

Mackintosh, Prudence. From "The Dallas Woman," published by *D Magazine* in October 1999 and used by permission of Prudence Mackintosh. Prudence Mackintosh is the author of four books. She is collaborating on a fifth, which will trace the architectural development of the Park Cities, a Dallas suburb.

Marcus, Stanley. From *Minding the Store*, published by the University of North Texas Press and reprinted by permission of the Stanley Marcus Estate.

Meier, Joyce. From "A Good-looking Woman," from *Common Bonds: Stories by and about Modern Texas Women*, edited by Suzanne Comer, published by Southern Methodist University Press, printed by permission of Janet Cashen.

Milner, Jay Dunston. From *Confessions of a Maddog: A Romp through the High-flying Texas Music and Literary Era of the Fifties to the Seventies*, published by the University of North Texas Press, printed by permission of Jay Dunston Milner.

Montgomery, Vaida Stewart. "Cattle Brands," from *Year Book 1946*, Poetry Society of Texas; "To the Rattlesnake," from *Texas in Poetry 2*, Billy Bob Hill, ed. Reprinted with permission.

Montgomery, Whitney. "Death Rode a Pinto Pony" (poem), from *Hounds in the Hills*, Kaleidograph Press.

Murrah, David J. from *C. C. Slaughter: Rancher, Banker, Baptist*, published by University of Texas Press, printed courtesy of David J. Murrah.

Myers, Jack. "I Already Tried Gardening"; "The Gift"; "We Go Away at Home," from *As Long As You're Happy*, published by Graywolf Press, © 1986 and printed by permission of Jack Myers.

Nathaniel, Isabel. "On the Patio, Dallas" published in *The Texas Observer* and from

The Dominion of Lights, published by Copper Beech Press, copyright © 1996 by Isabel Nathaniel; "The Dig," printed by permission of Isabel Nathaniel.

Oliphant, Dave. From *Texas in Poetry: A 150 Year Anthology*, edited by Billy Bob Hill, published by the Center for Texas Studies and the Texas Studies Association, University of North Texas, printed by permission of Dave Oliphant.

Oppenheimer, Evelyn. From *A Book Lover in Texas*, published by the University of North Texas Press, printed with permission of Billie Billingsley.

Ornish, Natalie. From *Pioneer Jewish Texans: Their Impact on Texas and American History for Four Hundred Years 1590–1990*, published by Texas Heritage Press and printed by permission of Natalie Ornish.

Payne, Darwin. From *Big D: Triumphs and Troubles of an American Supercity in the 20th Century*, published by Three Forks Press, printed by permission of Darwin Payne; From *Indomitable Sarah: The Life of Judge Sarah T. Hughes*, published by Southern Methodist University Press, printed by permission of Darwin Payne.

Phillips, John Neal (with André L. Gorzell). "'Tell Them I Don't Smoke Cigars': The Story of Bonnie Parker," from *Legendary Ladies of Texas*, Francis Edward Abernethy, Ed. Publications of the Texas Folklore Society Number XLIII. Dallas: E-Heart Press, 1981.

Reynolds, Clay. Novelist Clay Reynolds is professor of arts and humanities at the University of Texas at Dallas. Excerpt from *Players*, published by Pinnacle Books and printed by permission of Clay Reynolds.

Roach, Joyce Gibson Roach. "High Toned Woman," From Texas Folklore Society Publication *Hoein' the Short Rows,* printed with permission of Joyce Gibson Roach.

Rogers, John William. From *The Lusty Texans of Dallas: Their First Hundred and Twenty-five Years*, published by E. P. Dutton.

Shrake, Edwin. From *Strange Peaches*, published by *Texas Monthly Press,* printed by permission of Edwin Shrake.

Shuford, Gene. "The Visit," from *Gene Shuford: Selected Poems*, published by University of North Texas Press and reprinted with its permission.

Siegel, Marcella, "Waiting Wife." Reprinted with the permission of Suzie Siegel.

Smith, C. W. From *Gabriel's Eye*, printed by permission of C. W. Smith, courtesy of Winedale Books.

Smith, Goldie Capers. "Ballad of a Bombadier from Texas," from *Texas in Poetry 2*, Billy Bob Hill, ed. Reprinted with permission.

Sneed, Larry A. *No More Silence: An Oral History of the Assassination of President Kennedy*, published by the University of North Texas Press, printed with permission by the University of North Texas Press.

Taylor, Pat Ellis (Pat LittleDog), From "Afoot in a Field of Men," printed by permission of Pat LittleDog, published in *Her Work: Stories by Texas Women*, edited by Lou Halsell Rodenberger, published by Shearer Publishing.

Terry, Marshall. From *Angels Prostate Fall*, published by Southern Methodist University Press, printed by permission of Marshall Terry.

Tinkle, Lon. From *The Key to Dallas*, published by J. B. Lippincott Company, printed by permission of Maria G. Tinkle.

Tolbert, Frank X. From *The Staked Plain*, printed in *Tolbert of Texas: The Man and His Work* edited by Evelyn Oppenheimer, published by Texas Christian University Press; "Glamour Girl Called Electra," published by the Texas Folklore Society in *Legendary Ladies of Texas,* Francis Edward Abernethy, Ed. Publications of the Texas Folklore Society Number XLIII. Dallas: E-Heart Press, 1981. Printed with permission of Kathleen Tolbert Ryan and Frank X. Tolbert 2.

Unruh, Leon. From *Final Destinations: Remarkable Cemeteries in Texas, New Mexico, Oklahoma, Arkansas, and Louisiana*, published by University of North Texas Press and printed with permission of the University of North Texas Press.

Vogel, Donald. From *Memories and Images: The World of Donald Vogel and Valley House Gallery*, printed with permission of Valley House Gallery Press.

Walker, Stanley. *The Dallas Story*. Reprinted from the *Dallas Times Herald.* Dallas Centennial Edition of Feb. 5, 1956.

Whitbread, Thomas. "November 25, 1962," From *Whomp and Moonshiver*, BOA Editions, 1982. First published in *Of Poetry and Power*, Basic Books, 1964, and reprinted with permission of Thomas Whitbread.

Wiesepape, Betty. From "The Makers of Dallas," From *Lone Star Chapters: The Story of Texas Literary Clubs*, published by Texas A&M University Press and printed with its permission.

Winegarten, Ruthe. "Belle Starr: The Bandit Queen of Dallas," from *Legendary Ladies of Texas*, Francis Edward Abernethy, Ed. Publications of the Texas Folklore Society Number XLIII. Dallas: E-Heart Press,1981.

Wood, Jane Roberts. From *Roseborough*, published by Dutton, The Penguin Group, and printed with permission of Jane Roberts Wood.

Woolley, Bryan. From *November 22,* published by Seaview Books, printed with permission of Bryan Woolley; "Burgers, Beer, and Patsy Cline," printed with permission of Bryan Woolley. For more than thirty years, Bryan Woolley wrote journalism for *The*

Dallas Times Herald and *The Dallas Morning News*. His novels are *Some Sweet Day*; *Time and Place*; *November 22*; and *Sam Bass.*

Wright, Lawrence, author, *The Looming Tower,* and staff writer for *The New Yorker.* Excerpt from *In The New World: Growing Up with America from the Sixties to the Eighties*, published by Vintage Books, a division of Random House and printed with permission of Lawrence Wright.

Acknowledgments

In basically alphabetical order, for they are all important:

F. E. Abernethy, who first helped start my publishing career with the Texas Folklore Society Publications, the hook on which my whole publishing career was hung. He has been a stalwart friend through thick and thin. There is only one Ab, and I am so fortunate to call him friend.

Judy Alter, Director of TCU Press, must again be acknowledged for her great friendship and support through the years—personally as well as professionally. She has been there when I needed her, along with . . .

Gayla Christiansen, Marketing Manager *par excellence* for Texas A&M University Press, and dear friend and roommate on many a trip to all sorts of places—New York, Los Angeles, and many Texas cities where meetings were held—who has counseled me so wisely over the years in all sorts of matters, including pieces for *Literary Dallas.* She, Judy Alter, and I, form a trio of women in publishing who have spent many a night rocking on Judy's porch and solving all sorts of problems over glasses of wine after a delicious dinner prepared by Chef Judy.

Robert Compton, great good supporter and friend who helped me immensely when I was a publisher and has been a huge asset in putting together *Literary Dallas.* He has read widely and somehow remembers all the books he has read and the interviews with the authors he has done—a remarkable man who honors me with his friendship.

Keith Gregory, Director of SMU Press and Kathryn Lang, Editor of SMU Press, both longtime friends, helped me immensely in combing their backlist for titles and in providing me with copies of titles when they found them and then met me for many lovely lunches over the years.

Susan Petty, my TCU Press editor, who has been very, very patient with me and most agreeable to work with, who helped on permissions and was always congenial through trials, tribulations, and my mistakes. I cannot thank her enough.

James Ward Lee, friend from the Texas Folklore Society before there was an E-Heart Press, then an author I published and finally the driving force, with A. C. Greene, in getting the University of North Texas to agree to start a press and asking me to come run it. It was a great ride—all of it. My deepest thanks to him for it.

Joyce Gibson Roach, compadre and supporter in so many efforts that I cannot begin to tell them all. We have made many a trip in whatever car she was driving at the time, all over the state. Lots of talk on those road trips to meetings and more talk in the hotels in the evenings. She has honored me in so many ways that there is no way to thank her for all she has meant to me over the years. For me, she is the "High Toned Woman" of the world, and a treasured friend.

Carol Roark, a jewel beyond compare at the Dallas Public Library, with great knowledge of Texas and Dallas history, who has helped guide me through many mazes and then topped it all off with lunches on numerous occasions at the Zodiac Room at Neiman-Marcus. She makes research at the Dallas Public Library a treat.

Ellen Temple, my touchstone in life, who is so valued and treasured it cannot be expressed it goes so deep, who has also helped in many ways over the years, from the time she was eighteen and first touched my life as she still does now—with wise counsel and a shoulder to weep on when needed.

Jane Roberts Wood, another treasured friend for many years, who has helped in so many ways they cannot all be enumerated, who has been there in the darkest hours and also always counseled wisely and gave another shoulder to weep on if it was needed. I love her dearly.

Bill and Mary Etta Moreau, who, should I call right now for help, would be here as fast as they could. Long time friends and supporters whose help and advice has meant the world to me. They, too, were there when I needed them and still are.

Marilyn Manning, childhood friend who sticks with me no matter what, and there has been a lot of "what" over the years. She is my own personal therapist and therapist to my children and probably grandchildren as well, who has tried to guide me through hazards involving "my disposition," and helped me get out of the scrapes when I ignored her warnings. What would I do without her?

I would be remiss in not acknowledging Ross Vick Jr. and his parents Ross Sr. and Mary Randall Vick and cousin Neva Randall Smith—all born in Dallas. Their family before them are all buried in Dallas and helped build this city. They first introduced me many years ago to the city that would become my home. Their support was invaluable over the years, particularly Ross Jr., who was a helpmate and confidante for many years.

Joseph Patrick Brannen, my brother, who has entertained me all my life. Our morning phone talks are the highlight of my day. He is absolutely one in a million. There is certainly no one close to being like him. He is unique, delightful, incredibly brilliant, and I adore him. How lucky is that, to have such a brother who also lends his support when it is needed and is always perfectly honest with me?

And finally my children who helped me immensely through the years in all my publishing and writing endeavors—Karen Vick Cavazos, Ross Vick III, Patrick Vick (who once asked me why I didn't go into ping pong balls instead of publishing after he tired of toting boxes of books for me). They have been there to help at book signings, to host book signings and, yes, to tote books. And they, too, have been there with all the support they could muster whenever I needed them. I am so pleased and proud of these grown children who have turned out extremely well, it seems to their mother, in spite of numerous attempts by their parents to sabotage their dreams . . .

Index